SEEKERS

FOUND

Atonement in
Early Quaker
Experience

SEEKERS FOUND

Atonement in Early Quaker Experience

BY

Douglas Gwyn

PENDLE HILL PUBLICATIONS
WALLINGFORD, PA 19086

If ever there was a time for tears without, and grief of spirit within, this seems the season: when after such an expectation of Light and Glory, of Settlement and Establishment in the things of God, such thick darkness, such universal shame, such dreadful Shatterings, have so apparently overtaken us, and are so likely daily more and more to overtake us. Not only our Superstructure, but our very Foundation is shaken; and when we have striven and tryed to the utmost to settle again, we may be forced at length to confess, that there is no settling any more upon it, but we must come to a deeper bottom, or sink for ever.

—Isaac Penington
A Voyce out of the Thick Darkness (1650)

TABLE OF CONTENTS

PREFACE

This book completes a trilogy of studies in early Quakerism. The first, adapted from my doctoral thesis at Drew University, was *Apocalypse of the Word: The Life and Message of George Fox* (Friends United Press, 1986). That was a biblical-theological analysis of Fox's thought, finding its organizing principle to be an experiential form of apocalyptic eschatology. But that book barely suggested the sociopolitical dimensions of early Quakerism. I soon began work on a second book, *The Covenant Crucified: Quakers and the Rise of Capitalism* (Pendle Hill Publications, 1995). Covenant was the biblical-theological language that early Friends used to articulate the social and political vision concomitant to their revolutionary language of apocalypse. The present book takes one more look at early Quaker witness from a third angle, the spirituality of early Friends as it developed out of the milieu of English Seekerism. Atonement as an integrative reconciliation of alienated parties emerges as the key theological dynamic.

These three studies are intended to be complementary. Each stands alone; but together, they do more justice to the striking vision and prophetic witness of early Friends. Each represents further development in my work as a student of early Quaker history. At the same time, all three are written from an unabashedly Christian Quaker viewpoint, and with a view toward the challenges of our own times.

During the three years of intensive work that went into this study, a number of individuals and groups provided valuable help. I want to thank the Lyman Fund and the Elizabeth Ann Bogert Memorial Fund for small grants that were generous during a time without personal income. A full scholarship year at Pendle Hill and a year as Friend in Residence at Woodbrooke afforded the opportunity to research and write in the middle of vibrant and supportive Quaker communities. Along the way, Janet Shepherd and Margaret Fraser at Pendle Hill and John Sheldon at Woodbrooke helped find ways to keep the work going. Emma Lapsansky, Betsy Brown, and Diana Petersen at the Haverford College Quaker Collection, Mary Ellen Chijioke and Jerry Frost at the Friends

Historical Library of Swarthmore College, Josef Keith of the Library of the Society of Friends in London, Seth Kasten and Drew Kadel at the Union Seminary Library (New York)—all offered counsel, friendship, and help along the way. Ben Pink Dandelion at Woodbrooke helped develop certain ideas along the way. Basketball buddies on two continents helped me stay fit and sane through it all. Peter Bien and Larry Ingle offered important editorial improvements. Rebecca Mays and Eve Beehler have encouraged, prodded, and polished this project to its publication. My gratitude and friendship abides toward all of these.

Finally, this book represents a season of personal as well as intellectual growth, for which I give thanks to God. Along the way, I have experienced much joy over the past five and a half years finding and being found by my soul-mate, Caroline Jones, now my wife. To her this book is lovingly dedicated.

—Douglas Gwyn

INTRODUCTION

To be is to seek. Always and everywhere, the search for a fuller relationship with God continues. A century ago, the Quaker Rufus Jones wrote,
"Man's search for God is as plain as his search for food. He has, beyond
question, blundered at it and frequently missed the trail, but that man in
all lands and in all times has maintained some kind of search for an
invisible Companion is a momentous fact."[1] Even where the reality of
God is doubted, humans seek the god of Reality.

Seeking is the horizon of our existence. Even an individual with a
profound sense of religious identity and a fulfilling experience of God
must continue to seek. Morally, one must search for divine wisdom in
new situations. Intellectually, one must search for further implications
of the truth one has embraced. Communities of faith must search corporately for a place of integrity where they can stand and face new challenges on a changing cultural terrain. To stop seeking is to stop living
faithfully, to neglect the treasure that one has found.

But by no means does everyone seek in a condition of secure religious
identity. In all times and places, there are individuals dissatisfied with the
religious practices and interpretations they have known. Many become
unhappy enough to start looking for alternatives. Some even create alternatives of their own. Along the way, they may arrive at religious outlooks
that others find spurious or silly. In some cases, their views and practices
may be actively attacked as blasphemous, subversive, or dangerous.

But in certain times and places, particular historic situations of social
upheaval and religious ferment will inspire mass mobilizations of
seekers. During periods of crisis or rapid change, the apparent givenness
of normative beliefs and the assumed validity of religious practices
may lose plausibility in the eyes of many. The religious authorities and
institutions that once held the universe together no longer do so. Their
humanness—perhaps even their banality or hypocrisy—suddenly
becomes all too apparent. The experience of anomie, of living in chaos,
becomes overwhelming, leading individuals either to reaffirm the old
truths with greater zeal—and perhaps aggressive vehemence—or to begin
wandering in search of new truths.

1

Most of us in North America have lived through such an acute age. In many ways, we are still experiencing it. The 1960s were a decade of disorienting cultural shifts, jarring political conflicts, and scattering religious energies. The sixties inspired many, especially the young, to hold utopian hopes for a new, Aquarian age of "peace, love and understanding." The disappointment of those hopes left many of the same individuals bitter and confused, casting about for a more adequate faith and a more meaningful way of life. Many found answers in Eastern religion, neo-pagan practices, feminist spiritualities, or the human potential movement. For these, the rainbow of the "New Age" has offered some fulfillment of the promise of the sixties. There is a sense of a "new paradigm" coming into place. Nevertheless, the new order always seems just a bit further off, perhaps lacking just one more "missing piece" of truth.

The same sixties inspired fear and heartbreak for others, including many young people. For some, misadventures in the realm of psychedelic drugs or free love cast a pall over the enthusiasm of youth; for others, the good qualities of mainstream American life far outweighed the bad qualities. To see traditional religion and morality crumble in the face of widespread rebellion and experimentation made these Americans grieve for a lost innocence. For them, the sixties (and much of the seventies) were a time of mass *apostasy*, a falling away. Many have devoted great energies to repairing the breaches in the American cultural consensus, working for a renewal of traditional virtues, family values, and biblically based religion.

Thus, many of us who lived through the sixties, especially those who came of age during that time, have found ourselves on a *spiritual quest* of one kind or another. Whether we search among various "alternative" spiritualities or try to find our way back to the solid ground of traditional religion and self-evident truths, we share the same *seeking* condition. As sociologist Steven Tipton has expressed it, we are still trying to get "saved from the sixties."[2] The mass mobilization of religious seeking has been the subject of fruitful studies in recent years. Wade Clark Roof has investigated the religious journeys of American babyboomers, "a generation of seekers."[3] Robert Wuthnow has charted the "restructuring of American religion," the changes in religious institutions developing in tandem with the seeking phenomenon.[4] In *Habits of the Heart*,[5] Robert Bellah and his team of sociologists have pondered the decline of religious commitment that has become widespread in the post-sixties seeking culture. Christopher Lasch views the breakdown of corporate religious and cultural forms as leading to a "culture of narcissism."[6] James Davison Hunter and others have characterized post-sixties religious and political conflict as an ongoing "culture war" between conservative and progressive forces within religious groups and in American political life at large.[7] More recently, Martin Marty has called for a recommitment to constructive dialogue among the new religious and political positions staked out over the past 30 years.[8] Finally, Douglas Jacobsen and William Vance Trollinger have identified various instances in which Protestant groups throughout the 20th century have sought to reconcile polarizing positions and "reform the center" of their faith traditions.[9] All these examinations of contemporary American religious life deal directly or indirectly with the continuing phenomenon and legacy of seeking since the sixties.

These various sociological studies add perspective to the spiritual dramas of individual seekers. They suggest that a given individual's path of seeking and finding may not be as unique as it seems. They also pose important critical questions: To what extent is religious seeking today a form of consumerism? When does the shift from the institutional allegiances of traditional "religion" to the more individualistic dynamics of "spirituality" express a lack of commitment, even a narcissistic tendency? What do new religious forms produced in this era add to more traditional observances? Can the unprecedented range and scope of seeking today eventually produce new, constructive religious practices in American society?

REDEFINING THE SEEKING PHENOMENON

While seeking often leads one to abandon a precious religious affiliation, it also leads often to new associations. Seekers desire a deeper association (experience of, relationship with) the divine. Simultaneously, nearly every seeker hopes to associate with others who share that renewed sense of connection with divine reality. Thus, paradoxically, seeking is more about association than disassociation. It leads to disassociation for the sake of a more adequate association. For this reason, it would be useful to redefine the seeking phenomenon as a re-associative movement. We will be aided here by the analysis of the late British political scientist, Michael Oakeshott.[10]

According to Oakeshott, there are two fundamental modes of human association, *civil* association and *enterprise* association. Humans associating together in pursuit of some common, substantive goal combine in an enterprise association. Their rules promote action appropriate to their guiding purpose. The purpose might be religious fellowship and outreach (as in a church), profit-making (as in a business), stamp collecting (as in a hobby club), or national defense (as in an army). By contrast, humans associating together for the sake of a just and moral order combine in a civil association. Here rules exist not as instruments employed for the sake of some goal but as boundaries for the maintenance of good order. Whatever enterprises individuals or groups may choose to undertake, the civil mode of association defines the conditions and provides the rules, setting the limits on what actions may be taken without breaching the peace and equity of human society. Civil association defines the *rights* and *responsibilities* of each person living within its jurisdiction or participating within its boundaries. Each person participates as a formal equal within the civil association.

Although the political apparatus that defines civil association is the secular state, every association within the state's jurisdiction embodies some aspect of civil association. For example, a conservative Christian group may be concerned to "rechurch" America and thereby reclaim the normative Christian values that accompanied the founding of the United States and much of its history. That concern is a substantive purpose, defining an enterprise association. But it is simultaneously a concern to enhance the civility of American life (assuming that the rights of no individual or group are trespassed on in the effort to Christianize American society anew). As a counter-example, a more liberal religious group may be concerned with matters of civil rights, racial equality, and interfaith cooperation. These too are substantive purposes, inspiring programmatic action on both religious and political fronts. But the concern is also civil, seeking a fuller realization of the values enunciated in the Constitution of the United States. Finally, the political apparatus of the United States government is by no means a pure case of civil association, since it is also authorized to fulfill substantive purposes like economic health, public safety and national security. Indeed, Oakeshott makes the point that the enterprise association and the civil association are ideal types that do not exist in pure form in any actual institution. All particular associations combine both modes in one manner or another.[11] The sum total of associations produces a *civil society*. The political apparatus of the state alone cannot form or maintain a civil society, which is a complex fabric, the interweaving of all sorts of associations: religious, educational, economic, cultural, ethnic, etc.

Sorting out the modes of association can help us clarify religious seeking. Oakeshott's two modes of *association* suggest two modes of *seeking*. When we seek individual consolation, redemption, or enlightenment, we are engaged in a religious quest, a spiritual *enterprise* that will often associate us with other individuals seeking in the same vein. Similarly, when groups seek to organize themselves faithfully around a body of doctrine, a form of worship or meditation, or to propagate their faith more widely in society, they too are engaged in *enterprise*. But there is a *civil* dimension to these aims. The enterprise may keep them tightly sequestered in sectarian purity from all other religious groups, or it may lead them ecumenically into joint enterprises with other religious groups. But both sectarian isolation and ecumenical cooperation may be ways to maintain civility in the larger social whole while seeking the satisfaction of substantive purposes.

The other mode of seeking begins with the concern for civility. It is the search for the *conditions of relationship* that make for balanced individuals, healthy communities, and an equitable society. Certainly, this mode of seeking inevitably undertakes enterprising ventures such as the protest against injustice, work for moral renewal, or lobbying for more equitable laws. But the primary mode of seeking here is for an overall *quality* of religious community and public life that transcends any particular private *concern*. Oakeshott reminds us that the Latin word for "public concern" is *respublica*. The republican ideal has animated the political imagination from Plato and Aristotle down to the present.

In the biblical tradition as well, we find both modes of association embodied within the rubric of *covenant*. Oakeshott offers the following characterization of civil association *versus* enterprise association in biblical terms:

> [Civil association's] theological analogue is the freedom enjoyed when God is understood to be a "law-giver" and the believer is not only necessarily left to subscribe to his obligations the best way he may but can do so only in self-chosen actions, in contrast to a divine Will to which he must submit

himself and his conduct or join the part of the devil, or to a
divine Purpose, to which his conduct willy-nilly contributes.[12]

In the biblical drama of God's successive covenants with humanity, we
find both modes of association, civil and enterprise, witnessed. God is
portrayed as a law-giver, establishing Israel as a new form of civil society. But God is also portrayed as advancing a divine will to reconcile all
alienated humanity back into unity. To that end, a divine purpose is seen
to course through human lives and world history, notwithstanding many
human apostasies along the way.

In its fullest expression, covenant defines not only the terms of association with God but also the terms of association among humans and
between humans and the rest of creation.[13] For example, the covenant
with Israel through Moses is strongly weighted toward the civil mode
of association. Despite the far-ranging scope of its hundreds of laws,
the Mosaic covenant basically lays out the cultic, moral, and civil boundaries within which Israel is free to pursue its own ends. The major substantive purpose of the loose confederation of Israel's tribes is simply to
consecrate Israel to the Lord so that its communal life may testify on
earth to its divine liberator. But after two centuries of life in Canaan, the
threat of Philistine takeover led Israel to adopt a king and a standing
army for defensive purposes. Consequently, under the revised arrange-
ments of God's covenant with David, Israel was defined increasingly as
a royal-military enterprise association. That shift of emphasis gradually
caused Israel's civility to deteriorate (through socioeconomic exploitation and greater reliance upon military forms of security). Breaches of
the quality of covenantal association led to the Hebrew prophets' severe
indictment of Israel's royal and priestly establishments, a covenantal
lawsuit on God's part against Israel.

The biblical tradition suggests that seeking takes place not only on
the human side of the religious equation. Through a succession of
covenantal initiatives, *God seeks as well*. This two-sided drama Rufus
Jones called *The Double Search*.[14] As divine and human seeking are
reconciled, mutually fulfilled, and as the two forms of association move
into balanced expression of harmonious purpose, an *atonement* is
achieved between human and divine, among humans of differing identities and purposes, and between humanity and God's creation. The New
Testament witnesses God's seeking, in an initiative to extend covenan-

tal partnership to all humanity. As Moses and the prophets were sent as suffering servants of God's covenantal order and purpose toward Israel, Jesus was sent as the suffering servant of a new covenant toward all peoples of the earth. (The paradoxical role of suffering in atonement will be explored in later stages of this book.) And as the tribes of Israel formed a confederation of covenantal order in the Promised Land, the international network of Christian communities spread a new order and promoted a new divine purpose throughout the ancient world.

Later in Christian history, during the 16th-17th centuries, a renewed awareness of the covenantal tradition of the Bible was a major energizing influence among the Protestant reformers, as they began to renew the church and envision the modern political state. As the Reformation gave way to the Enlightenment, covenantal (or federal) theology combined with the classical Greek ideas of Plato and Aristotle, giving rise to liberal contractarian philosophy. These ancient influences can be seen in the writings of Thomas Hobbes and John Locke, as well as in the Constitution of the United States.[15] Thus, deep structures of biblical and classical tradition undergird and interlace religious and political discourse in American life. Despite their apparently insurmountable contradictions, the Christian fundamentalist and the liberal civil libertarian argue with one another drawing upon a common stock of religious and philosophical motifs. There *is* a basis for a fruitful dialectic, for a *sustained drama of seeking and finding together*.

SEEKING AND FINDING

We have seen that all seeking, like all association, embodies some combination of substantive purpose (seeking toward some end) and civil concern (seeking the conditions of relationship that make such substantive purposes meaningful). Thus, as we seek toward some end, we seek from a certain *point* of reference. That is, our *aim* implies a specific view toward a certain goal. That point of reference will tend to dictate the framework of reality around its goal. But as we seek with a more public concern for the general conditions of civil society and peace, we seek within a certain *frame* of reference. For example, to "seek first the kingdom of God" is to commit oneself to a biblically derived framework of moral and social values that qualify and shape whatever specific enterprises one undertakes. In the course of seeking, the point and frame of reference constantly inform and redefine one another. As we move forward toward the goal, the larger view of reality changes. And as our larger view changes, it reinterprets where we have been and where we are headed. That interaction constitutes the dialectical process of seeking—whatever trajectory of seeking we may follow.

Just as this process has two referents, so it has two alternating moments. The first is *errantry*: moving from one point toward another. Movement may be inspired by the satisfaction of some substantive purpose and the need to move on toward new ends. Or it may be inspired by the unfruitfulness of a particular point of reference, as in dissatisfaction with inherited religious truths and services. Thus, errantry may be well-focused action guided by a clearly defined aim—like the storied knight-errant going off to battle. Or it may be aimless wandering, in which the only point of reference is the one that has been rejected and left behind. But this movement is best called errantry because even where ends are well defined and direction carefully calculated, the journey will transform the significance of its destination. *The process of seeking alters the meaning of what is found*, even if one has aimed straight at it. Conversely, *finding alters the meaning of seeking*, as one looks back upon the journey. Seeking is also errant in the other sense: making mistakes. In both purposeful action and aimless wandering, errantry inevitably includes wrong turns.

The second dialectical moment of seeking is *standing still*. This moment may arrive with the attainment of some aim of seeking and be a time to consolidate newfound wisdom. Or standing still may embody a resistance to forces of change. As noted earlier, some responded to the crises of the sixties by reaffirming traditional religious faith and practice, sometimes with vehemence or even violence. Finally, standing still may arrive as a moment of cumulative fatigue and frustration with wandering among many different truths. It may dawn as a radically new moment of seeking, the transformation of seeking to another level. In biblical terms, it is sometimes described as "waiting upon the Lord." In Buddhist terms, it has been called "the wisdom of no escape."[16] But even this moment is not the final moment of seeking. For the great "finders" of religious history, once endowed with new wisdom or new revelations, embark upon a new vocation of errantry, of "spreading the word" to a new generation of seekers. And as new finders are gathered into that new revelation, they will enter a season of standing still, consolidating and institutionalizing the truth that they have found—or that has found them.

So the dialectic of seeking and finding, of errantry and standing still, is a constant conversation—indeed, a constant *conversion*—just as the civil and enterprise modes of association continually qualify one another along the path we follow as individuals, as faith communities, and as a larger society. It is unsettling at times to realize that the truth is a living, moving reality that we cannot finally capture, formulate, contain, or possess. We can only strive to be faithful partners with God and with one another in the ongoing conversation.

Seekers of Other Eras: What Can We Learn from Them?

The study of seeking in history reveals patterns that are instructive for us today. The seeking phenomenon of our time is not entirely unprecedented. Other cultural moments in history have elicited similar mass seeking movements. And these mobilizations have often produced important new religious expressions. For example, the saga of Abraham and Sarah portrayed in Genesis represents the emergence of a new vision of God amid the protracted upheavals of the ancient Near East during the second millennium B.C.E. Again, the Greco-Roman world of the first century C.E. set the conditions for unprecedented cultural exchange and religious exploration, factors favorable to the emergence of Christianity. Finally, in 17th-century England, at the dawn of our modern era, the bellicose final stages of the English Reformation produced a breakdown of Protestant consensus and the appearance of thousands of troubled young Puritans called Seekers.

This book aims to discover the larger historical dynamics behind the seeking phenomenon as we know it today. It makes use of the dialectical historical method that was defined by Marx in modern times[17] but that can be seen at work more implicitly in the writings of the classical and apocalyptic prophets of biblical literature. The first step of the method is to define the key dynamics at work in the present-day phenomenon of seeking. The second step is to move from the present to the past, discovering the preconditions that have helped shape contemporary seeking. Here the revolutionary period of 17th-century England is particularly illuminating. Not only was there a mass phenomenon of questing individuals actually called Seekers, but they prefigure the two dialectical tendencies found among seekers today. The book then takes another (decidedly non-Marxist) step, much further into the historical past, to view the biblical dynamics of seeking. The literature of the Bible is the single most formative cultural influence in Western culture. The structures of seeking we find there have shaped the intellectual understanding and narrative framing of Jewish, Christian, and secular seekers down to this day. The final step is to return to the present with an enlarged sense of the historical dialectics of seeking, in order to suggest a reconstructive, atoning practice of seeking today, at the dawn of a new millennium.

Most of the book's chapters are devoted to England's revolutionary decades, the 1640s and 1650s. That was a period of profound conflict and change, somewhat similar to the upheavals of the United States in the 1960s. Moreover, those two decades in English history mark the beginnings of the modern period of Anglo-American culture. Some of the most important religious and political tendencies of our modern era were briefly rehearsed by the inspired individuals and groups of that intense period. It was a moment of such ardent exploration that a mass phenomenon of young, questing men and women blossomed during the English Civil War. They were dubbed "Seekers." They will be the central focus of our study, for the vibrant seeking scene of the 1640s generated some of the most colorful religious and political groups of the period: Levellers, Diggers, Ranters, and Quakers. That last group will receive our sustained analysis in the latter half of this book, because the Quaker movement was the major convergence among English Seekers, forged through a powerful experience of atonement, of finding *and* being found. A brief overview of the chapters ahead will sketch our overall trajectory.

Chapter 1 examines the seeking phenomenon in American culture since the 1960s. Utilizing a variety of current social studies, it finds a basic bifurcation among the large numbers of religiously seeking Americans today. That split expresses itself as a conflict between different religious sensibilities, political aims, and class interests. It manifests the dialectical tendencies of seeking and association that we have sketched in principle above. It also represents an ongoing evolution of the same dialectic we will discover in our historical and biblical chapters.

Chapter 2 establishes the overall Reformation context for our study of English Seekers and Quakers. After a brief sketch of the historic situation that gave rise to the Reformation and its various branches, we focus on the life of two lesser-known Protestant reformers, Caspar Schwenckfeld and Sebastian Franck. Schwenckfeld is important to our study because, already within the first decade of the Reformation, he was the first to proclaim the bankruptcy of the entire Protestant project. Seeing the proliferation of alternative Protestant doctrines, church governments, and sacramental observances, Schwenckfeld recognized that only confusion and violent conflict would ensue. Thus, he called for a *Stillstand*, a moratorium in which earnest Christians would wait for an authentic practice of the Lord's Supper to be revealed. His decision to withdraw from church-building, combined with his deep spiritualist sense of inward communion with Christ, made Schwenckfeld the prototypical seeker of the Reformation period. We will note how his option to *stand still* paradoxically propelled him into a life of religious *errantry*. Sebastian Franck was another spiritualist reformer, whose message and ministry shared much with Schwenckfeld's. But his proto-liberal understanding of progressive revelation and his unconcern for a visible, institutional church make him representative of a second dialectical position among seekers of the Protestant era. Other important Reformation figures and movements related to Schwenckfeld and the *Stillstand* will also be mentioned.

Chapter 3 moves on to an overview of the English Reformation, from Henry VIII's break with Rome in 1534, through the Puritan movement for more thoroughgoing reforms, down to the English Civil War and the first appearance of the Seeker groundswell in the 1640s. We will see how royal intransigence, Puritan religious renewal, radical Separatist agitation, Baptist sectarianism, and utopian political fervor clashed in the 1640s, producing a breakdown of spiritual authority and religious consensus. That crisis sent thousands of young, idealistic Puritans retreating from all the competing religious options of the day, to wait for a more adequate faith and a more uniting church to be revealed. We will see two basic types of Seekers emerge. The first type, radical Protestants following Schwenckfeld's trajectory, waited for new apostles, like those of the Book of Acts, to show the way back to the purity of the primitive church of New Testament times. But a second type of Seeker also flourished, especially in the later 1640s. This type looked not to the primitive church of ancient days but to the emergence of a new age of the Spirit, a new "spiritual Christian," and a new form of church devoid of Christendom's institutional and sacramental trappings. This second position, founded upon doctrines of progressive revelation and a highly internalized experience of Christ, embodied something closer to Sebastian Franck's vision of an invisible church. Its impetus was incipiently liberal.

Chapter 4 profiles two leading figures from the seeking scene of the 1640s, John Saltmarsh and William Erbury, following their trajectories from orthodox Puritan divines to prophets of the new age of the Spirit. The chapter also examines the advanced spiritualism and radical politics among the ranks of the Parliamentary army, where both Saltmarsh and Erbury served as chaplains.

Chapter 5 explores the politics of Seekerism in the latter 1640s, with the rise and fall of the Leveller and Digger movements. The Leveller initiative for religious freedom, legal reform, an expanded political franchise, and a constitutional republic drew the support of many Independents, Baptists, and Seekers. In particular, we will follow the Leveller career of William Walwyn, whose paradoxical combination of Puritan faith and liberal political rhetoric made him suspect in most circles. Though Walwyn does not fit the classic Seeker profile of that period, he does exemplify the trajectory into early liberalism that many Seekers were to follow in the years to come, as spiritualist Christian religion was transmuted into rationalist political philosophy in the early Enlightenment. We will also track the meteoric career of Gerrard Winstanley, whose passage through Baptist and Seeker phases led to a utopian communal experiment in 1649. This so-called "Digger" commune was far beyond the political conversation of its day. But Winstanley's trenchant, intuitive critique of state religion and private property opened realms of political radicalism that Marx and others would chart later.

With the defeat of the Levellers and the dispersion of Digger experiments by early 1650, the prophetic spirituality and radical politics of the Seekers and others were thrown into disarray and disillusionment. *Chapter 6* narrates the outrageous and brilliant trajectories of three leading figures of the Ranter explosion of 1650. Laurence Clarkson and Joseph Salmon, in particular, present us with profiles of Seekers whose despair by 1650 sent them into fits of notorious language and conduct. The scintillating rhetoric and deep theological insights of these writers suggest that the initial burst of Ranterism was an important prophetic moment in the Seeker saga. Though Ranter behavior quickly degenerated into reflexive gestures of rebellion and revel, the initial moment signaled the entrance of Seekerism further into the depths of *via negativa* spirituality. Despite the intense conflicts between Ranters and Quakers in the 1650s, the Ranter eclipse was a powerfully formative moment along the way to the Quaker breakthrough.

Though most of the Seeker writers and leaders we know were men, a few women's voices survive from that period when the strictures of patriarchy were somewhat loosened. *Chapter 7* looks at two women whose lives and writings are at least partially known to us. Anna Trapnel was an esteemed prophet who moved in the radical Independent scene around London in the 1640s and eventually became a firebrand of the Fifth Monarchist movement in the 1650s. Although she remained attached to an Independent congregation, she passed through the classic doubt and disillusionment that most Seekers shared during the period. We will also look at Sarah Jones, whose life is almost entirely unknown to us, except for two remarkable tracts and a few traces of her activity in the Quaker movement of the 1650s. Such women were not merely a sidelight on the male-dominated Seeker drama of the 1640s. Though they remained peripheral in that earlier decade, they became central, inaugurating figures in the Quaker movement of the 1650s. George Fox's alliance with several gifted women prophets is an important key to the deep, cathartic energies that were unleashed in Quaker spirituality and the radical social agendas that early Friends revived.

Chapter 8 explores the turn from penitent Seekerism and rebellious Ranterism to the fiery baptism of Quaker spirituality through the lives of several men and women who recorded their spiritual journeys in later years. By no means did all Seekers and Ranters became Quakers in the 1650s. But nearly all of the earliest Friends underwent classic Seeker phases before becoming Friends, and the earliest Quaker preachers found their most receptive audiences among those mournful "travellers after Sion." Through their stories and a sketch of the early ministry of George Fox, we will note how the errant years of despair and wandering from group to group finally came to a moment of impasse, a standstill that produced either the brilliant flame-out of Ranterism or the sustained fire of Quakerism.

Chapter 9 follows the brilliant seeking careers of Isaac and Mary Penington. The Peningtons' wealthy London circumstances afforded them the leisure to dabble among doctrines and languish in spirit beyond the more humble situations of most Seekers. Both Peningtons chronicled their spiritual journeys through hope and despair, through a serious engagement with Ranterism in 1650, and on to eventual Quaker convincement in the mid-1650s. Isaac Penington's extensive Quaker writings are augmented by his significant corpus of pre-Quaker writings, giving us our most detailed Seeker-to-Quaker saga.

Chapters 10 and *11* shift our focus to the gradual definition and organization of the Quaker movement from the 1650s to the end of the 17th century. We will discover the formation of a viable Quaker movement most centrally in Fox's mediating role, interlacing the concerns and discoveries of both kinds of Seekers (as we discovered them in Chapter 3), between northern and southern Quaker constituencies, and between male and female leadership. What ensues is a drama of *atonement* in which the conflicts within an inherently fractious movement of long-term dissenters are slowly resolved and healed. The transformation from a prophetic and apocalyptic grassroots movement to an organized Religious Society of Friends was one that most Seekers-turned-Quakers happily embraced. Few wished to revisit the long travail through *anomie* that they had experienced as Seekers. But we will also follow the trajectories of a few Quakers who decided to go back to seeking when the Friends movement became too organized and uniform for them. For some of these, Quakerism proved to be the last station before dropping out of all forms of organized religion. Along the way, we note how the Seeker demand that religious doctrines be validated by one's own personal experience intersected with Friends' insistence that faith possess an overall doctrinal and practical coherence. Some Friends clung to the idiomatic quality of their own personal experience and resisted the normative patterns emerging corporately in the Quaker movement, eventually feeling obliged to leave. But most found it preferable to embrace corporate coherence even at the expense of some cherished personal truths. Through this process a hard-won, corporately defined sense of truth emerged.

Finally, the study's *Conclusion* summarizes the formation of the Quaker movement out of the Seeker milieu of the 1650s. Early Friends called themselves "Friends of Truth." We can recognize four mutually informing aspects, or "moments," of truth at work in the early Quaker process of self-definition during the latter half of the seventeenth century. These have correlates in four classic philosophical accounts of truth. Together, they form a powerful dialectical model, a framework for defining faithfulness. "Truth" remains a divine characteristic. But *faithfulness* to truth can be reckoned in human lives and within the historic circumstances of religious and philosophical traditions.

Because early Quakerism drew much of its language and logic from the Gospel and Epistles of John (for example, key terms such as "Friends," "light," and "truth"), the Conclusion moves on to review the use of the word "truth" in the Fourth Gospel. We find the same four "moments" of truth played out dramatically in John's narrative. A *quadrinity* emerges, with the community of Christ's "Friends" as partners with the Father, Son, and Spirit of truth. Quakerism is interpreted today from various competing perspectives. But when the deep structures of biblical theology are recognized undergirding the witness of early Friends, the full resonances of their language are better heard.

We return at last to the present moment of seeking, at the beginning of the twenty-first century. The polarized trajectories of seeking that we traced in Chapter 1 are essentially the same two tendencies we found among early Seekers. These were mediated and refocused by George Fox and the Quaker movement, forging a powerful prophetic witness out of the many diverging horizons of Seeker experimentation. Unfortunately, our present polarization between these two principal seeker tendencies has reached a level that nearly precludes constructive dialogue. We conclude by applying the four "moments" of truth recognized among early Friends, philosophical theory, and the Gospel of John, to see if reconstructive conversation can be devised. It is not for us to make proprietary claims for the truth in this postmodern era. But we can endeavor to become more faithful to the truth as we know it, and recognize the integrity of faithfulness in other people of other traditions in following the truth as they know it. Only the bare beginnings of such dialogue can be suggested here. But our four-part framework could prove useful for dialogue as we struggle to reclaim civility in religious life and to work across our differences toward a more peaceful and just society.

Notes

1. Rufus M. Jones, *The Double Search: Studies in Atonement and Prayer* (London: Headley, 1906), 10.
2. Steven M. Tipton, *Getting Saved from the Sixties: Moral Meaning in Conversion and Cultural Change* (Berkeley: University of California Press, 1982).
3. Wade Clark Roof, *A Generation of Seekers: the Spiritual Journeys of the Baby-Boom Generation* (San Francisco: HarperCollins, 1993).
4. Robert Wuthnow, *The Restructuring of American Religion: Society and Faith since World War II* (Princeton: Princeton University Press, 1988).
5. Robert Bellah, et. al., *Habits of the Heart: Individualism and Commitment in American Life* (Berkeley: University of California Press, 1985).
6. Christopher Lasch, *The Culture of Narcissism: American Life in an Age of Diminishing Expectations* (New York: Norton, 1979).
7. James Davison Hunter, *Culture Wars: the Struggle to Define America* (New York: Basic Books, 1991).
8. Martin E. Marty, *The One and the Many: America's Struggle for the Common Good* (Cambridge: Harvard University Press, 1997).
9. Douglas Jacobsen and William Vance Trollinger, Jr., *Reforming the Center: American Protestantism, 1900 to the Present* (Grand Rapids: Eerdmans, 1998).
10. I will draw principally on two works by Michael Oakeshott, "Talking Politics," in his *Rationalism in Politics and Other Essays*, new and expanded edition (Indianapolis: Liberty, 1991), 338-61; and Oakeshott, *On Human Conduct* (Oxford: Clarendon Press, 1975).
11. Oakeshott, *On Human Conduct*, 109,121.
12. Oakeshott, *On Human Conduct*, 158.
13. See my previous work on covenantal theology, *The Covenant Crucified: Quakers and the Rise of Capitalism* (Wallingford, Pa.: Pendle Hill, 1995). The introduction and first two chapters give basic background on covenant and its history in the Bible. For further background on covenant, from a political science perspective, see Daniel J. Elazar and John Kincaid, eds., *Covenant, Polity, and Constitutionalism* (New York: University Press of America, 1980).
14. Rufus M. Jones, *The Double Search*.
15. For more background on the covenantal roots of modern political theory, see Elazar and Kincaid, *Covenant*, as well as Charles S. McCoy and J. Wayne Baker, *Fountainhead of Federalism: Heinrich Bullinger and the Covenantal Tradition* (Louisville: Westminster/John Knox, 1991), Chapter 5.
16. Pema Chodron, *The Wisdom of No Escape, and the Path of Loving-Kindness* (Boston: Shambala, 1991).
17. For an introductory sketch of Marx's historical method, see Bertell Ollman, "Why Dialectics? Why Now?" *Science & Society*, 63, no. 3 (Fall 1998): 338-57.

CHAPTER 1

A LOOKING-GLASS FOR SEEKERS
THE AMERICAN CULTURE OF SEEKING TODAY

During certain historic periods of cultural transition, when institutions and forms of authority are in flux, religious seeking can become a mass phenomenon. We are living through such a period; it became acute in the 1960s, but continues down to the present. During the 60s, when economic growth and expectations for the future ran high in the United States, a number of cultural conflicts broke out: civil rights, the antiwar movement, the sexual revolution, and the women's movement, to name just four. These crises of conscience rocked American institutions and authorities. Religious institutions and authorities were no exception. The postwar religious consensus, one of the strongest in American history, began to founder.

Baby boomers, just coming of age during the 60s, were particularly prone to the full impact of these conflicts. But the shock waves were felt throughout American society. Many left their religious homes to seek more adequate answers and authorities. Often, their seeking took them away from mainstream Christian and Jewish faiths to explore various "alternative" outlooks: Eastern, Native American, and neo-pagan, for example. Others, feeling overwhelmed by the conflicts around them, found reassurance by "staying home" religiously. But they too realized that the rapidly changing social terrain would require that their inherited faith adopt a new stance, with new answers for a new era. Thus, even traditionalists became seekers, forced to search for new ways to convey old truths.

Over three decades since the 60s, both major seeking types (and many gradations in between) have continued to seek. Traditionalists continue seeking to reconstruct the religious and moral consensus they saw fall apart in the 60s. Seekers of alternative truths continue to explore a widening array of spiritualities, still confident that a "new paradigm" of faith and morality is emerging, still hopeful that a "new age" of religious consensus will finally displace the old one. Sociologist Steven Tipton has argued that, in different ways, Americans continue trying to get "saved from the 60s."[1] For some, it is the search for final deliverance from the religious conformism of the early 60s, which they found personally stifling and morally bankrupt. Meanwhile, others seek deliverance from the legacies of the "counterculture," from the moral chaos and personal confusion they found so disturbing in the late 60s.

Tipton characterizes the countercultural revolt of the 60s as a crisis of meaning and morality in the face of accelerating technological innovation and bureaucratic organization in American society. The counterculture reacted against both the normlessness of utilitarian individualist ethics and the moral concessions made by biblical religion. Technological advances had expanded production, consumption, and leisure, thus increasing Americans' time and opportunity for self-expression. Personal relationships became more intimate and affective, providing much of life's meaning and gratification. These factors, combined with a period of unprecedented economic growth and high birth rates following World War II, produced an epiphany of middle-class life. An intensification of family intimacy and privacy took place under these conditions, further heightened by the introduction of home entertainment electronics such as television and high-fidelity music systems. Moreover, the registers of consumer desire were expanded by the advancing techniques of advertising. The huge baby-boom generation was targeted by Madison Avenue as the first age-specific market in history. All these factors combined to make the middle-class nuclear family a new realm of near-utopian levels of expectation.

Tipton describes two paradoxes issuing from these changing conditions. First, while individuals experienced an expanded freedom to construct private realms of meaning and morality, these often began to feel unreliable, even artificial. There was no quality of *necessity* to give them a compelling force. Even religious commitment lost its self-evident importance. Second, intrinsic values held within the private sphere became less tenable outside its boundaries. They became vague and platitudinous as solutions to the wider problems of society. As a result, mainstream religion, the moral consensus that had constituted the evident wholeness of American social life, lost its plausibility for many. One of the memorable expressions of this crisis of plausibility in the 60s was the scandalous assertion that "God is dead." Another expression was the off-hand but equally sensational remark by John Lennon that the Beatles had become "more popular than Jesus Christ." The "sacred canopy" of religious meaning over American society was seriously ruptured. By the mid-60s, the stage was set for religious seeking of unprecedented scale and scope.

Owing to sustained economic growth and the demands of a highly technological and bureaucratized society, baby-boom youth went to college in unprecedented numbers. The cultural optimism of the period made young people view ongoing social problems more critically than their parents' generation had. The blights of racial inequality and poverty were seen as intolerable travesties of the American dream. In that light, the social conservatism of most of American biblical religion and the self-serving motives of utilitarian individualism became equally untenable. Baby boomers looked upon the religion and morality of their parents' generation as sheer hypocrisy, palpable venality. They had been raised on values of interpersonal sensitivity and individual worth, values that were clearly not operative in the wider social realm. Many hoped to work for a better society through their educational advancements, aspirations that spilled out into more immediate involvement in the civil rights movement and other social causes. The patent racism and unequal opportunity of American society came to popular attention as never before.

On the other hand, college life distanced youth from involvement in mainstream work and family. It detached them from the economic, political, and public sectors of society. The academic environment only heightened the sense of critical distance from society at large. This social alienation was catalyzed into outright countercultural revolt most of all by the Vietnam War. This far-off, slowly escalating imperialist conflict not only threatened the very lives of baby boomers through the military draft; its vague objectives and high-tech weaponry, combined with gruesomely intimate television coverage, made it emblematic of "technical reason gone mad."

New, *personalist* politics began to emerge during the 60s. James J. Farrell[2] has identified this element as an important key to understanding changes in politics and spirituality in postwar America. Personalism can be characterized as an outlook in which everyday life is a political arena, where everyday choices have political implications, and that political participation changes not only policies but participants. Personalism began to emerge in the 50s as a new style of dissent, in which people responded to racism and to the nuclear threat on the authority of their own personal experiences, aspirations, and fears. Personalism rejected the power realism and conventional politics of the old liberal consensus in favor of new political values and methods. These included the inviolable dignity of persons, especially the poor and marginalized in society, and a suspicion of systems, both the liberal market economy and the socialist state, for their dehumanizing tendencies. Personalism proclaimed an emergent revolution of the heart through the personal practice of morality. A purely private life is incomplete; communities and small-scale institutions fulfill our true human potential and work for the common good through decentralized dynamics. Individual changes in consciousness are the building blocks of social change. Small-scale communities and institutions help form that new individual consciousness and mediate between individuals and society as a whole. Personalist politics opted for a philosophical anarchism advocating not disorder but more cooperative, less coercive institutions. Finally, the means of social change should be in harmony with its stated goals. Thus, violence is not an option for creating a harmonious and equitable society.[3]

As the baby-boom generation came of age during the 60s, these expressivist politics found mass appeal. American youth questioned social, political, and religious authorities with unprecedented audacity. They spoke boldly to national and global concerns out of the authority of their own experience and feelings, forming mercurial networks of cooperation and social action. Out of these networks, the counterculture formed, a utopian vanguard whose lifestyle and politics were thought to prefigure a new era that would enact the love ethic of the Sermon on the Mount and vindicate the Bill of Rights. The "credibility gap" between American rhetoric and social norms was challenged as never before.

The counterculture sought to replace utilitarian pursuit of *self-interest* with a post-materialist pursuit of *self-expression*. As Tipton summarizes it, the countercultural individual existed to experience, know, and simply be: "the way to do is the way to be." A pastiche of introspective modes—psychological, pharmacological, mystical, and literary-academic—was assembled under the rubric of self-awareness as the way to personal growth and social change.

The subject-object, means-ends dichotomies of technical knowledge and capitalist enterprise were rejected in favor of a *monistic* sense of the unity of all things. Biblical religion's cosmic and moral dualisms were dismissed almost without mention by many, who viewed the churches as hopelessly subverted by the imperatives of an acquisitive society. The "irrelevance" and lack of ecstatic experience in mainstream religion demonstrated its deadness. The acosmic monism of Buddhism appealed strongly to many in the counterculture. Techniques of meditation and emphasis upon awareness of the interconnectedness of reality harmonized with the countercultural watchword—"peace." Psychedelic drugs offered easy access to the realm of the numinous, a dimension so lacking in mainstream organized religion.

As personalism expanded into mass politics in the 60s, the acuity of its vision was inevitably blurred and at times trivialized. Key insights, derived in many cases from Christian and other religious traditions, were diluted into empty slogans: "All you need is love!" "Give peace a chance!" Despite its rhetoric, the counterculture's ethics often became utilitarian, even exploitative in personal and sexual relationships. But such inconsistencies were often wrapped in rationalizations suggesting that any loving, affectionate act contributed to the transformation of American culture from death-dealing to life-affirming values: "Make love, not war!" Ethics were couched in an expressive imperative to "do what you feel," presupposing a positive assessment of human nature. Indeed, all nature became a world to encounter feelingly, rather than analytically and exploitatively. Daisies pushed down the barrels of rifles at the Pentagon epitomized the countercultural sensibility. At the same time, however, ethical evaluation was vaguely prescribed, couched in psychological principles of healthy expression as a human need, not simply a desire.

Given these expressive emphases, the social vision of the counterculture opted in favor of small-scale, intimate, collegial, consensual forms of human organization. The blights of mainstream society were seen to generate from its large-scale, hierarchical, impersonal bureaucratic forms. The commune served as the garden test plot for a new order. The "happening" and "be-in" constituted cathartic events confronting the business-suit world of the mainstream with foretastes of an imminent Aquarian Age. These characteristics of the 60s counterculture may seem callow, simplistic, and transparently self-serving when viewed from this distance in time. But the rebellion from the bankruptcy of mainstream American life generated many trenchant criticisms of the existing order and mapped many of the alternative realms that seekers have explored far and wide in succeeding decades.

Finally, it is important to note that the cultural shifts of the 1960s were set in motion not only by the rapid advance of techno-capitalism in North America itself. In retrospect, we can see that this was a moment when capitalism was beginning a fundamental global restructuring.[4] The decolonialization that accelerated through the 1950s set the stage for a multinationalization of capital. Corporate enterprise was no longer tied to the imperialist designs of national interest; it existed at last in its own right, across all kinds of political boundaries. Colonialism stood out as the embarrassing and unnecessary vestige of another era. As the colonial template was lifted from developing nations, the "Third World" emerged to American awareness as a social world, an economic condition and a human experience in its own right. The misery of exploited peoples was popularized in the West by books such as Franz Fanon's *The Wretched of the Earth*. This Copernican shift in global consciousness contributed to the counterculture's revulsion toward the Vietnam War. It epitomized the naked imperialism of the old order.

Of course, the exploitative mechanisms of capitalism by no means ended with this new phase. A "neocolonial" control over developing nations by multinational corporations began to displace the old nationalist imperialism. Simultaneously, a new cultural logic emerged, one that has profoundly altered all realms of our existence. Since the 60s, multiculturalism has gradually deconstructed the Eurocentric worldview of American culture. The unique, idiomatic perspectives of the African-American, Native-American, Hispanic, and Asian-American experiences have challenged American institutions and authority structures with multiple reference points for reform. Moreover, the Immigration Reform Act of 1965 opened doors to non-Europeans, bringing practitioners and teachers of Asian and Islamic religion to America as never before. This "supply-side" aspect of broadening cultural and religious diversity in America (that is, government deregulation stimulating new sectors of growth) has been often overlooked.[5]

Finally, and no less profoundly, as more women went to college and the market began to demand their labor and stimulate their independent consumptive powers, the traditional androcentric worldview of patriarchal society also has been challenged. Feminism has thus offered another fundamental perspective to the new world-view within the multi-national phase of capitalism. These new, earthshaking cultural patterns all gained ascendance in the 1960s, and they continue to work their way through society in ways that are bracing for some and jarring for others. Under these conditions of a rapidly shifting cultural terrain, religious seeking of one kind or another becomes incumbent upon everyone. There is no territory left untouched by the seismic changes that jolted society in the 60s. Even the most traditional religious practices are transformed in meaning by the new landscape.

The cultural spasms of the 60s mark the beginning of our postmodern era. Western modernism had celebrated a progressive triumph of the new over the traditional, promising ever more utopian bliss through economic growth, technological advancement, and mass cultural consumption of arts and entertainment. The accelerating progress of the new reached a fever pitch in the 60s. But as modernization evolved different forms in other cultures, and as other cultures came to be encountered in their own right, the Eurocentric reference point for the *new* disintegrated into the multiculturalism of the *many*. (In that last respect, perhaps our condition could be termed "metamodern" as easily as postmodern.)

THE AFTERMATH OF 60S COUNTERCULTURE

The counterculture wound down in the early seventies as the military draft ended, the liberal "Great Society" program stalled, and baby boomers entered the workforce and started families. By their very numbers, baby boomers devalued their educational assets as they entered the labor market. Finally, recessionary inflation, exacerbated by the energy crisis, further deflated countercultural politics. Tipton emphasizes that the counterculture's own fragility also contributed to its demise. It had existed almost entirely in the lived moment, unable to institutionalize its chaotic energies. Farrell's personalist analysis is more sympathetic, emphasizing that, whatever the strengths and failings of the counterculture, it was simply no match for the superior forces of the techno-capitalist mainstream.[6]

But while the counterculture's protest was soon ground down by the wheels of "the system," the latter also lost its moral authority. The counterculture seriously damaged the credibility of utilitarian culture and its institutions: governmental, legal, economic, religious, and domestic. The conflict of the 60s "left both sides of the battlefield strewn with expired dreams and ideological wreckage. It resulted in the disillusioned withdrawal of young and old, hip and straight, away from active concern with public institutions and back into the refuge of private life. But this has been no simple return to normalcy."[7]

Tipton's study charts various courses taken by discontented and disillusioned 60s youth, as they sought alternative religious options during the 1970s. He emphasizes that this was a matter of moral survival and a recovery of meaning and purpose for many who felt bereft entering adulthood. He offers in-depth examinations of three representative alternatives pursued by young adults in California during the seventies.

First, he describes a neo-pentecostal congregation combining many features of traditional biblical religion with a new emphasis upon ecstatic experience. The group ecstasy of tongue-speaking replaced the numinous experience of psychedelic drugs for young converts, many of whom came from lower-middle-class and less educated backgrounds. But a strong emphasis upon the Bible and the pastor's (in this case a woman's) leadership balanced intensely subjective experience with a stable, external authority structure. A millennial emphasis upon the coming end of the world articulated a continuing disillusion with the institutions of secular society and with the staidness of mainstream, denominational religion. For members of this congregation, the objective truth of the Bible's teaching would soon be painfully clear to all in God's judgment upon a morally bankrupt society.

Second, Tipton examines a Zen center, offering a monastic Buddhist regimen of life for a few live-in "students," as well as training in meditation and religious teaching for a larger network of nonresidents. Here many 60s youth found confirmation of the antinomian monism of the counterculture. The Buddhist emphasis upon a nontheistic, acosmic unity of all things fostered an all-embracing attitude of compassion. There were some rules, or precepts, for living; but the individual was taught to live more by expanded awareness than by rules. In this sense, then, countercultural antinomianism was preserved within a new, disciplined framework. In a sense, the "rules" existed only if transgressed. Otherwise, one lived in awareness primarily of reality itself, not its rules. Authority was strongly, almost autocratically embodied in the *roshi*, or resident teacher. Yet this authority was neither dogmatically asserted nor bureaucratically situated; it was rather the charismatic authority of one whose disciplined life exemplified his teachings.

The socioeconomic profile of Zen students in Tipton's study was more upper-middle-class and more educated. In the 60s, these youth experimented with drugs as a path of expanded perception (as opposed to the group catharsis many of the future neo-pentecostals in Tipton's study had sought). In many cases, they were not raised religiously as children. Through long-term involvement in Zen practice, many remained relatively "dropped-out" from mainstream American life, often working in lower-paying menial or service jobs. Tipton found a continuing countercultural disenchantment with mainstream institutions, including most Western theistic religions. The larger social and political vision of the Zen student was likely to be ecological in its outlook—a holistic, compassionate concern for all "sentient beings"—in opposition to the instrumentalist ethics of technocratic civilization. Such an outlook would better express the non-egoistic "Big Self," or "Buddha Self": the transpersonal nature of reality.

The third alternative religious movement examined by Tipton was *est,* the Erhard Seminars Training, that burgeoned in the 1970s as a major expression of the human potential movement. *est* restored the consequential ethical style of utilitarian individualism, but on a new, countercultural footing. It posited the expressive value of "aliveness," a sense of well-being, as the fundamental interest of every individual. It also confirmed the romantic rebellion from the institutions and authorities of mainstream culture. In addition, however, it also demanded a return to a mental toughness that recognizes that the "rules" governing institutions are a key to "getting what you want." So while *est* shrugged off the cultural standards of the mainstream, it embraced mainstream rules on a pragmatic, utilitarian basis. Life is a game. Playing by its rules and contracting effectively with others to do the same will maximize aliveness. This fusion of an expressive sense of the good and a consequential definition of the right aided many youths, particularly from the middle-middle-class sector, to make the transition out of the undisciplined ethos of the counterculture and into the bureaucratic structures of corporate America. If there is a line that can be drawn from 60s hippie to 80s yuppie, it surely passes through *est*, among other utilitarian human potential teachings.

That is not to say that *est* advocated an acquisitive lifestyle heedless of others. The individual was thought to create his or her own world, thus taking responsibility for the entire world, at least in subjective terms. The most responsible act of the *est* graduate was to recruit others to take the training and get a grip on life. But *est* also ran seminars in prisons and developed the Hunger Project in the late seventies, an initiative to motivate individuals on a mass basis to end world hunger by the year 2000.

Tipton finds a common thread among these alternative religious movements of the post-counterculture era: the combining of new expressive ideals with reasserted moral norms of authority, rules, and utility. He grants that these new syntheses were not always good, alluding to Jonestown and the brainwashing cults of the seventies. But in many cases during the seventies and eighties, stable alternatives, whether neo-Christian, neo-Oriental, or human potential-based, have offered a reconstructed moral universe for many seekers who, in one way or another, "dropped out" in the 60s.[8]

Religious Seeking in the 80s and 90s

As we approach the present situation of religious seeking in America, we come to a second important sociological study, Wade Clark Roof's *A Generation of Seekers: The Spiritual Journeys of the Baby-Boom Generation*.[9] Roof examines American patterns of religious exploration and commitment in the 80s and into the 90s, focusing particularly on baby boomers, those born between 1946 and 1964, comprising about a third of the population of the United States today. He cites the work of Karl Mannheim, who singled out generational dynamics in sociological research. Mannheim notes that, especially during times of intense social change and dislocation, a generation that is coming of age will be set apart, sharing a "common location"—certain unifying experiences—in the social process.[10]

Mannheim's theories seem to find particular confirmation in the baby-boom generation and its religious life. Through the extensive polling and interviews conducted by Roof's team, many different social factors such as race, class, ethnicity, gender, and region intersect in the religious movement of individuals. But the key connection Roof found among them is the experience of growing up in the 60s. Strong experiential themes of high expectations and deep disappointments during that period define the moral and religious vision of those who came of age in the 60s and early seventies.

One strong feature of the "boomer" generation is continued unsettledness, an ongoing search for personal meaning combined with a low level of community involvement, suggesting to some that the old "Me Generation" tag is still apt. In *The Culture of Narcissism* (1979),[11] Christopher Lasch criticizes a self-absorption in American morality. In *Habits of the Heart* (1985),[12] Robert Bellah and associates (including Steven Tipton) ponder American individualism and difficulties in commitment. Robert Wuthnow explores religious attitudes toward work and money in *God and Mammon in America* (1994),[13] finding utilitarian individualism still alive and well among religious and secularist Americans alike. Roof offers a more optimistic reading, suggesting that boomers are engaged in a fundamental quest: to discover a new grounding for religious and interpersonal commitments, a basis for community stronger than the one that fell apart before their eyes in the 60s.

Roof's study confirms many impressions of baby boomers in the 60s, but adds a new perspective. Many tried drugs, were sexually active, and went to rock concerts and political protests. But many did not. Half of those surveyed say they did not try drugs; a third never attended a rock concert; and 80% were not politically active in that period. On the whole, Roof finds boomers to be nearly evenly divided between traditionalist and countercultural affinities.

One of the strongest features of this generation pertains to institutional religion. During young adulthood, more than 60% dropped out for two years or longer from active involvement in religion as young adults (these figures are nearly even between women and men). That departure took place against a background of very high levels of religious involvement in childhood. Ninety percent of those surveyed had attended religious services weekly or more often as children eight to ten years old. By their early twenties, however, only about a quarter of them were still that active. The great majority had dropped out altogether or attended only occasionally. Roof notes that some level of dropping out is a steady feature in American culture. But the levels among those growing up in the 60s and seventies were exceptionally high.[14]

The suspicion of institutional forms that motivated the religious dropouts of that period is still active among boomers. Roof finds a continu-

ing passion to unmask hidden repression, violence, deceit, and evil
lurking at various levels of American life, including religious life. But
he sees behind this negative program a deep motive that is not fundamentally suspicious: the continuing search for God. Indeed, the boomer
profile as religious consumers "shopping around" in the marketplace of
faiths is confirmed by statistics: 60% agreed that it is better to explore
many different faiths than to stay with one. Explorers tended to be more
numerous among the more educated. However, boomers were divided
evenly on the question of whether all religions are essentially the same.
Only half had seriously doubted the existence of God. A
quarter of respondents said they could imagine God as a mother.[15]

Roof's study posits three basic religious types among boomers: dropouts, who have either continued exploring alternative religions or left
religious activity altogether; loyalists, who never left traditional religious institutions; and returnees, who eventually came back to mainstream religion, though not necessarily the same one. A brief review of
Roof's profiles of these three groups is useful.

Among the dropouts, Roof defines one group as "highly active
seekers." Comprising about 9% of the baby-boom generation, they are
deeply involved in their own personal quests and tend to view themselves as "spiritual" rather than "religious." The socioeconomic profile
of these boomers is older, white-collar, and professional (though often
in lower-paying work, such as teaching, nursing, and counseling), more
female, less likely to be married, politically liberal, often switching careers or jobs. Highly active seekers are less likely to have come from
highly religious homes. They exhibit less "relationship density" than
boomers in general: that is, fewer of their friends know each other.

Highly active seekers tend toward a mystical sense of spiritual life,
an emphasis upon direct, inward spiritual experience. Their religious
world-view is typically universalist in rejecting the exclusive truth-claims
of any single religion; monistic in affirming the oneness of all reality;
immanentalist in emphasizing God within or the continuity of God and
self; and syncretistic in adapting myths, concepts, and practices from a
wide variety of religious traditions. In their embrace of mysticism, highly
active seekers place particular value on peak, ecstatic experience. Roof
sees a number of strengths among this small but influential segment of
the boomer generation. But he notes that the mystical approach also
exhibits certain weaknesses. It is hard to sustain, requiring new con-

firming experiences on a frequent basis. And without a strong, stable social base to make an individual accountable to others, it can be hard to make lasting breakthroughs in personal transformation. Mysticism typically lacks shared rituals, an affirming community, and a sense of belonging, making it difficult to pass on a parent's values to children.[16]

While the highly active seeker fits the cultural archetype of the "wanderer," the profile of the "loyalist" is closer to the "orphan" archetype. The loyalist typically looks back ruefully at the 60s as a time when traditional values, religious allegiances, and family ties were swept away by irresponsible rebellion and false freedom. Thus, feeling orphaned by the turbulent storm of the counterculture, the loyalist devotes considerable religious energy to reclaiming and reconstructing a sense of "family" in personal relationships and religious community.

In this case, the seeking quest is not an open-ended odyssey but a focused effort to "walk with the Lord" in obedience, bringing all aspects of one's life into "right relationship" with God. In contrast to the monism of the highly active seeker, the loyalist sees the self not as continuous with God but in sinful alienation. Dying to self, in traditional Christian terms, is the challenge. Along with this distrust of subjectivity comes a renewed allegiance to external authorities: the Bible and its authoritative interpreters. The loyalist socioeconomic profile is more managerial and small-business oriented, less professional, less educated. One hears a rhetoric against materialism and status-seeking, but the profile is more upwardly mobile.

The new evangelicalism has attracted many boomers, bringing conservative faith back from the margins to the mainstream. It is an amalgamation of traditional Protestantism and newer, post-60s emphases, making the conservative baby boomer actually less ingrained in traditional ways than is usually supposed. For example, we noted earlier Tipton's portrayal of the neo-pentecostal combination of fundamentalist Christian doctrine and morality with the experiential power of ecstatic worship. Among neo-evangelicals generally, "personal salvation" has become more individualistic and experiential. As a result, the church as an institution appears to have less value as an entity unto itself, but is evaluated on utilitarian terms, according to what expressive outlets and other services it offers the individual. Consequently, being a good Christian is less linked to church attendance among boomer evangelicals. They are also less likely to pray or to read the Bible as regularly as

earlier generations of evangelicals. The emphasis on traditional family
values is often a fairly pragmatic one, freely mixing psychological concepts and changing gender norms with traditional biblical standards.
Here Roof sees a strategy that sets limits on lifestyle variation, while at
the same time accommodating it. Meanwhile, "recovery" spiritualities
aim to help the faithful to struggle against addictive patterns and abusive histories. As Roof concludes, the new evangelical is as much on a
quest for a renewed sense of self as is the dropout. They are both seekers, but in different modes.[17]

Finally, the "returnees": they tend to be moderates, standing between
the "born again" religious conservatism of the loyalists and the New Age
quests of the highly active seekers. These account for one quarter of Roof's
survey. They frequently use language of "shopping" religions and churches,
basing decisions upon subjective criteria of "how it feels." But family
considerations are most frequently cited by returnees. Many come back
for the sake of harmony with a spouse or the wider family. Concern over
children's religious training is most frequently cited among those interviewed. Roof postulates that concern for the children may often be
the guise for the parents' own struggle with feelings of emptiness or
loneliness.[17] Return to organized religion is sometimes a move made in
desperation, to save a marriage, reform children, or recover from addiction or abuse. Sometimes strains develop in congregations between the
loyalist and returnee contingents, between those who resisted the counterculture all along and those who have come back from it. Again, Roof
finds the 60s experience decisive. Those who were most caught up in the
counterculture are the least likely to return to organized religion, or will
have the most difficulty in reintegrating with it.[19]

"CULTURE WARS" AND THE GREAT RELIGIOUS DIVIDE
IN AMERICA

Roof posits four basic realms of religious polarization among baby
boomers. First, the conception of the self: a quest for personal fulfillment or a submission to God's will? Second, religious authority: immanent
or transcendent? feelings or Scriptures? Third, systems of meaning:
mystical, tending toward monism, or theistic, tending toward dualism?
Fourth, spiritual styles: let go or hold on? These are distilled tendencies

that may not exist in pure form in any individual or group, but they do characterize a great spiritual divide in American religious culture today.

But Roof also sees common themes among boomers of all types. Among these are a strong insistence upon personal preference in religious commitment; an imperative need for personal growth and wholeness; a valuation of "spiritual" over "religious"; a predominance of addiction, dysfunctional family, and abuse issues and metaphors; and a strong sense of victimhood and the need for healing or recovery. Finally, at both ends of the seeker spectrum, loyalist and drop-out seekers alike tend toward a millennial view of the future. Whether God is coming to judge the iniquity of this age, or environmental decay will overwhelm the planet, or some form of "harmonic convergence" will renew the cosmos, various "end of this world" scenarios proliferate.[20]

Many boomers across the spectrum manifest an outlook that Roland Delattre has described as "supply-side spirituality": a deep conviction that God or the universe offers an abundance of all things material and spiritual.[21] The only obstacles to our partaking of that abundance are the limitations that we place upon our consumption. The obstacles may be described in biblical terms as sinful alienation from God's grace, or in psychological terms as repression of personal feelings and interests. The individual may be encouraged to take responsibility for removing the obstacles or to make others responsible for them. But the underlying assumption is one of consumptive abundance. Delattre shows this theme to be well established in American culture, going back at least as far as Emerson. But it has grown as a theme in our consumptive, acquisitive society, reaching an apotheosis during the era of economic growth that culminated in the 60s. Supply-side spirituality has contributed much to the counterculture's utopian rhetoric.

But in subsequent decades, with a tightening of the American economy, the assumption of abundance often turned from utopian to belligerent, as Americans vented their frustration over lowered or failed expectations. Given their expanded subjective and expressive registers, boomers are already more likely to consider themselves wounded by defects in their religious upbringing. When religious institutions or leaders fail their expectations today, boomers are all the more likely to feel cheated, wounded, or even victimized.

In his *Genealogy of Morals*,[22] Friedrich Nietzsche formulated the classic analysis of *ressentiment* as a negative moral energy. Out of resentment of the social status or class standing of another individual or group, a negative self-identification emerges: "We are not what they are." Resentment becomes particularly strong when one's own objective well-being or subjective equilibrium is threatened by the position or actions of one's shadow-opposite. On an individual level, this can quickly lead to a negative self-identification as "victim," or the "low self-esteem" complaint that became widespread in the 90s. Unresolved resentments and victim-oriented politics preoccupy and often damage the effectiveness of many religious organizations today. Under these conditions, negativity shifts from a guilt-based mentality of personal responsibility to a shame-based mentality of "shame-and-blame." It is an interesting question whether the countercultural liberation from the guilt-based Christian conviction of human sinfulness has actually led us into a more paralyzing morass of shame-based rhetoric and behavior.

On a wider social basis, the same spirit of resentment has become the driving energy of the so-called "culture wars" portrayed in the popular sociological study of James Davison Hunter.[22] Hunter analyzes the well-publicized issues that rage in the public arena and tear apart many religious communities today: conflicts over abortion, women's rights and roles, homosexuality, sex education, public funding for the arts, and others. He finds the conflict played out between two fundamentally different sensibilities: orthodox and progressive. In Hunter's treatment, the constituencies that embody these two sensibilities correspond fairly well to Roof's loyalists and dropouts. Hunter notes that, in principle, both parties are willing to tolerate or ignore each other's existence in a pluralistic society. What often draws them into active conflict is the perception, real or imagined, that the other constituency is gaining ground politically or socially.

Peter Berger offers a class analysis of the conflict.[24] The cultural frictions we experience today are symbolic expressions of a struggle for power between two middle classes, the traditional business class and the emergent knowledge class. (Roof's profiles of religious loyalists and dropouts have already indicated this demographic split.) Cultural symbols are key weapons in class struggle. Issues such as abortion and gay rights have a symbolic dimension in the current class conflict, besides their own inherent meaning. Thus, Berger suggests, the spiteful energy of these conflicts derives as much from class resentment as from the intrinsic moral or political convictions being debated.

These class frictions intensify during periods of a tightening economy, the shrinking horizon that so threatens the "supply-side spirituality" of boomers in particular. Thus, it is "those religious right-wingers" who threaten the freedoms, cloud enlightenment, and obstruct the social destiny of the progressivist party. Or it is "those New Agers and liberals" who stand in the way of the orthodox program to rechristianize America and save the family. There may indeed be objective truth to some of these accusations. But the shadow projections from both sides make it clear that the dynamics of resentment are at work. The "family values" of the right certainly reassert some traditional American mores; but they just as certainly are formed out of resentment of the sexual freedom enjoyed by many since the 60s. Likewise, the "freedom" celebrated and defended by the left would lose much of its gusto without the perceived "strait-laced" sexual repression of conservative religion as its foil. In my years of ministry in the Religious Society of Friends (Quakers), on both sides of the American cultural conflict, I have heard the rhetoric of the endangered minority utilized countless times. Among evangelical Friends, the "mainstream" and rhetorical foil is pandemic liberal humanism. Among liberal Friends, it is the juggernaut of the religious right, or even the church in general. This resentment in the Nietzschean sense is the double negative that neutralizes moral evaluation, constructive action, and spiritual renewal across the religious spectrum today.

Orthodox and progressive factions live in each other's unexamined shadow. The utopian vision of each contingent, whether it be the multicultural rainbow of the left or the family values of the right, blocks the vision of each to the other's truth, sense of the sacred, and basis for hope. Worse, the foreign logic of the other's rhetoric easily becomes a screen upon which we project our fears. Again, there may be real, objective reasons for concern over the social aims of either the right or the left. But much of the resentment, conflict, and occasional violence generated by our current culture wars emerges from our own unexamined internal shadows. If we would seek a fuller vision of the truth, we must also seek one another. Religious and moral reconstruction in America will necessarily involve some kind of *atonement* across present battle lines.

Toward that reconciliation and restoration of covenantal wholeness, it is important to remember that the dialectic of seeking and finding, of standing still and wandering, is greater than all of us. Martin Marty has recently described the rebuilding of American civil society as a vast conversation, an epic argument, and an unfolding story in which all of us must engage.[25] It is an argument because we take different positions, some of which are contrary or even contradictory. The dialectic requires position-taking. It cannot be a give-and-take between vague wafflings. At some moments, the positions will be irreconcilable, incommensurable; at other moments, subtle shifts will open up new possibilities for the argument to become a conversation. Dialectic is converted to a conversation when we become curious enough to ask why others believe and act as they do, and when we talk about the experiences, dispositions, hopes, and fears that underlie our own religious positions. Inevitably, the conversation includes telling our stories, the journeys that have led to our present choices. In the process of the deeper listening afforded by conversation, we may find ourselves *converted* to our neighbor. That does not necessarily mean converted to our neighbor's position; rather, it means becoming neighborly, committed to one another. Our positions may be far-flung, but we are neighbors because our stories, our seeking, and our finding, weave our lives into some larger pattern. Here we begin to discover dialectic as a larger story, unfolding through the interplay of all our arguments, conversations, and stories. For example, although we have been arguing about many of the same questions throughout the 60s, 70s, 80s, and 90s, and although we will no doubt continue into the new millennium, the style and terms of the argument have not remained the same. They continue to evolve as we continue to seek and find, seek and find—seeking God and finding one another; seeking one another and finding God.

SEEKING WITHIN A CAPITALIST DEMOCRACY

Throughout this chapter, the economic dimension of contemporary seeking has hovered in the background. Occasionally, there has been explicit reference to economic factors, such as the globalization of capital that catalyzed the deep cultural shifts of the 60s. More often, there have been metaphorical evocations of the economic dimension, such as references to "supply-side spirituality," "religious consumerism," and the tendency to "shop" religious options. Our examination of seeking today would be incomplete (in fact, misleading) if we did not say a little more about the economic dimension of religious currents, particularly in the hyper-capitalist culture that exists in the United States. A market culture is by definition a seeking culture. We have already sketched the economic factors that "inspired" so many baby boomers to leave their religious homes and begin seeking in the latter 60s. I do not wish to reduce all social phenomena, even religious life, to a crude economic determinism. But we ignore the economic factors of our existence at our peril. They will rule us more fully if we remain unconscious of their pull upon us.

What are the signs of a capitalist dynamic at work in our seeking situation? When suburban mega-churches begin to look like office parks, their ministers functioning like CEOs, and their elders making decisions like boards of directors, corporate capitalism has surely made its mark upon church life. For many, such as the numerous business-class believers who flock to these new churches, this development seems entirely appropriate. To others, often those of the knowledge-class sector, such patterns indicate the continuing cultural captivity of the church.

As a counter-example, when "highly active seekers" take on the behavior of fickle, fashion-conscious shoppers, eagerly tasting every new spiritual flavor, a kind of consumer mentality seems to take over. The mystifications of a supposed "new spirituality," "a new consciousness" or a "paradigm shift" barely veil market logic at work. To what extent is our seeking moved by divine intimations? To what extent are we simply nudged by the "hidden hand" of the market to explore new "brands" of religion? And to the extent that we recognize that influence upon us, do we agree with Adam Smith that this "hidden hand" works for our good, and for the general good of all? In other words, how "civil" is the market?

Michael Oakeshott, whose analysis of human associations I utilized in the Introduction, notes a common misconception that equates the civil mode of association with democracy or capitalism. He responds by characterizing democracy as a "constitutional shape," not a mode of association *per se*. It may serve republican virtues with particular aptitude, but should not be equated with *respublica*, public concern. Likewise, "free enterprise" cannot be identified with the civil mode, which is not the mode of enterprise, free or otherwise. In the civil mode of association, the individual is a subject of obligations and a possessor of rights, not a bargainer for satisfactions.[26]

Civility is a quality of life held in trust by all participants, a covenantal peace that must be entered into as much in spirit as by the letter of its obligations. Thus, democratic political processes may serve that purpose but are not the concern itself. For their part, political actors may choose to pursue narrow self-interest rather than civil concern. Likewise, capitalist economic processes have remarkable flexibility and vitality, but function in the mode of enterprise. Capitalist enterprise may ruthlessly exploit weaker partners in production or heedlessly degrade the natural environment in the pursuit of substantive ends. Insofar as the stock-holding corporation dominates economic life, the narrowly defined aim of profit-making tends to filter out civil concern.

We may conclude that there seem to be affinities between a democratic capitalist society and a widespread religious mood of seeking. Free speech, religious liberty, and a free-market of religious options are conditions tending to maximize religious inquiry. But does increased seeking promote a more civil society?

With the preceding considerations in mind, we may make two general observations on the nature of seeking in a capitalist democracy. First, seeking that forms associations strongly in the enterprise mode, with only peripheral commitment to the civil mode of public concern, will often be captive (explicitly or implicitly) to capitalist democracy's agendas for the maximization of growth and the concentration of power. For example, the neo-evangelical movement, with its strongly enterprising imperative to church growth and world missions, tends toward an uncritical affirmation of capitalist expansion and multinational corporate power. This movement has formed the central contingent of the religious right, which has been extremely influential in American political life through coalition politics, direct mail campaigns, and political action committees. The religious right has been strongly supportive of federal government in its enterprise aspects, such as militarism and national interests abroad. Its civil concern tends toward a narrow insistence that traditional Christian moral virtues should be normative for all Americans. Thus, seekers who find their home in neo-evangelical churches tend to embrace simple, straightforward doctrines and morality that allow them to get on with the business of evangelism and missions. They will tend to find harmony between an entrepreneurial mode of church growth and the general market culture of capitalism. Their democratic values will often adapt to the imperative to Christianize American society and support policies to spread and defend capitalist democracy around the world.

The point here is not whether some economic system other than capitalism or some political system other than democracy would be better or worse than what we have today. Since capitalist democracy is the system that dominates our world, the point is to be aware of its far-reaching influence both within and around us, and to be more clearly intentional in how we choose to operate within that system. When Jesus held up a coin and said, "Render to Caesar the things that are Caesar's, and to God the things that are God's" (Mark 12:17), he was not offering a simple answer to a simple question about taxes. He intended to induce in every hearer a crisis of conscience—a deep, troubling reflection upon life as we find it within the dominant system of our time. In some respects, it is only appropriate that religious life should adopt forms idiomatic to the prevailing social and economic structures of its day. In other respects, however, the role of religious life is surely to confront the prevailing culture with a message, morality, and mode of operation that show another way.

The second and converse observation is that seeking that moves strongly in the civil mode of association, with a more peripheral concern for the substantive ends of an enterprising faith, will tend to be captive to the *processes* of capitalist democracy. Its political energies will tend to be neutralized by the weakness of its substantive ends, just as its spirituality will be enervated by the vagueness of its commitment to a transcendent God, a divine that is beyond the realm of human differences. For example, those whose seeking leads them to more religiously "liberal" associations will often be motivated by concerns for ecumenical, interfaith, or multicultural dialogue. The *process* that such interchange takes will be of paramount importance, while the desired *product* of the exchange will often receive only sketchy, qualitative definition (in contrast to the quantitative ends typically sought in the enterprise mode). While the chosen process of dialogue may appear immaculate within its own frame of reference, it may in fact be captivated by democratic and capitalist contractualism and fall short of true, covenantal civility.

For example, if civility is too strongly identified with democratic processes, then true seeking and conversion to one's neighbor will tend to be subverted. Caucus politics or the contest of interests may usurp the conversation. In a parallel fashion, a narrow-minded concern for the *procedures* of a religious association ("good order"), when it precludes attention to the *content* of the faith itself, may lead to a situation where the *means* of faith dictate and reshape the *ends*. This amounts to religious technocracy. In such a case, those most adept at manipulating the processes take control of the association, while its larger vision and purpose are lost. A conversion to neighbor that lacks a concomitant conversion to God creates a process without a *Telos*—a practical means without a transcendent End, or purpose. Where the larger purpose of faith is lost, even the most civil processes become sterile. We can see the captivity of liberal politics everywhere, as "political correctness" translates to political impotence against the more narrowly based but better focused coalition politics of the right.

A loose, syncretistic universalism that aims to tolerate and include all religious and cultural positions in an undifferentiated jumble is a barely disguised religious approximation of the free market. And while such an unrestricted field of play is prerequisite to public concern, it does not produce social health in the final analysis. The dialectical process of argument, conversation, and unfolding story *requires* a fair and open field of play but does not *consist* in it. A socially constructive and spiritually transformative process requires a disciplined and sustained dialogue between seriously considered and passionately held positions. The drama of faith, when it is played out upon a level civic stage of public concern, requires that each actor enter the scene fully immersed in his or her role or position in the drama, but also fully recognizing the improvisational reality that "the play" will dramatically alter the apparent meaning of each position and the evident direction of each role of the drama. Again, we see the ongoing interaction between seeking and finding. This sense of *dialectical* universalism is crucially different from the syncretistic universalism and obliquely market spirituality of the liberal left as well as the enterprising universalism of the Christian right, bent upon monopolistic domination by one faith.

We will return to these turn-of-the millennium issues of seeking, albeit from a different angle, in our Conclusion. But first, the bulk of our study will focus on seeking at the dawn of the modern era. In the next chapter, we will examine two leaders on the radical fringes of the Protestant Reformation. These two figures are paradigmatic of the seeking option during that tumultuous period on the continent of Europe. We will then move on in succeeding chapters to find their two seeking trajectories played out at the end of the English Reformation.

NOTES

1. Steven M. Tipton, *Getting Saved from the 60s: Moral Meaning in Conversion and Cultural Change* (Berkeley: University of California Press, 1982).
2. James J. Farrell, *The Spirit of the 60s: the Making of Postwar Radicalism* (New York: Routledge, 1997).
3. Farrell, *60s*, 6-8. Farrell portrays the roots of personalist politics as two main sources. The Catholic personalism of Emmanuel Mounier in France during the 1930s sought a third way beyond capitalism and Marxism. His influence came into the United States through Peter Maurin and his influence on the Catholic Worker movement. The other source is a stream of Methodist personalism articulated by figures such as Parker Bowne, Edgar Brightman, and Harold deWolf at Boston University. This stream attracted the young Martin Luther King Jr. to Boston University for his PhD studies and affected him profoundly. Important personalist innovators before the 60s counterculture include King, Dorothy Day, A. J. Muste, Kenneth Rexroth and some of the Beat poets, Bayard Rustin, Barbara Deming, and others. Farrell traces the development of personalist politics through the civil rights, ban-the-bomb, free-speech, antiwar, early feminist, environmental, and human potential movements. Something like the Spiritualist stream of the Reformation, which we will trace to the Seeker and Quaker movements in England, personalism is an important key to understanding the rise of mass seeking in our own time.
4. I am indebted here to the work of Fredric Jameson in *Postmodernism, or, the Cultural Logic of Late Capitalism* (Durham: Duke University Press, 1991). For another, more extensive use of Jameson's work I have made previously, see the Conclusion of my *The Covenant Crucified: Quakers and the Rise of Capitalism* (Wallingford, Pa.: Pendle Hill, 1995).
5. See Roger Finke and Laurence R. Iannaccone, "Supply-Side Explanations for Religious Change," in *Religion in the Nineties*, ed. Wade Clark Roof, *The Annals of the American Academy of Political and Social Science* 527 (May 1993): 27-39.
6. Farrell, *60s*, 258. While Farrell is realistic about the infirmities of personalist politics, he emphasizes that it permanently altered American politics even as it failed. Personalist politics are "Sisyphean" and must perennially wage struggle in the face of apparent futility.
7. Tipton, *Saved*, 29.
8. Tipton, *Saved*, 30.
9. Wade Clark Roof, *A Generation of Seekers: The Spiritual Journeys of the Baby-boom Generation* (San Francisco: HarperCollins, 1993).
10. See "The Problem of Generations," in Karl Mannheim, *Essays on the Sociology of Knowledge* (London: Routledge & Kegan Paul, 1952), 276-320.
11. Christopher Lasch, *The Culture of Narcissism: American Life in an Age of Diminishing Expectations* (New York: Norton, 1979).
12. Robert Bellah et. al., *Habits of the Heart: Individualism and Commitment in American Life* (Berkeley: University of California Press, 1985).

13. Robert Wuthnow, *God and Mammon in America* (New York: The Free Press, 1994).
14. Roof, *Seekers*, 54-56.
15. Roof, *Seekers*, 71-76.
16. Roof, *Seekers*, 79-88. On the mystical need for confirming experiences on a regular basis, see also Louis Dupre, "Spiritual Life in a Secular Age," in *Religion and America*, 3-13.
17. Roof, *Seekers*, 115.
18. Roof, *Seekers*, 158.
19. Roof, *Seekers*, 170-71.
20. Roof, *Seekers*, 128-33.
21. Roland A. Delattre, "Supply-Side Spirituality: A Case Study in the Cultural Interpretation of Religious Ethics in America," in *Religion and the Life of the Nation: American Recoveries*, ed. Rowland A. Sherrill (Urbana: University of Illinois Press, 1990), 84-108.
22. Friedrich Nietzsche, *On the Genealogy of Morals*, Walter Kaufmann, ed. (New York: Vintage, 1967).
23. James Davison Hunter, *Culture Wars: The Struggle to Define America* (New York: Basic Books, 1991).
24. Peter L. Berger, "From the Crisis of Religion to the Crisis of Secularity," in *Religion and America*, 14-24.
25. Martin E. Marty, *The One and the Many: America's Struggle for the Common Good* (Cambridge: Harvard University Press, 1997), Chapter 8. I do not find Marty's civil religion paradigm always helpful. He does not seem to honor the integrity of strongly held positions in the overall scheme of republican life, but prefers that all moderate toward a more semi-detached sense of civility. Also, his vision for civil religion does not take into account the powerful determining force of capitalist economics in American life.
26. Michael Oakeshott, "Talking Politics," in his *Rationalism in Politics and Other Essays*, new and expanded edition (Indianapolis: Liberty, 1991), 456-57.

Chapter 2

Caspar Schwenckfeld and Sebastian Franck
Seeker Formations in the 1520s and 1530s

The 1520s were a decade of revolt throughout much of Europe. Conceived of today as the Protestant Reformation, this widespread rebellion took many forms and was spearheaded by a generation of young leaders who could no longer tolerate the moral compromises and institutional inertia of the religious establishment. Many were inspired and given courage by Martin Luther's confrontation with the church's hierarchy. Luther was a half-generation older than many Reformers who emerged in the 1520s. But although the boldness of Luther's protest and the power of his religious synthesis caught the imagination of these younger Reformers, they soon developed reforming agendas very different from his. The crisis of Renaissance Catholicism and the different responses that crisis elicited require a brief review here.

In his classic study of the Reformation,[1] Roland Bainton emphasizes that by the 1520s the impetus for reform had become so urgent and widespread that movements cropped up more or less spontaneously in many places. A number of social, economic, and political factors converged to create the upheavals of this period. Nationalism had weakened the political consensus of the Holy Roman Empire. The theocratic power of the Papacy had become increasingly reactionary as the church's economic base crumbled. The economic individualism of new commerce drastically undercut the communal world-view of medievalism. And Renaissance arts and sciences drew increasingly from classical antiquity to recast the human individual as both subject and object of rational study. All these factors are important to our understanding of the great ruptures across European society during the sixteenth century.

But most of all, Bainton stresses that the Reformation must be recognized as a popular religious revival. In that respect, it was the last in a series of resurgences of grassroots Christian piety that had coursed through medieval Europe. The Reformation renewed Christendom by making popular devotion central again. At the same time, however, because this cumulative spiritual ground swell finally overwhelmed the institutional structures of classical Christendom, it marks the end of the medieval Catholic consensus.

It will be useful to review Bainton's summary of the great historic forces that had come to such fatal contradiction by the 16th century. It is important to remember that the spread of Christianity in the West is uniquely tied to the collapse of the Roman Empire as a political structure. In the face of barbarian invasions, the church assumed the role of Caesar, recreating political society on the basis of religious conversion. A complex process of educating and civilizing the invaders, pacifying feuding tribes, and integrating northern and southern European cultures took place from the 5th–11th centuries. In order to advance this enormous project, the church required great material resources. Through the mass conversion of whole tribes, it gained not only the religious devotion of large populations but enormous holdings in land as well. As much as half the territories of Germany and France came under church control. To be sure, these spiritual and material appropriations were as much the product of the coercive power of tribal chieftains as of popular religious awakening.[2] Through this process, the church became central to the European feudal system.

Paradoxically, as Europe became more Christian, the institutional logic and leadership of the church became more secular. There were certain advantages to this development, even a need for it. In a period of weak and unstable political structures, the church could maintain a certain degree of social order and carry culture forward where local political structures had collapsed. But, inevitably, the church's enormous power and wealth invited compromise and corruption on many different institutional fronts. For example, bishops sometimes doubled as lords, even marrying. While the monasteries maintained greater distance from these secularizing forces, there was a general laxity in monastic discipline.

By the 12th century, the need for reform being generally felt, Pope Gregory VII inaugurated an ambitious program embracing church life in all its aspects. Among religious orders, he tightened discipline. Among priests, he made chastity mandatory and abolished hereditary priesthood. Among the laity, he sought to end interminable civil warfare by focusing aggressive energies on an external enemy: hence, the Crusades.

Politically, Gregory sought to purify the church by wresting it from the manipulative designs of princes who had sometimes deposed popes to fulfill their own political designs. Henceforth, control of the church would lie exclusively in ecclesiastical hands. Finally, Gregory's new ecclesiastical and political synthesis was complemented by a new theological synthesis. Here the chief architect was Thomas Aquinas, who fused biblical revelation and classical philosophy into one integrative intellectual system and melded feudal and ecclesiastical hierarchies into a unified cosmos, one Great Chain of Being, a corporate sense of all reality.

Gregory's program was visionary and largely successful. Yet its very success activated forces that eventually shattered Christendom. The intensification of discipline made monasteries into seedbeds for the renewal of piety and "think-tanks" for reform. The Crusades engaged the world of Islam and opened up new realms for cultural exchange and commerce. Meanwhile, expanding trade gradually increased money's role as the medium of exchange, eroding the land-based wealth of the church. The decisive sundering of clerical and lay realms concentrated such theocratic power in the Papacy that the secular power of the Holy Roman Empire was undercut and nationalism was awakened.

While popes enjoyed unprecedented power, they were cash-poor. A new financial structure and new forms of income were required to maintain the church's institutional apparatus. The most controversial and morally compromising of the solutions devised was the sale of indulgences. An entire penitential system was elaborated, requiring monetary gifts to the church in exchange for the remission of sins. Indulgences became an enormous industry for the church. Emerging nations resented the extraction of so much wealth by Rome, particularly as a large portion went to finance papal wars and the acquisition of more church lands.

THE FRIENDS OF GOD AND BRETHREN OF THE FREE SPIRIT

The 14th century witnessed major crises and fresh initiatives for renewal. Upon the death of Fredrick II, two rivals proclaimed themselves the new Holy Roman Emperor. In 1324, the Pope chose Fredrick of Austria and excommunicated Louis of Bavaria and all who remained loyal to him. Louis had large popular support from independent states, particularly those in southern Germany. The Pope's Interdict against Louis banned official church services and sacramental rites wherever Louis was supported. Many priests were sympathetic to Louis, but obeyed the Interdict. Meanwhile, various calamities—earthquakes, plagues, and violent storms—heightened the general sense of crisis, infusing the times with an apocalyptic *angst*. Each new calamity was seen as further divine judgment upon an ecclesio-political order whose internal conflicts and corruptions were painfully evident. Mass marches of common people roved southern Europe, calling for repentance and warning of further divine judgments. Jews and others were increasingly scapegoated for society's malaise.

Amid this atmosphere of crisis and emerging from the sacramental hiatus of the Interdict, grassroots movements of Christian renewal blossomed. They drew from the mystical writings of Meister Eckhart as well as women mystics of the preceding two centuries: Hildegaard of Bingen, Mathilda of Magdeburg, Elizabeth of Schoenau. They formed no definite organization, but expanded as a network of small, local groups, interconnected by traveling prophets and letters. They had support from many in the priesthood, especially Dominicans. Some convents served as unofficial centers. These *Gottesfreunde*, or "Friends of God," were especially strong in the cities of Strasbourg, Basel, and Cologne. They practiced a quiet, ascetic life, questioned the sacramental formalism of the official church, preached the light of Christ as an indwelling presence, placed clergy and laity on equal footing, and had a number of women leaders.[3] Leading figures like Johann Tauler (ca. 1300-1361), a Dominican priest and a student of Eckhart, who itinerated around southern Germany and emphasized the "experiential wisdom" imparted by the Holy Spirit. Regarding the sacramental suspension of the Interdict, he wrote, "If the holy church wishes to deprive us of the external sacrament, we must submit. But nobody can take from us the privilege of taking the sacrament spiritually."[4] This internalized, highly sacramental consciousness did not reject the official church, but flourished without its services.

The anonymously written *Theologia Germanica* summarized the teachings of Tauler and the Friends of God, enunciating a shift in mysticism that might better be termed *Spiritualism*. For example, Eckhart had affirmed that knowledge of nature and of God are the same. His student, Tauler, countered that while they are the same, the connection between natural knowledge and spiritual knowledge is more a paradox than a simple unity. To know God is to know nature, but in a profoundly different manner. While Eckhart's mysticism was incarnational in emphasis, Tauler's stressed the transforming experience of knowing Christ's crucifixion and resurrection. While Eckhart could more or less merge human and divine into a form of Neoplatonic speculation, Tauler maintained a more absolute difference between human and divine, who encounter one another in an existential crisis and rebirth. Eckhart's mysticism aimed at union with the Father or Son; the Spiritualism of Tauler and others emphasized union with the Holy Spirit. A sustained immersion in the Spirit could in some cases lead to claims of moral perfection.[5]

While the Friends of God remained loyal to the official church, other grassroots groups did not. Most notably, the Brethren of the Free Spirit, many of whom had begun as Friends of God, lapsed into despair and skeptical materialism. At first, they advocated asceticism as a path toward God but soon they began to divinize the self as a divine, transmoral being, free to do anything. Only less developed Christians were still bound by morality; the Free Spirit moves the Christian beyond all mores. The Free Spirit movement questioned the existence of hell, purgatory, and the devil. With libertinism, the movement quickly exploded in numbers and notoriety. Although the Family of God denounced the Brethren of the Free Spirit, the church hierarchy tended to confuse and anathematize both movements.

These 14th-century developments did not result in permanent ruptures and reformations comparable to the Protestantism of the 16th century. But they charted new territories that later reformations would retrace. As we shall see, the dynamics of the Friends of God and the Brethren of the Free Spirit would be replayed among the Spiritualist reformers of the sixteenth century in southern Germany, and again among Seekers, Ranters, and Quakers in seventeenth-century England.

By the 15th century, unrest proliferated everywhere, from disaffected princes to popular heretical movements. Popular devotion flowered among the common people and mysticism thrived in the monasteries. New currents of individualism questioned the metaphysics of the Great Chain of Being. The humanism of the Renaissance advanced an inductive approach to study in all realms, emphasizing experimental techniques and experiential data over against speculative and metaphysical schemes. Hebrew and Greek philology advanced as the Bible began to be studied and translated in its own right, apart from church traditions of interpretation and canon law.

Resistance theologies, exposing the corruption of the church, grew out of these developments. For example, predestinational theology was popular among rebel Franciscans and others. Predestination posited the true church to be constituted only of the elect, those chosen by God before the foundation of the world. The elect could be discerned only by their moral regeneration, if at all. The elect were clearly not always those in civil and ecclesiastical power. Therefore, the institutional church, with its corrupt leadership, was a false church. Moreover, a false church was spiritually bankrupt, unable to dispense efficacious sacraments. In the sacramental universe of medievalism, this was the most serious challenge to the church. Wyclif and Huss, for example, denied that priests' words transubstantiated the bread and wine of communion. Apocalyptic movements abounded, predicting the end of the world and identifying the Papacy with the Antichrist, ripe for God's fiery judgment.

Thus, out of the static metaphysics of the medieval *Corpus Christianum* a jarring sense of history was emerging. The world was going somewhere, and the church, constrained by the imperious policies of the Papacy, was being left behind. As Bainton summarizes, just as predestination cut the church off from the ultimate past of God's Creation, apocalyptic annunciations of the present order's imminent end cut the church off from the ultimate future of God's kingdom.[6]

Many sought renewal from within the institutional structures of the church, founding new orders, renewing spiritual life and moral rigor. This loyalist renewal within Catholicism, sometimes known as the Counter-Reformation, is a powerful story unto itself. But reformers, in varying degrees, viewed the institutions of Christendom as fatally flawed. We must next examine the different critiques and solutions these Protestant reformers offered, leading us to focus on the seeking option.

Types of Protestant Reformation

Bainton offers a four-fold typology of the Protestant Reformation.[7] Each is a response to the religious and political crisis of Christendom. The first two types are Neoconstantinian, or Magisterial: they renewed the political marriage of the church to civil power that had begun in the 4th century. In these cases, the old political logic of empire was replaced by the new imperatives of the national state.

First, the *Lutheran* type was born out of its founder's own inner struggle, producing a deep personal piety rooted in the assurance of God's mercy. But Luther's social outlook was strongly pessimistic. The kingdom of God cannot be constructed on earth. At best, evil can be restrained by the state. The church therefore renounces the secularizing theocratic power of Catholicism, but retains a civic role by nurturing obedient citizens of its sponsoring state. One can appreciate Luther's position in terms of his need for a sympathetic prince to defend him from the Papacy's attack and to create the political space for his reforms. But the conservative, enfranchising politics inherent in Luther's position soon became clear in his harsh repudiations of other reformers and his advocacy of savage reprisals against the Peasant Revolt (1524-25).

Like the Lutheran type, the second type of Protestant Reformation also linked religious and civil authorities. Perhaps owing to the different political tradition of Switzerland, the *Reformed* churches founded by Ulrich Zwingli and John Calvin were more optimistic that God's kingdom could be established on earth. In their scheme, predestination provided a key middle term between the religious experience of the individual and the secular power of the state. The elect constituted a body within society that, if rightly identified and placed in positions of leadership in both church and state, could both inspire and enforce God's order on earth. The economic leadership of the pious burgher, whose commercial achievement was reckoned as a sign of God's election, assumed a place alongside leadership of pastor and magistrate in this Reformed settlement of church and society. The Reformed settlement of the church was more idiomatic to the incipient new order of capitalism than was the Lutheran. From Zurich and Geneva, the Reformed movement spread to several nations across the Continent. It also found expression in the Puritan movement in England.

The third and fourth types, the *Anabaptist* and *Spiritualist* Reformations, are often considered together as the Radical Reformation, due to their rejection (in most cases) of the Constantinian option. Because these movements were not politically enfranchised, they present us with a chaotic array of theologies and church orders—a kind of "banyan tree" effect, as Rufus Jones aptly put it.[8] Here the *countercultural* resonances of the gospel come most clearly to the fore, inspiring mercurial leaders and prophetic movements that frightened civil authority. Radical reformers faced a precarious existence without protection from civil powers. They encountered routine persecution and martyrdom from Protestant and Catholic powers alike, who sometimes even collaborated to stamp out these threatening reformations "from below." In mapping this complex realm, we will follow the typology of George Huntston Williams.[9]

Radical reformers, especially as they viewed the compromised politics of the Lutheran reformation, emphasized the general apostasy of the church. Some identified the apostasy with the Constantinian settlement of the 4th century, while others detected hints in the New Testament that decline was beginning even before the apostolic generation had passed. The crisis of the church inspired two different orientations among radical reformers. Anabaptist reformers looked more intently to the past, to find ecclesiastical blueprints in the New Testament and exemplary Christian martyrs from the early Christian era. Spiritualist reformers looked more to the future, for decisive action to reestablish the true church. Some aimed to achieve this by revolutionary human effort while others suspended all striving, to await divine intervention or to content themselves with an invisible church fellowship transcending all boundaries of time and place. To be sure, Spiritualists assiduously studied Scripture, and Anabaptists often looked for an imminent end of the world, but their primary orientations toward past and future, respectively, are clear.

Williams sees three types of Anabaptist manifestation in the 15th century. *Revolutionary Anabaptists* drew equally upon Old and New Testaments to derive a vision of the church as God's new Israel, a theocratic commonwealth. This logic led to rigid legal codes and repressive enforcement in their effort to establish the millennial kingdom of God on earth. At the same time, charismatic Spirit-possession was also a mark of the movement, especially among its leaders. Revolutionary Anabaptists were inspired by the writings of Melchior Hoffmann, though the latter was not himself a revolutionary. The peaceful Anabaptist takeover of Munster (1533-35) was viciously quashed by Lutheran and Catholic forces. Thereafter, Munster became the brush with which state-sponsored reformers tarred all populist reformations in the 16th and 17th centuries.

Contemplative Anabaptists are polar opposites to the revolutionaries and are best represented by Hans Denck, who preached the presence of the Word of God in all humans in all times and places. In 1524, he denied the value of external religious ceremonies, including the sacraments, asserting the primacy of the inner Word, or Teacher, over Scripture. In 1525, Denck was intensely involved with a variety of budding Anabaptist groups in and around Augsburg, but then withdrew. Expelled from Nuremberg and Strasbourg for his teaching, Denck became a homeless wanderer, succumbing to the plague in Basel in 1527. His dying testimony included these words: "I am heartily well content that all shame and disgrace should fall on my face, if it is for the truth. It was when I began to love God that I got the disfavor of men."[10]

Finally, we come to the *Evangelical Anabaptists*, the largest and most lasting sub-type. These centered their Reformation squarely upon the New Testament as normative for doctrine, ethics, and church order. Early experiences in the chaotic first stages of Anabaptism soon made them distrustful of charismatic and prophetic forms of leadership. Distilled out of ferments in Switzerland, Germany, and Holland, they all shared the conviction that the true church is a visible church, a gathering of confessing believers that can never be coterminous with the local population or the governing state. Renouncing state sponsorship, they did not contemplate the Christianizing of society as a whole, but gathered as countercultural islands amid the alienation and hypocrisy of the mainstream. They viewed infant baptism as the key symbol of the unholy alliance between church and state. Therefore, all confessing adult believers must be rebaptized through total immersion in water (thus the name, Anabaptist, "rebaptizer").

Moral rigorists, the Evangelical Anabaptists advocated a literal understanding of and compliance with the Sermon on the Mount as the standard for Christian living. This included a rejection of all forms of violence. They adopted congregational use of the ban and shunning to deal with lapses in their midst. Key figures include Ulrich Stadler (a founding figure among the communistic Hutterites), Balthasar Hubmaier, George Blaurock, Conrad Grebel, Michael Sattler, Dietrich Philips, and Menno Simons (founder of the main surviving body of Anabaptists, the Mennonites).

Williams offers an analogous tripartite typology for the Spiritualist reformers, all of whom stressed the inner, unmediated action of the Spirit or Word of God as foundational for any future hope of a true church.

Revolutionary Spiritualists emphasized the driving, catalyzing force of the Spirit among believers. Thomas Muntzer is the key representative of this position. His preaching helped catalyze the Peasant Revolt in Saxony in 1524, when he reportedly advocated a slaughter of oppressors. While he is often identified as an Anabaptist, his teaching did not fit their pattern. Like Anabaptists, he repudiated infant baptism, but did not advocate adult, believer's baptism. He instead stressed baptism as an inner work of the Spirit. Muntzer's preaching of the inward Word, or living voice of Christ's Spirit (which he derived from reading the medieval mystic Tauler) was a key influence upon Hans Denck in 1524.

  Rational Spiritualists are best represented by Paracelsus, Valentine Weigel, and Sebastian Franck. Like Denck, Franck emphasized the inner Word as a seed sown in all humanity. By 1530, he refused to be identified with any existing visible church. He prophesied a coming new work of God that would end all outward ceremonies, church offices, and Anabaptist bans, gathering from among all peoples an invisible, spiritual church governed only by the Word of God within, as the church in the apostles' days had been. Spiritualists like Franck stressed the unmediated work of God's presence, a universal sense of kinship among all morally regenerate individuals, and an interest in the belief systems of various peoples and faiths. These emphases strongly anticipate the rationalism of the later liberal Enlightenment. But they did not make life comfortable for Franck, caught in the middle of strongly politicized reform movements, as we shall see later in this chapter.

  Finally, *Evangelical Spiritualism* rounds out the typology of radical responses to the crisis of the 16th century. Here we do not find Franck's despair of a visible church, but a chastened approach. Evangelical Spiritualists gathered together Christian fellowships, but not formal sects or state-sponsored churches. These communities served as an interim church until new revelations clarified and reunited the rapidly splintering doctrines and practices of the Reformation. The leading exemplar of this option, Caspar Schwenckfeld, saw his approach as a "Middle Way" between Catholicism, Lutheranism, and Zwinglianism. Williams observes that Schwenckfeld's approach also offered mediation between Evangelical Anabaptism and Rational Spiritualism. Indeed, he had many connections to, as well as debates with, Anabaptist communities and was both an ally and critic of Sebastian Franck. Both for his central position among radical reformers and for the singularity of his vision, the life and thought of Caspar Schwenckfeld will be a major focus of this chapter, as we look for the roots of the seeking spirituality in 17th-century England and today.

CASPAR SCHWENCKFELD AND THE *Stillstand*

Caspar Schwenckfeld was born in 1489 of the lesser nobility of Silesia, an ethnically and culturally German region that is today part of Poland. The typical career for a young man of his rank was to become a courtier to one of the regional overlords. For this purpose, he went to university at Cologne in 1507, most likely studying law, not theology. Schwenckfeld's early career as a courtier imprinted his personality as an incisive but diplomatic reformer whose writings were generally more pastoral than polemical in tone.

His first spiritual awakening occurred in 1518, leading him to become a follower of Martin Luther. As with most radical reformers, Schwenckfeld's initial enthusiasm for Luther cooled by 1525, when the latter's political compromises and harsh attitude toward the Peasant Revolt became clear. After some heated conversations with Luther that year, Schwenckfeld realized he would have to go his own way.

The crucial point of departure concerned the theology and practice of the Lord's Supper. After a summer of intense study and reflection in 1525, he concluded that all the existing interpretations of the Supper were erroneous, unscriptural, and a root cause of schism. Perhaps most critically, he viewed the sacrament as an object of abuse, most of all by Lutherans. They insisted upon the sacrament as the real presence of Christ, but their state-sponsored church allowed unrepentant and unregenerate sinners to receive the bread and wine. Moreover, many participants were indulged in a superstitious belief that the sacrament had power to save regardless of the individual's moral condition. Thus, far from the outward sign of inward communion with God in Christ, the Lord's Supper had become the epitome of Christian hypocrisy and idolatry.[11] Schwenckfeld feared that the Lutheran eucharist would surpass Catholic indulgences as an invitation to cheap grace and false security for nominal Christians. That keen moral sense of hypocrisy and institutional laxity is key to understanding the Spiritualist sensibility in general, and the seeking spirituality in particular.

Under the sponsorship of Friedrich of Liegnitz, Schwenckfeld was leading a reformation in that city when his break with Luther came. This was a "comprehensive" reformation in that citizens were not compelled to participate and other religious options were tolerated. But the Liegnitz Reformation took a historic step in the autumn of 1525 when the church issued a statement advocating a general suspension of the Lord's Supper until unity and peace could be restored through a correct interpretation and a purified practice. This suspension, a *Stillstand*, was initiated immediately by the Liegnitz church. As Schwenckfeld later summarized,

> In the meantime we are zealous, by the grace of God, that we may observe the Supper daily, with the Lord Christ, be fed with His body and refreshed with His blood, through the spirit of living faith. This eating is dependent on no external thing. We beg that we be not reproached nor molested, as though we rejected the Lord's Supper, when for conscience's sake we abstain at this time in order that, having perceived the truth, we may not be a party to error, idolatry, and misuse.[12]

Thus, far from disdaining the outward ritual of the sacrament, Schwenckfeld scrupulously sought to protect its integrity by suspending its inept practice. A reader of Tauler and the *Theologia Germanica*, Schwenckfeld interpreted the crisis of multiple Protestantisms as a parallel to the Interdict of 1324, which had suspended sacramental services in some areas and gave rise to the Friends of God.

What began as a scruple over the Lord's Supper quickly elaborated. By the spring of 1526, statements from Liegnitz framed the *Stillstand* in terms of the general apostasy of the church. In June of that year, Schwenckfeld answered critics who urged the Liegnitz church to enact its own understanding of the Lord's Supper, and not worry about other interpretations. He replied that when there were true Christians and a true church to gather them, it would be easy to reinstitute the symbols. But that would require a new work of the Spirit of God. "We wait, therefore, eagerly and with sighs until Christ invites his guests through his spirit."[13]

As biographer Emmet McLaughlin concludes, Schwenckfeld's position derived less from metaphysics than from an intense fear of idolatry in regard to symbols and a strong aversion to hypocrisy in the church.[14] Therefore, Schwenckfeld did not follow Franck's course of disengagement and historical speculation, but maintained a sense of historical tension, eagerly awaiting the resolution of an intolerable state of affairs in the church. That sustained tension is one key to the dynamic energies of seeking spirituality.

Schwenckfeld does not seem to have imagined resolution coming in eschatological terms, such as the end of the world and the coming of God's kingdom on earth. He apparently viewed history in more cyclical terms, seeing periods of spiritual decline followed by divine visitation. In that sense, he looked for a decisive new work of the Spirit to overcome the stalemate of the Reformation. His own ministry of a "middle way" was evidently intended to prepare Christendom for this new work (much as John the Baptist sought to prepare Israel for its Messiah). The *Stillstand* spread to some churches beyond Liegnitz, though it is hard to assess how widely it was adopted. In his *Chronicle* (1531), Franck mentions that "some are ready to allow Baptism and other ceremonies to remain in abeyance [*stillson*] until God gives a further command and sends true laborers into His harvest-field. For this some have great longings and yearnings and wish nothing else."[15] Apparently, the suspension took hold even among some Lutheran congregations and was hard to root out.

Meanwhile, the Liegnitz church set out to regularize its new approach. In the autumn of 1525, a catechism was written. This was a key document, since Schwenckfeld felt that the gospel needed to be taught intensively, and not only proclaimed. While Luther's catechism clearly aimed to make good citizens of Christians, and while Luther did not blush at the use of secular force to impose his catechism upon the people, the Liegnitz catechism was conspicuously silent regarding the power of magistracy and the good of the state. Overwhelming emphasis was placed on teaching the gospel and achieving moral conversion.

Nevertheless, the Liegnitz Reformation soon fell victim to the vagaries of Reformation politics. When the Hungarian regional overlord was killed in battle against the Turks in August 1526, Silesia's political and religious situation suddenly became precarious. Friedrich of Liegnitz had to accept Ferdinand of Austria, a Catholic, as the new overlord, placing Liegnitz in crisis. The only political option of resistance would be to appeal to the Lutheran powers for help.[16] In August 1528, Ferdinand issued a ban on all heretics harbored in Liegnitz, especially Anabaptists, on pain of execution. Friedrich had no power to protect his Protestants. He tried to form an alliance with the Lutherans, but they demanded total submission to their religious program. By early 1529, Ferdinand had singled out Schwenckfeld as a heretic. Though he was ready to remain and face martyrdom, Schwenckfeld was convinced by Friedrich to leave for the sake of the church. He left Silesia by the spring, to begin a life of exile and ostracism, sojourning with supporters, traveling at times under assumed names. It is a paradox of Schwenckfeld's life that soon after he took his prophetic stance with the *Stillstand*, he embarked upon a vocation of errantry.[17]

Settling in Strasbourg for the next five years, he itinerated around southern Germany, gaining adherents. But in the spring of 1534, reformer Martin Butzer utilized the unfolding crisis at Munster to convince Strasbourg's city council to ban local Anabaptists and ask Schwenckfeld to leave. The latter was shocked and embittered by this turn of events. He moved briefly to Württemberg and began to oppose Butzer in public. Butzer, more a political strategist than a religious leader, aimed to create an alliance among Protestant powers as a bulwark against Catholic aggression in southern Germany. This "eucharistic concord" was to be worked out at the expense of Anabaptist and Spiritualist groups. Certainly, the *Stillstand* had no part to play in this bargain. Schwenckfeld saw Butzer's Protestant alliance as a clerical conspiracy to seize the Reformation away from the people and to bully magistrates into enforcing the alliance's policies. The fact that Butzer and Zwingli sought the alliance of Luther, who had categorically denounced them, proved that their ambition was to reestablish clerical hegemony over a passive and disenfranchised laity.[18]

In 1535, Schwenckfeld settled in Ulm, which remained his base for the next four years. The patronage of a leading *burgermeister* there assured his position. A large and open Schenckfelder movement developed in the area. Adherents met without use of sacraments or the ban, gathering for Bible study, prayer, prophecy and to wait for a new Pentecost to renew the church. (The Schwenckfelder movement, strongest in southern Germany, continued and grew beyond its founder's lifetime and was transplanted to America in the 18th century due to continued persecution. It observes the *Stillstand* to this day.) Caspar Schwenckfeld set an egalitarian tone, with a consistent concern for the poor and an attentive encouragement of women's leadership.

At this point, we may move from further narration of Schwenckfeld's life (after many more years of persecution and flight, he died in Ulm in

1561) to consider more fully his thought and its significance for later developments. In many respects, Schwenckfeld fits well in the Spiritualist mold with his strong sense of the dichotomy between inward and outward realities. As his thinking developed after Liegnitz, he went on to affirm with Muntzer, Denck, Franck, and others that outward ceremonies cannot themselves communicate any spiritual benefit. He too emphasized the primacy of the "inward hearing" of the Word within over the outward hearing of human preaching or the reading of Scripture (a sensibility that may have been intensified by his own hearing disability[19]). Like Muntzer and Franck, he gained his viewpoint in part from reading Tauler.

Pursuing the further implications of his suspension of the Lord's Supper, Schwenckfeld argued that the flesh of Christ is only in heaven, which he defines not as a place but as a mode of existence. Heaven is the realm of divine Presence beyond the categories of time and space. Thus Christ is available wherever people seek him. The redemptive Word, the celestial bread of life, does not come down from heaven into physical bread; instead, the believer ascends to heaven, partaking of Christ's essence.[20] The celestial bread is broken inwardly by the reborn believer, just as Christ was broken on the cross in history. Unlike the natural physical bread that we eat and assimilate to ourselves, this bread, when we feed upon it, assimilates us into Christ's celestial nature.

In this regard, Schwenckfeld, like other Spiritualists and Anabaptists, utilized the early church doctrine of Christ's *celestial flesh*. While much of his writing on this subject sounds like metaphysical speculation, his emphasis may be understood as more existential. The crux of the issue for Schwenckfeld was that Christ, as a sinless individual, the incarnate Word of God, could not be anything less than a fundamentally new kind of human being. Schwenckfeld posited two dimensions of the Word of God. The creative Word generates all things in nature from the beginning to the present. But the redemptive Word draws us from heaven, from a diametrically opposite mode of existence grounded in the resurrection, the future.

That latter work begins with the incarnation, life, crucifixion, and resurrection of Jesus Christ. Schwenckfeld's motto was "God became man in order that man might become what God is." So, through an inner, mystical feeding upon the celestial flesh of Christ, and through concretely moral participation in Christ, the believer moves into an utterly different realm of existence. Schwenckfeld rejected Luther's teaching of justification as a forensic righteousness imputed to believers by Christ's historical death. He insisted that justification, sanctification, and regeneration are all of one piece in Christ's action within the believer. This would seem to suggest that the believer in Christ might attain to Christ's moral perfection. Schwenckfeld did not take that step, however. The new existence in Christ does not take over, but wages constant battle with the old creature. Only in eternity does Christ's celestial existence utterly define us. Until then, we are defined by hypocrisy and inconsistency.[21]

This point is important to note briefly for later reference. Schwenckfeld developed the doctrine of celestial flesh mainly as a clarification on the perfect life of Christ. But we will see later in this study how George Fox and other early Friends developed the same doctrine to speak of the perfecting power of Christ in their lives, with far-reaching moral, social, and even political implications.

The Spiritualism of both Schwenckfeld and the early Friends derives from similar existential grounding and moral passion. Their dualism between inward and outward, spiritual and formal, is based not on metaphysics but on an intense aversion to hypocrisy, the contradiction between nominal righteousness and the actual sinfulness, alienation, and pride. The Constantinian politics of the Reformation goaded this sensibility unbearably among individuals of uncommon introspection and scrupulosity. It drove them to reject all the formal observances and institutions of Christendom—all the mediations that offered relief from the tension between inward and outward. For these Spiritualist seekers, the only mediation that did not stink of hypocrisy was a morally transformed life, a life raised to the level of sacrament. This was not just a life moral in one's own eyes, but a life infused with the flesh and blood of Christ, whose sinless life and death fifteen centuries before had mediated between heaven and earth in history. With Schwenckfeld, as with the first Friends in the 1650s, the highest sacramental expression of this moral mediation was to follow Christ in self-expenditure, even martyrdom, advancing the mystery of the gospel further into an alienated and violent human society.

The *Stillstand* thus introduced a powerful, lived tension into Radical Reformation spirituality. Rather than simply abandoning sacraments and the visible church, those adopting the *Stillstand* lived in this unbearable tension: they demanded an authentic, visible church and yet knew that it could come only as a gift of God. Schwenckfeld came very close to, but ultimately rejected, the proto-liberal position that Franck took—namely, that Christians had outgrown the church founded by the apostles. However, he knew that n*othing less than a new Pentecost and a new apostolate* could renew the church. In the meantime, Christians could gather together in conventicles, exhorting and teaching one another. These were not to be understood as churches or sects. *They existed to wait upon the Lord.*[22]

SEBASTIAN FRANCK AND THE INVISIBLE CHURCH

If Caspar Schwenckfeld's *Stillstand* represents the ultimate Protestant sense of the church's radical apostasy, Sebastian Franck manifests the emergence of a post-Protestant, incipiently liberal stance. Ten years younger than Schwenckfeld, Franck was born in Bavaria in 1499 to a family of weavers. He was educated at Heidelberg, where he was influenced by the humanism of Erasmus and others. He met Luther in 1518 and was allied with the Lutheran movement by 1527, when he took up pastoral work near Nuremberg.[23] His first published work, a tract *On the Detestable Vice of Drunkenness* (1528), expresses the growing frustration of a young reformer already disappointed by the Lutheran movement's moral laxity. The institutional compromises of the magisterial Reformation were intolerable to Franck, with his burning passion for personal and social transformation. It seems that he was also positively influenced in those early years by Anabaptist congregations, which were numerous around Nuremberg. The tract ends with a call for the use of the Anabaptist-style "ban," a shunning of fellowship, against immoral church members.

By 1529, Franck had resigned his pastorate and left both Lutheranism and Anabaptism behind. In 1530, now married and living in Strasbourg, he expressed a nearly total despair of the Reformation and the world itself. "For the first time I experience and understand that the world is not only dark but darkness itself, as John 1 says, and that the Devil is its god and prince. . . . Behold now how many beliefs, sects, and parties exist only among those who are Christians. . . . It is impossible that one God . . . baptism, Supper, and gospel can exist in so many repugnant churches."[24] Thus, like Schwenckfeld, Franck found the sheer multiplicity of Christian claims to the true faith a convicting sign of spiritual bankruptcy. Indeed, Schwenckfeld was already in Strasbourg when Franck arrived and no doubt became a ready ally. At that time, Franck began to write of Spiritualism as an emerging fourth way, moving beyond the Lutheran, Zwinglian, and Anabaptist settlements of the church. But his approach to Spiritualism was not an interim *suspension* of outward forms of church order, but a permanent *supersession* of them by this fourth way. The outward church forms ordained in the New Testament era were right for those circumstances. But fourteen centuries later, Franck saw outward ordinances of church order, even at their best, as outmoded. The outward church was corrupted by Antichrist soon after the apostles' days. At that point, the true church was taken up into heaven, where it lies concealed in God's Spirit and truth. The true, spiritual church thus exists in a different dimension that must remain scattered and hidden to human reckoning until Christ comes (soon, Franck was sure) to gather the saints from among the peoples.[25] That view suggested a more individualized faith. For Franck, the true church exists on earth only as it is sought and found, a spiritual unity discerned here and there among *all peoples*. It is a morally defined fellowship, unencumbered by outward forms of religious belief and organization.[26]

Having withdrawn from the field of church politics, Franck reframed his thinking in his massive *Chronicle* (1531), a spiritual history of the human race beginning with the biblical patriarchs, who set the example of living by inner guidance. The book exposes the injustice and hypocrisy of all forms of political and religious authority. Given the categorical bankruptcy of institutional religion, true Christians subsist as a few kernels in a mountain chaff.[27] The heretics of church history are the inheritors of the true spiritual tradition of inner guidance. Erasmus is included on Franck's heretical honor role.

But the *Chronicle* also offers a constructive program for alternative spiritual authority, based on human experience. Experience includes not only the inner work of the Holy Spirit and the observation of nature in one's personal life, but the larger scope of collective experience recorded as history. The total scope of experience is "an open book and a living Bible, in which you may study, without any previous introduction, the science of God and learn his will."[28] Just as the Spirit gives the individual a personal understanding of Scripture's meaning, so history offers an objective and final interpretation. Because events fulfill and elucidate the meaning of biblical prophecy, they make clear by experience what was only darkly taught by the letter. Whereas credal distillations of Scripture's witness remain dead letters, history, even in recorded form, lives.[29] Franck's *Chronicle* thus provides a startlingly prescient statement of liberal rationalism and historicism.

Not surprisingly, the book was denounced by nearly all parties—even by Erasmus, who was no doubt alarmed to find himself portrayed as a heretic. Martin Butzer led the way in arousing official action against Franck, as he later did against Schwenckfeld. Local copies of the *Chronicle* were confiscated and Franck was briefly imprisoned, then expelled from Strasbourg at the end of 1531. Henceforth, he was increasingly marginalized and insecure.

In 1533, Franck was given permission to settle in Ulm, upon promising not to cause any trouble. He worked in a printing house and was eventually able to go into business for himself. Before long, more stunning treatises emerged. His *280 Paradoxes or Wondrous Sayings* (1534) soon aroused complaints from Ulm's Lutheran forces.[30] His *World Book* (also 1534) compiled descriptions of countries, peoples, religions, customs, and doctrines from around the world, including America.[31] Clearly, the universal scope of his interests and theology continued to grow. For these and other provocative writings, Franck was soon under attack again and nearly expelled from Ulm in 1535. Upon further promises of good behavior, he was allowed to remain. But conservative forces, fearing that he and Schwenckfeld (who had arrived in 1535) sought to establish a new church, could not abide their presence. Both were expelled from Ulm in January 1539. Franck and his family moved immediately to Basel, another haven of relative tolerance.

There, Franck continued to write. As a pacifist, he attacked religious leaders who justified the warfare (*The Little War Book*, 1539). In a letter to "the Christians in Lower Germany" (probably intended mainly for friendly Anabaptist congregations there), he urged the broadest mutual toleration:

> Consider as dear people all who tolerate you in your faith and conscience and are willing to admit you as God-fearing citizens besides themselves . . . even if they preach Christ and nevertheless walk in error . . . do not separate yourselves in any other respect than from their ungodly life. . . . In brief, do not seek Christ here or there, and do not mistakenly think

that he is more with us than with you. . . . He is equally close to every nation even if they are outwardly called heathen, Jews, Turks, or Christians. Anyone who lives right and well, let him be to you a true brother, flesh and blood in Christ. It must be thus, Christ's sheep must lie among the wolves to the end of the world, as Luke 21 clearly shows.[32]

Franck had arrived at a position where faith claims no special territory on earth, yet finds its community in all places.

In *The Seven-Sealed Book* (also 1539) Franck offered the following statement of his seeker's quest. It summarizes his position beyond the frontiers of the Reformation:

The longer one travels toward the city he seeks the nearer and nearer he comes to the goal of his journey; exactly so it is with the soul that is seeking God. If he will travel away from himself and away from the world and seek only God as the precious pearl of his soul, he will come steadily nearer to God, until he becomes one spirit with God the Spirit; but let him not be afraid of mountains and valleys on the way, and let him not give up because he is tired and weary, for he who seeks finds.

Nobody is the master of my faith, and I desire to be the master of the faith of no one. I love any man whom I can help, and I call him brother whether he be Jew or Samaritan. . . . I cannot belong to any separate sect, but I believe in a holy, Christ-like Church, a fellowship of saints, and I hold as my brother, my neighbor, my flesh and blood, all men who belong to Christ among all sects, faiths, and peoples scattered throughout the whole world—only I allow nobody to have dominion over the one place where I am pledged to the Lord to keep as pure virgin, namely my heart, and my conscience.[33]

Having been harried to that inner sanctuary of resigned serenity, Franck spent the last three years of his life in relative quiet, dying in Basel in 1542. In 1540, a declaration by state-sponsored reformers at Smalcald had condemned both Schwenckfeld and Franck as "vagabonds,"[34] permanently excluding them from the official Protestant consensus in lower Germany. Luther commented bitterly in 1545 that Franck "is a fanatic or spiritualist who likes nothing but spirit, spirit, and who thinks nothing of Word, sacrament, and the office of preaching. . . . He has wandered through all filth and suffocated in his own filth." Though he was soon forgotten in Germany, Franck had an enduring influence among Anabaptists. His writings had a major effects upon Menno Simons, Galenus Abrahams, and the Collegiants.[35]

In Schwenckfeld and Franck, we find the two fundamental modes of seeking described in the Introduction. Schwenckfeld's *Stillstand* exhibits the enterprise mode of seeking and association, albeit paradoxically, in a suspended state. Schwenckfeld by no means gave up on the Reformation project to establish a true, visible, institutional church. And while he did not feel that the moment had arrived for that new order of church to be revealed, he worked enterprisingly to gather fervent seekers into the fellowship of waiting upon the Lord, a church-in-suspension. That stance carried with it a strong civil mode, in that Schwenckfeld was concerned for peaceful coexistence among the many conflicting churches of his day—in sharp contrast to Butzer and others who turned the Silesian nobleman into a religious refugee. But the enterprise mode of association remains primary. By contrast, in Franck's invisible church we find the civil mode to be primary. Franck was concerned to establish peaceful, constructive relations not only among all Christians but all peoples, religions, and cultures. His enterprise was mainly writing, sketching a new frame of reference for a new age of seeking. Once he left the Lutheran movement, he did not seek to draw a specific, visible community of followers to his teaching. These two seeking stances will manifest themselves again when we examine the English Seekers of the 1640s.

THE COLLEGIANTS IN HOLLAND

The Collegiant movement in Holland in the 17th century constitutes another significant phenomenon of seeking as a group quest during the Continental Reformation. Rufus Jones tells the story of this movement as an important flowering of seeking spirituality and a vibrant expression of Dutch religious toleration.[36]

The freedom that Holland achieved and offered to religious fugitives in the seventeenth century derived from developments in the 16th century. Dirck Volckertsz Coornhert was an important figure in those developments. A self-educated engraver from Amsterdam, Coornhert was involved in the political struggle for freedom in Haarlem in the 1550s. William of Orange made him a high-ranking government official in 1572. Having seen religious persecution at first hand, he used his position to influence the course of freedom. He was critical of the Calvinist mainstream of the Dutch Reformed Church, finding too much emphasis there upon doctrinal purity and sacramental technique. He viewed the Reformers as generally too fixated upon externals. He had read the Spiritual Reformers and was particularly fond of Sebastian Franck's writings. Consequently, he emphasized the inward quality of true religion and the living Word of God. He viewed all faithful individuals and groups everywhere as constituting the invisible church, that had existed in all ages, but had been stunted by humanity's preoccupation with externality. In this regard, he was critical even of the Anabaptist Mennonites for their insistence upon a visible church and their congregational use of the ban to keep it pure.

In summarizing Coornhert's position, Jones states that, rather than start yet another organization,

> he pleaded for freedom of conscience and for the right to live in the world undisturbed as members of the invisible Church, using or omitting outward ceremonies as conscience might direct, waiting meantime and seeking in quiet faith for the coming of the new and divinely commissioned apostles who would really reform the apostate churches, unite all divided sects, and gather in the world a true Church of Christ. Meantime, while waiting for this true apostolic Church to appear, Coornhert approved of the formation of an *interim-Church*. This Church, according to his programme, would accept as truth, and as true practice, anything plainly and clearly taught in the canonical Scripture. . . . This interim-Church was to have no authoritative teachers or preachers. In place of official ministry, the members were to edify one another in Christian love with the reservation that they would welcome further illumination out of the Scriptures wherever they had made a mistake or gone wrong. All persons who confess God as Father, and Jesus Christ as sent by God, and who in the power

of faith abstain from sins, may belong to this interim-Church. For the sake of those who are still weak and spiritually immature, he allowed the use of ceremonies in the interim-Church, but all ceremonies are held as having no essential function for salvation, and the believer is at liberty to make use of them or to abstain from using them as he prefers.[37]

Again, we hear the hope for a renewed visible church, to be instigated by nothing less than new apostles. It seems likely that Coornhert's ideas were informed at least partly by Schwenckfeld's writings. He used the term *stilstandskerk* for the interim-church he envisioned.[38]

Coornhert's vision did not find embodiment until early in the 17th century, owing to a crisis in the Dutch Reformed Church. In the first decades of the 1600s, Jacob Arminius of Leyden challenged the Calvinist establishment on the question of predestination. He argued that it qualified Christ's death on behalf of all humanity. Not only did it fence most of humanity out of God's salvation, but it fostered the impression that those deemed among the chosen could ultimately do no wrong. This challenge was quashed at the Synod of Dort in 1619, leading to the expulsion of 200 Dutch clergy with Arminian sympathies. One hundred were banished. A congregation in Warmund lost its pastor to this purge. Rather than bear with a new minister in whose orthodox teaching it did not believe, the congregation chose to meet without any minister. Members gathered simply to read Scripture, pray, and share Spirit-led messages of edification. Some became opposed to professional ministry on principle, arguing that it stifled the prophetic gifts in the group as a whole.

A congregational split occurred, with one faction opting to have a pastor and the other determined to do without one. The latter group began to call itself a *Collegium*, or "gathering." It attracted a number of Mennonites, who introduced Anabaptist traditions such as resistance to the swearing of oaths, refusal to fight, rejection of state involvement in religious matters, greater equality between women and men, women's ministry, and a plain, simple lifestyle. They baptized adults, but affirmed the true baptism to be inward, by the Spirit. They often met in silence, waiting for new revelations. Their meetings were subdued in tone, though tears were viewed as a sign of true prayer. The movement spread to Leyden, Rotterdam, Amsterdam, and elsewhere in Holland.

Like Schwenckfeld and Coornhert, the Collegiants waited for a new dispensation of the Spirit and new apostles to restore the true church.

THE ROOTS OF SPIRITUALISM IN ENGLAND

The exact path by which Spiritualist ideas moved into England has long been a quandary to scholars. Rufus Jones tried in vain to establish clear lines of influence from Continental mysticism and the Spiritualist Reformers. Subsequent scholarship has been able to establish only dotted lines at best. Still, it seems clear that, either directly or indirectly, the writings and ideas of the Radical Reformation were circulating quietly in England during the reign of Elizabeth I.

Continental Anabaptism entered England during the mid-16th century through immigration. It is known that a number of Anabaptist textile workers settled in Norwich. But state suppression drove their religious activities underground and apparently to extinction. Only in the early 17th century did a more lasting Anabaptist influence establish itself. We will note that later development in our next chapter.

Selina Gerhard Schultz ponders the affinities and possible lines of influence between Schwenckfeld and the English Quakers. She notes that the explicit influence of his writings can be traced only as far as the Collegiants in Holland. However, the interchange of religious trends that went along with commercial trade between Holland and England could easily have brought his ideas into England. She also speculates that members of the Silesian nobility, dispersed by the Thirty Years' War, may have brought Schwenckfeld's influence to England. The English tended to lump Spiritualists together with Mennonites and others under the general epithet of "Anabaptist," so a specifically Schwenckfelder gathering would not show up in English official records. Moreover, considering the religious policies of Tudor and Stuart England, Schwenckfelders may well have chosen not to call attention to themselves.[39]

The Radical Reformation doctrine of the general apostasy of the church is detectable in English writings as far back as 1590, when Henry Barrow published *A Brief Discovery of the False Church*, asserting that Catholic and Anglican sacraments alike were void of spiritual power. In *A Brief Exposition of the Thirteenth of Revelation* (1619), John Wilkinson wrote that the overwhelming confusion of the present church manifested its illegitimacy. During the 1620s and 1630s, John Everard was an important conduit for Spiritualist thought into England. A doctor of divinity from Cambridge, he translated Denck, Franck, and others (though apparently not Schwenckfeld) into English and preached their ideas in London—at least when he was not in prison.[40]

Rufus Jones and others have speculated much on the influence of Jacob Boehme (1575-1624) on Seekers and Quakers in England.[41] Boehme was a Lutheran mystic and alchemist born in Silesia fourteen years after Schwenckfeld's death. We know that he read and was influenced by his Silesian spiritual forebear. English translations of his writings appeared by the late 1640s and groups of "Behemenists" met to read and discuss his ideas. Signs of his probable influence can be seen in writings of the Seeker John Saltmarsh and the Quaker George Fox, among others.

In terms of religious ideas, then, Jones is right to draw lines between Boehme and the Seekers and Quakers. However, Boehme remained a loyal (though ostracized) Lutheran all his life. Like Franck, he was more interested in the invisible church than the visible one that was often scandalized by his vivid "flashes" of revelation and far-reaching cosmological speculations. Thus we do not find the same *held tension* in Boehme that is so palpable in Schwenckfeld and in the Collegiants. Nor do we detect the same *sense of moment* that catalyzed events in the 1520s on the Continent or the 1640s and 1650s in England. Following the themes established in our Introduction, this study will differ from previous work on 17th-century English Seekers by devoting primary attention to the religious and political sense of moment and the generational dynamics of the times, rather than the pedigree of particular Seeker and Quaker ideas (which of course remain important to our concern).

We will see that, much like the American counterculture of the 1960s and the Continental Radical Reformation of the 1520s, deep shifts in English culture during the 1640s inspired creative and sometimes desperate responses among the young idealists who came to be known as Seekers. Their sense that a fundamentally new order was emerging infused them with a strong sense of crisis. Those who neither ran for the cover of traditional piety nor fled into private mysticism or nihilistic cynicism remained in an unbearable tension, a suspended world that finally became apocalyptic in the truest sense. Religious seeking takes many forms. But in that kind of cultural situation, it reaches a privileged moment that is better narrated than described. That narrative will occupy the next nine chapters.

Notes

1. Roland H. Bainton, *The Reformation of the Sixteenth Century* (Boston: Beacon, 1952). Also see more recent studies by Peter Brown: *Authority and the Sacred: Aspects of the Christianization of Late Antiquity* (Cambridge: University Press, 1995); and *The Rise of Western Christendom: Triumph and Diversity, AD 200-1000* (Oxford: Blackwell, 1996).
2. In this regard, note the major new study detailing the many different circumstances and motivations of first-millennium conversions by Richard Fletcher, *The Barbarian Conversion: From Paganism to Christianity* (New York: Holt, 1998).
3. Bengt Hoffman, Introduction to *The Theologia Germanica of Martin Luther* (New York: Paulist, 1980), 7-8.
4. Quoted by Rufus M. Jones in *Studies in Mystical Religion* (London: Macmillan, 1909), 275.
5. See Hoffman's Introduction to *Theologia Germanica*, 14-20. These differences are largely unnoticed and glossed over in Rufus Jones' work on mysticism (cited earlier) and his subsequent interpretation of Quakerism as a form of mysticism. Jones' vague and liberal definitions of mysticism may have developed under the influence of Adolf Harnack's work, which tended to lump all mystical and heretical movements together into a single antithesis to the institutional church, according to Hoffman (footnote from p. 14). Jones was studying at Harvard when Harnack's *History of Dogma* (7 vols.) came out in English editions in 1899-1900. For a brief summary of Joachim Wach's distinctions between mysticism and Spiritualism, see George Arthur Johnson, "From Seeker to Finder: a Study in Seventeenth-Century English Spiritualism before the Quakers," *Church History* 17 (1948): 299.
6. Roland Bainton, *Reformation*, 19.
7. Roland Bainton, *Reformation*, 77-78.
8. Rufus M. Jones, *Spiritual Reformers in the 16th and 17th Centuries* (London: Macmillan, 1914), 17.
9. *Spiritual and Anabaptist Writers: Documents Illustrative of the Radical Reformation*, ed. George Huntston Williams (Phila.: Westminster, 1958). See Williams' Introduction, 19-38.
10. Rufus Jones, *Spiritual Reformers*, 30.
11. Selina Gerhard Schultz, *Caspar Schwenckfeld von Ossig: Spiritual Interpreter of Christianity, Apostle of the Middle Way, Pioneer in Modern Religious Thought* (Norristown, Pa.: Schwenckfelder Church, 1947), 110.

12. Selina Gerhard Schultz, *Schwenckfeld*, 113-14 This quotation actually comes from shortly before his death, but is typical of his position from the beginning.
13. R. Emmet McLaughlin, *Caspar Schwenckfeld, Reluctant Radical: His Life to 1540* (New Haven: Yale University Press, 1986), 75.
14. McLaughlin, *Schwenckfeld*, 76.
15. Quoted in Rufus Jones, *Spiritual Reformers*, 86.
16. Emmet McLaughlin, *Schwenckfeld*, 111. I follow McLaughlin in narrating the biography as well as some of the theology of Schwenckfeld.
17. It is no doubt this dynamic in Schwenckfeld's life (along with Kierke-gaard's reflections on Abraham) that inspires the title of Joachim H. Seyppel's book, *Schwenckfeld, Knight of Faith: A Study in the History of Religion* (Pennsburg, Pa.: Schwenckfelder Library, 1961).
18. Emmet McLaughlin, *Schwenckfeld*, 142.
19. Joachim H. Seyppel, *Schwenckfeld, Knight of Faith*, 31.
20. Emmet McLaughlin, *Schwenckfeld*, 72.
21. Paul L. Maier, *Caspar Schwenckfeld on the Person and Work of Christ* (Assen, Netherlands: Van Gorcum, 1959), Chapter 11.
22. Emmet McLaughlin, *Schwenckfeld*, 139.
23. For biographical sketches of Franck, see articles in *The Oxford Encyclopedia of the Reformation* (New York: Oxford University Press, 1996), 2:134-35; and *The Mennonite Encyclopedia: A Comprehensive Reference Work on the Anabaptist-Mennonite Movement* (Scottdale, Pa.: Mennonite Publishing House, 1956), 2:363-67.
24. Quoted by Steven E. Ozment, *Mysticism and Dissent: Religious Ideology and Social Protest in the Sixteenth Century* (New Haven: Yale University Press, 1973), 140.
25. George Hunston Williams, *The Radical Reformation*, third edition (Kirksville, Mo.: Sixteenth Century Studies, 1992), 695-96.
26. *Mennonite Encyclopedia*, 2:363.
27. Ozment, *Dissent*, 141-44.
28. Ozment, *Dissent*, 148.
29. Ozment, *Dissent*, 149-50.
30. Williams, *Radical Reformation*, 697-98 calls Franck's *Paradoxes* a work of "dialectical mysticism," related to Denck's thought and the *Theologica Germanica*. The paradoxes laid out consist of seemingly antithetical Scriptures and Scriptural doctrines that can be transcended only through spiritual interpretation. He states flatly that literalist interpretation is the sword of Antichrist, producing nothing but heresies and sects.
31. *Mennonite Encyclopedia*, 2:364
32. *Mennonite Encyclopedia*, 2:365.
33. Rufus Jones, *Spiritual Reformers*, 52.
34. Williams, *Radical Reformation*, 762.
35. *Mennonite Encyclopedia*, 2:366.
36. Rufus Jones, *Spiritual Reformers*, 104-32.
37. Rufus Jones, *Spiritual Reformers*, 113.
38. For more on Coornhert, see Williams, *Radical Reformation*, 1186-88.
39. Selina Gerhard Schultz, *Schwenckfeld*, 407-10.

40. Rufus Jones, *Mysticism and Democracy in the English Commonwealth* (Cambridge: Harvard University Press, 1932), 64-68. For more on Everard, see Christopher Hill, *The World Turned Upside-Down: Radical Ideas during the English Revolution* (New York: Viking, 1972), 149.
41. Rufus Jones, *Spiritual Reformers*, 151-227.

CHAPTER 3

"SION'S TRAVELLERS"[1]
THE ENGLISH REFORMATION UP TO THE
APPEARANCE OF SEEKERS IN THE 1640S

The Sect of Seekers grows very much, and all sorts of Sectaries turn Seekers; many leave the Congregations of Independents, Anabaptists, and fall to be Seekers, and not only people but Ministers also; and whosoever lives but a few years (if the Sects be suffered to go on) will see that all the other Sects of Independents, Brownists, Antinomians, Anabaptists, will be swallowed up in the Seekers, alias Libertines, many are gone already and multitudes are going that way....

—Thomas Edwards, *Gangraena*, 1646[2]

The English Reformation charted a vexed course that defies Roland Bainton's typology of Protestant reformations. Bainton calls the English Reformation a "divergent type" combining a Lutheran approach to church-state relations and liturgy with a Calvinist sense of doctrine.[3] Much of the difference between English and Continental reformations derives from the very different motives that initiated them. Continental reformations of the 1520s erupted as popular religious renewals that translated into revolts against the institutional inertia and corruptions of the church. Even where reform took a "magisterial" turn and enlisted state sponsorship of the new church, popular spiritual ferment provided much of the impetus. For its part, England had a rich spiritual ferment of its own. But Henry VIII's break with Rome in 1534 had nothing to do with religious devotion at the grassroots. It was instead a shrewd nationalization of the English church for the sake of royal prerogative. Far from harnessing popular piety, the English Reformation tended to snub it.

Henry's desire to divorce and remarry was only a precipitating factor in his autocratic revolt from Rome. By making himself Supreme Governor of the church, he accrued enormous gains in political power. Not only did he have at his disposal a powerful instrument of ideological promulgation and social control; he also took over the enormous land holdings of the church. Henry and his successors liquidated these vast resources to reward political allies and to finance wars and other operations.[4]

As Supreme Governor, Henry exercised control of the church through the royal appointment of bishops. The political and liturgical reformation of the church was thus subject to a conservative bias from above. But Henry did not assume responsibility for doctrine. This lack of royal attention left open a window to more popular forces for renewal. Over the remainder of the 16th century, the Protestant stream that dominated doctrinal conversation in the English church was the Reformed tradition of Calvin's Geneva and the Rhineland.

A contradiction was thus built into the Henrician Reformation. In terms of church governance, it was nothing less than Erastian (subjection of the church to state control and purposes), placing the church *under* the crown. Meanwhile, the popular religious discourse of pulpit preaching, Bible lectures, and family devotions came increasingly under the influence of the Reformed tradition, which (as we noted in the preceding chapter) took predestination as its starting point. To the Reformed mind, social renewal had to come through the agency of God's elect people, rising to godly leadership in both civil and church government. Henry's Erastian policy subjected the church to unabashed political pragmatism while the Reformed faith struggled toward a theocratic hope of a godly society. Over the long term, England's ecclesiastical anomaly proved untenable.

PURITAN AND SPIRITUALIST CURRENTS

The reign of Elizabeth I (1558-1603) succeeded in carrying Henry's formulation through the 16th century. She stayed the conservative course for church polity and liturgy. While this policy nurtured a stable church, and in turn a stable society, many of those inspired by Calvin and other Continental Reformers found the English church far too "popish": that is, still unsundered from Roman Catholic hierarchy and spirituality. But no major resistance developed in the sixteenth century, owing partly to Elizabeth's popularity. Nevertheless, the growth of Reformed doctrine among the clergy, as well as the popular piety of Bible study and family devotions, slowly infused the church. Many yearned to purge the church of traits that made it seem atavistic by Reformed standards.

This broad-based feeling began to find political representation in the "Puritan" movement. Puritans were those who favored an ecclesiastical purification of the church, a more free-market economy, and a consistently Protestant-aligned foreign policy. Over the course of Elizabeth's reign, they gained influence in Parliament. Their concern to reform church structure found expression in a Presbyterian Petition in the 1580s. The proposed plan would have adopted the ecclesiastical structure developed by Calvin's disciple, Beza. In England's case, bishops appointed by the monarchy would be replaced by presbyters approved by Parliament. Puritans also wanted parish clergy to be elected by local elders, rather than chosen by principal landowners. This would have allowed greater voice for new commercial wealth in the life of the church. These steps made sense within the Reformed vision for a collaborative leadership between religious, political, and economic sectors of God's elect. However, Elizabeth did not smile upon an initiative that took control of the church away from her. The Presbyterian Petition was withdrawn for the remainder of her reign.

For the mainstream of the Puritan movement, the stalemate was tolerable, particularly as Reformed doctrine and piety continued to spread. The Presbyterian Petition would eventually find its opportunity. But for growing numbers, the situation grew unbearable. Their impatience mostly simmered below the surface. Clandestine *Separatist* congregations met, choosing and supporting their own leaders, writing their own creeds and covenanting together to be faithful in terms more rigorous than a local parish could ever institute. Sympathetic parish clergy sought to co-opt this voluntaristic spirit back into the life of the established church. But for many impassioned reformers the compromises were too great; only separation would do, even if it came at personal risk. The government countenanced little overt religious dissent, and a few Separatists were prosecuted. Some chose to emigrate to Holland and America.

Other groups explored different options. The *Family of Love* was a strongly heterodox underground network during the latter half of the

16th century. Drawing upon the writings of Dutch Spiritualist Hendrik
Niclaes (Anglicized as Henry Nicholas), Familists taught that heaven,
hell, judgment day, and the resurrection are present realities, that God
dwells in all creatures, that every day is the Sabbath, that university
education does not itself equip a person to interpret Scripture, and that
the power of the Holy Spirit can lead believers to perfection. The proliferation of these ideas caused alarm and suppression during the 1570s.
Nevertheless, Familist ideas continued a subterranean life in England
and later influenced Seekers and other Spiritualists of the 1640s. The
Family of Love was a conformist group, however. While they met secretly in homes, often at night, they were also committed members,
even leaders, in their local parishes.[5] Therefore, they exerted some
influence in terms of religious ideas, but did not manifest the kind of
crisis mentality and the turbulent spiritual quest that we will find among
the Seekers.[6]

Despite state censorship and prosecution, a variety of heterodox
groups undoubtedly subsisted below the surface of English life. The
few that became public represent the tip of a heretical iceberg, so to
speak. The Legate brothers, for example, actively preached by 1600
the general apostasy of the church and advocated the disuse of the
sacraments. Moreover, they advanced the Spiritualist idea that only
new apostles could renew the church. For such views, and for claiming
themselves to *be* the new apostles, two of the Legates were martyred.
Thomas Legate died at Newgate prison in 1604 and Bartholomew Legate
was burned at Smithfield in 1613.[7]

Puritans and the Stuarts

The accession of James Stuart, King of Scotland, to the English throne
in 1603 first appeared to Puritans as an act of divine providence. Surely
James, raised a Presbyterian, would readily sponsor a Presbyterian reformation of the English church. But James viewed the plan as dangerous to his position. To lose control of the church would be to lose control
of the country. "No Bishop, no King," he quipped. Seeking to bolster
his authority in a rapidly changing society and increasingly commercial
economy, James celebrated the archaic ideology of monarchical
"divine right." Such imperious rhetoric did not endear James to his loyal

but impatient opposition. Nevertheless, James added further impetus to England's devotional ferment when he authorized a new translation of the Bible, which appeared in 1611. Under these contradictory conditions, Separatism continued to flourish.

Anabaptist influence made its first overt appearance during James' reign. Separatists emigrating to Holland during the late 16th and early 17th centuries came in contact with Waterlander Anabaptist congregations, whose rejection of predestination and the state church appealed strongly. During the latter 16th century, the Waterlanders had tempered the moral and ecclesial rigorism of Anabaptism with the liberalizing tendencies of Spiritualism, especially the concept of the invisible church. More stringent groups called them the *drekwagen*, the "garbage wagon," of Anabaptism.[8] In 1612, Peter Helwys led a group of English expatriates back to England, founding the first *General Baptist* congregation there. They rebaptized adult believers, decried the general apostasy of the church, and proclaimed general redemption against predestination. In 1619, John Robinson led a second group back to England, founding the first *Particular Baptist* congregation there. These were less influenced by Anabaptism, retaining predestinational theology and rebaptizing believers within a more Calvinist outlook. At first they did not embrace the principle of separation of church and state, hoping for the reform of the Church of England. But during the 1630s, bitter persecution drove them to a fully Separatist position.

Neither group embraced the religious pacifism of the Continental Anabaptists. While only the General Baptists retained any serious degree of Mennonite influence, both groups were usually dubbed "Anabaptist" by outsiders, who assumed them all to be the same. In reality, however, protracted debate between their predestinational and free-grace doctrines generated great enmity between the two groups. While both groups grew quietly and steadily, their mutual antipathies neutralized some of their energies.[9]

The reign of Charles I (1623-42) rapidly eroded relations between the Puritan party and the Stuart throne. The forces for reform had become dominant not only within the church itself but through representation in Parliament. But Charles' obliquely Catholic sympathies, together with the decadence of his court, made it difficult for even the most loyal Puritan to see this king as the godly prince who could lead the nation in paths of righteousness. In foreign policy, Charles failed to align England with the international forces of Protestantism; in economic policy, he favored the monopolists; and in church policy, he appointed William Laud as his archbishop to root out and barbarously punish religious dissent.

When the conflicts between Charles and Parliament degenerated into outright stalemate in 1629, Charles dismissed Parliament and ran a personal government for the next eleven years. Many despaired of any significant reform of church or society. In spite of persecution, Separatism grew. Separated congregations were small, since they were limited to meeting in private homes. Murray Tolmie estimates that there were probably no more than 1000 Separatists in London, out of a total city population of around 250,000.[10] Some Separatists resorted to more dramatic action. Emigration, especially to America, soared in the 1630s. Meanwhile, the rhetoric of protest escalated. Dissenters denounced prelacy (the rule of bishops in ecclesiastical and even some civil spheres) as the rule of Antichrist, a relic of "popery" still flourishing in England. Such apocalyptic rhetoric indicates that, for some, an irremediable conflict between court and nation had developed. Still, the Puritan movement was by no means revolutionary in mood.

Besides those who dropped out of parish churches to join Separatist congregations, a larger phenomenon of informal Separatism grew as individuals participated in informal meetings for religious purposes. Such meetings included lay preaching, Bible reading, and group prayer. For example, Bristol witnessed a significant quasi-Separatist phenomenon beginning in the 1620s. A local parish minister named Yeamans attracted a large following that met regularly to fast and pray, often at night. The group featured a considerable participation by women. Only in the 1640s did this informal group decide to constitute itself formally as a Separatist congregation.[11] Bristol, England's second city, became a major center for Seekers and later for Quakers. Quasi-Separatists disliked the principle of formal Separation, but their exercise of options outside official parish services introduced a novel relativism into the established church. Their tendency to create inter-parochial networks of dissident ideas and experimental piety may have done more than outright Separatism accomplished in undermining the authority of the official church.

CIVIL WAR

In 1640, revolts in Ireland and Scotland forced Charles to call Parliamentary elections in order to raise an army. The new Parliament manifested a mature Puritan opposition that was ready to demand concessions from Charles. Popular expectation was suddenly renewed. Puritans entertained no thoughts of revolution, but saw an opportunity to force Charles' hand. Nevertheless, some left-wing Puritans interpreted the moment in millennial terms. The Separatist Thomas Goodwin, exiled in Holland, preached early in 1641 that Babylon's reign in England was about to fall and that Christ's kingdom would begin in 1650.[12] He understood Christ's kingdom to be the triumph in England of a gathered, congregational church. Separatists like Goodwin spoke of the "rule of the saints." This term implied the Reformed agenda: God's predestined elect must rise to leadership in the ecclesiastical, political, and socioeconomic sectors of English society. At this point, the Separatist position was primarily focused on ecclesiastical reformation, with only implicit political aims. But the millennialist rhetoric of leaders like Goodwin tended to become more political once open conflict with Charles erupted.

For his part, Charles had grown unaccustomed to outright political opposition over the past eleven years. In the face of strongly worded petitions arising in Parliament and riots breaking out in the streets of London, he grew more imperious. By 1642, he had raised an army and made it clear that he would treat opposition in England the same as insurgency in Scotland and Ireland. An astonished Parliament scrambled to raise its own military force and defend itself. Thus, an unthinkable English Civil War began.

Parliament had little difficulty recruiting men to fight. The pent-up resentment and reforming zeal in the country found a cathartic outlet in military service. But Parliament was ambivalent about waging war against Charles. The initial goal in this unwanted war was simply to force Charles back into political negotiation with Parliament. But Charles' intransigence and Parliament's ambivalence combined to create an intermittent and indecisive struggle. By 1643, Parliament feared it might lose the war and sought military aid from Scottish forces already alienated from Charles. While genuine insecurity was a primary motivation, Parliament's Presbyterian majority also saw the alliance as an opportunity to vouchsafe their agenda for reformation. In the Solemn League and Covenant that year, Parliament secured Scottish military aid in return for the promise to reform the English church "according to the Word of God and the best example of the Reformed Churches." Parliament and the Scots shared the opinion that the Presbyterian plan was that "best example."

Parliament moved to enact its part of the covenant by establishing the Westminster Assembly of Divines, a Puritan clerical elite, to formulate a creed, catechism, and directory of church order and worship. It soon became clear that Parliament planned to impose this revised parochial system upon the entire nation. If it had been carried out in the 1580s, when the Presbyterian Petition was first presented, such a plan would have received strong popular support. But by the 1640s, other agendas for reform competed vigorously with the Presbyterian plan. An Independent party was formed in opposition to the Presbyterians. Independents rejected the parochial system, advocating a nation of gathered congregations that would elect their own elders and ministers, even write their own creeds. Some envisioned this option enabling a continued national church, albeit on a decentralized basis; others saw congregational autonomy as a break between church and state, a warrant for religious pluralism. The more conservative Independents saw their plan for a congregational English church as the best route to true Protestant reform. But the more radicalized Independents held more millennial hopes for a total transformation of English society through the "rule of the saints" in state as well as church politics.

This moment is crucial for an understanding of the breakdown of the Puritan coalition and the proliferation of alternative religious agendas in the 1640s. The Independent party gave political focus to a considerable spectrum of Puritanism to the left of the old guard of Presbyterian leadership. In the confusion and uncertainty of the situation, however, the Independent movement itself tended to splinter into successively radicalizing groups. Just as Puritans had been able to unite in opposition to Charles only for a while, now Independents were able to unite only in opposition to the Presbyterian attempt to predetermine the outcome of the English Reformation. The spiritual energies of resentment fired the politics of the 1640s. Political unities generated mainly in opposition to perceived threats of religious coercion. Once a sense of parity or superiority was achieved in relation to a repressive power, the political unity dissolved. It is important to remember that in that environment, religious and political agendas were the same. "Presbyterianism" was not the matter of denominational preference we think of today, but a political platform for the religious destiny of the nation. Conversely, "Baptism" was a different political agenda, though defined mainly in opposition to any state-church apparatus, whether Presbyterian or Independent.

Likewise, it is important to recognize Parliament's army as more than a military force. It quickly evolved into something much more: a political actor in its own right and a cauldron of radical religious experimentation. From the start, many men enlisted in Parliament's cause with a religious sense of purpose. But Parliament's ambivalence and the traditional ranking of military leadership according to social position tended to blunt that sense of purpose. It was the political and military genius of Oliver Cromwell most of all that created a potent military, political, and religious force out of the army. By 1645, his innovations for a "New Model" of military structure, awarding rank according to leadership ability, began to take hold. Moreover, Cromwell enlisted a new wave of idealistic young soldiers to the cause with incendiary political rhetoric that transformed an unintended civil war into a millennial holy war, in which the army served as God's hand in history. This military agent would enact divine purposes that kings and parliaments resisted. Cromwell and other key leaders in the New Model army were strongly aligned with the Independent party. The army thus became a potent political force that outflanked the Presbyterian-dominated Parliament. Finally, the generals also enlisted some of the most radical and brilliant Puritan preachers as chaplains, ideological firebrands among the ranks of this galvanized military and political force. Henceforth, the army became a prime site of religious ferment, political radicalism, and utopian agitation in England.

One other radicalizing factor during the civil war is important to note: the suspension of censorship and of enforced attendance at parish services. Without active suppression of heterodox religious and political ideas, currents that had remained below the surface welled up in profusion. Meanwhile, without enforced attendance, many parishes were emptied, and the experiments in worship and ministry that had been previously extracurricular or underground moved to center stage. A seeking situation *par excellence* overwhelmed English society, particularly affecting a young, idealistic generation of Puritans swept up in the drama of events.

In our Introduction, we noted "supply-side" theories of religious change in American culture, in particular the effect of the Immigration Reform Act of 1965 upon religious diversity in the United States. The suspension of censorship and enforced parish attendance in the 1640s would seem to offer a similar example of government deregulation (in this case, more *de facto* than intended) opening new social space for religious seeking and innovation. The range of experimentation that unfolded during the 1640s was disturbing to some, exhilarating to others, and disorienting for all.

Hence, a great popular outcry was raised against the Presbyterian attempt to predetermine the religious outcome of the civil war. Even the Presbyterian Scots were scandalized by Parliament's attempt to impose church order by *fiat*. In effect, then, England's second attempt at reformation was as vexed as the first: it pitted a new Erastian superstructure, this time with Parliamentary control of the church, against a new popular religious ferment. Whereas Puritanism had developed through Reformed opposition to Tudor and Stuart Erastianism, now Independents, Baptists, and others formed the opposition to the new Puritan ruling elites. As the poet John Milton wrote at the time, "new Presbyter is but old Priest writ large."

By the mid-1640s, Parliament recognized that there was no politically viable way to impose their Presbyterian settlement of the church. One factor that doomed the project to failure was the suspension of censorship of the press. Religious ideas that before 1642 had circulated only below the surface, if at all, now reeled off presses in exponentially expanding numbers. Propaganda pieces, ranging from one-sheet "broadsides" to tomes hundreds of pages long were printed and sold at low cost.

One of the most notorious publishers of dissenting literature was Giles Calvert of London, among the first publishers in England who was not also a printer. Among his first publications was *The Soldier's Pocket Bible* (1643), sixteen pages of Scriptural quotations to strengthen "the inner man" to "fight the Lord's Battels." Like many idealists of that day, Calvert was soon disenchanted with Parliament's course and threw his support to more radical writers. He also published Spiritualist writings by Jacob Boehme and Henry Nicholas. Over the course of his career, he published more than 600 of the most radical tracts and books written in England during that period, including many of those that we will examine in succeeding chapters.[13] Calvert was questioned, fined, and imprisoned briefly on various occasions for his publishing activities, but was never really silenced. Once the door was opened for a free press, it was never to be effectively closed again.

INDEPENDENTS, SEPARATISTS, AND BAPTISTS

Amid the confusion and alarm of these unanticipated circumstances, all religious and political positions evolved rapidly. The Independent party in politics was complemented by Independent churches. These were gathered congregations, something like the Separatist churches before the war. But in contrast to the untrained Separatist ministers, Independent ministers tended to come from the traditional ordained clergy. The new Independent congregations flourished rapidly in the freedom of the new situation, and Independents saw themselves as enacting a new profile of congregational church life that would soon become standard in English life, either as a decentralized national church or as a confederation of churches sundered altogether from the state.

Meanwhile, Separatist congregations also burgeoned in the permissive atmosphere and even began to meet less secretly. For example, Praise-God Barbone, a leather merchant and Separatist lay preacher, opened a meeting of his congregation to the public in December 1641. But mob hostility sparked a riot involving thousands of people. Thus, Separatists encountered some popular opposition, even in the absence of official coercion, and returned to a low profile well into the 1640s.

Finding new space to operate in the political rift between Presbyterians and Independents, Baptists soon outflanked both mainstream parties.[14] Flourishing in public and exuding confidence, Particular and General Baptists became a political force in their own right. Both groups held political opinions well to the left of the Puritan mainstream. Particular Baptists were religious propagandists of unprecedented technique and success. Both groups seemed to thrive on conflict and commotion. Their sensational meetings and aggressive techniques of controversy and outreach were a focal point of religious fervor. Baptists were the first unabashed sectarians in England. Their agenda was not a vision for a national church. They took religious pluralism and free-market religious competition as assumptions and went out to make gains as quickly as possible. Baptists published and circulated popular, inexpensive tracts as no group had done before. They also gained ground by challenging local clergy to debates. These confrontations were so charged that they sometimes ended in riots and thus were banned by some local authorities. Such tactics set the tone for a new, rough-and-ready religious conversation in the 1640s and 1650s. Baptist congregations began to baptize their converts in public during the 1640s, drawing both derision and curiosity from outsiders, who gave them the nickname "Dippers." Preaching by the immediate leading of the Holy Spirit, untrained Baptist "mechanic preachers" tapped into new realms of popular religious sentiment and brought lower social echelons into the arena of religious renewal and political conflict.

The Calvinist-minded Particular Baptists held public debates in the early 1640s, challenging the Puritan mainstream's practice of infant baptism. In the radicalized atmosphere of the new situation, the critique of infant baptism as the dead ordinance of a state-sponsored religion galvanized many young Puritans. As a result, large numbers of Independents and Separatists were drawn into the Particular Baptist movement.

Separatists scrambled to respond to the Baptist onslaught. Some of the more radical Independent ministers offered adult baptism as an option to congregational members, alongside a continued use of infant baptism. In 1642, Praise-God Barbone formulated an important rebuttal to the Baptists. In *A Discourse Tending to prove the Baptisme*, he argued that Baptists had no authority to reinstitute an adult baptism. Such an innovation could be established only by someone, like John the Baptist or the early apostles, with a divine commission.[15] Barbone's argument turned on the standard Puritan assumption that the apostles had operated by extraordinary inspiration, whereas succeeding generations of Christians knew only an ordinary level of the Spirit's work. His tract proved useful in fending off the Baptist attack. But for some Independents, Separatists, and Baptists, it raised a larger question. Many of the most idealistic young Puritans had concluded that a general apostasy had degenerated the church over most of its history. The question raised by Barbone regarding adult baptism was applicable to *the entire life of the church*. Ordinary Christians could not reform or reconstitute the church and its ordinances. This momentous juncture required divine intervention through extraordinary figures. A nagging uncertainty began to grow in some hearts. It cast all the competing reformations into doubt, leading to the Seeker despair regarding all present options.

The Mennonite-inspired General Baptists also posted rapid gains in the new situation. Because they were not Calvinists, they were not simply Puritans taking one step further to the left. General Baptists were a more disturbing phenomenon. They drew well from the lower-middle classes and often converted individuals still attending their local parish. Their organization was loose and their ministers tended to be laymen whose charisma made up for lack of training. Thomas Lambe, a "soapboiler," was a leading General Baptist minister in London and an evangelist who moved extensively around the country. His congregation's meetings were sensational events—public religious theater that drew large crowds, especially women and young people. All positions had opportunity to be heard and debated. Sometimes several different discussions continued at the same time. Perhaps drawing upon the description of early Christian worship in 1 Corinthians 14, Lambe allowed two or three men to speak in succession, with hearers free to offer counterpoint.

In 1645, Lambe published The *Fountain of Free Grace Opened*, offering the fullest General Baptist statement to date. In it, he rejected both Calvinist predestination and Arminian free-will. Christ died for everyone. The individual is free to reject or ignore this free gift—and must bear personal guilt for doing so. However, the power to accept Christ's death and to grow in grace derive not from human freedom but from the work of the Spirit. (Tolmie notes that this understanding of general redemption comes close to the later Quaker preaching of the light of Christ within all people. But in contrast to Quakers, General Baptists remained intensely focused on the Bible as primary authority.[16]) Hence, General Baptists insisted on the term "free grace," rather than "free will."

This was a real alternative to the whole range of Puritan positions, even Particular Baptist preaching. The theological heterodoxy and congregational anarchism of the General Baptists was matched by their political radicalism, particularly as they rallied to the Leveller cause (see Chapter 5). They also gave more hearing to women's voices than did most other groups. Though only men could speak before the congregation, women were allowed to speak at certain times from the congregation, or in separate women's meetings. A Mrs. Attaway was a member of Lambe's congregation and a notorious woman preacher in London. She began holding special meetings for women, where she lectured much in the manner of a Puritan divine. These sessions were soon opened to all interested persons and became highly charged events. Mrs. Attaway never gained the approval of her congregation for her independent ministry. In January 1646, she ended these meetings, telling her audience that she was in the wilderness, waiting for a new outpouring of the Spirit. Until the new Pentecost, no one was commissioned to preach the gospel.[17] She then disappeared from the General Baptist scene.

Tolmie summarizes: "The position of the General Baptists on the frontiers of organized sectarianism exercised a powerful attraction for enthusiasts who in their search for religious fulfillment passed from Church to Church and from sect to sect."[18] It was the last station on the journey that many took from Puritanism to Seekerism by the mid-1640s. Beyond their contribution to the Seeker phenomenon of that decade, the General Baptists are a key precursor to the Quaker movement, which gathered so many radicals together in the 1650s. Besides preaching general redemption and allowing women's ministry, General Baptists also were known to refuse the swearing of oaths before magistrates (a position already established in Continental Anabaptism), to marry only within their fellowship, and to keep their businesses open on Sundays. These practices carried over into the Quaker movement.

The Commodification of Religion

For a generation of young, earnest Puritans, the 1640s combined rising expectations with crushing disillusions. Their experience of the Parliamentary cause is analogous to the disappointment some had felt in the 1520s regarding Martin Luther's reforms. No sooner had one form of religious repression finally been removed than another ecclesiastical franchise took its place, attempting to quash all competing agendas for reform. The appearance of outright sectarianism—not one but two Baptist groups rapidly growing in England—was a liberating alternative to the Presbyterian-Independent contest for political dominance. Yet, as we will see pointedly in later chapters, many young Puritans who turned Baptist experienced further dissatisfaction, even revulsion, in the realm of sectarian faith.

While none would have been able to articulate it in these terms during the 1640s, the novel experience of sectarianism placed a radically different frame around Christian faith. From the fourth century onward, the history of Christendom had been dominated by a monopolistic church establishment. Alternatives (Christian, Jewish, pagan) of course flourished in varying degrees around the edges and below the surface, but their existence was played out against the foil of a powerful church establishment. With the suspension of church establishment and the growth of sectarianism, a dizzying experience of religious relativism came over the faith, a wide-open competition of truth-claims and religious services complementary to the free market system emerging in economic life. Religious market competition inaugurated the experience of religion as a commodity. (For example, the young George Fox in 1649 heard church-bells ringing and "it struck at my life, for it was just like a market-bell to gather people together that the priest might set forth his ware to sale."[19])

The avid propagandist techniques rapidly developing among Baptists were both exhilarating and disturbing. As we shall see, all parties, reactionary as well as reformist, experienced a certain queasiness in this unprecedented historic moment. In later chapters, we will see this queasiness grow to full-fledged *nausea* in the case of the Ranters. For now, however, we simply note that, beyond the traumatic military, political, and religious conflicts raging between England's ruling interests in the civil war, something more subtly unsettling was creeping into religious consciousness, especially among those most fervent for personal and social renewal. For conservatives, on the one hand, the dominant response was one of fearful squeamishness at what was perceived as chaos and libertinism erupting from the lower social orders. For radicals, on the other hand, it was the disconcerting sense that all religion was turning into *forms* that could offer only fleeting satisfaction. This is an early modern experience of "addiction formation" in relation to the commodified form, so integral to the experience of life in a capitalist society.[19]

Anabaptist and Spiritualist ideas had been seeping quietly into England since the latter 16th century. We have seen that the doctrine of the general apostasy of the church appeared in print by the 1590s, followed soon after by the Spiritualist doctrine of the nullity of the sacraments and the need for a new apostolate to reinstitute a valid church. These ideas suddenly found new space to circulate with a free press. They also found new currency in the 1640s, as all competing agendas did their best to discredit one another. Just as Caspar Schwenckfeld in his Liegnitz

Reformation rejected the option to go ahead and establish one more practice of the sacraments, a new generation of English Spiritualists did not have the stomach to add one more brand to the new religious market.

EARLY SIGHTINGS OF SEEKERS

In the early to mid-1640s, the names "Seeker," "Expecter," or "Waiter" began to crop up in religious literature. These arose among the many colorful nicknames of that period. Rarely, however, did individuals or groups embrace the epithets they received. It is hard to find anyone in the 1640s who claimed, "I am a Seeker." But the term was frequently applied as short-hand for an emerging religious position amid the tumult of military conflict and religious competition. Just as Schwenckfeld's *Stillstand* came into focus owing to a crisis regarding the Lord's Supper, the Seeker position coalesced in response to a crisis regarding baptism. The sensational Baptist immersions and the Puritan response to them precipitated a question of legitimacy that neither Baptists nor Puritans had anticipated. Describing the situation in 1644, the Independent Sarah Jones (from whom we will hear more in Chapter 7) commented that "some are seekers out of a Baptisme looking for Elyas [or] John the Baptist to bring it from heaven, forsaking all fellowship til Christ shall send for new Apostles."[21] Rather than join the sectarian fray by adding yet another formulation of Christian faith and practice, Seekers distinguished themselves by their renunciation—a chastened willingness to wait for divine intervention.[22]

The most extensive early description of Seekers comes from one of their most hostile critics. In 1646, Thomas Edwards published *Gangraena* in three installments. The title suggests the author's sense of an advancing contagion and spiritual decay in society. The subtitle bills the book as "A Catalogue and Descovery of many of the Errors, Heresies, Blasphemies and pernicious Practices of the Sectaries of this time, vented and acted in England in these last four years." A strict Puritan minister of the Presbyterian party, Edwards hoped to rekindle political resolve for the Presbyterian plan by arousing public alarm regarding the proliferation of heterodox groups. Thus, he wrote not so much against any one faction or doctrine as against sectarian growth in general, a "many headed monstrous Hydra"[23] about to ruin England's reformation.

Edwards lists some 176 doctrinal errors floating at large in England.[24] Heading his list is the Spiritualist assertion that Christ alone, not Scripture, is God's authoritative Word. Apparently some went so far as to disparage Scripture as a human "invention." Heresy number 45 is universalism: one may be saved "without Christ"; "the very Heathens are saved if they serve God according to the knowledge God hath given them." Number 50 on the list is the old Familist doctrine of human perfectability under the power of the Spirit. Number 148 is the separation of church and state: "that Christian Magistrates have no power at all to meddle in matters of Religion . . . but in civill only, concerning the bodies and goods of men." Number 153 is the communistic assertion that all the earth belongs to the saints; the estates of gentlemen and rich men should be shared among all the saints. Number 158 is the scandalous idea that Christians may not fight to defend religion, for "Religion will defend itself." Some also denied that Christians should fight to defend their nation or their civil rights.

From this brief sampling, we hear of wide-ranging religious and political ideas being "vented" by assorted individuals and groups. But Edwards concludes that the Seeker phenomenon embodies the general trend of these ideas. Heresy number 97 defines the Seeker position succinctly:

> That there ought to be in these times no making or building of Churches, nor use of Church-ordinances, as ministering of the Word, Sacraments, but waiting for a Church, being in readiness upon all occasions to take knowledge of any passenger, of any opinion or tenet whatsoever; the Saints as pilgrims do wander as in a Temple of smoak, not able to finde Religion, and therefore should not plant it by gathering or building a pretended supposed House, but should wait for the coming of the Spirit, as the Apostles did.[25]

The "temple of smoak" imagery had been used by two Seeker writers in 1646, Lawrence Clarkson and John Saltmarsh. It derives from Revelation 15:8, which states that the smoke will not clear from the heavenly temple, and no one can enter it, until the seven plagues are completed. Spiritualists and other radicals of the moment saw the current military and ideological warfare as the apocalyptic conflict envisioned in Revelation. England was enduring seven plagues of God aimed to bring the people to repentance (that is, true reformation). Saltmarsh argued that churches must not be settled until a new coherence emerged from the present confusion, until everyone in his or her own way had come out of Babylon.[26] Edwards disagreed. If matters were allowed to continue drifting in the present fashion, faith would only degenerate further.

Edwards took delight in naming not just heresies but individual heretics. His writing is also peppered with lively anecdotal accounts of their excesses in word and deed, offering us valuable glimpses into those "salad days" of English radicalism. Among those he identifies as heretics and seditionists are Saltmarsh, Clarkson, William Erbury, William Walwyn, John Lilburne, and the publisher Giles Calvert. In his second installment, Edwards sneers that Walwyn has been "touchie" about being described as a dangerous Seeker.[27] Such notoriety was harmless enough at the moment, when no government policy on religion had been established. But it would single out individuals for persecution if a state church were reestablished.

Edwards finds various pernicious doctrines breaking out in various groups, creating an incoherent, "linsey wolsey compounded Religion."[28] One can hear sincere panic in some sections:

> This Land is become already in many places a Chaos, a Babel, another Amsterdam, yea, worse, we are beyond that and on the high way to Munster (if God prevent it not) but if a general Toleration shall be granted, so much written and stood for, England would quickly become a Sodom, an Egypt, Babylon, yea, worse than all of these. . . . A Toleration is the grand designe of the Devil, his Master-peece and chief Engine to work by at this time.[29]

He adjures magistrates to inflict exemplary punishment on the most notorious individuals as well as on those who publish their writings. That will rein in heresy and sedition until church and state can be reconstituted.

Edwards sees the Presbyterian moment of opportunity passing. Parliament's hesitation to impose its settlement will prove disastrous, for

> who can read all the errors, heresies, and blasphemies catalogued here and not say it is time to settle Government? what [will] these things come unto if let alone a little longer? and

what will we do in the end thereof? what will not men fall
into, what will they not preach and do if Government is not
quickly settled? There is need for a *Ne ultra* set up.[30]

The epigraph at the head of this chapter summarizes Edwards' fear that
the trend of the situation will eventually make Seekers of everyone to
the left of Presbyterianism. But he goes on to prophesy that this trend
will not stop with the Seekers. People will drift on "from Seekers to be
Antiscripturalists, and Sceptiks, yea, Blasphemers and Atheists."[31]

John Saltmarsh, one of those most strongly attacked by Edwards,
answered him in print that year with *Groans for Liberty*. He chided him
for his "jeers" against his brothers: "have you no gnawings, no flashings"
of conscience? Having met Edwards by chance on the street in London,
Saltmarsh was not altogether put off by him, but felt concern for his
condition: "your face and complexion shews a most sadly parched, burnt,
and withered spirit . . . I told you at parting I hoped we should overcome you by prayer."[32]

Indeed, there is great fear and revulsion, mixed with very little
Christian charity, in *Gangraena*. Yet, apart from his severe judgments,
Edwards' reportage offers some of the best information we have on the
early seeking scene of the mid-1640s. His reactionary politics notwithstanding, Edwards made a number of compelling points. He stressed that
religious toleration would translate into disruption of all social
institutions. Moreover, Edwards' conviction that Seekerism would lead to
general skepticism was borne out in many cases over decades to come.
Tolmie describes Edwards' *Gangraena* as "an underestimated minor classic
of the English revolution, a new form of popular journalism of great power,
deliberately conceived and executed to influence public opinion."[33]

Early Interpretations of Seeking

Reactionary writers attributed various causes to the Seeker phenomenon.
Some viewed it as the outcome of too much questioning. Edwards interpreted seeking as a cloak of humility for political agitation and generalized rebellion. The great Puritan divine Richard Baxter, who could write
with wisdom on other topics, was prone to conspiracy theories when it
came to Seekers and other dissenters. To Baxter, such groups were simply

clever fronts for Jesuit infiltrators and other secret Catholic agitators aiming to destabilize Protestant England.[34] The Seekers were thus really Catholic "Hiders," he quipped, "among whom I have reason to believe the Papists have not the least of their strength in England at this day."[35]

His conspiracy theories aside, Baxter's *Key for the Catholicks, to Open the Jugling of the Jesuits* (1659) supplies a useful six-fold typology of Seekers.[36] Ranging from the most moderate to the most extreme, he begins with those who seek the true church among proliferating competitors. They still believe that a true church exists, but have not found it. Next, some doubt whether there should be any organized church, but have not yet denied institutional religion in principle. Third, there are those who, holding to the theological principle of the general apostasy, deny the validity of any organized church. Fourth, and more grievously, come those who deny all visible churches, seek a universal, invisible church, and cast serious doubts on the truth of Scripture and the validity of any ordained ministry. Given the general state of apostasy among the churches, no one is obliged to believe anything in Scripture without its truth being certified by miracles like those wrought by the first apostles. Baxter finds it hard to imagine anyone silly enough to believe this. Who would believe in a Christ who came to set up a faith that lasted only a little while before collapsing?

> Who will not despise Christ that thinks he came on such a low design? . . . It's most evident therefore that . . . such are either Infidels or Papists. Infidelity is the thing professed, and therefore that we take them for Infidels, they cannot blame us.[37]

This fourth position represents a final dissolution of the Protestant outlook. It had experienced the undoing of Christendom through civil war, sectarian uproar, and the decay of scriptural authority through the multiplicity of interpretations. Within his loyally Protestant frame of reference, Baxter can see it only as infidelity. He does not, however, recognize the great desolation experienced by the soul that has come to this position. He can only see it as "silly."

Fifth in Baxter's typology of Seekers are those

> that own the Church and Ministry, and Ordinances, but yet suppose themselves above them: for they think that these are but the Administrations of Christ to men in the passage to a higher state, and that such as have received the Spirit and

have the Law once written in their hearts, are under (as they
call it) the second Covenant, and so are past the lower form
of Ordinances, Scripture, Ministry, and visible Churches.[38]

Here we can recognize the Spiritualist position of the type we found in
Sebastian Franck. An incipient liberalism is audible in the abandonment of visible church order for a mystical union of faithful souls in all
times and places, a claim to a "higher," more abstract truth.

This tendency is more abundantly realized by the sixth and final
position in Baxter's scheme, those

that think the whole company of believers should now be
over-grown the Scripture, Ministry, and Ordinances: For they
think that the law was the Father's Administration, and the
Gospel Ministry and Sacraments are the Son's Administration and that both these are now past, and the season of the
Spirit's Administration is now come, which all must attend,
and quit the lower forms.[39]

Here a fully progressive sense of history is revealed: these Seekers
see themselves as the vanguard of a new age dawning on all humanity.
Their abandonment of organized churches is "the wave of the future."
This doctrine of the three ages extends at least as far back as Joachim of
Fiore in the 12th century, and can be found among subsequent writers,
including Jacob Boehme.[40] Clearly, these last two Seeker types manifest an optimism that does not attend the first four. Their outlook is
clearly post-Reformation, and incipiently post-Christian.

Writing in 1659, Baxter had more perspective on the Seeker phenomenon than was enjoyed by Edwards. He admitted that "a great while
I knew not what to make of this close Generation." But eventually he
concluded that Seekers and other English dissenters "have long had a
design . . . to overthrow the Gospel, and set up Infidelity and meer Deism." If there is some paranoia evident in these judgments, Baxter still
made a sincere effort to map the diverse ideas and actions that were
lumped together as "Seeker" in the 1640s and 1650s. Certainly, he was
right that these pilgrims, both the desolate and the triumphalist, had
come to the "Land's End" of Protestantism.

What Baxter could not supply was a positive definition of the new
territory Seekers had entered. One commentator of the period attempted

a sympathetic interpretation. *A Sober Word to a Serious People* (1651) was published anonymously by John Jackson. Clearly, Jackson had moved among Seekers, although he did not claim to be one. He bemoaned the many condemnations spoken and written against Seekers. At the same time, he observed that many individuals impatient with the stalemate of the church had left their congregations and moved among Seeking groups, only to be disappointed in their actual numbers, unimpressed with their spiritual attainments, and eventually weary of waiting for God to reveal the new church. These often went back to their churches, saying, "come, let us go back to Egypt for bread."[41]

But Jackson defended the seeking impulse. It was a common experience for sincere Christians to find themselves going through the motions of a form of worship and then suddenly questioning the entire enterprise. The Seekers Jackson defended were those who, rather than claiming to be against or beyond the ordinances of the church, sought a better understanding of their basis in Scripture. Such a Seeker would fit with the first and second types in Baxter's model. Jackson maintained that the more advanced types were not truly Seekers but "Attainers," since they felt that they had moved on to some new dispensation of the Spirit.[42] Jackson argued that the present ministry and sacraments of the church were still valid, but that Scripture shows that these are not the only avenues of God's work. When Israel languished in Babylon, prayer and waiting for redemption were true forms of faithfulness. So the present "mourners of Sion" should not be faulted for emulating that example during these troubled times. The overall tendency of Jackson's argument suggests a confidence that, over time and with sufficient Bible study, all would converge at some fairly orthodox faith.[43] The tract does not evince a Spiritualist sense of the teaching and gathering power of the Word of God within the believer.

Oliver Cromwell had an orthodox but tolerant attitude toward Seekers, similar to that of Jackson. His daughter, Elizabeth, had become a Seeker in 1646, probably under the influence of William Erbury. Writing to her concerned sister, Bridget Ireton, Cromwell saw the potential for much growth:

> She sees her own vanity and carnal mind, bewailing it; she
> seeks after (as I hope also) that which will satisfy. And thus
> to be a seeker is to be of the best sect next to a finder; and

such an one shall every faithful humble seeker be at the end. Happy seeker, happy finder."[42]

So, with Jackson and Cromwell, we hear a more sanguine assessment of the seeking phenomenon. They recognized that in times of social upheaval and/or early adult spiritual formation, seeking to deepen one's foundation in faith can be a healthy step. Both writers assumed that the Seeker would return home again to orthodox faith. But this was by no means the outcome in many cases, including that of Elizabeth Cromwell.[43]

A Seeking Nation:
From "Fundamentalists" to "Atheists"

The penitential spirituality of those called Seekers was not the only tack that English men and women tried during the 1640s. Of course, the majority stayed in their parish churches, which offered some reassuring stability in a "world turned upside down." But other currents were moving as well. Bernard Capp has researched the growth of popular millenarianism during the 1640s and 1650s.[46] The upheavals of war and religious uncertainty stimulated millenarian speculations concerning the end of the world, the return of Christ, and the kingdom of God on earth. These circulated particularly in the lower strata, but in varying degrees across the entire social spectrum. "Chap-books" of the period (an early form of newspaper) are rife with astrological speculations as well as stories of miraculous events and messianic births, not unlike the tabloids of our own day. Given England's growing commercial and military power, it was a small step for many to imagine themselves living at the dawn of a new age of Protestant imperialism. These nationalistic desires did not necessarily move in the direction of democracy. The longing for more secure, reassuring times led some to predict the resumption of the Stuart throne as a messianic force in the world. Capp finds prophecies of the glorious reign of Charles II beginning as early as 1649, the year Charles I was beheaded. According to some prophecies, a Stuart world monarchy would lead to the conversions of Jews to Christ and Irish Catholics to Anglicanism! Visions of a coming age of material surplus were all the more delicious given the economic dislocations and crop failures of the 1640s.

These utopian dreams, often conservative and nationalistic in bias, finally found political expression with the rise of the Fifth Monarchist movement in the 1650s. Galvanized by a sense that political leaders, especially Cromwell, had betrayed God's cause in England, Fifth Monarchists were a force in the Nominated, or "Barebones," Parliament of 1653. But their absolutist politics were ultimately self-defeating. One Fifth Monarchist faction, led by Thomas Venner, eventually resorted to impotent insurrectionary attempts in 1657 and 1661. Some of their political objectives overlapped with those of many Seekers, Levellers, Quakers, and others—for example, the abolition of tithes and sweeping legal reforms. But they also held a theocratic dream of "the rule of the saints" that would have placed government in the hands of Independent and Baptist religious leaders. And while they would have ended the death penalty for theft, some would have instituted it for adultery, blasphemy, and Sabbath-breaking. They enthusiastically supported private property, trade protectionism, the war against the Dutch (England's chief trading rival), and even dreamed of conquering Rome. But the Fifth Monarchists were only a loose coalition whose unity consisted more in resentment against political enemies than in any coherent agenda of their own. Still, this early "religious right," which drew major support from radical Independents and Particular Baptists, became a force on the political scene. (We will return to the Fifth Monarchist movement in Chapter 7, when we examine its leading prophetess, Anna Trapnel.)

At the other end of the spectrum, religious skepticism, total retreat from church life, and even principled atheism also grew. Christopher Hill has attempted some estimate of the role of "irreligion" in this period.[47] At the popular level, particularly among the poor, much irreligion was passive, a quiet disobedience toward the laws requiring parish church attendance. With such laws left unenforced during this period, nonattendance surely grew. A more philosophical irreligion can be found among the upper classes. It was not uncommon in some circles to hear the existence of God denied. In the late 16th century, the dramatist Christopher Marlowe had cynically remarked that Jesus was either a bastard or a homo-sexual, and that he deserved his fate.[48] Some spoke candidly of religion as a force to protect property and keep the poor in fear. Even many Puritans held a pragmatic view of the church as an organ of social control.

There was popular hostility toward the clergy in the 1640s. Parish ministers in particular were subjected to outright scorn in the streets of London. Gerrard Winstanley, whom we will study later, formulated the most principled and categorical rejection of "Church-made" religion during this period. "We will neither come to Church nor serve their God," he wrote against the clergy. He also began to substitute "Reason" for God. Yet a strong theistic sense seems to have remained in Winstanley's case, despite the fact that the growing popularity of science and naturalism led some to conclude that "all things come by nature." Finally, despair over England's future, issuing forth in nihilistic expressionism, overcame many during this period, in particular those dubbed "Ranters." One of them, Thomas Webbe, cracked, "no heaven but women, nor no hell save marriage." (We will devote Chapter 6 to the Ranters.) Conservative commentators like Edwards believed that atheism would only continue to grow until religious conformity was enforced again. By 1660, Richard Baxter was ready to support a restoration of monarchy and episcopal church government in order to bring popular heresy back under control.

SEEKERS THEN AND NOW

One is struck by the appearance of many movements in this period that are prescient of religious and political developments in our own time. From the incipiently "fundamentalist" politics of the Fifth Monarchists to the "post-Christian" skepticism and protests of Ranters and others, the English Interregnum period (1642-60) presents us with a historical mirror to help us gain perspective on the excesses as well as the insights of our own times.

Wade Clark Roof's interpretation of religious seeking since the 1960s includes the entire spectrum of baby boomers, from conservative loyalists to New Age neo-pagans. Similarly, everyone caught in the upheavals of the English Civil War can be considered a religious seeker of some sort. There was no place to "hide" from these revolutionary changes. There was simply no ground left unmoved. Even the most passionate traditionalist looked for some way back to "the bosom of the Church." And even the merriest Ranter sought out the company of like-minded nihilists.

But our focus of study will center mostly on those who at least for a while fit somewhere within Baxter's taxonomy of "Seekers," those who longed keenly for a renewed church fellowship yet who refused to "go back to Egypt to eat bread" in their former congregations. Some of these were basically religious conservatives whose moral scrupulosity and spiritual idealism drove them to a radical renunciation of all existing options. Others were incipient liberals, who believed that the age of Christendom, whether Catholic or Protestant, was over, and that a new age of the Spirit was dawning. They did not look for new apostles to reconstruct the New Testament church; nevertheless, they too "waited upon the Lord" together for some new Pentecost appropriate to the new age.

These two basic Seeker types form the axis of our study. They are polar opposites in some respects. In various ways, however, both occupy the spiritual "place" where the unbearable tension is lived between visible churches and the invisible church, the particular and the universal, the already and not yet, the conservative and progressive. As with Schwenckfeld's *Stillstand*, this was the place where stopping became moving on, but at a different level. This tension was maintained somewhere between the theocratic machinations of the Fifth Monarchists and the superior disdain of outright skeptics. Some Seekers held millennial hopes in common with Fifth Monarchists but remained grounded in a sense that God's glorious new work would be enacted by the faithfulness of ordinary men and women. Some Seekers also shared the skepticism held by "Antiscripturalists" but continued to derive new meanings from the ancient texts. Within that tension, which grew unbearable at times, the Seeker matrix engendered some of the most creative responses to the crisis of the civil war, generating movements such as the Levellers, Diggers, Ranters—and, finally, the Quakers.

Thus, it is the view of this study that the Seekers were not just one more colorful group among others. As a mass phenomenon of idealistic, radicalized, and often young Puritans who had come to the end of all present options and had found them wanting, the profile of the Seeker in the 1640s defines the posture of extremity that generated so many important experiments in that period. Indeed, seeking, levelling, digging, ranting, and quaking were activities that briefly sketched many of the major political and religious options of the ensuing modern period.

Notes

1. This is the name for Seekers given by Charles Marshall, who was one of the numerous Bristol Seekers in the early 1650s, before becoming a Quaker in 1654

while still a teenager. See *Sion's Travellers Comforted, in A Collection of Works and Epistles of that Faithful Minister of Christ Jesus, Charles Marshall* (1704). Note that in 17th-century English usage, to "travel" could imply movement and/or suffering (i.e., "travail"). The narratives of Marshall and many others suggest that the Seeker quest entailed both.

2. Thomas Edwards, *Gangraena* (1646), Part II, 11.
3. Roland H. Bainton, *The Reformation of the Sixteenth Century* (Boston: Beacon, 1952), 78.
4. For more details on Henry's Reformation, see my most recent book, *The Covenant Crucified: Quakers and the Rise of Capitalism* (Wallingford, Pa.: Pendle Hill, 1995), 68-72; also see Christopher Hill, *Puritanism and Revolution* (New York: Schocken, 1958), 29-49.
5. For more information on the Family of Love, see Christopher W. Marsh *The Family of Love in English Society, 1550-1630* (Cambridge: University Press, 1994); and Jean Dietz Moss, *"Godded with God": Hendrik Niclaes and His Family of Love* (Philadelphia: American Philosophical Society, 1981).
6. However, William Penn, a second-generation convert to Quakerism, claims that Seekers were sometimes referred to as the Family of Love. This is the only such attestation I have found. See Penn's Preface to George Fox's *Journal,* in the latter's collected *Works* (Philadelphia: Goold, 1831) 1:ix.
7. Champlin Burrage, T*he Early English Churches in Light of Recent Research (1550-1641)* (Cambridge: University Press, 1917), 1:215-16.
8. George Huntston Williams, *The Radical Reformation,* third ed. (Kirksville, Mo.: Sixteenth Century Journal, 1992), 1188-90.
9. J. F. McGregor, "The Baptists: Fount of All Heresy," in *Radical Religion in the English Revolution,* ed. McGregor and Reay (Oxford: University Press, 1984), 23-63. Also see Murray Tolmie, *The Triumph of the Saints: Separate Churches of London, 1616-1649* (Cambridge: University Press, 1977).
10. Tolmie, *Triumph,* 37.
11. Tolmie, *Triumph,* 29-30.
12. Thomas Goodwin, *A Glimpse of Syons Glory,* cited by Tolmie, *Triumph,* 86.
13. For more information on Giles Calvert, see "Giles Calvert's Publishing Career," *Journal of the Friends Historical Society* 35 (1938): 45-49. This short article is a summary of a larger paper by Althea A. Terry, a Columbia University librarian.
14. J. F. McGregor, "Baptists," 26.
15. Praise-God Barbone, *A Discourse Tending to prove the Baptisme,* 3-11, cited by Tolmie, *Triumph,* 54.
16. Tolmie, *Triumph,* 73. Note the similarity of Lambe's position with the statement to "Free-Willers" by the Quaker Edward Burrough in *A Trumpet of the Lord Sounded forth in Sion* (1656), quoted in *The Covenant Crucified,* 103. For a detailed exposition on the later Baptist-Quaker controversies regarding these similarities and differences, see T. L. Underwood, *Primitivism, Radicalism, and the Lamb's War: The Baptist-Quaker Conflicts in Seventeenth-Century England* (New York: Oxford, 1997), especially chapters 2,4, and 7.
17. Tolmie, *Triumph,* 81.
18. Tolmie, *Triumph,* 78.
19. George Fox, *Journal,* ed. John L. Nickalls (Cambridge: University Press, 1952), 39.

20. My previous work on the spirituality of capitalism in this early period, as well as reflections on life in our advanced capitalist society, can be found in *The Covenant Crucified.*
21. Sarah Jones, *To Sions Lovers* (1644).
22. Nigel Smith offers the same general definition of Seekers in the 1640s in *Perfection Proclaimed: Language and Literature in English Radical Religion 1640-1660* (Oxford: Clarendon, 1989), 7-8.
23. Thomas Edwards, *Gangraena* (1646), Preface.
24. Edwards, *Gangraena*, Part I, 15-31.
25. Edwards, *Gangraena*, Part I, 24.
26. John Saltmarsh, *The Smoke in the Temple* (1646).
27. Edwards, *Gangraena*, Part II, 23.
28. Edwards, *Gangraena*, Part II, 13.
29. Edwards, *Gangraena*, Part I, 57-58.
30. Edwards, *Gangraena*, Part I, 54.
31. Edwards, *Gangraena*, Part II, 164.
32. John Saltmarsh, *Groanes for Liberty* (1646), included in a collection of controversial tracts, *Some Drops of the Viall* (1646), 112.
33. Tolmie, *Triumph*, 131.
34. Richard Baxter, *A Key for the Catholics, to Open the Jugling of the Jesuits* (1659), 331.
35. Baxter, *Key*, 332-34.
36. Baxter, *Key*, 334.
37. Baxter, *Key*, 334.
38. Baxter, *Key*, 334.
39. Boehme wrote of the age of Mosaic law as the Age of the Nettle, the age of Christ as the Age of the Rose, and the age of the Spirit as the Age of the Lily, in which the joy and love of God becomes fully internalized in humans. See A. L. Morton, *The World of the Ranters: Religious Radicalism in the English Revolution* (London: Lawrence and Wishart, 1970), 127-28.
40. John Jackson, *A Sober Word to a Serious People* (published anonymously, 1651), Preface.
41. Jackson, *A Sober Word*, 2.
42. Jackson, *A Sober Word*, 60 (62).
43. Quoted by J. F. McGregor, "Seekers and Ranters," in *Radical Religion*, 127.
44. It appears that twelve years later, at the time of her death, Elizabeth Cromwell, then Lady Claypole, was still in a seeking state. During her last months, when illness had troubled her spirit, she was ministered to by various Quakers, including George Fox. See Fox's *Journal*, Nickalls, ed. (Cambridge: University Press, 1952), 346-48.
45. Bernard Capp, "The Fifth Monarchists and Popular Millenarianism," in *Radical Religion*, 165-89.
46. Christopher Hill, "Irreligion in the 'Puritan' Revolution," in *Radical Religion*, 191-211.
47. Hill, "Irreligion," 195.

CHAPTER 4

JOHN SALTMARSH AND WILLIAM ERBURY
THE JOURNEY FROM ORTHODOXY
TO ANTINOMIANISM

And thus I say, that in my own sense I did not preach at all,
Preaching is for edification; mine was for destruction . . . to
pour out a Vial, full of the wrath of God, even a Plague upon
all the Churches, who say, they are in Gospel-order and are
not, but doe lye in Babylon. And there not they onely, but all
the scattered Saints this day do dwell, and I also with them
waiting for deliverance.

William Erbury, *The Honest Heretique*, 1652[1]

We began by viewing the Seeker phenomenon from the outside. First, we sketched more than a century of English history leading up to the civil war and the first appearances of Seekers. Then we drew upon assessments of Seekers by hostile critics and fellow travelers of that day. Now we are ready to look at Seekers on their own terms. It is important to note first that seeking suggests a *trajectory*, rather than a defined *position*. We best understand the English Seekers by reconstructing their stories and considering faith statements they made along the way. These next six chapters will be devoted to these stories and statements.

We begin in this chapter with two of the best known (or most widely reputed) Seekers of the day, John Saltmarsh and William Erbury. We will follow their classic journeys from orthodoxy to what many considered antinomianism (life beyond the constraints of religious, moral, or civil law). Along the way, their life stories will also allow us to continue the saga of the vexed English Reformation. The events that were decisive for these two figures also shaped a whole generation of young, idealistic Puritans.

John Saltmarsh

In his brief biography of Saltmarsh, A. L. Morton describes him as"perhaps the most talented and influential of all the preachers of the antinomian left. Yet little is known of his antecedents or early life, and little would lead us to anticipate his later developments."[2] Indeed, the religious and political territory Saltmarsh covered during his meteoric last years, 1642–1647, is startling. As late as 1640, he was a conventional parish minister and devotional writer.

Since he is thought to have died at age thirty five, he was probably born around 1612. We know that he graduated with a Master's degree from Magdalen College, Cambridge in 1636 and that he published a small volume of metaphysical poetry that same year. By 1639, he had become rector at Hasterton in Yorkshire (most likely his home county). He also published that year *The Practice of Policie in a Christian Life Taught by Scriptures*. Totaling over 300 pages, this compendium contains 486 maxims for Christian life, each supported by biblical citations. Nothing outside Puritan orthodoxy appears yet.

But the events of 1642 quickly rallied Saltmarsh to the cause of religious freedom. He later recalled that he was at first a "stickler in Yorkshire for the Parliament."[3] But the Solemn League and Covenant in 1643 soon led him to qualify his support. That year, he hurriedly published *Examinations*, a reply to a published sermon of Thomas Fuller. Fuller had urged citizens to pray for Parliament and the Westminster Assembly of Divines as they set about to reform the English church and state. But he advised them not to meddle in this great work. Reformation was the business of supreme authority alone. Moreover, people should not build up hopes for a perfect reformation or a utopian society. After all, latter-day divines did not enjoy the same level of inspiration possessed by the apostles. (We recall that conservative Puritan doctrine from the preceding chapter.)

Saltmarsh countered that all English people had an interest in reform and a role to play in it. He further asserted that the apostles had light for their times; the English people were presently receiving new light for new times. He concluded that, with the startling events now unfolding, "who cannot think that we are rising to that age where God shall pour his Spirit upon all flesh?" Thus, we detect here not only a concept of progressive revelation (successive veils taken away from truth through the ages, as he stated it), but also a utopian sense that God was doing something unprecedented in England, fulfilling the prophecy of Joel 2:28, re-enacting the Pentecostal origins of the early church (Acts 2). Saltmarsh appears already moving toward one of the two basic Seeker outlooks: either that new apostles must come, with a new revelation and a new Pentecostal beginning for the church, or that the new age of the Spirit was about to dawn. There was debate in Parliament regarding Saltmarsh's tract. Some found it extreme while others defended it heatedly.

In October 1644, Saltmarsh published another short political tract, *A Peace but No Pacification*, urging Parliament not to compromise with Charles but to fight on and vanquish him. Meanwhile, his own ministry continued to evolve and radicalize. That same year, he concluded that tithes were unchristian and renounced his parish post at Hasterton, even returning his past year's income. Not long after, he accepted the rectorship at Brasted, Kent, where he refused tithe support. For the first year, he accepted voluntary contributions. Thereafter, he accepted no financial support at all.[4]

The beginning of 1645 saw the release of his most advanced political statement, *Dawnings of Light,* the first to be published by Giles Calvert. Though dedicated to Parliament, the tract clearly looks beyond:

> unless we be more sanctified, our enemies do not fall by any divine favor toward us, but by the provocation of their own sins . . . then their ruin will scarcely be our salvation, but they will only be the first to fall.[5]

What follows this prophetic warning is an intriguing meditation on the interaction of divine and human interests in reformation. Saltmarsh admits that his musings merely wander "in the unbounded wafts of Theology," but he imagines that a "transcendent science" can be devised, using exact and particular methods of inquiry. Generally, the interests of Christ need to be separated from those of the state. Mixing the two only darkens Christ's kingdom and subverts established government.

Saltmarsh urges orthodox Puritans to study the Scriptures anew, in order to see how much latitude they offer both in both doctrine and practice. That should discourage them from trying to impose their understandings upon others. Meanwhile, for their part, dissenting groups should be just as concerned to contribute to the common good as they are to promote their particular sectarian agendas. As in all his writings, Saltmarsh retains a generous and even-handed approach. He pleads for an inclusive sense of the body of Christ, one that allows different degrees and manners of reformation ("coming out of Babylon") to coexist. Name-calling only accentuates division and weakens the nation against its common enemy. Groups withdrawing into their own conventicles should not be labeled as schismatic or sectarian. In line with Schwenckfeld's *Stillstand*, Saltmarsh prefers the term "suspension" to "separation."[6]

Seeking must be everyone's vocation at this time:

> When tidings of publique calamity are abroad, then is the season of seeking God, and enquiring after sin, and putting God in minde of covenants, and engagements that he stands in to his people.[7]

Thus, God is not some inert object to be groped after; our very seeking stimulates God's own faithful response.

Its tangled prose aside, *Dawnings of Light* is an intriguing treatise of Christian political philosophy, brimming with optimism and fresh intellectual currents. Its discussion of the "interests" in reformation, and its incipiently free-market approach to religious diversity breathe the hopeful spirit of nascent capitalism. Its advocacy of scientific methods of analysis in religious matters suggests a social-scientific outlook far ahead of the times. Saltmarsh was well on his way into uncharted regions.

At the end of 1645, Saltmarsh took a more theological tack with *Free-Grace*, subtitled *The Flowings of Christ's Blood Freely to Sinners*. Published by Calvert, this book went through eight printings by 1661. It deserves some detailed attention here, for it prompted critics to call Saltmarsh an antinomian and libertine. Such accusations were inspired by his attack upon the casuistry that had overtaken much spiritual counsel by Puritan ministers. The doctrine of predestination, affirming that souls were either elect or damned from the beginning of time, implied that salvation was a status to be *inferred* rather than sought. Thus, individuals were directed to examine themselves for signs of their election. For example, moral virtue and industry might be signs of God's grace at work. Puritan divines reassured anxious souls that even the *desire* for salvation might be a hopeful indicator. That approach worked well enough for many average parishioners. But for more introspective and morally scrupulous souls, it became a maddening hall of mirrors.

Free-Grace purports to be the experience of a soul wracked by feelings of guilt and unworthiness. Morton believes this to be Saltmarsh's own story, but the prose is so ambiguous and garbled that this reading is impossible to confirm. It may just as easily be someone Saltmarsh interviewed, as the text states, or a composite portrait of several persons he had known. In any case, the individual was haunted by an accusing conscience. He went to hear sermons, but with no relief. He feared not going to church; he feared going as well, since it would be an abomination for an unregenerate soul to take communion. He went to ministers for help. They generally told him that his troubled conscience was a sign of God's work in him. But rather than preaching Christ and salvation to him, they prescribed "religious duties" (prayer, church attendance, Bible study, etc.). He complained that he could not make himself pray. The minister answered that even the desire to pray was prayer. This didn't help: what if his desire to pray was simply for his own sake and not for God's glory? The minister responded that even *the desire to desire to pray* was a sign of grace![8]

The poor soul concluded that he was not really sorry for his sins, but simply afraid of hell. This was a legal sorrow, a merely slavish terror, not the sorrow of a true child of God, with brokenness and meltings of the heart. Ministers went through the Bible with him, reading the promises of salvation there, to see if they stirred some hopeful feeling in his heart. This common practice was called "applying the promises."[9] But he could feel only his own miserable, selfish spirit. Slowly, the individual became suicidal, attempting to take his own life at least once. But messages of God's love slowly came into his heart. He began to see that God had already pardoned his sins. *Free-Grace* concludes by advising others not to resort to Puritan regimens of religious exercise, "lest you perish in the sparks you kindle, as I almost did." In other words, trying to *infer* one's salvation from self-induced "sparks" of hope is a futile exercise. Saltmarsh urges ministers to preach the gospel of Jesus Christ first and foremost, rather than prescribe legalistic "duties."[10] Otherwise, doubt will consume some souls.

Saltmarsh summarizes: God covenants with us *in Christ*, not on the basis of any human merit. We love God because God loved us first. Christ died for all. Just as all are dead in Adam, all that live are alive in Christ.[11] At times in this book, Saltmarsh still holds out for predestination, insisting that it remains a "secret thing." But he is willing to use the term "general redemption" as well.[12] To the Calvinist mind, Saltmarsh had undermined God's sovereignty in human redemption. Christ's death for all, without qualification, seemed to place freedom on the side of human decision to accept or not (though Saltmarsh insisted that salvation was all God's work). Moreover, if the "duties" of Christian piety were swept aside, then how was spiritual and moral regeneration to occur? After all, anxious self-doubt provided the fuel for a great deal of Puritan self-improvement and social betterment. Such concerns underlay the accusations against Saltmarsh of being an "antinomian" and "libertine." Much like Thomas Lambe's General Baptist manifesto, *The Fountain of Free Grace Opened*, published the same year (and noted in our preceding chapter), Saltmarsh's work maintained a paradox that steadfastly resisted simple reduction to either God's election or human freedom.

Ironically, the preaching of free grace in the 1640s served much the same countercultural function that predestinational theology had served in the late Middle Ages. Just as the latter had placed God's elect outside the hierarchies of institutional Catholicism and feudal society (see Chapter 2), free grace now placed Christ's activity beyond the tidy formulas of the new Puritan religious establishment. This was a key theological element for the General Baptist and Seeker movements. As a left-wing Independent, Saltmarsh had been won over to it as well. In some cases, the theology of free grace may have contributed to the libertinism that Edwards and others reported. It was also easily mistaken for an Arminian theology in which the individual's "decision for Christ" was a simple matter of human choice. But we shall see that the Spiritualism of the most advanced Seekers like Saltmarsh did not actually place redemptive freedom in human hands. Salvation was not to be *appropriated* by human will, nor obliquely *earned* by Puritan religious duties, but *received* through a radical surrender of the self and all its designs. We shall also see, through the narratives of Seekers who went on to become Quakers, that Puritan casuistry indeed tormented many of England's most sensitive souls during the 1640s.

During this period, Saltmarsh functioned as a leading figure in the Independent movement. He was part of the younger generation of Independent ministers, orthodox in their university training, but rapidly moving beyond Puritanism. Murray Tolmie finds Saltmarsh among the leaders mentioned at an Independent gathering in London, held in 1645 or 1646. The meeting debated whether Independents should continue involvement in their local parishes or join the Separatists in complete withdrawal.[13] Saltmarsh's participation in the decision against separation fits with his overall attitude of mutual toleration, despite the rapid radicalization of his views.

In January 1646, Saltmarsh returned to political pamphleteering with *The Smoke in the Temple,* mentioned in the preceding chapter. This piece marks his first mention by name of Seekers, among the various groups in conflict over the sacraments. He strikes a distinctly Spiritualist note, warning all contending factions that in striving over the cup, the wine may be spilled. The ordinance of Christ must not become a substitute for Christ himself. The truth of every dispensation, or religious form, should be seen in the light of Christ in us, "for where the Sun is, there will be every beame with it." He argues again for a moratorium among diverse churches during this transitional time: "We may be Friends, though not Brethren: and let us attaine to Union, though not to Unity."

He goes on to describe the position of each faction, then to offer a critique of each based on Scripture. In his critique of the Baptists, he takes the Seeker position against their adult baptism: "the time is not yet come for Ordinances: for as there were several seasons for the givings out of Truth before, so now," citing the steps in Acts whereby the early church was first constituted. He then summarizes the Seeker position thus: because of the general apostasy, there is no legitimate church at present. Any new founding of the church will be accompanied by miraculous works, like those described in Acts. While civil war and religious oppression continue, the new dispensation of the Spirit cannot begin. Moreover, he reports, many Seekers suspect corruptions and additions in the canonical text of the Bible, leading them to conclude that new tongues of the Spirit will be needed to reveal the original purity of Scripture and guide the way to true church order.

Saltmarsh criticizes the idealism of this position with no less than seventeen points. He suggests that even centuries of spiritual apostasy are not powerful enough to corrupt biblical texts materially. Scripture, whatever its textual corruptions, still offers a clearer revelation of faith than reason alone can attain. Even if more glorious dispensations will someday come, everyone should still follow as many of the traditional forms as they conscientiously can. In particular, he attacks the assumption that new miracles are necessary to confirm any new dispensation of the Spirit. If we need miracles to believe, he argues, then we will need them continually. The truth of a new revelation should be self-evident.

Outward signs convince only the outward mind. The glory that is coming is secret, invisible, inward, spiritual.

Thus, Saltmarsh maintains his Christian statesmanship, affirming the dignity of all forms sincerely professed and practiced. He dismisses biblical skepticism and censures the idealism that imagines an unmistakable faith certified by visible signs and wonders. (We will find this question of miracles to be a key issue among Seekers and a factor in the gathering of Seekers into the Quaker movement.) Nevertheless, Saltmarsh also clearly shares the hope of a coming dispensation, albeit in more subtle, spiritualized terms.

Up to this point, Saltmarsh maintained a balance between agitation and mediation. He made a steady stream of attack upon the Presbyterian plan, but was critical of all groups, pleading for a moratorium among them. He held many views in common with the Seekers, but still served a parish church as an Independent minister.

But in June 1646, Saltmarsh's life took a momentous turn. He left his position at Brasted and accepted an invitation to serve as a chaplain in the army. This began a year of intense activity resulting in less publication but a in quantum leap in vision. Some of the most radical preachers in the nation—William Erbury, William Dell, John Webster, Henry Denne, Jacob Bauthumley, and others—had been appointed chaplains. Other advanced spirits populated the ranks of officers and soldiers, generating intense religious energies. Saltmarsh was radicalized by this vanguard. We can also imagine that he added much from his own deep insights. Later reports of his army chaplaincy suggest that he meddled little with politics but "labored to beat down sin and exalt Christ," earning great esteem among soldiers and officers alike.[14]

In May 1647, Saltmarsh published his definitive statement, *Sparkles of Glory*. This large work opens with a continuing advocacy of suspension of the national church, but quickly moves on to much more annunciatory realms. Spiritualist influence, which was rife in the army, becomes much more overt here, no longer tinctured by pragmatic political arguments for mutual toleration.

With a clearly post-Reformational perspective, Saltmarsh summarizes the basic flaws of a state-sponsored church. First, there is no single, clear model for church order to be derived from Scripture. Any attempt to impose one reduces Christians to bondage all over again. But more than that, it amounts to a "finer kind of idolatry" to suppose that God enters into outward forms and conveys divine power through them. Nevertheless, he allows that sacraments and other forms are useful as *parables* of spiritual things. They are not to be rejected any more than the disciple Thomas was rejected for needing to see in order to believe. But blessed are they who do not see and still believe (John 20:26ff)![15]

The bulk of the book is an expansion upon two fundamental principles of Spiritualism. First, there are two creations, natures, or seeds— flesh and spirit. Though the apostate church has lapsed back into the former nature, the future of Christian faith is in the latter. Second, the one true church consists in the one true baptism of the Spirit into one body of Christ. Hence, the true church is an *invisible* church, though visibly gathered churches are not derogated here.

This leads to stunning assertions of the reign of Christ on earth: "the true personal reign of Christ is spiritual." It is a glory that defies all representation. But it manifests itself in human lives. "Christ reigns already in everything that is put in subjection under him, but we see not all yet put under him. Jesus Christ reigns in Spirit, only his reign appears not yet, now we are sons of God, but it doth not appear what we shall be; but when he shall appear, we shall be like him."[16] Saltmarsh now speaks with a strong sense of moment, even apocalyptic moment. Christ is already starting to enter the world through human bodies. The revelation is not yet fully realized; Christ has not yet fully appeared. But there is a sense of imminent transformation. Through this humanized sense of Christ's return in the bodies of believers, we find a psychologically, socially, and historically dynamic sense of apocalyptic fulfillment. The return of Christ is seen in Presence-centered terms. Saltmarsh cautions that the Bible's prophecies of Christ's return are allegories, allusions, parables that are not to be understood in terms of any political system as such.

Adapting dispensational schemes from Jacob Boehme, Saltmarsh continues that each Christian's life is intended to reenact the three ages or spheres described in Scripture: the Law, the Gospel, and the Spirit.[17] Just as Christ was born under the good dispensation of law and circumcision but had to be crucified to it, so the Christian is born under the outward Christian dispensation of baptism, bread, and wine but must be crucified to it in order to rise to the spiritual realm. There, one comes to know the true Lord's Supper, the very body and blood of Christ in Spirit. On this level, one knows Christ as the true spiritual minister, apostle, pastor:

> Jesus Christ is the true spiritual prophet that teaches his people
> so as they are all taught of God, and so called in Scriptures a
> prophet, which the Lord God raised up, in stead of Moses
> (see Dtr. 18:18).[18]

The experience of Christ's Presence has become so complete here that it
has obviated the need for a clergy. Christ is the true shepherd of the flock.
This Christology is compatible with Schwenckfeld's teaching that true
communion raises the believer to the heavenly, spiritual plane, rather than
Christ descending again into physical bread and wine (see Chapter 2).[19]

The earth-shaking theological statements keep coming. He moves on
to assert that true, spiritual "gospel order" (good order in the church) is

> "that spirituall Distinction and Variety in the Body of Christ,
> wherein one member differs from another in Measure of Spirit
> and Glory, and Power, and yet all compleat and make perfect
> that Body of Christ in the Spirit."[20]

Thus, visible church order is not abandoned along with formal ordinances of church worship and government, but is achieved by Christ's
direct action, bestowing different gifts to various individuals to perform
different services. "True spiritual Government is Christ reigning in the
Saints in Spirit, ordering them in Thought, Word, and deed . . . which is
a Sceptre of Righteousness against Flesh and Blood, Principalities and
Powers."[21] The covenant consists in this intimate relationship, in which
God's law is inscribed directly upon human hearts (see Jer. 31:31-34).

Therefore, "the Christian is one, who hath the incorruptible seed in
him, or the Word which liveth and abideth for ever, which Word is the
Lord Jesus Christ."[22] The seed within functions as a key metaphor in the
Spiritualist vision of advanced Seekers and Quakers. The seed represents
the last hope of reformation, indeed of all utopian prospects, now completely separated out from state-sponsored reformations and even sectarian congregations. It now lies beyond the reach of all human striving,
political or individual. This seed rises within to reign only through radical
surrender, the death of self and its will. Saltmarsh admits that figures such
as Wycliffe, Luther, and Calvin were beginning to receive glimmerings of
this revelation, but were still deep in the dark night of apostasy.

All these reformers were attempting to "return to the Gospel-Day,"
the church of New Testament times. But that was not possible, for God

had already "laid it by." Just as Christ came not to restore the priesthood again but to lead onward, true reformation must move on. There is no way back. But a period of purification from old idolatries is required. Like Israel coming out of Egypt, this is a time of the church in the wilderness (see Rev. 121-6). Christians must retire in Spirit into that wilderness. The emergent, spiritualized faith is a new dispensation of light. In time, it will cover the earth, swallowing up all former dispensations. Thus, Saltmarsh suggests the beginning of a new, universal revelation of God, a universal light of Christ. Those who have come into this light, or Spirit, discern the "same Spirit in others, as in Prayer, Preaching, Prophesying, Conference, Conformity to Christ, Spiritual Conversation, so as Christians can in a manner say . . . here I taste, and see something of God."[23] Hence, beyond all definable boundaries of church membership and doctrine, each individual in the light of Christ recognizes it (or the lack of it) in the actions of others.

Clearly, these statements issued from some profound experience that Saltmarsh found among the army ranks, even some sense of incipient church order. It now led him to conclusions startling within a military setting. For Saltmarsh adds that war is the work of nations, the natural impulse to self-preservation and just retaliation. Many Christians fight alongside "natural" men under this law. But as Christ is more fully manifested in Spirit, the Christian is taken up, out of such activity. Christian perfection is to lay oneself down "to rest in the bosom of whatever providence God opens." Left to its own devices, the human will leads individuals to lust, desire, and plot, even to kill one another. Peace is to be "willing to be gathered up by God from one Way and raised up to a higher one." God moves from one tabernacle to another. The Christian must move with God. This inner surrender leads to outer surrender, a willingness to receive the enmity and oppression of others into oneself. There, one quenches the violence, destroying it in the Spirit.[24] *Sparkles of Glory* stops short of a generalized principle of nonviolence or conscientious objection to military service. Saltmarsh was apparently still hopeful that God might yet accomplish something earth-shaking through the army. But a clear principle of Christian withdrawal from warfare was emerging.

Sparkles places greatest emphasis upon the work of Christ at large among the people. "The Lord Jesus hath a day and time to be revealed in, which is his coming in the Saints when he will judge the World, and then shall Antichrist be consumed" (see Rev. 20:1-10).[25] God's indulgence of false worships will end and worship in Spirit and truth will replace them. But this comes only through what Saltmarsh calls the "Fiery Tryall."[26] Unfortunately, we do not pass on easily to higher revelations of God. The old vision of God must die: "the fiery tryall is the Spirit of God burning up or destroying" the old truth. What was good and righteous before must be consumed and crucified. He notes that these trials are "Prophecy of the last judgment" experienced in the Spirit here and now. Thus, Saltmarsh witnesses an apocalyptic sense of personal transformation, in which the believer experiences *now* what the world at large will experience later. In that process, one is so changed as to become a *new creation* in Christ.

He clarifies that this transformation does not imply that one's earlier faithfulness was bad: Christ's life embodied the best of the law's righteousness. Still, that body was crucified in order to be raised up to a new sphere. "So every Christian is to take up his crosse, and to bring his highest and choicest . . . to this crosse, and to have them all crucified to higher discoveries of God, this is the knowledge of Christ Crucified, or self-deniall."[27] Christians often mistake this experience for God's absence. It is rather God's presence, making the old wither in order to bring in a fuller glory.

Sparkles concludes with Saltmarsh's classic description of Seekers. He reviews the dilemma of apostasy and confusion in the churches, as we have already heard articulated in a number of ways. Seekers wait for the coming of the Spirit with power. In the meantime, they worship

> onely in Prayer and Conference [religious discussion], pretending to no certain determination of things, nor any infallible . . . interpretations of Scriptures. They wait for a restauration of all things, and a setting up of all Gospell-Officers, Churches, Ordinances, according to the pattern of the New Testament. They wait for an Apostle or Angel, that is, some[one] with a visible glory and power . . . to give visible demonstration of their sending, as to the world. . . . This is the highest of their Attainment.[28]

"But," he adds, "some speak of a further discovery, and more spiritual than this of the Seekers." He now articulates the new Spiritualist sense that must have been emerging at that time. According to that view, the New Testament church was only a transitional form. Apostasy aside, it was intended to pass away in any case. All dispensations are but for a season, and they are never restored. Therefore, to await the restoration of New Testament church order is antichristian. There is nothing in Scripture to warrant it. The truth is that Christ, the eternal seed, is already in all true Christians. All true reformation, growth, and improvement of the church can take place only by Christ himself working through his people. The world will see Christ come in the saints, but it will be "in a day of conviction and spiritual judgment upon themselves." Far from being a day of signs, wonders, and glory, the day of the Lord will be perceived by most people as a day of consternation. This point has much in common with the prophecy of Amos 5:18: "Woe to you who desire the day of the Lord! Why would you have the day of the Lord? It is darkness and not light."

So we find in Saltmarsh a confirmation, at least in general terms, of the various Seeker classifications we reviewed in the preceding chapter. There are two kinds, according to Saltmarsh, who does not even consider the second type to be Seekers anymore. The first still awaits a renewal of the New Testament church. The second has moved on to "a further discovery, and more spiritual." He prefers to leave this new position unnamed. But Saltmarsh has already sketched many important points that we will see defined more fully in the Quaker movement. Clearly, developments in the army and elsewhere by 1647 had given Saltmarsh much reason to hope for momentous things to come.

One reason for optimism was the army's eventual defeat and capture of Charles. Parliament quickly moved to disband the army, fearing the latter as a threat to the Presbyterian settlement and even Parliamentary sovereignty itself. But the army refused to disband, causing still greater concern in Parliament. In June 1647, *A Letter from the Army* appeared, Saltmarsh's last publication. He reported on the mood among the ranks, seeking to allay fears of an army takeover of the government. In various counties where army regiments had moved or been stationed, people appealed to them to act as mediators between themselves and Parliament. Though Saltmarsh did not state it explicitly, everyone knew that the present Parliament would enact only modest political reforms, was still determined to impose Presbyterianism on the nation, and might even return Charles to the throne.

So the army sought to satisfy some "just grievances" before disbanding, to insure that members would be "estated in a free and clear capacity" both as soldiers and as citizens.[29] This probably meant two things. First, that no one would be prosecuted for acts of war, whatever the ensuing settlement might be. This was an important point, especially if Charles regained the throne. But more broadly, it also meant that the army intended to coerce from Parliament political freedoms that would "flow down," as Saltmarsh states it, to all fellow subjects. Once their civil rights were established, he was confident the army would do whatever Parliament commanded.

Saltmarsh witnessed "a mighty spirit for Justice and Righteousness raised up in the Army."[30] He assured Parliament that the army did not wish to impose an Independent church settlement on the nation, or challenge the rule of law. "I know no designe here appearing, but Peace to the Kingdom."[31] Saltmarsh may have been innocent at that point of more revolutionary designs moving among the regiments. Some were plotting by this time actions that would have overruled by force not only Parliament but the generals as well.

The army formulated its position in a "Solemn Engagement," adopted earlier in June, formally stating its refusal to disband; instead, it organized an Army Council that included not only the generals but representatives elected from the regiments, possessing full voting rights. Here was a democratic organ of self-government for the army that also aimed to influence the direction of civil government in England. Saltmarsh's letter thus came at a moment of great resolve within the army. That was also around the time he left, probably for reasons of health.

Unfortunately, this unity did not last long.[32] Parliament rescinded its demand that the army disband, and Cromwell and other generals sought a compromise between the two rival powers. The generals, lacking sympathy with the more far-reaching political demands coming from the ranks, soon scuttled the democratic processes established by the Solemn Engagement. Both within the army and in London a new faction had emerged to press a republican agenda for reform in England. This party, nicknamed the "Levellers," was led by Lieutenant Colonel John Lilburne, Richard Overton, and William Walwyn. They formulated their proposals in *An Agreement of the Free People of England* in October 1647. (We will review that document in the next chapter, when we study Walwyn's life and thought.) On October 28th, this provisional constitution was debated by the Army Council at Putney, near London. The debates were inconclusive. The generals, seeing that they were losing control of the army, arrested Leveller leaders and quelled demonstrations among the ranks.

In failing health at home in Ilford, Essex, Saltmarsh followed these events with alarm. He wrote three letters—to General Fairfax, Oliver Cromwell, and to the Army Council as a whole—deploring their actions, and calling upon them to return to the promises made in June.[33] But Leveller leaders remained in detention.

On December 4th, Saltmarsh got out of bed and told his wife that he had been in a trance, seen a vision, and received the command to go to the army and speak God's Word to them. He left that evening for London.[34] Mid-morning on the 6th, he reached Windsor, where the Council sat. He entered the session and told them that, although God had worked with and for them previously, divine favor had left them. They had betrayed God's cause in imprisoning God's innocent servants. His eyes fixed in an otherworldly countenance, he confronted General Fairfax without removing his hat, telling him that he would not honor him; he had honored him too much in the past. In the hallway, he rebuked Cromwell for imprisoning the Levellers and abandoning positions affirmed as late as June. This apostasy would lead to division and ruin. With his usual candor, Cromwell admitted that things were not going well and that he had received similar criticism from others.

Saltmarsh returned the next day with further oracles of judgment. He was asked if he would advise faithful members of the army to leave. He replied that he would not; God still had a great work to be done, making use of *members* of the army.[35] Evidently, he believed that some remnant in the army might still prove useful to God's cause—perhaps the Leveller faction or those worship groups that met to "wait upon the Lord." He took leave of the officers, telling them he had finished God's errand and would never see them again.

He reached home on the evening of the 9th, apparently cheerful and well, reporting his activity to his wife. The next day, telling her he had finished his course, he took to his bed. He died peacefully the afternoon of the 11th. These remarkable last days were reported by an anonymous author in a tract entitled *Wonderful Predictions* (1648). The details of the story had been confirmed by the Council itself. It is testimony to Saltmarsh's renown in the army that the Council was willing to receive his bizarre visitation. In fact, ten days after that confrontation, the Council released the Leveller leaders in a momentary relaxation of the conflict.

Thus ends an amazing life and prophetic vocation. The brilliance of Saltmarsh's witness and the utter lack of self-righteousness or resentment in it make him perhaps the most impressive figure from the Seeker scene of the 1640s. It is hard to say where he might have progressed from *Sparkles of Glory* and from the army if he had lived longer. But his influence was great, both before and after his death. Richard Baxter was disturbed by his influence. Writing in criticism of *Free-Grace*, Baxter commented, "I saw how greedily multitudes of poor souls did take the bait, and how exceedingly the writings and preachings of Saltmarsh and many of his fellows did take with them."[36] After his death, Saltmarsh's writings exerted influence on a number of Seekers, including future Quakers such as Richard Farnworth.[37]

OTHER WRITINGS FROM THE ARMY

We know that the Spiritualist worship groups in the army continued in some regiments, at least through 1648. This fact is evidenced by a remarkable collection of documents by army members written in 1647 and 1648. The first and best piece in the collection is Joseph Salmon's *Antichrist in Man*, which we will review in Chapter Six, where we deal with the life of that notorious Ranter. In *The Man-Child Brought Forth in Us* (1648), John Lewin reflects upon the Reformation: the true people of God become a shrinking minority as layers of church tradition and formality continue to be pared away. Now, those who wait upon the Lord, as presently done in some quarters of the army, are the smallest minority the true church has ever been—and the most hated. None of these army writers describes what this waiting was, but it probably involved some form of silent worship. Lewin describes the rigors of this spirituality:

> I know nothing but my owne spirit; and speake nothing but
> my owne experience: I will not lay any exhortation upon any
> mans spirit: I have been a while, and not long, waiting for the
> appearance of God; that God might be manifested in my flesh,
> and doe cry in paine to be delivered: Now in this time, my
> thoughts are carried out after too many things, and not upon
> this only, to wait for God; and this hath bin my weaknesse: I

> have been and am so troubled at what one man, another, and
> the world will say, and [how] to answer all these . . . I say this
> is our weaknesse. If we could but waite upon God untill he
> be manifest; and then all men shall fall.[38]

Their worship and their desperate longing for God apparently raised questions and provoked derision among those who observed them. The "Man-Child," a figure of Christ, born of the heavenly woman in the wilderness (Rev. 12), is a collective entity, born through the flesh of those who wait, like a woman in labor. Lewin prophesies, "when God appears in the saints, then many more shall come in, and God will appear in them."[39] Thus, the tiny minority waiting to deliver Christ into the world will be joined by many more once the birth begins.

In *Christ Coming in the Cloudes* (1647), Robert Westfield sounds the same theme, Christ coming in the saints. This new revelation renews the "manifestation of God in our elder brother and fore-runner, whose flesh was crucified at Jerusalem."[40] The manifestation of Christ is "that light which lighteneth every man, or which every man walketh by which cometh to God" (this is a formula that will be heard repeatedly from Quaker writers of the 1650s).[41] This "glorious dispensation" comes in four steps. First, one dies to all things below God, so that nothing is left alive but the divine nature. Second, one must be buried and remain in the grave until the last day. Third, one rises again—or at least the divine nature rises, while everything else stays in the grave. Fourth, the saints ascend into glory—full enjoyment of God. Here, God's light replaces all temples, teachings, and sacraments (Rev. 21:22f). So those who wait upon the Lord come to know Christ's Passion reenacted in their own bodies. The Spiritualist typological interpretation of Scripture, translating outward events recorded in the Bible (history) into inward personal experience (mystery), is very evident here. (Robert Westfield, or Wastfield, is among a number of army Spiritualists who merged into the Quaker movement in the 1650s.[42])

Nicholas Couling, an army officer, makes explicit the perfectionist implications of this spirituality in *The Saints Perfect in This Life or Never* (1647). "I propound that a Saint in this life, without any addition hereafter, is perfectly just, perfectly holy, completely glorious in this life." He supports this claim with New Testament quotations, such as the injunction of Jesus, "be ye perfect." Couling anticipates heated responses to his tract. He prefaces his remarks by stating that our corrupt nature wants to keep others in misery with us. If prisoners see one of their group try to escape, they warn the keeper. So it is in spiritual things: if anyone begins to leave Babylon, the others cry out in alarm.

Indeed, perfectionist teaching especially threatened the Puritan clerical establishment. If Christ's direct teaching and power within the believer could perfect the individual, that person escaped being a client of human teachers. Likewise, civil authorities feared that individuals convinced of their perfection might do anything. Some fifty-two London ministers united to attack Couling in print after his tract appeared.[43]

The most polished and complete statement to come out of this ferment was *The Saint's Travel to the Land of Canaan* (1648) by one R. Wilkinson. As with most of these writers, we know nothing of Wilkinson other than the designation on the title page, "a member of the army." It may be the Robert Wilkinson who debated Quakers in 1654, sounding very much like a Ranter.[44] It is curious that other modern scholarship on Seekers does not take note of Wilkinson, whose book is comparable to Saltmarsh's *Sparkles of Glory*, but is more coherently written.

The *Saint's Travel* is a highly distilled devotional guide. With the slight air of superiority typical of the army Spiritualists, Wilkinson urges the reader to accept as much as possible of what follows and let the rest be; God will eventually reveal more of its truth to the honest soul. If anything is "above thy experience, be silent in it and wait to know it, if it be of God."[45] The basic thesis is this: there are lower and higher workings of God in the individual. Whatever level one achieves, one thinks to have "arrived" in spiritual Canaan, the land of rest. But any rest that is below complete communion with God sooner or later proves false. Wilkinson affirms that even false rests are God's dispensations, a series of temporary resting places on the journey, leading the creature on toward God.

Most of the book is devoted to describing seventeen false rests, rang-ing from mere civility, through zeal for the truth, legal righteousness, "strange castings down of the Spirit," knowledge of Christ according to Scripture, "great, strange and excellent flashes of God," and even "extraordinary gifts of the Spirit." All of these attainments stop short of the true rest in God. God dwells in all of them for a while, but then moves on, leaving them empty. The creature no longer finds rest there and is forced to move on. As one who admits to having spent too many of his years in these false rests, Wilkinson acknowledges the pain, confusion, and abandonment one feels at times along the way.

He goes on to describe the true rest in various ways. It is a gift of God within us, but from beyond us; nothing the creature can attain of itself will remain a rest for long. Christ is an unalterable being, or substance; once the creature is centered in Christ, above itself, it rests securely, beyond all fears. This "centering up" of the creature brings full contentment in God's inexpressible glory. The experience of Christ within is the peace of God. The will is centered up into the will of God, so God's will becomes the will of the creature (perfection). The mind and emotions are also centered up, resting from their busy machinations. This is heaven. Wilkinson acknowledges the exalted tone of such claims: "Some think this a very high state, yet experience and Scripture do testify that it is a state enjoyed, or to be enjoyed, by all or most true saints in these our days."[46]

The writings of Saltmarsh, Wilkinson, and other army Spiritualists bear witness to great breakthroughs. We can hear many key points of future Quaker preaching and practice already in place by 1648: Christ as a heavenly prophet risen in the flesh of ordinary human beings; the universal light of Christ within; the apocalyptic day of the Lord as a "fiery trial" of judgment experienced within; perfection bestowed upon those who weather through the spiritual trials; "gospel order" as Christ's direct government among the faithful; even the name "friends" and the first steps toward a Quaker renunciation of war and violence. The seed was forming that would carry forward the genetic code of radical Christian hope. But it would mature only through mortifying disappointments and betrayals. The seed of this fecund Spiritualism would rise to new life only after the flower of the English Reformation had truly faded and died.

WILLIAM ERBURY

We see the flowering and fading of Seeker hope poignantly in the figure of William Erbury, whose writings mirror events up to his death in 1654.[47] Another orthodox divine, Erbury was born in Glamorganshire, Wales in 1604. He graduated from Oxford with a bachelor's degree in 1623 and returned to Wales, taking a parish post in Cardiff. Hostile sources claimed that he was always "schismatically affected." Indeed, by 1634, his preaching was under attack from his bishop. When he would not submit, proceedings were taken against him and he was ejected in 1638. By 1640, he had begun preaching against episcopacy and advancing Independency. He became a chaplain to the Parliamentary army early in the civil war, but left before the time of great Spiritualist awakening there.

As a leader in the radical wing of the Independent movement, Erbury felt free to preach eclectic views. We know of him attending a meeting of Independent leaders of London in May 1644, where they debated what to do about the defection of one of their ministers (William Kiffin) to the Particular Baptists.[48] For his part, Erbury had left all set ecclesiastical agendas behind. Early in 1645, he was preaching in London, where he was attacked for allegedly denying the divinity of Christ. He moved to the Isle of Ely and led a congregation there for a while.

He continued to itinerate widely among many groups. A trip to Bury, for example, is noted by two different sources. Lawrence Clarkson, who would become a leading Ranter in 1649, was a Baptist imprisoned at Bury in 1645. He was visited by Erbury, who convinced him that baptism amounted to burning brick in Egypt. By the time he was released, Clarkson considered himself a Seeker, ready to embrace spiritual wilderness.[49] In *Gangraena*, Thomas Edwards related reports of Erbury's preaching in Bury that same summer. According to Edwards' information, Erbury preached general redemption (free grace) and prophesied that soon God would raise up new apostles with spiritual powers not seen since New Testament times. He spoke against gathering churches, enjoining listeners to

> wait for the coming of the Spirit, as the Apostles did; look as in the Wildernesse they had Honey and Manna, but not circumcision and the Passover till they came into Canaan; So now we may have many sweet Things, Conference and Prayer, but not Ministry and Sacraments.

He predicted that the arrival of the new apostles would lead eventually to the fall of Rome and the appearance of the new Jerusalem, a unified faith.[50]

Theologically and geographically, Erbury was now moving quickly and sometimes erratically. He briefly settled in Oxford, where in January 1647 he debated an orthodox preacher named Cheynel. Shortly afterward, Erbury published an account of his side of the debate in *Neither Truth nor Error*. The debate seems to have centered on Erbury's grand theme, the indwelling of Christ. He concludes with the following enigmatic reflection:

> Well, when wise men err, and the Princes of Zoan are be-
> come fools [Isa. 19:13]; that is, the chief leaders in (spiri-
> tual) Egypt [e.g., his attacker] are causing to err and wander,
> there is a way, a high-way that way-faring men, though fools,
> shall not err therein. If any man would be wise still, he dares
> not call him a fool: But as for him who hath found himself a
> fool already, and sees himself bewildernessed as a way-far-
> ing man seeing no way of man on earth, or beaten path to
> lead him, let him look upward and within at once, and a high-
> way, the Way is found, Christ in us, God in our flesh. Wait
> here a while for that Spirit and power from on high to appear
> in us, walking in the Spirit of holiness, love, and peace; and
> at last, within a little, we shall be led forth out of this confu-
> sion and Babylon, wherein we yet are not clearly knowing
> Truth nor Error, Day nor Night; but in the evening there shall
> be light [Zech. 14:7].[51]

Erbury was never afraid to admit that he was groping his way and was willing to be a fool in the wilderness, rather than be counted wise in Egypt. His sense of errantry was perhaps the keenest of all the Seeker writers. In his advice to look both inward and upward we find a parallel to Wilkinson's theme of "centering up." This spiritual practice led him in many directions across the barren wastes of ruined religion in the 1640s and 1650s. His peripatetic ministry and impulsive statements caused him a great deal of trouble. Controversy arising from his Oxford debate prompted authorities to ask him to leave town.

Back in London, Erbury preached for a while at Christ Church, Newgate Street, where he followed Spiritualist and Leveller develop-ments in both the army and the city. Like Saltmarsh at the end of 1647, Erbury began to see God's purposes moving past the army leadership to the "saints" scattered throughout the army and elsewhere. In *The Lord of Hosts* (1648), he declared that "God is now rising as a man of War in the Saints, by whom he will destroy all the Oppressors, and Oppressions of men." "God owns his saints as his Army," he continues. Christ the true King "is coming, meek and lowly, riding upon an ass . . . this is God in the saints, base, despised, dull fellows . . . men have made mere asses of the saints, laying burdens on them." But when God rides upon them and is revealed in them, they shall reign as kings on earth.[52] God's favor toward these saints is the only reason the nation has not utterly perished, Erbury adds.

So, according to Erbury, the army had run its course. It had served to defeat the king and to cradle a new political actor, Christ risen in the saints. The language is so metaphorical and the writing so garbled at times, it is not clear whether he envisions the saints waging military or spiritual warfare. It is also unclear what kind of political organization he imagines the saints coming to embody. As we noted in the preceding chapter, Independent preachers generally avoided giving definite political shape to "the rule of the saints." But Erbury clearly asserts that they will not impose their order from above, forcing conformity as princes and magistrates have done. Rather, they will establish the new order from the midst of the people.[53] This egalitarian sense is consistent with his preaching of the new age of the Spirit,[54] the dispensationalist scheme we found also in Saltmarsh. Erbury's writing breathes the desperate hope that he and other radicals envisioned during the last struggles against King Charles and as the Levellers continued to agitate and organize for a republican future in England.

Little is known of Erbury's activity over the next three years. He may have been overwhelmed by the defeat of the Leveller initiative and the general non-fulfillment of radical hopes. He may have spent that period back in Wales.[55] But early in 1652, he was again in trouble for his preaching. A Parliamentary committee called him to answer accusations of heresy. He offered an orthodox statement, but the committee was incredulous and imprisoned him briefly. He published a summary of his response to Parliament in *The Honest Heretique* that year. He acknowledged

> that I am a man in Babylon, with all the gathered Churches, and scattered Saints [Seekers]: my own continued Confessions, both in Print, and Publique [speeches], shew the same. Besides, my acknowledged Confusion in my apprehensions, and present attainments, may be a just Apologie, at least a Motive, to your Honours Indulgence over all my weaknesses.[56]

We hear Erbury's chastened spirit more clearly, as many of his hopes faded. "Babylon" had expanded its city limits to annex all those who had thought they were escaping.

Indeed, the political situation had deteriorated by 1652. The Levellers had been defeated and dispersed by mid-1649 (more on that in the next chapter). The army was transformed from a liberation force and hotbed of spiritual discoveries to an organ of control over Parliament and the nation. Many of its most radical spirits dropped out and withdrew. After renewed civil war in 1648, Charles was recaptured, then executed in January 1649. Army troops forcibly purged the Long Parliament of a hundred Presbyterian members. The pared-down body that survived was nicknamed the "Rump." But no political consensus seemed attainable between the army and even a purged Parliament.

By 1652, Erbury viewed the English nation as broken, like Babylon, into three parts (see Rev. 16:19): monarchy, aristocracy, and democracy. The king and episcopacy had represented the first, Parliament and presbytery represented the second. The third was best represented by the Independent and Baptist churches, where authority rested in the voting power of whole congregations. Parliament and the army claimed to be democratic, but were not. Erbury concluded with a shrug that the vials of divine wrath were still not empty (i.e., the time of conflict and chaos was not over yet; see Rev. 16), but that God would eventually appear in everyone, turning darkness into light and divisions into love.[57] In such prophecies, we hear his hope becoming vague and dispirited.

Cromwell finally expelled the Rump in April 1653. The Army nominated a new Parliament of one hundred forty men, some of whom had been elected by Independent congregations. A dozen or so were Fifth Monarchists, a faction now at its zenith of influence and agitation for a theocratic state (see Chapter 7 for more on the Fifth Monarchists). This experiment, more formally known as the Nominated Parliament, earned the nickname "Barebones," based on the name of Praise-god Barbon, the colorful Separatist preacher of London who became one of its members.

Erbury drew back from the triumphalist hopes and coalition politics of the Fifth Monarchists. *A Call to the Churches* was published in February 1653, chastizing the Independents and Baptists, who thought they were rising to power at last. While they rejoiced, the "scattered saints" (Seekers) mourned: "by the waters of Babylon they sit down and weep [Psa. 137:1] while you are dipping in them." Seekers had confronted the bondage of self. "We your brethren are not alive, but dead in Babylon . . . will ye not yet dye for us?"[58] He concluded,

> the greatest work that God hath to do with you this day, is to make you see you are dead; that's the end why he does dash

and divide you, disquiet and destroy all your comforts; for I
know you are shaking already, and 'tis a mercy to you, that
God will disquiet the inhabitants of Babylon, that you shall
have no rest, till you return to his land, even to the Lord that
lives within you . . .though the Body be dead.[59]

Events bore out his grim prophecy. The Barebones Parliament was a
stillborn creature. After months of impotent squabbling, it dissolved
itself in December 1653.[60] The army produced a new provisional constitution, the *Instrument of Government*, which created a new executive,
the Lord Protector, a nearly dictatorial post to which Cromwell was
named. Henceforth, Cromwell became the only constant in English
political life, until his death in 1658.

Erbury's last statement, *The Great Earthquake*, was published in July
1654, shortly after his death in London. There, he testifies once more to
the apostasy of all the churches. In that regard, he notes that the Reformation had identified the Papacy or various state-church establishments
as the Antichrist. But Antichrist is the alienation from God played out in
every human. It simply manifests itself most painfully in the life of
churches. His own prophetic ministry has focused primarily on the apostasy as it developed among the Independent churches.[61] We will find the
same theme of an inner Antichrist in an earlier publication by Joseph
Salmon (see Chapter 6). In the relocation of Antichrist from Rome to
the human heart, Christopher Hill sees the political collapse of English
radicalism.[62] But later in this study we will find that it forms the starting
point for the Quaker resurgence of radicalism in the 1650s. Concomitant with the theme of the seed within, it indicates that revolutionary
struggle must henceforth begin within.

John Webster, a former army chaplain and ally of Erbury's, wrote
prefaces to *The Great Earthquake* and to *The Testimony of William
Erbury,* a collection published posthumously in 1658. His observations
summarize Erbury's life sympathetically. Writing in 1654, Webster asserted that although Erbury was branded as a heretic and antinomian, he
was neither. Webster admits, however, that some followers misunder-
stood Erbury's doctrines and took license. He thrived on silent prayer
among earnest believers, having renounced all external demonstrations
of piety. He loved Scripture, not for its "bare letter," but for the truth
hidden there like treasure buried in a field. He was against all pretended

ministry—better none at all. Indeed, in the abiding situation of apostasy, no regular ministry could be legitimate: "in this darkness he had rather sit down and wait in silence, than be beholding to the pretended light and direction of deceivable guides."[63]

Reflecting again on Erbury four years later, Webster concludes that many are anxious to proclaim the end of spiritual captivity, laboring to fulfill their prophecy and redeem themselves by their own efforts. In so doing, they "rivet themselves" all the more strongly to their bondage.[64] But for his part, Erbury, like Jeremiah, had prophesied that the time in Babylon would not be short. Following Jeremiah 29, Erbury counseled saints to work and pray for the peace of the city of their captivity, knowing that their bondage to vanity was ordained by a greater power. Thus, the wisdom of the saints is to make captivity as comfortable as possible, without being drawn into the idolatries, interests, and privileges of the powers. "Be patient therefore Brethren until the coming of the Lord. As for this friend, his memory will be pretious in the hearts of many."

Erbury exemplifies the trajectory many Seekers followed through the 1640s into the 1650s. In the mid-1640s, his preaching sounded many of the confident utopian themes we heard in Saltmarsh. Erbury parallels Saltmarsh's antinomian, proto-liberal tendency, preaching the new age of the Spirit, an end to Puritan legalism. But later, in the years after Saltmarsh's death and in light of the defeat of the Levellers and other radical groups, we see a more chastened spirit in Erbury. The captivity of the church is not about to end so easily or quickly. Here, Erbury seems to revert to the more traditional Seeker position, mourning in Babylon, worshipping in penitent silence, waiting for a new revelation that will revive primitive Christianity. This mournful sense of captivity could not simply celebrate the secret glory of an invisible church; it ached for a visible, gathered church. Such Seekers were still formed in the Protestant tradition, even though they refused to stand within it any longer.

Erbury's sentiments are similar to those of many Seekers who became Quakers in the 1650s. But the Quaker mission did not arrive in London until the summer of 1654, around the time of Erbury's death. So we do not know what his response to Friends might have been. We do know, however, that Erbury's widow, Mary, and daughter, Dorcas, were well known by Quaker leaders by the end of that first summer.[65]

John Saltmarsh, William Erbury, and John Webster are figures cited by a number of early Quakers as precursors of and influences upon early

Friends. In a 1693 letter, the second-generation Quaker convert, William Penn, mentioned all three as "forrunning Friends appearance."[66] We will find the ideas that they preached in the 1640s erupting with new force in the Quaker resurgence of English radicalism in the 1650s.

Notes

1. William Erbury, *The Honest Heretique* (1652), reprinted in *The Testimony of William Erbury* (1658), 337-38.
2. A. L. Morton, *The World of the Ranters: Religious Radicalism in the English Revolution* (London: Lawrence and Wishart), 45.
3. John Saltmarsh, *A Letter from the Army* (1647), which we will review later.
4. Saltmarsh described these developments later, in *An End of One Controversie* (1646), when he was attacked with false accusations regarding his past forms of income. His accuser, John Ley, characterized Saltmarsh as unstable. The latter replied that if putting off the old man, coming out of Babylon, and growing in the stature of Christ amount to instability, so be it.
5. John Saltmarsh, dedicatory preface to *Dawnings of Light* (1644).
6. Saltmarsh, *Dawnings*, 33.
7. Saltmarsh, *Dawnings*, 68-69.
8. John Saltmarsh, *Free-Grace: Or, the Flowings of Christ's Blood Freely to Sinners* (Tenth Edition, 1700), 23.
9. Saltmarsh, *Free-Grace*, 25.
10. Saltmarsh, *Free-Grace*, 37-45.
11. Saltmarsh, *Free-Grace*, 106.
12. Saltmarsh, *Free-Grace*, 106.
13. Murray Tolmie, *The Triumph of the Saints: Separate Churches of London 1616-1649* (Cambridge: University Press, 1977), 123-24.
14. From the "Preamble" to the anonymously authored *Wonderful Predictions* (1648), which we will review a little later.
15. John Saltmarsh, *Sparkles of Glory: Or, Some Beams of the Morning-Star* (1647), Epistle to the Reader.
16. Saltmarsh, *Sparkles*, 18.
17. Saltmarsh, *Sparkles*, 52-53.
18. Saltmarsh, *Sparkles*, 66. I had long thought that George Fox was first to crystallize this prophetic Christology in such experientialist terms. But this is a very clear statement in 1647.
19. Indeed, in *A Survey of the Spiritual Antichrist* (1648), Rutherford wrote partly in response to *Sparkles of Glory*, finding in Saltmarsh's thought a combination of Schwenckfeld, Henry Nicholas, and Familism. See Jean Dietz Moss, *"Godded with God": Hendrick Niclaes and His Family of Love* (Philadelphia: American Philosophical Society, 1981), 58-63.
20. Saltmarsh, *Sparkles*, 68.
21. Saltmarsh, *Sparkles*, 68.
22. Saltmarsh, *Sparkles*, 78.

23. Saltmarsh, *Sparkles*, 108.
24. Saltmarsh, *Sparkles*, 112-15.
25. Saltmarsh, *Sparkles*, 185-86.
26. Saltmarsh, *Sparkles*, 189-93.
27, Saltmarsh, *Sparkles*, 193.
28. Saltmarsh, *Sparkles*, 114-15.
29. Saltmarsh, *A Letter from the Army* (1647), 1.
30. Saltmarsh, *Army*, 2.
31. Saltmarsh, *Army*, 3.
32. I am largely dependent on Morton's account of these next stages of development in the army during the second half of 1647. See *Ranters*, 63-66.
33. These were published after his death under the title *England's Friend Raised from the Grave* (1649).
34. Reported by Anon., *Wonderful Predictions, Declared in a Messages as from the Lord . . . by John Saltmarsh . . .* (published hurriedly, before the end of December 1647), 1.
35. Anon., *Wonderful Predictions*, 6.
36. Quoted in A. L. Morton, *Ranters*, 57-58.
37. See Hugh Barbour, *The Quakers in Puritan England* (New Haven: Yale University Press, 1964), 89.
38. John Lewin, *The Man-Child Brought Forth in Us: Or, God Manifest in the Flesh* (1648), 19.
39. Lewin, *Man-Child*, 22.
40. Robert Westfield, *Christ Coming in the Cloudes: Or, The Dawning of the Day* (1647), Preface.
41. Westfield, *Cloudes*, Preface.
42. In Joseph Smith's catalogue of Quaker writings (2:988), Robert Wastfield's 1647 pre-Quaker publication is included, along with Quaker publications of 1657, '59, '62 and '63.
43. We are aware of this attack through Couling's response, *A Word to the 52 Ministers of London, Shewing that the Most Zealous Professors have been the Greatest Persecutors of Christ and His Most Spiritual Members* (1648).
44. The Quaker Richard Farnworth summarizes a debate he and other Friends had with a Robert Wilkinson in September 1654 in Leicestershire; see Farnworth's tract, *The Ranters Principles and Deceits Discovered and Declared against, Denied and Disowned by Us Whom the World Calls Quakers* (1655).
45. R. Wilkinson, *The Saint's Travel to the Land of Canaan* (1648), Preface. This is an extremely rare book. The Wing catalogue of seventeenth-century English literature knows of only one extant copy of the original edition, and only four copies of the 1650s edition. There were subsequent editions, however, in 1703 and 1874. My source is the 1874 edition, which notes that the 1703 edition identified R. Wilkinson as Robert Wilkinson.
46. Wilkinson, *Travel*, 194.
47. The outlines of Erbury's life are derived here from the article on him in the British *Dictionary of National Biography* (Oxford: University Press, 1921), 6:801-02.
48. Tolmie, *Triumph*, 122.
49. See A. L. Morton, *Ranters*, 131-32.

50. Edwards, *Gangraena* (1646), Part 1, 24-25.
51. William Erbury, *Neither Truth Nor Error, Nor Day Nor Night, But in the Evening There Shall Be Light* (1648), reprinted in *The Testimony of William Erbury* (1658), 17-18.
52. William Erbury, *The Lord of Hosts* (1648), reprinted in *Testimony*, 24.
53. Erbury, *Hosts*, 39.
54. Erbury, *Hosts*, 36.
55. In 1652 Erbury published *The Sword Doubled*, addressed to civil and religious authorities in Wales, against tithes. He confesses there to his own inner struggles before he had finally renounced tithe support as a parish minister, though he does not indicate when. *A Call to the Churches* (1653) is addressed specifically to Welsh Independent and Baptist ministers.
56. William Erbury, *The Honest Heretique* (1652), reprinted in *Testimony*, 315.
57. William Erbury, *The Sword Doubled* (1652), reprinted in *Testimony*, 63.
58. William Erbury, *A Call to the Churches* (1653), reprinted in *Testimony*, 230.
59. Erbury, *Call*, 233.
60. Erbury published *The Babe of Glory* in November 1653, as the collapse of the Nominated Parliament drew near. He articulated the chastened sense of radical politics in that moment, reaffirming that Christ indeed dwells in the saints, but that this reality will find no concrete political expression for the moment. The only expression it finds for now is humility and patient waiting. The glory of Christ is revealed through the suffering of the saints, as it was revealed in the suffering of Christ. See *Testimony*, 93-95.
61. William Erbury, *The Great Earthquake* (1654), reprinted in *Testimony*, 271.
62. See Christopher Hill, *Antichrist in Seventeenth-Century England* (Oxford: University Press, 1971).
63. John Webster, Preface "To the Truly Christian Reader," to Erbury, *Earthquake*, 263.
64. John Webster, Preface "To the Christian Reader," to Erbury, *Testimony*. Webster probably alludes primarily to Quakers here. We know that by 1657, Webster left London for a post at Clitheroe. Early Quaker Robert Widders mentions a brief, partial convincement of a "priest Webster" near Skipton (the two towns are about fifteen miles apart). See *The Life and Death of Robert Widders* (1688), 5; cited by Geoffrey F. Nuttall, "The Last of James Nayler: Robert Rich and the Church of the First-Born," *Friends Quarterly* 60 (1985): 527-34.
65. Two letters written to Margaret Fell by John Audland and John Camm, who had been in London during the summer of 1654, send greetings to Mary Erbury and her daughter (A. R. Barclay MSS., 157, 158, Friends House, London. Both letters were written in September 1654). As a Quaker, Dorcas Erbury became embroiled in the Nayler crisis of 1656.
66. William Penn letter, 1693, quoted by Geoffrey Nuttall, *The Holy Spirit in Puritan Faith and Experience* (Oxford: Blackwell, 1946), 13. The Quaker schismatic Robert Rich listed all three among those who "longed to see this day of the Son of Man; but could not, he vanishing out of their sight." See Nuttall, *Spirit*, 184. Finally, an October 5, 1685 entry in John Locke's diary mentions a conversation with the Quaker Benjamin Furley, who believed that Saltmarsh was the first to refuse to remove his hat to social superiors to use plain language toward them. Again, see Nuttall, *Spirit*, 83.

CHAPTER 5

WILLIAM WALWYN AND GERRARD WINSTANLEY
TWO POLITICAL EXPRESSIONS OF
THE SEEKER QUEST

Many there are, who have run themselves quite out of breath, in searching after peace, and rest, in the various waies of these Churches, and from one Church way to another; but find none to comfort them, nothing to establish them; confessing that . . . instead of power . . . they find only formes, fashions, likenesses, and imitations . . . not without the countenance of corrupt authorities, and oppressive Statesmen; who find it (as it hath ever proved) a notable means to devide the people, making use thereof, to their wicked and tyrannous ends.

—William Walwyn, 1649[1]

In his journals, Søren Kierkegaard observed that, in the Reformation, every movement seemed religious, yet turned out to be political.[2] We have found this axiom borne out at every turn thus far. Even Spiritualists like Caspar Schwenckfeld and Sebastian Franck could not escape the politics of the Reformation. And while the Seekers moved beyond Protestantism, they still followed the Reformation impulse to politicize their religious convictions. No group could afford *not* to be political. In a climate where religious toleration had by no means found a political consensus, every religious group struggled for its existence in a "winner-takes-all" arena.

But the millennial hopes inspired by the civil war raised the stakes even higher. For groups on the left end of the religious spectrum, utopian visions of the kingdom of God on earth, Christ reigning through the bodies of his saints, demanded a democratized political apparatus.

Seekers held onto these hopes with an acute intensity, as they sought to further God's purposes by transforming not only themselves but English society as a whole. They lived out the decade of the 1640s following each unfolding event of the civil war, constantly teetering between Eden's bliss and the Abyss of despair.

As we saw briefly in the preceding chapters, many young Puritans, having been quickly weaned from their hopes in Parliament, shifted their political hopes to the army. By 1647, many of the most radicalized— those who became Separatists, Independents, Baptists or Seekers— pinned their hopes upon the political fortunes of the Levellers, an alliance of republican-minded activists chiefly in London, Bristol and the army. We saw John Saltmarsh, otherwise congenial and charitable, confront Oliver Cromwell and the other generals with prophetic indignation at their repression of the Levellers late in 1647. We then followed William Erbury's descent into a twilit wilderness after the last Leveller hopes faded by 1649.

It is now time for us to explore the lives of two key political innovators in the Seeker milieu. In some respects, William Walwyn and Gerrard Winstanley are much alike, the latter being simply more radical in vision and action. In other respects, however, they are nearly polar opposites, at least within the realm of alternative politics in the 1640s.[3] In the long run, both were easily overpowered and outmaneuvered by Cromwell's canny politics. Among England's highest soarers in the heady atmosphere of the 1640s, both became flightless birds thereafter.

WILLIAM WALWYN AND THE LEVELLER SAGA

William Walwyn was born in 1600 into Worcestershire's landed gentry.[4] But as a younger son, he did not inherit family lands. Surprisingly, given his intellectual ability, he was not even sent to university; he was instead apprenticed in 1619 to a London silk merchant. When he completed his term of seven years, he went into business for himself. In 1627, he married Anne Gundell, a woman who bore him no fewer than twenty children. Walwyn was successful enough to support his family comfortably.

He was an avid reader not only of Christian literature but of classical writers as well, and frequently quoted Montaigne. Still, the Bible was his great text. He was often troubled by the abstruse biblical expositions of some Puritan divines, but was equally critical of those whose speculations led into wild notions without solid Scriptural foundation. He maintained that a sincere and diligent reading of the Bible should lead an individual to a relatively simple Christian faith, centered on the doctrine of Christ's death for the sins of the world. Acceptance of this truth should lead to concrete ethical applications, such as helping orphans and widows, clothing the naked, feeding the hungry, and visiting those in prison.[5] Like other Leveller leaders, Walwyn often expressed Christian piety in terms of such socially concerned action. The Golden Rule was a guiding maxim for Walwyn. He believed it not only to be derived from Jesus' words in Scripture but also to be "a rule of reason and pure nature."[6] In this and many other instances, Walwyn exhibits an early liberal attitude. His republican political ideals were founded on his belief in universal principles of human reason. Yet he was still very much at home in a basic, commonsense approach to Christian faith.

For these reasons, Walwyn does not fit the classic Seeker mold of the period. He was less concerned to discover the true church than to explore all the competing religious positions. Hence, for Walwyn, seeking was a matter not of agonized, bewildered utopianism but of good-natured curiosity and a love of debate. Instead of renouncing one church form in favor of another, he visited many groups, listening to and debating their preachers. He pursued a Socratic style of engagement in both religion and politics, critiquing and comparing many different positions. But in the hothouse atmosphere of the 1640s, his equanimity was viewed with suspicion. Ironically, his reasonable, urbane manner made him the least trusted of the Leveller leaders.[7]

While Walwyn rejected all religious labels, he was politically a congregational Independent: that is, he advocated a loose, nonparochial confederation of freely gathered churches. Thus, he could accept Parliament's Solemn League and Covenant of 1643, but not as a mandate for an enforced Presbyterian national church. The vow to reform the English churches "according to the Word of God" meant to Walwyn a renunciation of all religious compulsion. Religious diversity would persist as long as religious understandings remained imperfect (Saltmarsh articulated the same view, but on more apocalyptic grounds, utilizing the Book of Revelation). He believed that the state was free to establish a church, and he could even support a continuation of parish churches and professional clergy; but he rejected the use of state-enforced tithes for their maintenance. Financial support must be voluntary.[8]

Like many Seekers, Walwyn had gone through an "extream affliction of mind" regarding predestination in an attempt to discern his eternal election.[9] He worked through this crisis by means of careful Bible study, coming to embrace Christ's free grace to all humanity, a religious position more complementary to the universalism of his republican political convictions. This drew him into contact with the General Baptists and their teaching of general redemption. For a while Walwyn was close to the leading General Baptist preacher, Thomas Lambe. But Lambe soon drew back from Walwyn, suspicious of his unwillingness to join a gathered congregation.[10]

Not surprisingly, Walwyn was one of the prime targets of Thomas Edwards' 1646 attacks in *Gangraena*. The first of the book's three installments identified Walwyn as "a Seeker and a dangerous man."[11] It also attacked Walwyn's associate, John Lilburne, as "a darling of the Sectaries," notorious for his "insolency and contempt of Authority."[12] Edwards apparently did not know the epithet "Leveller" at this time, but he predicted that the political activities of these figures, if not checked, would lead inevitably to rebellion and chaos. Thus, according to Edwards, arguments advanced by Walwyn and others for religious toleration were part of the devil's grand design against the English Reformation.[13]

Walwyn devoted much energy in 1646 to clearing his name and justifying his cause against Edwards' sensational slanders. In *A Whisper in the Ear of Mr. Thomas Edwards* published that year, Walwyn replied,

> I a seeker, good now; whose our author? Am I one because I know many, and have been amongst them often, that I might know them fully; so have I been with all other judgements, but carry with mee in all places a Touch-stone that tryeth all things, and labour to hold nothing but what upon plain grounds appeareth good and usefull: I abandon all niceties and useless things.[14]

We detect here Walwyn's liberal, utilitarian individualist attitude toward religious truth, commensurate with his zest for a good debate. Still, the "Touch-stone" he carried with him was probably his Bible. He countered that in his movements among Edwards' so-called "sectaries" and "Seekers" he found morally upright people who were friendly toward all good government. He had even been open-minded enough to go hear Edwards preach, "which few seekers will do, but never but once, for I was not so blind a seeker, as to seek for Grapes of thornes, or Figgs of thistles."[15]

His efforts at self-defense, however, only provided new ammunition for the second salvo of *Gangraena*. Edwards jeers that Walwyn is "touchie" about being labeled a dangerous Seeker.[16] He expands his attack, calling Walwyn "a Seeker and Libertine, a man of all Religions, pleading for all; and yet what Religion he is of no man can tell."[17] This expresses the widespread suspicion of Walwyn's wily Socratic style and his generous acceptance of all groups. Edwards also renews his attack upon Lilburne, whose "abuse and insolence" toward authority epitomize the sectarian agitation that will turn England into another Munster.[18]

Given the political realities of the 1640s, liberal views like Walwyn's could find no political representation other than popular agitation through pamphleteering, leafleting, and informal meetings. The Leveller movement coalesced out of the convergence of Walwyn with other republican pamphleteers.[19] John Lilburne was the most charismatic of these figures. He first rose to notoriety in 1638 when he was flogged through the streets of London for pamphleteering against the Episcopal state church. Religiously, Lilburne was a fairly orthodox Puritan whose affinities to the Separatist congregations of London led him to advocate complete separation of church and state. Cromwell had him released from prison and he soon became an officer in the Parliamentary army. By 1644, he had risen from captain to lieutenant colonel. He left the army in 1645, in part because he could not swear to the Solemn League and Covenant. After engaging in more political debate around London, Lilburne was imprisoned again from the summer of 1646 until the autumn of 1647.

Richard Overton spent part of his youth in a refugee congregation of English Baptists in Holland. By 1642, he had become a writer and printer of illicit political tracts in London. As the 1640s wore on, his targets of attack turned from episcopacy to presbytery. He was imprisoned in the summer of 1646 for publishing the first general republican platform, *A Grand Remonstrance of Many Thousand Citizens*. Overton was not a very public figure, but a strong intellect and sharp satirist with a large following among General Baptists. Given that Walwyn was an excellent debater and Lilburne possessed a gift for the political theater of confrontation and self-dramatization, each leader contributed distinct qualities and represented a certain sector of English radical religion. Together, they aroused the imagination of thousands to the political possibilities of England's situation. Toward that end, they innovated several modern techniques of political activism, such as pamphleteering and leafleting, mass demonstrations, mass petitions, and lobbying. Over the next three years, the Leveller agenda came to include the following points: the sovereignty of the House of Commons, expansion of the electoral franchise to include all male heads of households,[20] biennial elections for Parliament, religious toleration, legal reform, abolition of tithes, an end to military conscription, stabilization of tenure for copyholds, and democratization of guilds.[21]

Overton's and Lilburne's actions in 1646 induced a rapid escalation of popular agitation over the next year. In the opening months of 1647, a number of reform petitions were presented to Parliament. The Commons vote to burn the largest of these made it clear the Levellers would not be invited into the legislative process. That summer, when the army refused Parliament's order to disband, Levellers shifted their energies toward the army. There was already plenty of radical sentiment among the ranks. Already in the spring, each regiment had elected two "Agitators" to represent its concerns in the Army Council, introducing a democratic process to future decision-making. Lilburne was a natural link between Levellers in London and Agitators in the army.

The unfolding interactions between Parliament, King Charles, the generals, and the Levellers are extraordinary and can only be summarized here. It would seem that nearly every possible alliance was formed and betrayed, especially by the generals. First, they tried to negotiate their own constitutional agreement with the defeated king, after stealing him from Parliamentary custody. The Agitators and Levellers drafted an alternative, non-monarchical provisional constitution. In late October 1647, the two constitutions were debated by the Army Council at Putney, near London. After the debates, the generals jailed key Leveller and Agitator leaders. That elicited nearly mutinous demonstrations in two regiments by mid-November. More arrests and one execution followed. Meanwhile, Charles escaped custody. Some thought he had been aided by disgruntled Levellers.

The year 1648 was dominated by Charles' renewed military actions and the army's efforts to defeat and capture him again. With the Agitators expelled from the Army Council, Leveller activities refocused upon Parliament. In September, a *Large Petition* was presented to Parliament, assailing its betrayal of the republican cause. The moderate language of the petition suggests that Levellers still desired some rapprochement with Parliament. But, as G. E. Aylmer states, the upper-class interests represented in Parliament were simply unwilling to bargain with a qualitatively different political movement.[22]

Late in 1648, just as the Levellers' hopes seemed lost, the Army Council reopened negotiations with them, apparently concerned to counter a possible treaty between Parliament and the king. Initially, Walwyn was excluded from the negotiations owing to his unpopularity among London Independents. He eventually found his way into the debates at Whitehall, which continued into January 1649. But Levellers withdrew in disgust at the generals' tactics, which they viewed as Machiavellian. Still, the army had adopted a number of Leveller proposals, and now moved forward resolutely to execute Charles, abolish the House of Lords, and purge Commons of its Presbyterian majority.

The oligarchic control now exerted by the Army Council and the "Rump" remnant of the Long Parliament moved Levellers to denounce the new regime in *England's New Chains Discovered*, published in two parts during February and March. Facing renewed tumult in London and in the regiments, Cromwell succinctly posed the Leveller threat to the regime: "You must break these men or they will break you."[23] The army moved quickly to arrest the Leveller leaders in their homes in the early hours of March 28. The final catharses of the drama were soon played out. A small mutiny of soldiers occurred in London during April, resulting in one execution. From the Tower, the Levellers issued a final draft of their proposed constitution, *An Agreement of the Free People of England*, dated May 1 and published by Giles Calvert. Mass petitions for the release of the Levellers were refused. A large mutiny began at Oxford, becoming a force of about a thousand soldiers, apparently heading toward Bristol, where civilian support was strong. But they were easily defeated at Burford on May 14. Except for scattered expressions of outrage, the Leveller cause was finished.

Over succeeding months, army leadership acted to neutralize dissent within the ranks. Some regiments were sent off to Ireland and elsewhere, away from London. Malcontents were purged over succeeding years. But perhaps most crucially, according to Aylmer, the backpay owed to troops was finally settled; soldiers were paid through grants of land formerly owned by the crown. This eliminated one of the key grievances motivating regiments to agitate. In succeeding months, officers bought up soldiers' land rights at bargain prices and resold them for large profits, adding a pall of cynicism to the general mood of disillusion.

Why did the Levellers fail? In cities like London and Bristol, where large-scale support was repeatedly demonstrated, popular sympathies never quite coalesced into sustained political resolve. To some extent, support was oriented more toward the leaders themselves, especially Lilburne, than toward the Leveller agenda as such. Walwyn was despised in many circles. Christopher Hill and some others believe that internal differences of personality and political vision may also have hobbled the Leveller leadership.[24]

Why did the Levellers fail to bring the left wing of the religious spectrum together as a united bloc of support? The case of the Baptists, who had become quite strong in London in the 1640s, is telling. As we noted in Chapter Three, Baptist leaders hesitated to go very far into political advocacy, fearing they would be associated with the notorious revolutionaries of Munster. Having been vigorously repressed for so long, the Baptist movement did not readily expand into the freer political atmosphere of the 1640s. Further, the Levellers' republican rhetoric of natural rights, which posed the secular state as a legitimate sphere of moral action, was foreign to biblical theology. It was antithetical to the politics of Independents and Particular Baptists, who embraced predestination and the political destiny of God's elect saints to rule over society at large. The General Baptists, with their general redemption theology, were the group most congenial to Leveller political ideology[25] and demonstrated the most consistent support. By contrast, Particular Baptist leaders viewed with dismay Leveller agitation in their congregations and were quick to repudiate Levellerism once mutinies erupted in the army during the spring of 1649. They proved to be more prone to the millennial rhetoric of the Fifth Monarchist movement, whose radical politics succeeded those of Levellers during the 1650s (see Chapter 7).[26]

In the final analysis, over the course of a civil war that no one had anticipated to begin with, the popular political conversation simply did not catch up with revolutionary events quickly enough to form coherent support for the Leveller agenda. Moreover, given the clout and vehemence of conservative opposition, the Leveller constitution could have been imposed only by armed force. The rejection of the Leveller constitution by the generals after the Putney debates in October 1647 was thus a key turning point.

From the Tower of London, William Walwyn followed the events of early 1649 in despair. During March, he published anonymously *The Vanitie of the Present Churches*,[27] a lament over the degenerating situation of religion and politics. There, he attacked both Presbyterians and Independents for their efforts to gain religious hegemony over the nation by political force. His attack upon Independents (many of whom had turned against him personally and the Levellers generally) was very strong. Though they had "scumm'd the Parish Congregations of most of their wealthy and zealous members," they now turned and spat venom at all who separated from them, calling them atheists, antinomians, and Seekers, hankering for the power to repress them.[28]

But Walwyn was equally disgusted with groups to the left of the Independents. New sects and doctrines continued to generate and debates raged endlessly and fruitlessly. He devoted much criticism to the Baptists and Spiritualists, contingents that had proven too divided, ambivalent, and distracted to support the Leveller cause. He noted their current vogue of preaching and praying *ex tempore*, following the direct leading of the Spirit. Poorly developed ideas passed for new revelations by virtue of the confidence of speakers and the superstition of their hearers.[29] Religious controversy kept many sincere hearts in perpetual suspense and doubt. Some became strident, plunging into malicious and envious wrangling; others claimed great revelations beyond Scripture, leading their followers to neglect the Bible. They would not test their opinions by the text, but instead interpreted the text according to their opinions and experiences.[30] Here Walwyn's Puritan biblicism clearly set him apart from the Spiritualist trend among Seekers, where the living Word within became the decisive authority in personal and church life. He suspected Spiritualists to be enthralled by "the Germans madde mans Divinity"[31] (probably meaning the writings of Jacob Boehme).

Walwyn trenchantly analyzed a degenerative tendency inherent in so much overheated mystical writing and prophetic utterance. In that setting,

> prophets dared not question one another's claims, lest they should break the golden chaine of their own honor and profit, for whoever assumes himself to be taught by the Spirit dares not condemn the false assumption of the Spirit in another, lest he

should thereby condemn himself, since both have only their bare affirmations for their foundation, neither being able to manifest by any thing extraordinary the real possession thereof.[32]

Thus, Walwyn found a wasting malaise in the Seeker scene, where a lack of critical dialogue could easily indulge delusion. Speaking from his own experience among Baptists and Spiritualists, he observed that any critical response caused these mystics to condemn him as unenlightened and ask him to go away.[33] Walwyn found that tendency defeating to both the Leveller political cause and coherent church life. He also sounded a theme we have heard before, that any real fresh outpouring of the Spirit would be accompanied by "extraordinary" signs and wonders to authenticate it. He suggested that if these self-styled heralds of the new age were really endowed with the Spirit, they couldn't hide it even if they tried.[34]

Individuals became so immersed in delusion as to believe they were the darlings of God, so exalted, they could hardly be convinced of their mistake. Some soared so high, they maintained that there was no such thing as sin or evil—all things were good, all things one, and to believe otherwise was a grievous lack of enlightenment.[35] This is an early report of the Ranterism we will examine in the next chapter. At this point, it had not been branded with that nickname. But these nihilistic ethics and monistic worldview became hallmarks of the Ranter rhetoric that exploded in England later in 1649. Walwyn offered probably the most telling critique of religious seeking in the 1640s. Notwithstanding the many inspired individuals and brilliant insights that enlivened the Seeker scene, it easily digressed from concerted political resolve into dangerous self-absorption. As Walwyn noted in the passage placed as the epigraph to this chapter, seeking thus unwittingly served the political designs of corrupt, entrenched powers. (A similar degeneration and neutralization of personalist politics in the 60s counterculture was noted in Chapter One.) These pitfalls to the Spiritualist tendency were to become key challenges to the Quaker movement over the next decades, as leaders like George Fox sought to balance the Spirit's authority in individual consciences with the need for corporate unity of vision and consistency in moral standards. (We will take up these themes in Chapters 10 and 11.)

Walwyn laid some blame for these developments upon those Puritan clergy whose overcomplicated doctrines led people into obscure notions. Like many critics of Puritanism, he charged that divines had taken this course to elevate themselves and keep the people in subjection. Walwyn insisted that the truth of Christ does not take long to learn— but there is no profit in it! He suggested that more open discussion and debate would help everyone attain better understanding. The truth of Christ's sacrifice for sinful humanity inspires a simple faith, which in turn inspires love, which in turn inspires us to help others.[36] But "if you exceed the plain, indisputable doctrines of the Gospel, you will be ever to seeke."[37] In conclusion, he pleaded for the English Reformation to return to a spirit of love, tolerance, and forgiveness.[38]

Incidentally, Walwyn's views on the simplicity of religion complement his attacks against lawyers and the overcomplexity of the law. In other writings, he advocated that laws be simplified enough to fit into a single book, translated into English. This would reduce everything to "common equity and right reason," bringing law to the "nearest agreement with Christianity."[39]

Walwyn's parting shot projects a fine critique of the entire religious spectrum in 1649. He felt defeated by the generals and betrayed by all the churches. While his wide-open curiosity and debate with all parties made him a Seeker of some kind, his was not the variety of seeking that usually garnered that epithet. Like Socrates, whose style of questioning infuriated religious leaders of an ancient time, Walwyn was feared as a seducer of the people, an enemy to faith. He poses an unusual paradox for the 1640s: a man who longed for a return to the traditional Protestant faith in the Bible; at the same time, an early liberal who expressed great confidence in the powers of human reason and the possibilities of social betterment; and, finally, a man who yearned for more "practical Christians" who would roll up their sleeves and do good works in their community.

As a Leveller, Walwyn hoped to create a republic that would reflect and nurture the best of the Reformation experience in England. A. L. Morton suggests[40] that the Leveller constitution, the *Agreement of the Free People of England*, was the political expression of congregational church order. Over preceding decades, thousands of English Separatists and Independents had gathered into new congregations, signing covenants that stated a shared creed and defined the specific rights and duties of participants. The Leveller *Agreement* proposed to extend that covenantal process on a national scale. It was proposed as a provisional constitution, to be signed by all consenting male heads of households, constituting the English nation as a covenanted people. As such, the Leveller platform was the crowning political outworking of the Puritan experience; it was the political expression of the deep religious desires that had been building for more than an century. But it was not to be.

After May 1649, Leveller leaders either withdrew or became involved in insurrectionary plots. John Lilburne was eventually tried and impris- oned again in 1653 for plotting with the future Charles II against the Commonwealth. He remained in the Tower until his death in 1656. During his last year, he became a Quaker and renounced all forms of violence.[41] Overton was involved in work both for and against the gov- ernment during the 1650s.[42] Walwyn, after his release from the Tower, resolutely retired from political life. He continued his textile business, enjoyed his large family, contributed to the life of his local London parish, and developed a considerable interest in herbal medicine. There- after, his published polemics were limited to attacks upon the applica- tion of "Purgers, Vomitters, Bleedings, Issues, Glisters, Blisters, Opium, Antimony and Quicksilver"[43] in contemporary medicine. This herbal interest developed among a variety of Spiritualists of the period. The Seeker John Webster, the Ranter Abiezer Coppe, and Quakers such as George Fox and Charles Marshall all pursued interests in that direction, particularly after the revolutionary decades of the 1640s and 1650s.

GERRARD WINSTANLEY AND THE DIGGERS, OR TRUE LEVELLERS

The name "Leveller" was another of the colorful epithets of a tumultu- ous decade. It expressed the fears of some that these early republicans wanted not only to expand the electoral franchise and to achieve reli- gious freedom, but to redistribute wealth as well. Thomas Edwards' 1646 list of current heresies alleged that some in England espoused such ideas. But Leveller leaders consistently denied such accusations. The thirtieth point of the final Leveller *Agreement* explicitly prohibited any attempt to "level mens Estates, destroy Propriety, or make all things Common" in a future Commonwealth. As early liberals, Levellers affirmed the sanctity of property. Far from redistributing wealth, they sought politi- cal representation for the emerging class interests of small property owners such as independent traders, artisans, and yeoman farmers, who struggled against the oligarchic forces behind the Presbyterian party and the more conservative wing of the Independents. There was little in the Leveller agenda to benefit the poor directly.

Meanwhile, the plight of England's poor was growing increasingly dire. The 17th century saw increasing numbers of marginal families run off the land by the accelerating capitalization of agriculture, the draining of the fens, and the opening of new "waste lands" for tillage. The enclosure of "common lands" by wealthy landowners isolated pasture traditionally open for local residents to graze their livestock. There was only limited concern for the poor to be found in the political conversation between royalty, aristocracy, gentry, and new commercial interests. Still worse, the civil war created many sudden economic dislocations. Finally, a series of poor harvests boosted food prices and added to the general climate of desperation. In some counties, pestilence and outright starvation were reported.[44]

Alms-giving was a staple of Puritan piety, and a more substantial parish-based poor relief system was a serious component of both Presbyterian and Independent reform schemes. Baptists were outstanding in their aid to the needy in their congregations. Levellers like Walwyn urged more voluntarism to aid the poor and downtrodden. Later, Ranters and Quakers were well known for their severe invectives against the rich and their passionate advocacy for the poor. And as they began to organize over the course of the 1650s, Quakers were noted for their networks of mutual aid as well as their assistance to other needy individuals and families.

But among all these movements, only one brief experiment aimed straight at the issues of poverty and wealth. The "Diggers," or "True Levellers," were a spontaneous blossoming of perhaps ten communes in central and southern England. None of them lasted very long. If the Levellers were ahead of the political consciousness of the period, the Diggers were a disturbing apparition straight from the political unconscious. They were sensationalized in the "press-books," the early newspapers of the day, and repeatedly attacked by local gentry and clergy. But they did not attract any serious following among England's poor, who were probably too hard-pressed and demoralized to be mobilized.

The key figure and exponent of the Digger experiment was Gerrard Winstanley, another shadowy form in the gallery of obscure heroes and heroines of this period.[45] He was probably born in 1609 in southern Lancashire, into a family at the edges of the gentry class. His parents had been in trouble for religious nonconformity even before his birth. He had no formal education and was apprenticed in 1630 to a tailor in London. After finishing the usual seven-year term, he went into business in London for himself, probably before 1640, the year he married Susan King. His business failed in 1643, owing to the economic stresses of the war, he later wrote. He and his wife moved to Surrey that year, where he herded sheep and was aided by friends.

How much this business failure affected his later communistic ideas is unclear, but his faith began to shift in a pattern typical of many Seekers at that time. He later described himself as a one-time strict churchgoer, reckoned to be a good Christian by his ministers, but having only a secondhand knowledge of Christ. At some point during the mid-1640s he became a Baptist and may have been a lay preacher among them. But, like many Seekers in the making, he soon left the Baptists and all other gathered churches. He spoke to informal groups, "not customarily to make a trade of it, for fleshly ends, but occasionally as the Light is pleased to manifest himself in me."[46]

By 1648, Winstanley's ideas had advanced to such complex and radical conclusions that he shifted his energies from speaking to writing and found Giles Calvert a ready publisher. He produced four publications that year, all full of ideas and language from the Seeker milieu. In *The Saints Paradice*, he writes that

> I do not write anything as to be a teacher to you, for I know you have a teacher within yourselves (which is the Spirit) and when your flesh is made subject to him, he will teach you all things. . . . And this Spirit, or Father, which as he made the globe and every creature, so he dwells in every creature, but supremely in man. . . . [47]

We recognize the theme of divine indwelling as an inward teacher from Saltmarsh and other Seekers. But the panentheistic idea of God's dwelling in all creatures is a further development that will soon give his Spiritualism a new materialist and communist thrust.

In the same book, he expresses friendship with all whose "souls hunger after sincere milk" of divine teaching. These "few scattered ones" are the only manifestation of God's wisdom in England. The time is coming when the Spirit will appear in all flesh. The poor will be the first to receive the gospel, as wise men become fools and scholars become ignorant.[48] Winstanley attacks the alienated mentality that seeks divine wisdom from human teachers. This condition imagines a god somewhere beyond the skies; it also leads men to kill those who differ from them. He further asserts that this alienation from God and from other human beings is itself the devil; its misery is itself hell. So the devil is not a self-sufficient power distinct from God but is a mystery that will be swallowed up again into the mysterious unity of God. With the discovery of God within, the devil finds no place in us and we are free.[49]

He goes on to characterize four demonic aspects of the devil within: subtlcty, hypocrisy, envy, and cruelty. Winstanley finds these qualities manifested not only in individuals but also in Parliament, the churches, and the army. No power but Christ reigning within can free individuals or societies from these symptoms of alienation.[50] He defines the Spirit that knits all creatures together in love as reason.[51] He intends this not in the rationalistic sense that predominated during the next century, but, as George H. Sabine suggests, as a neutral term for the "incomprehensible spirit" he also calls "universal love."[52] Winstanley clearly connects reason to the Father, Son, and Holy Spirit of Christian faith, but seeks a language at least partially distinct from the alienated structures of traditional Christendom.

To Winstanley, the poor and uneducated are crucial to God's new work. Not only are they the most oppressed by an alienated society and its religion; they are also by implication those most ready to receive the immediate power of the gospel:

> The voice of Jesus Christ reigning in his Church comes
> first from the multitude . . . God uses the common people
> and the multitude to proclaim that the Lord God Omnipotent
> reigneth. As when Christ came at first the poor received the
> Gospel . . . so in the reformation of religion.[53]

In *The Breaking of the Day of God,* the same year, Winstanlcy is clearly caught up in the Leveller drama unfolding in London and in the army. He prefaces his work to his fellow Seekers, "the despised sons and daughters of Zion, scattered up and down the Kingdom of England." They are hated and scorned precisely because the light and beauty of God shines in them. He must have Levellers specifically in mind when he writes that they are "sentenced to death" as "Roundheads" (a popular nickname for radicals, because of their short haircuts) and accounted troublers of England. But they are in fact the nation's true peace-lovers. At the time of his writing in May, one Leveller agitator from the army had already been executed, and Leveller leaders were under indefinite detention. The woes of the "mourners after Sion" are acute but will soon end: "You that are children of light, must lie under reproach and oppressions of the world; that is Gods dispensation to you: But it shall be but for a little time . . . your redemption draws near."[54]

In preparation for this imminent redemption, Christ is shaking the kingdom, both within and without. This is the earthquake envisioned in Revelation. Without, it causes the oppressive powers to teeter and fall. Within, it shakes down the corrupt flesh in the saint, destroying Adam's constructed self in order to establish Christ's new anointing. He remarks that unbelievers scoff and laugh when they see this shaking in the bodies of the saints.[55] This suggests that Winstanley had been moving in circles where physical trembling was part of the public worship experience. This, together with the expression "children of light," further suggests that he may have been part of the same proto-Quaker network in which George Fox moved from 1646 to 1650. Fox's *Journal* also notes his experience of the earthquake in powerful meetings during 1648 (albeit in Nottinghamshire, not Surrey).[56] Moreover, Winstanley sounds a clear theme of pacifistic resistance to the powers:

> Wait patiently upon the Lord, let every man that loves God, endeavour, by the spirit of wisdom, meeknesse, and love to drie up Euphrates; even this spirit of bitternesse that like a great River hath over-flowed the earth of man-kinde. For it is not revenge, prisons, fines, fightings, that will subdue a tumultuous spirit: but a soft answer, love, and meeknesse, tendernesse, and justice, to doe as we would be done unto, this will appease wrath.[57]

Winstanley is among the first to see the hollow victory of the civil war. Any further violent struggle for freedom and justice will only beget more violence and oppression. (We will explore further connections between Winstanley and the ensuing Quaker movement at the end of this chapter.)

Though we can make only indirect inferences from his 1648 writings, Winstanley seems to have supported the Leveller political initiative. We also hear many Seeker themes, though in the context of a critique of religion even more sweeping than previous Seeker writings. He was consolidating a religious, political, and socioeconomic vision that affirmed what today's liberation theologies call God's "preferential option for the poor." It is the conviction that God's Spirit works most powerfully from the base of society upwards, partly because the poor suffer the most, and partly because they are less implicated in and favored by the alienated structures of an unjust society.

Howsoever the development of his thinking proceeded, his culminating moment of radicalization occurred in January 1649, during the most decisive events of the English revolution: the beheading of Charles I, Colonel Pride's purge of the House of Commons, and the abolition of the House of Lords. At this point, the political meaning of Winstanley's Seekerism came fully into focus. His support for the Levellers gave way to an abruptly different, vastly more radical position. That month he underwent some kind of trance experience, in which he heard the words, "Work together, eat bread together; declare this all abroad." He understood his trance as a clear Word from the Lord meaning several things: hired labor must be replaced by loving cooperation in creation, which is God's one household; anyone claiming to own a part of this creation is a destroyer who brings a curse upon the earth and its inhabitants; the market economy of buying and selling must cease; persons should control no more land than they can work themselves or with the voluntary help of others.

Winstanley published this revelation that same month, in a manifesto entitled *The New Law of Righteousness.* In a powerfully annunciatory preface, he declares that the object of so much seeking, God's new law of righteousness and peace, is rising up in the sons and daughters of God in order to take captivity captive. This is the "restoration of all things" foreseen by the prophets and apostles, purging the curse not only from human relations but from the four elements of creation itself. He reaffirms that violence will not produce this revolutionary transformation: the arm of the Lord alone shall accomplish it. The transformation will be peaceful but frightening: human hearts will tremble at a social order that exalts no one but God.[58]

The book's main text begins with the biblical account of creation and fall, describing the "evenness" that existed among the creation, humans, and God in the beginning. But this unity was "put out of order, through man's rejecting the Spirit to live upon objects."[59] That is, covetousness overcame the human soul, drawing it out from unity and composure in God. Property and the violent means of acquiring and protecting it ensued. God began to draw humans back into unity, first through the ministry of Moses and the nation of Israel. That work was extended to all humanity through the life and death of a single body, Jesus Christ. The third phase of this redemptive plan is just now beginning, as Christ becomes a "spreading Spirit," an anointing power that is "all in all in every person, the one King of righteousness in every one."[60] But this universal Spirit does not proceed without resistance. As Jews pleaded for privilege against the revelation of Christ, so Christians plead for privilege against this new "spreading power," envying and killing those who worship God in a new way. This teaching is much along the lines of the Seeker preaching of the third age of the Spirit, but tends to fuse spiritual and material realms more fully.

Winstanley affirms that, in a sense, Christ's power is already spread throughout the entire creation. But it has its "chief residence" in men and women, that through them this one Spirit may again rule the world it created. Despite the startling, creation-centered import of his message, Winstanley insists that this is no new gospel but the old one: God in us, manifest in the flesh (see Col. 1:28: "Christ in you, the hope of glory," a recurrent theme of William Erbury and other Seekers). Nevertheless, in view of the way the clergy and socially powerful leaders of the church have twisted the gospel into alienated forms, he is barely willing to share the word "God" with them. We can see that Winstanley's 17th-century Christian critique of the church anticipates the atheistic humanism Karl Marx later adopted in opposition to 19th-century Christendom.

In Chapter 6 he begins to spell out the social implications of this gospel. The mind of alienated flesh judges it right for some to be "clothed with the objects of the earth, no matter how they were gained," and for the poor to be their slaves, and for magistrates to maintain this disorder. But the spiritual mind judges differently: "Reason requires that every man should live upon the increase of the earth comfortably; though covetousness fights against Reason's law."[61] He hastens to add,

> I do not speak that any particular men should go and take
> their neighbours goods by violence, or robbery (I abhor

it). . . but everyone is to wait, till the Lord Christ do spread himself in multiplicities of bodies, making them all of one heart and one mind, acting in the righteousness to one another. It will be one power in all, making all to give their consent.[62]

This phrase of *Mine and Thine* shall be swallowed up in the law of righteous actions one to another . . . the Lord. . . will sit upon the throne in every mans heart.. . . The work of freedom is now in the hand of Christ . . . he hath begun to spread himself, and he goes on mightily . . . the poor receives the Gospel daily; he is calling . . . the world, to come to this great Battell, even to deliver the oppressed, and to destroy the oppressour . . . and so to lead captivity captive, and let the prisoners of hope go free.[63]

So, even if Winstanley renounces violent tactics, he acknowledges that such profound transformation will come through deep struggle, a "great Battell" both within individuals and throughout society. The new order unfolds from below:

The Father now is raising up a people to himself out of the dust, that is, out the lowest and despised people. . . . In these, and from these shall the Law of Righteousness break forth first, for the poor they begin to receive the Gospel.[64]

He goes still further in drawing the dimensions of the new order:

When this universall law of equity rises up in every man and woman, then none shall lay claim to any creature, and say, *This is mine, and that is yours, This is my work, that is yours*; but every one shall put to their hands to till the earth. . . and the blessing of the earth shall be common to all. . . . There shall be no buying or selling, no fairs nor markets, but the whole earth shall be a common treasury for every man, for the earth is the Lords.[65]

There will be no need for lawyers or prisons. Instead, those who break the law of righteousness shall be made servants until they know themselves equal to all and lord over none. Even execution for murder, which is just another murder, will end.[66]

When he counsels all to "wait upon the Lord" for the fulfilling of these prophecies, he does not mean a passive waiting. He understands his trance as a command to initiate the new order by starting a community of poor people that will "manure and work the common lands," eating bread together by the sweat of their brows. "I have an inward perswasion that the spirit of the poor, shal be drawn forth ere long, to act materially this Law of Righteousness."[67] He awaits specific guidance from the Spirit as to where and how to begin. While he expects many struggles ahead, he affirms that the greatest combat is within, when the King of Righteousness judges the individual's selfish flesh. "And though this be trouble and torment for a time to the Creature, yet Christ at last will sit down in him. . . . "[68] This language recalls Saltmarsh's witness to the "Fiery Triall," but with a more explicit material aspect to the inner, spiritual conflict. It anticipates the inward and outward conflicts early Quakers were to experience in their "Lamb's War," where spiritual purification was accompanied by a material simplification of life.

Winstanley makes several statements of mystical communion with God in nature; but he strives to go beyond this largely aesthetic appreciation. Right relations upon the earth bring objects and subjects together. This point is worth quoting at length:

> To see the Divine power in the Creation-objects is sweet; but to see him ruling in the heart is sweeter. . . . The first sight is at a distance far off, as to see him in meat, drink, cloathes, friends, victories, riches, prosperity, to see him in the Sun, Moon, stars, Clouds, Grasse, Cattle, and all the Earth, how he has sweetly caused every one of these to give in assistance to preserve each other Creature: Or rather how he himself gives forth preservation and protection from one another, and so unites the whole Creation together by the unity of himself. But now to see the King sitting in his banqueting-house, to see the Law of Righteousness and peace ruling and dwelling in the heart. . . . This is the Word of God; This is sweeter then the honey or the honey-comb, for this is to see him near at hand, even within the heart ruling and resting there. This is the Kingdome of heaven within you.[69]

One becomes part of the divine order of creation only as one finds the Creator within and lets divine wisdom rule. This is a vision of vastly comprehensive scope. He writes that he received it not from reading books but by direct revelation.[70] Indeed, while many of his ideas have precedents among other Spiritualist writers, his overall integration of them into a socioeconomic and ecological framework balances spiritual and material dynamics with unprecedented clarity and completeness. Like all of Winstanley's books, *The New Law of Righteousness* bristles with many more powerful insights than can be related here.

Winstanley initiated his communal experiment on April 1, 1649 on a commons at St. George's Hill, Surrey. An associate, William Everard, was a key ally in the early stages of the experiment. They were joined by about a dozen poor men from the area. Together they began to dig, preparing the earth for spring planting, and to build some rudimentary shelter.

The Leveller leaders had been rounded up and put in the Tower just four days earlier and the demise of their cause was clear. Later that same month, Winstanley published *The True Levellers Standard Advanced*, denouncing the government's treatment of Levellers in London and announcing the new, more radical program in Surrey. He excoriates both Parliament and the army for promising the people freedom while actually increasing their bondage.[71] From the Solemn League and Covenant onward, the powers have demonstrated bad faith to the very people who shed blood, paid taxes, and provided free quarter in their homes to troops.

Private property is the curse behind these continuing oppressions; those who own it have gained it by oppression, theft, and murder, going back to the Norman Conquest of 1066. England will not be free until the landless poor can till the common lands. The King of Righteousness is rising to rule over the earth. Therefore, break the bonds of private property and market relations. "*Let Israel go free*, that the poor may labour the Waste land, and suck the Brests of their mother *Earth*, that they starve not."[72] If the powers do not grant this freedom, God will plague them like Egypt. But if the people are united in community, England will become the strongest land in the world. Peace and liberty will be her only necessary defenses.

Local reaction to the St. George's Hill community was hostile from the start. On various occasions, the communal experimenters were driven away, taken prisoner, beaten, their crops trampled, and their livestock stampeded. Both sides appealed to General Fairfax for help. After meeting Winstanley, Fairfax was convinced that the army should not interfere. But, by the summer, lawsuits had been lodged against the community. Winstanley was fined but not forced to pay.

In June 1649, Winstanley's *Declaration of the Bloudie and Unchristian Acting* responded to these hostilities, announcing that the nature of England's civil war had changed, from a war between competing dragons to a war against the Lamb of God:

> Victories that are got by the sword, are but victories of the Murtherer, and the joy of those victories is but the joy of Caine . . . the Dragon hath fought against the Dragon, and one part conquered another . . . and the King of Righteousness hath been a looker on, and suffered them to break each other to pieces, that his power at last might come in. But now O England know this, that thy striving now is not only Dragon against Dragon . . . Covetousness and Pride against Covetousness and Pride, but thou now begin'st to fight against the Lamb, the Dove, the meek Spirit, the power of love, and wilt not willingly suffer the Prince of Peace to have a house to dwell in upon the earth (which is humane bodies), but seekst to imprison, beat, kill, or else to withdraw all assistance of favour from them . . . a few years now will let all the world see who is strongest, love or hatred, freedom or bondage.[73]

This is a powerful statement of the apocalyptic conflict he saw unfolding around the tiny, beleaguered settlement at St. George's Hill. The nonviolent "Lamb's War" language used here is a strong precursor of the language used by Quakers during the 1650s to describe their more widespread nonviolent conflict with the dominant order.

In the autumn, the community relocated in Surrey to another commons at Cobham Manor. By the spring, ten or more communes had been started in other counties. These proto-communists were dubbed "Diggers." Sensationalized by the press, they were threatened and vandalized by locals. Few people supported their cause, and sometimes those who did were as much trouble as the vandals.[74]

During this period, Winstanley continued to publish one remarkable tract after another, interpreting the Digger experiment and appealing for freedom to continue. By March 1650, however, he seemed to see the end coming. During that month, he had his first five tracts reprinted, restating his general principles. He also published a new work, *Fire in the Bush*, one more general statement of his vision, this time addressed to the various churches of England. As Christopher Hill remarks, *Fire in the Bush* may obliquely acknowledge defeat, but not surrender.[75] Winstanley reiterates his view that standard Christian faith and practice lead people out of themselves and into the realm of imagination. They imagine God in some far-off place called heaven, rather than within. But Christ is a seed abiding within each individual. "This Seed is he, that leads mankinde into Truth, making every one to seeke the preservation and peace of others, as of themselves; This teaches man inwardly to know the nature and necessity of every body."[76] The language here echoes Boehme and Saltmarsh, but also foreshadows the extensive seed language of Fox, Penington, and other early Quaker writers.

As Christ the seed is risen up within, "Mankinde begins to enter into himselfe againe, and to enjoy rest, and peace, and Life within, which is the resurrection of Christ."[77] This rest from contention for power and wealth reveals Christ's nature as the only true Leveller:

> When mankinde once sees, that his teacher and ruler is within him; then what need is there of a teacher [clergy] and ruler without; they will easily cast off their burden. ... Therefore you Souldiers, and you great Powers of the Earth, you need not feare that the Levellers will conquer you by the sword; I doe not mean the fighting Levellers, for they be your selves; but I meane Christ levelling; who fights against you, by the sword of Love, patience and truth...for Christ came not to destroy but to save.[78]

Thus, Winstanley by no means retreats from his apocalyptic annunications of the previous two years. *Fire in the Bush* is strongly critical of the clerical establishment. The clergy's teaching not only keeps people alienated from the true spiritual authority within them; it also upholds the economic, legal, and political institutions that oppress the nation. His renewed attack upon the clerical establishment may have been inspired in part by the leading role of local clergy at Cobham against the Digger community. Winstanley concludes by asserting that the parceling out of creation into private property is the greatest sin. The second sin, intimately related to the first, is to seize the earth by violence and then make laws to defend and hoard the land against the needs of others.[79] He dismisses England's laws as "the declarative will of Conquerours."[80]

In a manner befitting the alienated religious imagination of the commune's neighbors, the group was finally driven off and its site destroyed on Easter Sunday, 1650. The commune had never amounted to more than forty to fifty individuals. They had lived in family units, with family dwellings and household items understood to be private property.

So, at age forty-one, Winstanley withdrew from this period of increasingly intense activity during 1648-50. While his experiment in Surrey had inspired a smattering of like-minded communes, it had not galvanized the groundswell from below that he had prophesied. Still, the experience had generated further reflections he felt the need to publish in one more major statement. As Aylmer concludes,[81] the Digger experience apparently convinced Winstanley that, without governmental support, God's new order had no chance against mob violence, legal harassment, and clerical agitation. He now sought to balance his message of inner regeneration and his grassroots initiative with a proposal for governmental reformation.

In early 1652, *The Law of Freedom* appeared, a platform for the restoration of "true magistracy" in England, composed from notes Winstanley had made over the past two years. Its preface, dated November 5, 1651, was addressed to Oliver Cromwell. By this time, Cromwell had emerged as the key political actor in England. Winstanley could not have seriously expected the general to support a communist design of government. Still, like other radicals in the 1650s, Winstanley tried to appeal to Cromwell's well-known penchant to find God's hand in human affairs. Consequently, *The Law of Freedom* loads the weight of history on Cromwell's shoulders, claiming that God has honored him as no man since Moses, to become the leader of a people who have cast out Pharoah, the Norman conqueror. The task ahead is to restore English land and liberties to oppressed commoners. Events have shown that the key obstacle to this liberation has been not the king but the clerical and legal establishment. "Kingly power" thus remains, even without the king. The monarchies of the earth will "laugh up their sleeves" to see a *commonwealth* that operates by their rules. To Winstanley's mind, Parliament's acts of 1649—the abolition of monarchy and the creation of the English Commonwealth—mandated a profoundly new frame for society.

What follows is a comprehensive vision of English society inspired primarily by the Bible's description of Israel in Canaan before the Davidic monarchy. Winstanley observes that, while Israel was a tribal commonwealth, it was a terror to all nations, as a true English commonwealth would be. But when the leaders of Israel became proud and covetous, they forsook unity. As Isaiah had prophesied, the apostasy of the leaders was to bring ruin to the nation as a whole.

The Law of Freedom elucidates the larger political vision Winstanley had partially sketched in earlier writings. We find here a government based upon common treasury, rather than market economy. Family units remain intact, and in fact become the primary building blocks of the order, as they were in tribal Israel. Winstanley assumes the patriarchal family unit, in which the father is leader and representative to larger organizational units. Various local leaders include peacemakers (mediators who replace lawyers in the new order), overseers of the storehouses, and roving elders. Local governments in turn are aggregated under county governments, which take their place under a national, parliamentary government (with representatives elected annually). Despite his earlier pacifist affirmations, Winstanley sees an armed force as necessary to protect a free commonwealth from being retaken by oppressors within or overrun by invading armies from without.

His idea of parish life is intriguing. Ministers would be elected annually. Their role would be much like the Levites of ancient Israel, to read the laws of the land to the people on a weekly Sabbath. He would forbid any expansion beyond simple reading, as preaching tends to cloud minds. In addition to ministers reading the law, local experts would be appointed to speak on subjects of recent technical advancement or other areas of useful knowledge. Churches would be allowed, but would have no place in this governmental structure.

As Hill concludes, Winstanley's experience had taught him that England's transformation would not be as sudden as he had first believed. The "rudeness of the people," combined with the distracting pseudo-liberation of Ranters and other libertines, suggested that structural reform was necessary to enforce a change in consciousness. As in ancient Israel, "the law was added" to deal with the people's hardness of heart.[82]

Winstanley's final work is not written as clearly or as compellingly as his earlier pieces. While the ideas carry forward, they are not driven

by the same sense of imminent expectation. *The Law of Freedom* is by
no means as bitter as Walwyn's parting shot in 1649, nor as grim a
statement on the human condition as Thomas Hobbes' *Leviathan*, also
published in 1652; but it does reflect the darkening horizon most people
in England experienced by that time.

Thereafter, Winstanley dropped out of public view. He moved with
his wife to Hertfordshire, where he became an overseer and rent
collector for an eccentric aristocratic prophetess.[83] After his first wife
died in 1664, Winstanley married Elizabeth Stanley and moved back to
London in 1665, eventually becoming a grain broker.

The Quaker movement was just emerging as a recognizable phenomenon in the North during 1652. When Quaker preachers began to arrive
in London during the summer of 1654, Winstanley attended their meetings. In a letter dated that August, the Quaker missionary Edward
Burrough reported that "Winstandley says he believes we are sent to
perfect that worke which fell in their handes. He hath been with us."[84]
There is no information indicating how long or how extensively his
involvement with Friends continued. He was buried among Quakers
after his death in 1676. Christopher Hill finds it hard to imagine
Winstanley would have thrown his lot in with Quakers, concluding,
"where else could he go after it became clear that Christ was not going
to rise in Charles II's England?"[85]

Certainly, Friends did not arrive at positions as radical as Winstanley's.
Nor did they ever write any governmental platform as extensive as
The Law of Freedom. According to some of the earliest anti-Quaker
publications, some Friends advocated the abolition of property.[86] But
no early Quaker writer made a clear statement to that effect.[87] Friends
were not the ultimate radicals of the English Revolution. Nevertheless,
it is intriguing to ponder what Winstanley recognized in the Quaker
movement. It may well be that he saw the movement providing a crucial
middle term between his valiant attempt at local communism and his
utopian model for a democratic commonwealth. As I tried to show in
my previous study, *The Covenant Crucified*,[88] the Quaker Lamb's War of
the 1650s was a exponentially expanding network of preachers, agitators,
and local worship groups. It could not be bullied out of existence like an
isolated commune; nor did it resort to begging Oliver Cromwell to enact
its political ideas. The Quaker symbolic warfare of street preaching, plain
language, simple dress, advocacy for the poor, and attacks upon the

conspicuous consumption of the rich was not as radical *in principle* as the Digger renunciation of private property, but *in practice* its effects were much more threatening to the establishment. The Quaker genius for integrating Leveller, Digger, and Seeker ideas into practical moral-ity, symbolic codes, and a program of action made Friends a more pervasive challenge to entrenched interests than any of these precursors had been during the 1640s.

In 1678, two years after Winstanley's death, Thomas Comber pub-lished anonymously *Christianity No Enthusiasm.* An attack upon the abiding scourge of Quakerism, the book offers perhaps the first orga-nized research into its formative influences. Comber cites published state-ments of Friends to establish that the movement really began in 1648, not 1652, as most supposed. While he lists many precursors, including Schwenckfeld, Boehme, the Familists, and Seekers, he characterizes Quakers as an "off-set" of the Levellers. In the North of England where they started, Friends "sucked in" many heretical groups and ideas. "But the very draughts and even Body of Quakerism [lies] in the several Works of Gerrard Winstanley, a zealous Leveller, wherein he tells of the rising of new Times and Dispensations." Comber lists a full page of parallels between Winstanley's ideas and Quaker preaching. He suggests that Friends carried on Winstanley's economic levelling principles as best they could, by addressing everyone with the plain language of "thee" and "thou" and by refusing to use titles and other forms of civil respect. He even alleges that "at first they were for Community . . . and George Fox said, 'no man ought to be above another'" during a trial at Lancaster in 1652.[89]

But, Comber notes, most Quaker opinions are expressed in negative terms—"touch not, taste not, handle not"—these are "the distinctive Shibboleths of the sect." By the time Comber wrote in the 1670s, Quaker behavioral codes had indeed begun to take on a more definite sectarian tone and to exhibit some of the legalism that Comber describes. It is probably that long-term tendency that Hill is prone to impose on the Quaker movement from the start, and thus find Winstanley's allegiance puzzling. But during the first decade of the movement, while the politi-cal and religious destiny of England was still undecided, Quaker speech and dress codes, along with their simple lifestyle and confrontational public witness, implied open-ended, revolutionary meanings. As we noted earlier, the preaching of early Friends emphasized communal standards of morality and solidarity. The Quaker movement sought to build a network of communities engaged in radical spiritual and social practices, a middle term between personal morality and public policy. The failures of the Levellers and the Diggers (or True Levellers) by 1650 showed that true revolutionary transformation could occur only through the development of such a network.

It is difficult to establish Winstanley's writings as a formative influence upon early Friends.[90] No early Quaker leader wrote of acquaintance with Winstanley or even with his writings (other than the brief mention by Burrough cited above). George Fox was not one to admit the influence of any human source upon his vision, but instead insisted upon God's direct revelation to him. Still, the more one compares Fox's writings to those of radicals from the 1640s, the clearer it becomes that he was a powerful synthesizer of that decade's many powerful insights. It seems almost inevitable that Winstanley's writings, along with those of Saltmarsh, Erbury, and others, were an important part of that synthesis. George Sabine, the first modern collector and editor of Winstanley's writings, has found the resonances between Winstanley and early Quakerism most compelling.[91]

Perhaps the most important congruence between Winstanley and early Friends is the new, aggressive attack mounted by both against the churches. While Seekers generally just walked away from the churches, and Levellers courted the political support of the gathered congregations, it was Winstanley who focused the most devastating attack upon all existing forms of the church, and against the clerical establishment most of all. His preaching of a fundamentally different sense of community, based upon a profoundly different order of religious knowledge, anticipates the Quaker critiques of the 1650s. Early Friends furthered Winstanley's insight that the churches were the chief obstacle to social transformation on all fronts. But whereas Winstanley confronted the clerical establishment only in print, early Friends confronted clergy face-to-face, in parish churches all over England.

In *Fire in the Bush*, Winstanley wrote, "Stand still, and you shall see the downfall of *Pharaoh* and his company."[92] We hear Schwenckfeld's Spiritualist position restated in its most politically radical implications. Winstanley followed the *Stillstand* through Seekerism and into territory he was to chart virtually alone. Through the unmediated Spiritualism of inward communion with Christ the living Word, he explored a new spirituality that was materially engaged with all creation. From rejection of the eucharistic wafer, Winstanley moved to the renunciation of property. From rejection of a clerical teaching establishment, he envisioned the abolition of all forms of class privilege and legalized exploitation.

As we have noted, Winstanley's descent from the mountaintop of such breathtaking vision was not graceful. But there was no way for him to reenter an alienated society without jarring self-contradiction. Thus, the prophet of a propertyless society withdrew to become a rent-collector. As the turbulent 1640s came to a close and England's new rulers moved to consolidate power, not all Seekers accepted defeat and disillusion so quietly, however. We now move on to the Ranters.

Notes

1. William Walwyn, *The Vanitie of the Present Churches* (1649), 40-41.
2. Quoted as the epigraph to Harold Bloom's *The American Religion: The Emergence of the Post-Christian Nation* (New York: Simon and Schuster, 1992).
3. See George H. Sabine's reflections on Winstanley and the Levellers in the Introduction to *Works of Gerrard Winstanley* (Ithaca: Cornell University Press, 1941), 2-3.
4. Most available biographical information has been derived here from the Introduction to *The Writings of William Walwyn*, ed. Jack R. McMichael and Barbara Taft (Athens: University of Georgia Press, 1989).
5. William Walwyn, *The Vanitie of the Present Churches* (1649), 30-31.
6. William Walwyn, *Tolleration Justified* (1646), 14.
7. G. E. Aylmer, ed. *The Levellers in the English Revolution* (Ithaca: Cornell University Press, 1975), 19; Murray Tolmie, *The Triumph of the Saints: Separate Churches of London, 1616-1649* (Cambridge: University Press), 150.
8. McMichael and Taft, *Walwyn*, 13-14.
9. See William Walwyn, *A Whisper in the Ear of Mr.Thomas Edwards, Minister* (1646), 3; and *Walwyns Just Defence* (1649), 8.
10. Tolmie, *Triumph*, 150.
11. Thomas Edwards, *Gangraena* (1646), Part 1, 38.
12. Edwards, *Gangraena*, Part 1, 38.
13. Edward, *Gangraena*, Part 1, 58.
14. Walwyn, *Whisper*, 10.
15. Walwyn, *Whisper*, 11.
16. Edwards, *Gangraena*, Part 2, 23.
17. Edwards, *Gangraena*, Part 2, 21.
18. Edwards, *Gangraena*, Part 1, 57.
19. Aylmer, *Levellers*, 14ff; and Tolmie, *Triumph*, 144-72. I am indebted mainly to Aylmer for this summary of Leveller leaders and activity during the 1640s.

20. The actual extent of the Levellers' proposed expansion of the electoral franchise has been debated. It would have mandated somewhere between a two-fold and five-fold increase in participation. It would have continued to exclude women, indentured servants, and others at the margins; but a much broader range of the socioeconomic spectrum would have been brought into England's political process.
21. This summary is derived from Christopher Hill, *The Experience of Defeat: Milton and Some Contemporaries* (New York: Viking, 1984), 29-30.
22. Aylmer, *Levellers*, 38.
23. Quoted by Hill, *Defeat*, 31.
24. Aylmer, *Levellers*, 48-49.
25. Tolmie, *Triumph*, 144,151,171-72.
26. J. F. McGregor, "The Baptists: Fount of All Heresy," in *Radical Religion in the English Revolution*, ed. McGregor and Reay, (Oxford: University Press, 1984), 51-55.
27. Reprinted in McMichael and Taft, *Walwyn*, 311-333.
28. Walwyn, *Vanitie*, 11.
29. Walwyn, *Vanitie*, 8-9.
30. Walwyn, *Vanitie*, 13.
31. Walwyn, *Vanitie*, 16.
32. Walwyn, *Vanitie*, 16.
33. Walwyn, *Vanitie*, 17.
34. Walwyn, *Vanitie*, 18.
35, Walwyn, *Vanitie*, 14.
36. Walwyn, *Vanitie*, 18-24.
37. Walwyn, *Vanitie*, 32.
38. Walwyn, *Vanitie*, 47-48.
39. Brian Manning, "The Levellers and Religion," in *Radical Religion,* 67-68.
40. Morton, *Ranters*, 14-15.
41. See John Lilburne, *The Resurrection of John Lilburne* (1656). For a brief treatment of Lilburne's Quaker convincement in 1655, see my recent study, *The Covenant Crucified: Quakers and the Rise of Capitalism* (Wallingford, Pa.: Pendle Hill, 1995), 101-02
42. See "Richard Overton" in *The Dictionary of National Biography* (Oxford: University Press, 1921), 14:1279-81.
43. From the title page of Walwyn's *Physick for Families* (1674).
44. See Christopher Hill, *The Religion of Gerrard Winstanley, Past and Present* Supplement No. 5 (Oxford: Past and Present Society, 1978), 23. There were ten poor harvests from the last years of Charles I to the first years of Cromwell's Protectorate. Food prices soared by 50% between 1646 and 1650. See H. Larry Ingle, *First Among Friends: George Fox and the Creation of Quakerism* (Oxford: University Press, 1994), 11.
45. For biographical information on Winstanley, I draw chiefly upon the Introduction to George H. Sabine, *Works*; and G. E. Aylmer, "The Religion of Gerrard Winstanley," in *Radical Religion,* 91-119.
46. Gerrard Winstanley, *The New Law of Righteousness* (1649), 2; reprinted in Sabine, *Works*, 155.

47. Gerrard Winstanley, *The Saints Paradice* (1648), Preface. The tract is abstracted in Sabine, *Works*, 93-96.
48. Winstanley, *Paradice*, Preface.
49. Winstanley, *Paradice*, Ch. 3.
50. Winstanley, *Paradice*, Ch. 5.
51. Winstanley, *Paradice*, Ch. 5. Of course, the *logos* that created all things in John 1 can be translated "reason" as well as "word." But whether Winstanley would have known any Greek or intended a Johannine overtone here cannot be established.
52. Sabine, *Works*, 41.
53. Sabine, *Works*, 24-25.
54. Gerrard Winstanley, *The Breaking of the Day of God* (1648), Preface.
55. Winstanley, *Breaking*, 114-115.
56. George Fox, *Journal,* John L. Nickalls, ed. (Cambridge: University Press, 1952), 22.
57. Winstanley, *Breaking*, 126-27.
58. Gerrard Winstanley, *The New Law of Righteousness* (1649), Preface, dated January 26.
59. Winstanley, *New Law*, 3; Sabine, *Works*, 156.
60. Winstanley, *New Law*, 9-11; Sabine, *Works*, 161-63.
61. Winstanley, *New Law*, 36.
62. Winstanley, *New Law*, 38.
63. Winstanley, *New Law*, 38-39.
64. Winstanley, *New Law*, 42.
65. Winstanley, *New Law*, 39.
66. Winstanley, *New Law*, 50-51.
67. Winstanley, *New Law*, 54.
68. Winstanley, *New Law*, 99.
69. Winstanley, *New Law*, 103.
70. Winstanley, *New Law*, 66.
71. Gerrard Winstanley, *The True Levellers Standard Advanced* (1649), 11; Sabine, *Works*, 255.
72. Winstanley, *Standard*, 22.
73. Gerrard Wiinstanley, *A Declaration of the Bloudie and Unchristian Acting of William Star and John Taylor of Walton* (1649), 4-5.
74. See Winstanley's *A Vindication* (1650), in which he denounces the Ranters, whose immorality he detests, for trying to associate themselves with the Digger cause. Further, some Ranters had allegedly tried to raise money in support of the Diggers, funds which they had kept for themselves. We will look further at Winstanley's attack upon Ranters in our next chapter.
75. Christopher Hill, *The Religion of Gerrard Winstanley* (Oxford: Past and Present Society, 1978), 25.
76. Gerrard Winstanley, *Fire in the Bush*, 6.
77. Winstanley, *Fire,* 21.
78. Winstanley, *Fire*, 33-34.
79. Winstanley, *Fire*, 77.
80. Winstanley, *Fire*, 23.

81. Aylmer, "Winstanley," 111.

82. Hill, *Winstanley*, 41-42.

83. Aylmer, "Winstanley," 114.

84. Edward Burrough to Margaret Fell, August 1654, Caton MSS., 3/63, Friends House, London.

85. Hill, *Winstanley*, 51. Also see Hill, *Defeat*, 40.

86. See, for example, Francis Higginson's *A Brief Relation of the Irreligion of the Northern Quakers* (1653).

87. Benjamin Nicholson's *A Blast from the Lord* (1653) is a stinging attack upon wealth, especially the luxuries of the clergy and magistrates in particular, insisting that "the earth is the Lord's and the fulness thereof." But he does not state a clear principle that all things should be held in common. See Gwyn, *Covenant*, 142.

88. Gwyn, *Covenant*, Chs. 3 and 4.

89. I cannot confirm that remark from Fox's relation of the Lancaster trial in his *Journal* (134-35), but it is not unthinkable that he would have said it, especially in his early years.

90. Ingle, *First Among Friends*, 15 notes that Digger communes sprang up in Nottinghamshire and Leicestershire, where Fox was moving, in 1649-50. Moreover, Nathaniel Stephens, minister of Fox's home parish in Drayton-in-the-Clay, complained of the influence of Winstanley's writings. But Fox spent little time in his home village by the time Winstanley's writings appeared.

91. Sabine, "Introduction" to *Works*, 8-10, 33-49.

92. Winstanley, *Fire*, 57.

CHAPTER 6

ABIEZER COPPE, LAURENCE CLARKSON, AND JOSEPH SALMON
THE RANTER ECLIPSE

Eternal plagues consume you all, rot, sink and damn your bodies and souls into devouring fire, where none but those that walk uprightly can enter. Sirs, I wish you damnable well, because I dearly love you; the Lord grant we may know the worth of hell, that we may forever scorn heaven: For my own part I am ascended far above all heavens, yet I fill all things, and laugh in my sleeve to think what's coming. . . . [1]

—Joseph Salmon
Letter from Coventry Gaol
April 3, 1650

In 1938, Jean-Paul Sartre published *Nausea,* the first existentialist novel. Writing during ominous times in Europe, Sartre portrayed a man who enters a crisis of despair. He confronts the sheer terror of naked existence, stripped of all the formal qualities that normally distract human attention. In that moment, existence is swallowed up into nothingness, an all-consuming void that renders everything absurd. His mind searches in vain for meaning, for something to grasp. But he finds only a nauseating abyss, or impasse. Most of the novel follows the protagonist's failed attempts to restore meaning through travel, intellectual pursuits, contemplation, and sexual liaison. None of these helps. While the crisis is eventually overcome, Sartre portrays the protagonist's suffering more compellingly than his recuperation. Still, as Hayden Carruth observes, *Nausea* is important for its evocation of the 20th-century crisis of meaning—even if it skirts the line between jest and sermon.[2]

The Ranter phenomenon that erupted in 1649 combined many of the same elements: political despair, a nauseating experience of the absurd, nihilistic behavior, and language that is both silly and profound. The Ranters' outrageous antics earned denunciations from all sides and government repression. Their rhetoric, as the epigraph above illustrates, combined blind rage, nihilistic glee and, religious parody. Until recent years, scholarship agreed with the Puritan consensus, calling Ranters "degenerate," "the dregs of the Seeker movement."[3] But the Ranter moment is important to understand, particularly in relation to Seeker spirituality and the failure of its political hope in 1649.

In Chapter 3, we noted the queasiness that came over the English scene by the mid-1640s, as the proliferation of dissident groups overshadowed Presbyterian and Independent struggles for a national church establishment. The specter of religious *commodification* became particularly evident as Baptists openly competed for adherents in a free-market style. Conservatives like Thomas Edwards sought to force this chaotic growth back into the container of state-enforced religious uniformity. Radicals, caught up in the swirl of events and ideas, went reeling out of all religious affiliation, seeking new foundations that would go deeper, below the shifting sands of formal doctrine and observance. The Seeker John Webster wrote that religious observances are a veil preventing human consciousness from seeing its true condition. Once the veil is rent, the individual looks down and within to discern a bottomless pit of smoke and darkness, sin and misery.[4] For many, this experience of spiritual vertigo continued for years.

Despite such disorientation, Seekers clung desperately to the hope that the army or the Levellers would establish an open political space enabling the religious search to continue. They firmly believed that, if given time, some new religious consensus would emerge, one that would not require the hypocritical enforcement of religion upon the human conscience. But the rigors of such intensive spiritual search and political tumult inevitably took their toll. While the figures we have studied thus far did not succumb to the moral collapse of "libertinism," their antinomian preaching provided an excuse for some to cast off piety altogether. For example, Dorothy Howgill, who became a Quaker in 1652, wrote of reading Saltmarsh's *Free-Grace* in the 1640s. For a while, she took the emphasis upon Christ's death for sinners *as* sinners to be "liberty to walk in sin."[5] In Chapter 8, we will consider the testimony of other early Friends whose earnest seeking gave way to "wild and wanton" periods. It is important to remember that these men and women were "living on the edge" during a period when an entire nation was drunkenly lurching.

By 1649, the collapse of political hope had combined with the spiritual exhaustion of the Seeker quest in a number of the movement's most advanced spirits. Seeker queasiness turned into an outright *nausea* of despair, rage, resentment, and—paradoxically—nihilistic celebration. As such, the Ranter phenomenon is best understood, according to J. F. McGregor, as "more of a religious mood than a movement."[6] Ranters apparently made no attempt to organize, though their exhibitionist style naturally made group activity safer and more fun. The name "Ranter" was a hostile epithet, referring to their nonstop gales of railing, swearing, singing, or even whistling. But names they preferred for themselves included the "the Universality," "the Mad Crew,"[7] and "My One Flesh."[8] For the raging and brilliantly anarchic style of the Ranters at its most florid, we must begin with the individual who probably catalyzed the Ranter scene in 1649.

ABIEZER COPPE

Born in 1619 in Warwick, Abiezer Coppe evidently came from a comfortable background. He entered All Souls College, Oxford, in 1636 but soon became known for "grossly immoral" behavior.[9] Though he began as a loyal member of the Church of England, he soon inclined toward Presbyterianism and left school at the outbreak of the civil war. By 1646, he had turned Particular Baptist and was a successful preacher among the army garrison in Warwickshire. He later claimed to have baptized some 7,000 souls during that period, which also included fourteen weeks in prison.

Like many Seekers, Coppe abandoned Baptism by 1648. But he was too ebullient a character to remain long in the melancholy state of most Seekers. He began to associate with Richard Coppin, whose advanced Spiritualism, though still engaged with orthodox Christian doctrine, was moving toward a kind of Neoplatonist mysticism. Coppin's *Divine Teachings* (1649), for which Coppe wrote a Preface, shares with many Seeker writings the strong sense of divine indwelling, the saint as the temple of the Lord. But Coppin went further, tending to identify the saint with God.[10] Moreover, he advanced a monistic sense of God as a "fountain" from which all things sprang and to which all things shall return.[11] Here Spiritualism becomes more overtly metaphysical, going beyond the experiential or existential emphasis that earlier Seekers had maintained (recall the contrasts between the mystical Eckhart and his student, Tauler, in Chapter 2). Coppin later disclaimed Ranterism and even complained that he had been "persecuted" by pestering Ranters.[12] Moreover, his discourse is quite intellectual, nearly systematic, in contrast to the chaotic, expressionistic style of most Ranter texts.[13] Nevertheless, his *Divine Teachings* became a key source-book for Coppe and other Ranter writers.

Jerome Friedman describes Coppe as "ecstatic, spectacular, bizarre, and probably insane."[14] His first literary bombshell came early in 1649 with *Some Sweet Sips of some Spirituall Wine*, published by Giles Calvert. The title page is a call to "hasten to Spirituall Canaan (the Living Lord) which is a land of large *Liberty*, the House of *Happiness*." Coppe's prose contains many themes and biblical motifs in common with earlier Seeker writings, but without coherent development. Instead, one encounters a medley of ecstatic outbursts, incantatory riffs, and mirthful word-plays. Coppe calls all to

> Awake, awake, and watch; Seeke ye *Seekers*, Seeke ye, *Seeke* ye the *Lord* . . . Seeke him above, he is not *below*. (*He is not here, he is risen*—) . . . What? Is it Love, Sincerity, and Zeale mixt with weakness that sent thee, (*poor Mary*) to seeke him in the *Sepulcher*? . . . O that the love, sincerity, and zeale of true *Maries* indeed might be prevented with unexpected glory, and their weakness swallowed up in strength, death in victory. . . . [15]

We can hear some of the same annunciatory tone that marked Saltmarsh's *Sparkles of Glory*, Wilkinson's *Saints Travel,* and Winstanley's *New Law of Righteousness*. There is a sense of joyful breakthrough, together with a note of impatience with the sorrowful posture of many Seekers, who were looking in the wrong direction for God's new revelation.

The life in the Spirit beyond the law leads Coppe to startling new conclusions. Utilizing the typology of Abraham's two sons (Gal. 4:21-31), he announces that "the son of the *freewoman* is a Libertine . . . born after the Spirit . . . hissed at and hated."[16] From there, he shifts later to the two sons of the parable of the Prodigal Son. The younger son's redemption comes by way of "riotous liveing" which continues until his substance is exhausted, hastening him home to "the fatted calfe, ring, shoes, mirth, and Musicke, etc. which is the *Lords Supper indeed*."[17] Meanwhile, the elder brother "knows not what this meaneth, but is angry, and dogged, puffs and pouts, is sullen, snuffs, swells and censures without doors."[18] One suspects that Coppe's profligate life had already started to elicit censure from his Puritan neighbors.

Finally, we hear an echo of Coppin's Neoplatonism in the affirmation that the

> enmity within, and without shall be slaine,— Then shall all channels runne into the Ocean, live in the *river*, returne to the *Fountaine*, from whence they came: recreating themselves there . . . all that He made, which is *exceeding good*, shall returne to the (summum bonum) the chiefest good. . . . "[19]

Sweet Sips represents the first, heady draughts of a strange new wine Coppe now imbibed.

But by the middle of the year, perhaps prompted by the collapse of political hope, or perhaps simply following the course of spiraling mania, Coppe's delighted banter turned to raging fulminations. He experienced some kind of inner apocalyptic crisis that summer. As he would later describe it, his family disowned him and his wife became alienated (perhaps owing to his behavior).

> I was utterly plagued, consumed, damned, rammed, and sunke into nothing, into the bowels of the still Eternity (my mothers wombe) out of which I came naked, and whitherto I returned again naked. And lying a while there, rapt up in silence, at length . . . I heard with my outward eare (to my apprehension) a most terrible thunder-clap, and after that a second. And upon the second thunder-clap, which was exceeding terrible, I saw a great body of light, like the light of the Sun . . . whereupon with exceeding trembling and amazement on the flesh, and with joy unspeakable in spirit, I clapt my hands, and cryed out, *Amen, Halelujah, Haleluja, Amen.*

The voice of God within assured him, "Fear not, I will take thee up into mine everlasting Kingdom. But thou shalt (first) drinke a bitter cup, a bitter cup, a bitter cup." He was then commissioned:

> Go up to London, to London, that great City, write, write,
> write. And behold I writ, and lo a hand was sent to me, and a
> roll of a book was therein, which this fleshly hand would
> have put wings to, before the time. Whereupon it was snatcht
> out of my hand, & the Roll thrust into my mouth; and I eat it
> up, and filled my bowels with it, (Eze. 2.8; 3.1,2,3) where it
> was as bitter as worm-wood; and it lay broiling, and burning
> in my stomack, till I brought it forth in this forme. . . .[20]

That nauseating bitterness first erupted in the streets of London that summer of 1649, as Coppe careened around, preaching to the poor, charging at wealthy pedestrians, assaulting them with oracular deprecations, proclaiming the day of the Lord.[21] He preached in the nude at least once. His sermons were sometimes comprised of long chains of oaths. He recommended the swearing of oaths as therapeutic to Puritan consciences burdened by sin. This fit with his general belief that redemption comes through saturation in sin, rather than avoidance of it.[22]

A Fiery Flying Roll, published in two parts at the beginning of 1650, summarizes much of what Coppe was preaching and doing in London over the previous months. There, he raises the fallen standard of the Levellers, but makes it clear that they were "but shadowes of most terrible, yet great and glorious good things to come. Behold,

> I the eternall God, the Lord of Hosts, who am that mighty
> Leveller, am comming (yea even at the doores) to Levell in
> good earnest, to Levell to some purpose, to Levell with a
> witnesse, to Levell the Hills with the Valleyes, and to lay the
> Mountaines low. . . . And the LOFTINESSE of man shall be
> bowed down, and the haughtinesse of men shall be laid low.
> And the Lord ALONE shall be exalted in that day, and the
> Idols he shall utterly abolish. . . . And the Prime levelling, is
> laying low the Mountaines, and levelling the Hils in man.
> But this is not all. *For lo I come (saith the Lord) with a
> vengeance, to levell also your Honour, Riches, etc. to staine
> the pride of all your glory, and to bring into contempt all the
> Honourable (both persons and things) upon the earth, Isa.
> 23.9.* For this Honour, Nobility, Gentility, Propriety, Super-
> fluity, etc. hath (without contradiction) been the Father of

> hellish horrid pride, arrogance . . . yea the cause of all the
> blood that hath been shed, from the blood of righteous Abel,
> to the blood of the last Levellers that were shot to death.[23]

The experience of the Levellers and Diggers had shown that not only the political superstructure but the entire social infrastructure of wealth, power, and privilege stood in the way of true justice in England. The attack upon wealth and honor, and the emphasis upon spiritual levelling as the primary field of conflict anticipates much of the Quaker social witness of the next decade.

But Coppe's rage and political resentment gave rise to a logic opposite to the Quakers' moral austerity. An upside-down Ranter morality aimed to scandalize and rattle the Puritan establishment:

> Not by sword; we (holily) scorne to fight for anything; we
> had as live be dead drunk every day of the weeke, and lye
> with whores i'th market place; and account these as good
> actions as taking the poor abused, enslaved ploughmans
> money from him . . . for killing of men.[24]

Coppe fulminated against the burdens – tithes, war taxes, free quartering of soldiers – that the new regime laid upon struggling Englishmen. Yet, in contrast to Winstanley's constructive intitiatives, Coppe seemed content to rage against the powers and enact an inverted Puritan morality. He prophesied that God's liberation would not be achieved by the hollow victories of the civil war; rather, "God hath chosen base things, and things that are despised, to confound—the things [that] are" (see I Cor. 1:28). Family values and acts of piety, the things that "are" in standard Puritan piety, were thus to be confounded with "base" things.[25] Accordingly, Coppe set out to perform a series of prophetic signs in London: hugging and kissing a man's disfigured face, bowing before beggars, cripples, and rogues, giving away all his money, exchanging intimacies with "Gypseys and Gaolbirds." He summarizes:

> Yea, could you imagine that the quintessence of all visible
> beauty, should be extracted and made up into one huge beauty,
> it would appear to be meer deformity to that beauty, which
> through base things I have been lifted up into . . . which is
> my crown and joy, my life and love. . . . Though I have con-

cubines without number, which I cannot be without, yet this
is my spouse, my love, my dove, my fair one.[26]

Through this highly eliptical language, Coppe expresses his mad faith
that, by some divine alchemy, his prophetic acts will transform the
weak and despised, the base metals of society, into God's vessels of
glory. Friedman classifies Coppe among the Ranter "sexual libertines,"
of whom there were doubtless many. But Coppe's own words leave
the case ambiguous. The mention of "concubines" here appears to be
metaphorical.

Anyone airing such language in Puritan England was unlikely to
remain at large very long. Coppe was arrested and jailed at Coventry
within a month of the release of A *Fiery Flying Roll*. On February 1,
Parliament ordered all available copies burned. Presbyterians published
A Blow at the Root in March, finding this new "perfect Libertinisme" to
be the final fruits of Separation, which "perfects itself in Seeking, being
above the Ordinances, and Questioning everything revealed in the Scriptures, and in high Raptures and Revelation."[27]

By this time, a full-fledged Ranter phenomenon was exploding in
London and elsewhere. Typical Ranter tenets included: God is present
in every creature; the devil is only the "backside" of God; sin exists
only in the imagination; good and evil are one; in the Spirit, all women
and all men become one woman and one man, rendering all sexual
relations monogamous. Some rejected the Bible as contradictory and
false. Wild Ranter gatherings were reported, in which drunkenness, nude
dancing, and free sex celebrated liberation from moral law.

In June 1650, Parliament appointed a committee "to consider a way
for suppression of the obscene, licentous and impious practices used by
persons under the pretense of Liberty, Religious or otherwise." The committee investigated "several abominable practices of a sect called
Ranters." A Blasphemy Act was passed in August, punishing the public
espousal of various Ranter doctrines and practices. A six-month term of
imprisonment was authorized for first offenses; for a second offense,
banishment; banished Ranters returning to England would be executed.
Only "persons distempered in their brains" were exempted.

Evidently, Coppe was deemed mentally competent. He languished in
prison nearly a year before publishing a partial recantation in January
1651. His statement was too equivocal for the authorities, so in June he

published a fuller statement, *Copp's Return to the wayes of TRUTH*. Most of the text is taken up with a point-by-point repudiation of specific heresies. But most interesting is the Preface,[29] which describes the genesis of his Ranter episode, for which he says he is "exceedingly sorry." In classic Seeker fashion, he utilizes the typology of Israel in the wilderness, relating how God "took me by the hand . . . pitching and removing my tents from place to place. Setting, and seating me in various forms." Up to a point, this had been a spiritually refining quest. He mentions his high reputation and fourteen weeks of imprisonment as a Baptist.

But after a while, having "thought that I was shown a more excellent way," he left the Baptists, and was fed with spiritual "dainties, that the tongue of men & angels cannot express. Unfathomable, unspeakable mysteries and glories." But while in that state, "the terrible, notable day of the Lord, stole upon me unawares," a day of heat that flesh cannot withstand.

> And the cup of the Lords right hand, was put into mine hand, etc. Hab. 2. And it was filled brim full of intoxicating wine, and I drank it off, even the dreggs thereof. Whereupon being mad drunk, I so strangely spake, and acted I know not what. To the amazement of some. To the sore perplexity of others. And to the great grief of others. For I was (really, in very deed) besides my self. [30]

This sounds like the period from *Sweet Sips* to *Flying Roll*. He writes that he lost his reason, even his very humanity. "But these daies are ended."

He promises to go home to his wife and children and behave himself. As for sparking a popular revolt of anarchistic nihilism, he admits that there are "many spurious brats, lately born. . . . Some of them (indeed) look somewhat like my children." But he will indulge none of them. "I am resolved (by the grace of God) to give no offence (either in life or doctrine) to any."[31]

Abiezer Coppe toned down after his release from prison later in 1651. But he still moved in Ranter circles for some years. While under detention in London in 1655, George Fox was beset by Coppe and some of his associates. Fox grew impatient with their drinking, smoking, and exalted language and asked them to move to another room.[32] Later, after the Restoration, Coppe withdrew to Surrey and practiced "physic" under the name Dr. Higham (probably pronounced "i am."[33]) Other than preaching an occasional antinomian sermon, he maintained a low profile until his death in 1672.

Did Coppe suffer a from manic-depressive condition? Does his groveling recantation represent a shift to the depressive pole? The extremity of his Ranter phase makes one suspect some kind of imbalance. But there were quite a few in England who went through the same phase with him. The religious and political factors of that historical moment are too strong to ignore. We will see them played out more clearly in the saga of Joseph Salmon. We will also find in Salmon's recantation a more fully developed theological interpretation of ranting as the nauseating effects of the Lord's "cup of staggering."

But first we will examine another of the classic Ranters, one whose personal charisma and sexual exploits earned him the name "Captain of the Rant."

Laurence Clarkson

Born in Lancashire in 1615, Laurence Clarkson grew up in the Church of England. But from a fairly early age, his Puritanical conscience was afflicted by the establishment's "toleration of maypoles, dancing, rioting" on Sundays. Aged 28 when the civil war broke out, he followed the Seeker trajectory through Presbyterianism, Independency, and on to the Baptists by late 1644. He preached as a Baptist until he was imprisoned for his activity at Bury St. Edmonds in January 1645. He was visited there by William Erbury, who convinced him that baptism was a carnal ordinance and no longer valid.

When he was released after six months of detention, he immediately went to Ely, where he expected to find and follow Erbury. But Erbury was itinerating elsewhere. So Clarkson went to London, where he was sure to find more Seekers. There, he published his first tract, a Seeker statement entitled *The Pilgrimage of Saints, by the church cast out, in Christ found, seeking truth* (1646). Unfortunately, there are no extant copies of this piece, though Edwards alluded to it in *Gangraena* as a typical Seeker expression. The latter also reported on a Clarkson sermon delivered in London that year as a "Rapsody of nonsense."[35]

Clarkson continued to move restlessly, supporting himself by guest-preaching for various radical congregations. Like many other Seekers, he proclaimed of the perfecting power of the Spirit upon the saints. But secretly he suspected that "none could live without sin in this world."

> For notwithstanding I had great knowledge in the things of
> God, yet I found my heart was not right to what I pretended,
> but full of lust and vain-glory of this world.[36]

Easy notoriety and adulation led him from one place to another, and through successive sexual dalliances. None of them settled his spirit. Meanwhile, he continued to send money home to support his wife.

He became chaplain to a regiment stationed in London in 1649 and began to hear of a group calling itself "My One Flesh." Through the publisher Giles Calvert, he connected with Abiezer Coppe and other Ranters. He already had begun to believe that "there was no man could be free'd from sin, till he had acted that so called sin, as no sin." Among Ranters, he found many confirming opinions, even Scriptural proof-texts, isolated texts from New Testament letters: "nothing is unclean, but as man esteems it so" (Rom. 14:14); "to the pure all things are pure" (Titus 1:15). "Therefore," Clarkson concluded, "till you can lie with all women as one woman, and not judge it sin, you can do nothing but sin . . . so that I understood no man could attain perfection but this way . . . and Sarah Kullin being then present, did invite me to make trial of what I had expressed."[37]

Clarkson notes that while Coppe excelled at ranting and swearing, those were not his *forte*. The Song of Solomon was the principal text for his sexual path of knowledge. He soon became the focal point of many notorious Ranter "happenings"—if I may use the idiom of another period when sex, drugs, and spirituality combined recreationally. Ranter meetings were often held in ale-houses, where alcohol flowed freely, the air was thick with tobacco smoke, and free sex proceeded upstairs. Clarkson recalls that "men and women came from many parts to see my face, and hear my knowledge in these things, being restless till they were made free, as we called it." Hostile reports of the Ranter phenomenon may have exaggerated the sexual dimension. But in the circles around Clarkson, it was definitely a strong feature.

Nicotene as a stimulant used in religious meetings had been popularized first by some Baptists. Erbury evidently also found it useful. But it became best known among Ranters. For example, some years later, the Quaker Thomas Curtis wrote to George Fox of preaching to a group at

Dunstable. All the men had their pipes burning, with "smoke at their noses." Even after the meeting, he adds, they continued to smoke intensely, like swine at the trough.[39]

When an imminent government crackdown began to loom over the London meetings, Clarkson left to be with his wife for a while. But soon finding himself bored at home, he traveled with a group of Ranters to Surrey to visit Winstanley's Digger commune. Ranter celebrations offered an easier path to community; both Clarkson and Coppe advocated theft as a path toward personal redemption as well as economic justice. Clarkson tried to convince Winstanley that his Digger experiment was an act of personal aggrandizement.[40]

Winstanley reacted in March 1650 to these visitations with a blistering, eleven-point *Vindication* of his experiment against its supposed Ranter allies. He expressed his moral revulsion against Ranter covetousness, madness, gluttony, drunkenness, and "excessive copulation with women."[41] Ranters deeply offended Winstanley's strong sense of the family as the building block of social and moral order. He saw men taking pleasure with women and leaving them to deal with the consequences: "Therefore you women beware, for this ranting practice is not the restoring, but the destroying power of creation."[42] Moreover, he was disgusted by the idleness of Ranters, "wandering busibodies . . . cheating others that are simple and of a civil nature." He was particularly concerned for people of a "loving and flexible disposition wanting in strength of reason"; they were those most likely to be taken in by "this devouring Beast; the Ranting power."[43] Finally, he warned readers that some Ranters were taking up donations around the country, supposedly to aid the Diggers, but actually keeping the money for themselves.

Clarkson summarized his message in one of the principal Ranter works, *The Single Eye: All Light, no Darkness; or Light and Darkness One*, which appeared during the summer of 1650 and was a key provocation for Parliament's move against Ranters. He takes as his main text Isaiah 42:16, God's vow to "make Darkness Light before them." Clarkson posits light and darkness are two opposite powers coming from the same God, or nature:

> So that consider, though two Powers, yet they have but one womb, one birth; both Twins, both brethren, as Esau and Iaacob . . . one Flesh, one Nature yea, of the self same Nature

of God . . . Pharoah as Moses, Pilate as Jesus Christ: I say, although these be distinct, in reference to their several operations, as two streams runneth contrary ways, yet they are both of one Nature, and that from one Fountain: Herein it appeareth but a seeming opposition; instance the Tide, what striving for Victory; yet but one Water, yea and that from one Ocean. So is the case with these Powers, one opposite to the other, contending it for Victory, till at last, one overcomes another, as the Tide the stream. Thus, you may take nature from whence darknesse hath its rise, only from God.[44]

Clarkson goes on to argue that sin, either the act itself or the perception of the act as sinful, is the work of imagination. Imagination is power derived from God but does not exist in God: "so I say again, the very tittle Sin, it is only a name without substance, hath no being in God, nor in the Creature, but only by imagination: and therefore it is said; *the imaginations of your hearts are only evil continually.* [Gen. 8:21]"[45]

Accordingly, Clarkson viewed the forces dominating England as deriving their power from God, but exercising it according to their evil imaginations. In one paragraph, he obliquely but pregnantly sums up his Ranter solution to England's hopeless situation:

Being now surrounded with the black Regiment, whose Commander is the Devil, and the whole legion consisting of the imaginations of the whole Creation, I have no way to escape this Camp and bottomlesse guilt but by breaking through the Bulwark and strong hold fortified against me. So that being armed with a weapon of majesty, I doubt not but that God in me shall cast down those strong holds and imaginations, yea every thing that exalteth itself against the Power of the most high.[46]

The Ranter strategy was thus opposite to the ascetic strategies of the Puritans and Spiritualists. Puritan legalism had only served to multiply sin, adding to the burden of guilt. Seekers opted out of Puritan religious observance, but were still surrounded by "the black Regiment," the religious and political establishment. They waited for divine deliverance by way of miraculous apostles. Ranters were those Seekers who had despaired of supernatural deliverance. Their solution was a hedonistic assault upon the "Bulwark" of Puritan morality, to rend the very fabric of society, to shake down the religious and political foundations of the new regime.

Clarkson and other Ranters aimed to immerse themselves in everything held odious by respectable society, until they could experience and claim a kind of *sinful perfection*. This solution is somewhat akin to existentialist and Zen understandings of the "pure act," though neither of those traditions advocates immorality. Ranters must be understood in relation to Puritanism's momentary triumph in religious hegemony, political control, and moral consensus.

Looking back on this period ten years later, Clarkson summarized his state of despair:

> I saw all men spake or acted, was a lye and therefore my thought was, I had as good cheat for something among them, and that so I might live in prosperity with them. . . . So that the 18th and 19th verses of *Ecclesiastes* was the rule and direction of my spirit, to eat and to drink, and to delight my soul in the labor of my minde all the days of my life. . . . For this I conceived, as I knew not what I was before I came into being, so for ever after I should know nothing after this my being was dissolved; but even as a stream from the Ocean was distinct in itself while it was a stream, but when returned to the Ocean, was therein swallowed and become one with the Ocean . . . yet notwithstanding this, I had sometimes a relenting light in my soul, fearing this should not be so, as indeed it was contrary; but however, then a cup of Wine would wash away this doubt.[47]

This later perspective may be jaundiced, but it offers insight into the paradoxical combination of despair and elation felt by many Ranters during the twilight of radical hope. Far from being morally indifferent, Clarkson was a man who had once been offended by Maypoles.

The same summer, Clarkson was arrested and interrogated by a Parliamentary committee. By September, they had sentenced him to one month imprisonment, to be followed by banishment. Only the first provision was actually enacted. So, later in 1650, he was free again and left London for Cambridgeshire, "where I still continued my Ranting principle, with a high hand." He practiced astrology, physic, magic, "and made many fools believe in me, for at that time I looked upon all was good, and God the author of all."[48]

He continued in this nihilistic condition until 1658, when he met John Reeve and Lodowick Muggleton, leading lights of a small messianic sect in London. He was persuaded of their message and became a member of their group, popularly known as Muggletonians. It seems as if antinomians like Clarkson often gravitated eventually to groups with cult-like devotion to charismatic authority figures. To replace religious institutions with authoritative individuals was one way out of anomic drift during the 1650s. Similarly in our own time, the chaotic scene of the 1960s counterculture gave rise to the cults of the 1970s, gathered around figures such as Sun Myung Moon and Maharaj Ji. We will consider the role of charismatic leadership in the Quaker movement in later chapters.

Clarkson settled down with his wife and lived quietly, practicing various trades until the fire of London in 1666. He became involved in a money-lending scheme to rebuild houses in London. The scheme collapsed and Clarkson was imprisoned for debt at Ludgate, where he died of a lingering illness in 1667.

Joseph Salmon

Finally, we come to Joseph Salmon, whose writings probably best illustrate the movement from Spiritualist Seeker to Ranter and beyond. He also exhibits the political aspects of the Ranter divine madness most clearly. His background is unknown to us.[49] Like Coppe, he displayed an extremely broad and playful command of the English language, though he did not share Coppe's usage of Hebrew, Greek, and Latin. In any case, there are no university records of him at Oxford or Cambridge. There does seem to be a mutual influence of ideas, attitudes, and vocabulary between Coppe and Salmon, but we do not know if they were associated before their ranting period.

Salmon served in Ireton's regiment as both a soldier and a chaplain around 1647-49. He was evidently a leading figure among the Spiritualist worship groups, for his first published tract, *Antichrist in Man* (published by Calvert in 1648), appeared with the army pieces we reviewed in Chapter 4. *Antichrist in Man* is dated December 12, 1647—the same week John Saltmarsh had his dying confrontation with the generals.

Like the other army Spiritualists, Salmon evinced a strong sense that
he was part of a new revelation breaking forth. His preface exhibits the
same tension between humility and superiority we heard in Wilkinson
and others. On the one hand, he claims to know God beyond the formal
religion that his readers practice; on the other, he asks that they read
what follows with charity, for "I am a child in the things of God." He
assures readers that if they come to this new revelation, they will find
"your present light will be darkness and your form to be flesh." Salmon
makes it clear that his new revelation is nothing less than Christ's
second coming within.

The main text begins by looking back over the conflicted history of
the English Reformation. There has been a continual sense of Antichrist's
taint in the English church. Some have identified Antichrist with papacy,
others with episcopacy, and more recently others with presbytery. Thus,
all have found Antichrist on the outside and not the inside, in history
and not in mystery. These are deluded perceptions.[50]

Salmon uses the apocalyptic terms Antichrist and Whore of Babylon
interchangeably.[51] These masculine and feminine images of the demonic
both represent the "mystery of iniquity," the power that continues to
defeat personal transformation and social justice. In both cases, Salmon
defines this power as "fleshly wisdom," "carnal policy." The problem of
the flesh is not an innate evil of material existence but an outward way
(that is, both sensory and subjectively rational) of knowing. The apocalypse of Christ's second coming is known only within, although the saints
who receive the inward Christ will also enact the new age without. Like a
"mystical Herod," the demonic power aspires to kill every new appearance of God in us.[52] This work goes on by a variety of subtle operations in
the human heart. Religion often serves Antichrist's purposes best of all.
The whore "wears a religious dress" to seduce believers from true knowledge of Christ, captivating the mind in formal observances.[53]

Salmon stresses that everything reported of Christ in Scripture, in
history, must be known within, in mystery. He summarizes pungently:
the history of Christ is "Christ for us" while the mystery is "Christ in
us."[54] Scripture and sacraments take us only so far. Then we are crucified with Christ to them and suddenly the elements become bare water,
bare bread, and wine. The soul must be patient in this dead condition
and wait for the Comforter to come within. Therefore, to "wait upon the
Lord" is the order of this day of uncertainty. But in that very process of

waiting, the "still and small voice" will call the soul forth, beyond self and creature, allowing one to see the self as never before. In this movement, one is carried away in spirit beyond all former strength, strategy, and emotion— carried into a wilderness, a "lost condition." There, God will "ravish the soul" with beams of light, making one's vanity and deformity all the more clear. This is a time of great "amazement of spirit."[55] Here, the great battle of the Lamb begins against the mystery of iniquity, to defeat and cast it out. This is the day of judgment. Salmon epitomizes this Spiritualist sense of apocalypse: it is nothing to read about the last day prophesied historically in Scripture; it must be known mystically within.[56]

This cosmic battle of divine and demonic forces breaks out both within and without. There are wars and rumors of war. Salmon follows here the apocalyptic imagery of Revelation 12. As Christ is born within, the serpent is cast down from heaven (i.e., the demonic power loses its place within), causing it to rage and chase the true church, heavenly Jerusalem, into the wilderness. God will sustain her there until the day of salvation arrives. For Salmon, the wilderness church is comprised of groups, like those in the army, who gather to "wait upon the Lord." They are experiencing both intense spiritual warfare within and conservative Puritan attacks from without.[57]

This is where the true revolution is unfolding. The civil war has been a grand diversion from the real struggle for Christ's kingdom on earth. Therefore, Salmon exhorts, do not so much desire the downfall of the Pope, Presbyter, or any other state; desire the ruin of this mystical Babylon. He concludes that he has only sought to declare

> the manifestative minde of God unto me in all my mystical application of Scripture, I do not endeavor to overturn history [but] have only written about the history I have known verified in me, in the mystery.[59]

Thus, Salmon by no means discards Scripture; it is the historical code that identifies the forces working within the faithful. But in a culture saturated with biblical knowledge and debate, the work of liberation shifts toward knowing the revelation of Scripture enacted on an interior landscape.

Salmon's text shares much with Saltmarsh's and Wilkinson's writings at that tremulous moment. But there is a clarity in his apocalyptic vision and internalizing application of the Book of Revelation that we do not find in other writers, until George Fox in the 1650s.[60] Unlike Fox and the early Quaker apocalyptic message, Salmon does not possess the same sense of empowerment and socially transforming witness. But he has gone far to relate the inward, spiritual struggle of the Seekers with the outward, political events of the 1640s.

Salmon advanced his interpretation of inward and outward events further in his next bulletin from the army, *A Rout, A Rout*, subtitled, *some part of the ARMIES QUARTERS BEATEN UP, By the DAY of the LORD Stealing upon Them*. This piece appeared in February 1649, just after the beheading of Charles, the abolition of the House of Lords, and Pride's Purge of Commons. The generals were taking control and the Levellers were denouncing them in *England's New Chains*.

Salmon addresses a first preface to the generals, now at the height of their power:

> All that I have to say [to you] is this; That you go on as fast as you can with the work you have begun, for the time draws nigh that is allotted you . . . in this day of the Lords Wrath you strike thorow King, Gentry, and Nobility, they all fall before you: You have a Commission from the LORD to scourge ENGLAND'S Oppressors; do it in the Name of God, do it (I say) fully, hotly, sharply; and the same measure you mete, shall be met to you again; for the Lord ere long cast his Rod into the fire of burning and destruction: It will be a sweet destruction, wait for it.

This is ironic encouragement! Salmon invokes God's blessing, even commission, for the generals' strike against the competing powers of monarchy and Parliament. But he adds that their time is running out too, and the force of their violent actions will soon double back upon them.

The tract is really written for the "Fellowship (of SAINTS scattered)" among army's rank and file, whom he addresses in a second preface. The Spiritualists and Levellers he counts as brethren still hope to do God's work as members of the army. He responds therefore that

> I have fellowship with you in the Lord: but I am distant from your dark and fleshly enterprises. You are a scattered seed amongst tares, and it is your name that upholds the fame of the whole . . . if it were not for you, this power of the sword, would vanish and be annihilated. . . . Thus saith the Lord of Hostes,

> The Day is coming, and now is, when I will gather up my
> jewels in the Army (from under this dark and carnal form of
> the Sword) into my self . . . when they shall no more contend
> with the world for outward Interest, but beholding all in
> Divine Fulness, shall in the enjoyment of it sit down con-
> tented. And this I partly see fulfilled in my self and others.[62]

The army is degenerating as God's instrument on earth. The righteous
remnant is the only element saving it from God's wrath. But this will
not be for long. A final weaning away from political and personal
interest will soon draw them out. It sounds as if Salmon himself is already on his way out.

He expects nothing but censure and malice for his message. But he is
willing to bear it:

> I will own it all, being willing to become sin for you, though
> the Lord in me knows no sin; that you, together with me,
> may be presented in the Lord an eternal righteousness.[63]

These words may indicate the onset of Salmon's Ranter phase. He is
engaging in pure acts that others will regard as sinful, but the purity
within him knows no sin. Whatever malice or retaliation he suffers
for these acts will be a cross he must endure, a kind of atonement that
he hopes will ultimately draw others with him into a higher form of
righteousness. But at this point, as far as we can tell, the "sinful" act in
question is simply his prophetic message, not the outrageous behavior
that was soon to make Ranters notorious. Indeed, it is probably too soon
to call Salmon a Ranter.

In the main body of the tract, Salmon states his principle that God's
power moves from one dispensation or party to another, accomplishing
divine purpose in both religious and civil affairs. The power now rests
in the army. It is a low, dark form for God's glory.

> The Lord here besmears himself with blood and vengeance,
> deforms his own beauty, hides his amiable presence under a
> hideous and wrathful form. . . . Friends! Look about you, for
> the Lord is now coming forth to rip up your bowels, to search
> your hearts, and try your reins; yea; to let loose the impris-
> oned Light of himself in you.[64]

The army is now "far below the pure Light and Life of God." The men of God in the army must disentangle their hopes from the army's designs. Hope must rest in God, not this "beggarly thing." An army is animated by a "base, earthly Spirit" that "seeks after the ruine and blood of creatures, for the enjoyment of that which is at best bitter-sweet, a well-being subject to all manner of casualties."[65]

The Lord was content to work through such dark spirits up to this point, but now

> he is coming out of darkness, his secret place, into a light and open view . . . [and] in an holy shame, you will reflect upon your present Employments . . . the Lord hath shewed us . . . a more easie and sweet way of Victory; we can overcome by being conquered, we can lose all, and yet be savers in the conclusion. . . . Oh, that sweet and meek Spirit of Christ! Who, when he was reviled, reviled not again . . . you must shortly part with all; your name, fame, success and victory must all be forgotten, yea, you yourselves shall rejoyce at your own Overtures. . . . All things are not yet reconciled in you, earth and heaven are not yet agreed. . . . If you could see all men, all interests, all power in the Lord, you would be offended at none, you would not fear any.[66]

Salmon has clearly begun to articulate a pacifist Christian understanding beyond the first intimations we heard at the end of Saltmarsh's life. He has seen the cruelty and the vanity of war as an instrument of justice. While he is still willing to affirm God's hand in military struggles up to this point, he finds God's power shifting toward nonviolent means.

Salmon speaks for some kind of pacifist group that may be outside the army. It is not clear that this is the incipient Ranter party. There is no indication of the wild expressionism that will soon make Ranters notorious. But there is a rapturous sense of having moved into some realm beyond all present categories:

> We see and behold ourselves, (as in the Lord) without fear or jealousie, because we are really reconciled to all men, all designs, all interests; and all they that know us are carried forth in a spirit of Love towards us. The reason why we are hated, despised, and trampled upon, is, because the world

> knoweth us not, they know not the Father in us. In [their] state of ignorance we are the objects of scorn and contempt, and it is our Freedom and Liberty to be so. . . . the dyings of the Lord are manifested in us dayly: Here, O here's a way to bring forth peace and unity: the Lord is coming, (he is coming) to discover it. . . . [67]

Salmon makes inspired use of ideas and phrases from Paul and from John's gospel. Nevertheless, there is a sense of desperation here, from one who has moved to the edge and beyond. This becomes abundantly clear in the final sentences of Salmon's postscript:

> I was once wise as well as you, but I am now a fool, I care not who knows it: I once also enjoyed my self, but I am now carried out of my wits, a fool, a mad man, besides my self; if you think me any other, you are mistaken, and it is for your sakes that I am so. And now Friends, In him that was, is, and is to come, I take my farewel of you . . . The Lord was, when you were lowest; he is, now you are highest; and he is to come, when you shall be nothing. Even so, Come Lord Jesus, Come quickly.[68]

Adapting the "fool's speech" from Paul in 2 Corinthians, Salmon enters the Ranter eclipse. The entire Reformation project to restore "primitive Christianity," the Leveller hope for a free English republic, even the Seeker quest itself – these are all now swallowed into a strange, nether region. Salmon has charted the painful spiritual dialectics of this awful historical moment better than any other Spiritualist. But it has left him "a fool and a mad man, besides my self."

Little is known of Salmon's activities over the next year. He definitely was an associate of Coppe's in London and elsewhere during this period. According to reports, Salmon indulged in "wicked Swearing, and uncleanness, which he justified and others of his way, That it was God which did swear in them, and that it was their Liberty to keep company with Women, for their Lust."[69]

In February or March of 1650, Salmon went to Coventry, where Coppe had been imprisoned since January. He was arrested for preaching there in March. Salmon continued to defend his position for some months, preaching to crowds gathered outside his cell, and publishing his only true Ranter tract, *Divinity Anatomized*, which unfortunately is lost to us. The letter quoted in the epigraph to this chapter offers at least a taste of his outrageously playful and inverted state of mind. In particular, it exemplifies the Ranter practice of swearing oaths—that is, taking God's name in vain, invoking heaven and hell. The Ranter experienced captivity to a Puritan regime that had surely taken God's name in vain by invoking divine purposes in a revolution now subverted by the interests of a new ruling class. Ranter swearing was the purposeful degradation of that misused language, an outrageous parody of the covenantal formulas that had been intoned by Puritan divines to bless war, religious repression, and social inequality. The Ranter prolixity of oaths is actually quite related to the subsequent Quaker refusal to swear any oath at all. In very different ways, both served as symbolic repudiations of Puritan covenantal bad faith.

George Fox, the future Quaker leader, was still a fairly obscure figure when he visited Salmon in the Coventry prison sometime in the spring or early summer of 1650. He recorded the encounter twenty-five years later in his *Journal*. This was his first encounter with Ranters and he writes that he felt a great darkness when he entered their company. They began to "rant, vapor, and blaspheme," claiming to be God. With his typical tenacity, Fox replied that if they were God, they could tell him if it would rain. He reproved them and left.[70] Fox continued northward and was himself imprisoned at Derby in October under the Blasphemy Act.

It is not clear how long Salmon spent in prison. He was already free when his recantation was published in August 1651. *Heights in Depths and Depths in Heights* may have been influenced by Coppe's second recantation two months before. But there are significant differences. Salmon's repentance is less cringing, and he is able to articulate more fully the experience of Ranter mania. Neither piece was published by Giles Calvert, an indication that he had now distanced himself from Ranters. Starting in 1653, he became the chief publisher of Quaker literature.

The preface, "An Apologeticall Hint," explains to the reader that Salmon has employed "a homely Language" (in contrast to the exalted speech of his last couple of years) but adds teasingly that the tract "steales like a Thiefe upon the benighted world: However, bee not shy of it; for it shal take nothing from thee but what thou shalt bee made willing to part withall." Salmon has by no means lost his playful, ironic sense. He begins to explain his Ranterism, writing that after an initial, ecstatic experience of divine light (perhaps around the time of *A Rout*), he was suddenly covered with an "enigmaticall cloud of darknesse" that confused and disoriented him. Soon he was "posting most furiously in a burning zeal toward an unattainable end." That end is unfortunately not defined. He affirms that his behavior was justly deemed uncivil by authorities, at least "according to the present state of things." After six months of defiance, his imprisonment became "very irksome and tedious to my outward man."[71]

But prison has also been a cloister, a sanctuary from the clamor of the world, affording time to ponder his condition. He has summoned his heart before the throne of divine justice and seen that he acted destructively. Slowly, "I was led to consider that certainly Providence had some end in leading (or suffering me to bee led) into these appearances." He began to rise "above the most insulting and daring Fury," to see the Lord's purposes in his bizarre actions. Thus, "the rage of man shall turn to the praise of God." He writes appreciatively of two officers of the army, Major Beak and Colonel Purefoy, who helped him define and condemn his offenses, eventually gaining his release.[72]

The present publication honors his promise to make a public apology. He hopes to make this statement his last:

> I now am made to speak, because I am almost weary of speaking, and to informe the world that silence have taken hold of my spirit. The thunderstrokes of the Almighty have to purpose uttered their voices in me, heaven and earth have trembled at their dreadfull sounds: the Alarm being over there's silence now in heaven; for how long I know not. I lie quietly and secure in the Lord while I see the whole world consuming in the fire of envie one against another. I heare much noyse about me, but it serves onely to deafen me into the still slumbers of Divine rest. . . . Come then, O my Soule, enter thou into thy Chamber, shut thy doores about thee, hide thyself in silence for a season till the indignation bee blown over.[73]

With amazement, Salmon looks out upon the continuing wrath and contention of English society. He has finally been delivered from its grips. After a season in hell, overcome by furious rage, he has found the stillness of eternity.

The main text reaffirms the Ranter sense of futility, taking Ecclesiastes as its starting point: "Vanitie of Vanities, All is Vanitie saith the Preacher.

The highest piece of wisdom, is to see wisdom it self but Vanity. The whole world is a Circle, including nothing but emptiness." He reasserts the monistic principle of unity. Life in the world is a "State of variety," in which forms exist as mere shadows.

> To descend from the oneness or Eternity, into the multiplic-
> ity, is to lose our selves in an endlesse Labyrinth. To ascend
> from variety into uniformity, is to contract our scattered spir-
> its into their original center and to find ourselves where we
> were, before we were.[74]

We hear succinctly the Neoplatonic themes that Coppin had aired in 1649.

The intense idealism of the most spiritualized Seekers had already placed great emphasis upon finding all truth within. Only their moral scrupulosity and political hope had maintained their moorings in the world around them. The overwhelming experience of political defeat combined with spiritual exhaustion had resulted in a strongly *apophatic* (*via negativa*) mysticism[75] and a world-denying cosmology. Salmon's earlier apocalyptic dialectic between outward history and inward mystery was swallowed up in an all-consuming oneness that became both everything and nothing, idealism intensified to the point of nihilism.

Still, Salmon maintains some tension between biblical theism and world-denying monism. He echoes his earlier theme of *waiting* in a state beyond desire or self-interest. "How then shall a man attaine to a oneness, and communion with this inaccessible glory? . . . We must patiently expect its seasonable descenscion upon us; whose nature it is to consume us into itself, and melt us into the same nature and likeness." This advice is not that different from his earlier exhortations in *Antichrist in Man* and *A Rout*, or Wilkinson's guidance in *the Saints Travel*, but the outlook is no longer Spiritualist and apocalyptic. With a weary shrug, Salmon testifies,

> I have lived to see an end of all perfections; that which I now
> long for, is to see perfection it selfe perfected. I have bin led
> out to seek the Lord in manifold appearances, I must now
> (by himself) be found in himselfe, who is the good it selfe,
> and nothing but this can satisfie.[76]

This is the final, mystical phase of one Seeker's quest.

So how did he come to this rarefied state? Salmon narrates a classic Seeker saga from the Church of England, into Presbyterianism, Independency, Baptism, and beyond. He felt uneasy about drifting from one thing to another, and tried to settle down in Baptism. But the Lord called him out, saying "this is not your rest." Thus, he continued following Christ until he expired with him and was buried in darkness with him. Out of this state of waiting in death, he was raised to new life, embracing love and peace, overwhelmed by unspeakable joy. This must be the time of *A Rout*—late 1648 to early 1649. "I appeared to my selfe as one confounded into the abyss of eternitie, nonentitized into the being of being; my soule split, and emptied into the fountain and ocean of divine fulness: expired into the aspires of pure life."[77] Seldom has mystical ecstasy been described as well.

However, Salmon explains that proud flesh soon tried to claim a share of this glory, causing

> a suddain, certain, terrible, dreadful revolution, a strange vicissitude. God sent a Thorn immediately; hid himself from me by a sudden departure. . . . Angry flesh being struck at heart with the piercing dart of vengeance, begins to swell, and contracting all the evil humors of the body of death into one lump, to grapple with this throne of wrath, at last violently breaks out, and lets forth the very heart and coar of its pride and enmity. The rankor and venom of this subtil serpent, now discovers it self, and being sore sick with cup of pure wrath, disgorges its foul stomach upon the very face, and appearance of Truth. I . . . became a mad man, a fool amongst men. Thus tumbling in my own Vomit, I became a derision to all, and even loathed by those by whom I had beloved. . . . O the deep drunken bewitching, besotting draughts of the wine of astonishment that hath been forced upon me.[78]

Thus, Salmon's ego reasserted itself, seeking to wield, rather than yield to, this new spiritual power. This induced the inversion that Salmon interprets biblically as the Lord's cup of wrath, the wine of astonishment. We saw this image briefly mentioned in Coppe's recantation, citing Habakkuk 2:15f. This wine induces "shameful spewing" by those who are forced to drink it (vs. 16). The image is also found twice in Revelation (14:10; 16:19).[79] In addition, Salmon makes use of Paul's in 2 Cor 12:7-10, a "thorn in the flesh" that brings one's ecstatic flight back to earth. But unlike Paul, Salmon did not find the humility of spirit to accept the ongoing role of suffering. Instead, he fell into a state of uncontainable rage.

But the Ranter episode is not simply one man's tragedy; it is a sign, a warning to others. He chides readers for thinking themselves superior:

> You little think, and less know, how soon the cup of fury may be put into your hands: my self, with many others have been made stark drunk with that wine of wrath, the dregs whereof (for ought I know) may fall to your share suddenly. I speak not this either to extenuate my own evil, or to cast approbries in the face of those who have (to the utmost) censured me; but rather to mittigate the severity of peoples spirits, and to give a by-hint of that doom and judgement, that is at hand upon the world.[80]

Salmon returns to the apocalyptic worldview, to suggest that the craven despair that claimed him may overtake others—indeed, the entire nation. When one considers the arrogant cynicism and debauchery that attended the Restoration period, starting less than ten years later, this warning has a prophetic ring.

Salmon offers one more ironic commentary on his Ranter phase:

> I was indeed full sick of wrath, a vial of wrath was given me to drink; the heavenly pleasure would not excuse me a drop of it . . . Well—drink I must, but mark the riddle. 'Twas given me, that I might drink, I drank, that I might stumble, I stumbled, that I might fall: I fell, and through my fall was made happy. It is strange to think, how the hidden and secret presence of God in me, did silently rejoyce while flesh was thus manifested; I had a sweet rest and refuge in the Lord, even while my flesh was frying and scorching in the flames of ireful fury. I was ark'd up in the eternal bosome, while the flesh was tumbling in the foaming surges of its own vanity . . . and this I know is a riddle to many, which none but the true Nazarite can expound; and til he is pleased to unfold it, it pleases me it should lie dark.[81]

Salmon has not completely abandoned the Ranter doctrine of salvation through saturation in sin. It is not unlike his earlier affirmation that the violence of the English Civil War had served God's purposes up to a point. Truly, the role of sin and evil in the path of redemption remains a troubling riddle for all.

At last, Salmon has passed on to an unearthly repose:

> All the waves and billows of the Almighty have gone over me. I am now at rest in the silent deeps of eternity, sunk into the abysse of silence, and (having shot this perilous gulf) am safely arrived into the bosome of love, the land of rest. I sometimes hear from the world, which I have now forsaken; I see its Diurnals are fraught with the tydings of the same clamor, strife, and contention, which abounded in it when I left it; I give it hearing, and that's all. . . . My great desire . . . is to see and say nothing. I have run round the world of variety, and am now centered in eternity . . . I see partly what the end will be, but I must not declare, neither will the world hear it.[82]

The rest of the tract is given over to individual questions of blasphemy, which he renounces, citing biblical authority. Most interesting, perhaps, is his reaffirmation of the Trinity:

> Unity is the Father, the Author and begetter of all things; or (if you will) the Grandmother in whose intrinsecal womb, variety lies occult, till time orderly brings it forth. . . . In multiplicity they [Father, Son, and Spirit] are three, but in the unity or primary state all one, but one. I love the Unity, as it orderly discovers it self in the Trinity: I prize the Trinity, as it beares correspondency with the Unity; Let the skillfull Oedipus unfold this.[83]

Thus ends one of the most paradoxical pieces of English religious literature. Salmon may have regained his composure and civility, but he lost none of his impish genius.

After his release from Coventry, Salmon garnered a loyal following around Kent. He preached regularly on Sundays at Rochester Cathedral until he emigrated to Barbados around 1655. Richard Coppin succeeded him. J. F. McGregor believes that Salmon's followers provided the nucleus for the subsequent Quaker community in Kent.[84]

Our final sighting of Joseph Salmon comes in a letter from Barbados in November 1656. Henry Fell wrote to the Quaker leader Margaret Fell regarding the new Quaker mission there. Despite many promising developments, Henry Fell notes that

here is one Joseph Salmon who was a ringleader of the Ranters
in England and has gotten a chance to speak, he seems to
deny Ranting outwardly, but it is but to deceive the hearts of
the simple. And truly many are deceived by him . . . and
gotten into his image . . . he hath gotten the forme of truth in
words the most that ever I heard any, and very bould and
impudent . . . and yet his fruits plainly make him manifest
that he is not on the foundation. Truly he is a great enemy to
the truth. . . . I know not any such a one in England as he is.[85]

Fell concludes that he has tried to warn the congregation against Salmon,
but "many of them are sore bewitched with him . . . they will hear
nothing against him." Clearly, Fell was deeply disturbed by this notorious character whose preaching was so close to the Quaker gospel yet
whose "impudent" manner affronted the moral gravity of Quaker
sensibility. We will note this kind of confrontation repeatedly in later
chapters. In any case, it seems Salmon was either pushed out of the
Quaker meetings in Barbados or grew weary of them. Another letter
from Henry Fell the following April makes no mention of him.

EPILOGUE

Ranters continued to be a significant phenomenon in England through
the 1650s. A major source of information on them is Quaker correspondence and the spate of Quaker literature against Ranters, 1655-59. We
will consider the hostile attitude of early Friends toward Ranters later,
in Chapter 10. While Quakers did their utmost to distance themselves
from Ranters, such efforts themselves suggest some important overlap.
Many third-party observers viewed Ranters and Quakers as two versions of the same blight.

It is probably true that the Ranter phenomenon quickly degenerated
into reflexive bawdiness and blasphemy. Just as the hippie and punk
movements of the 1960s and 1970s soon became more attitude and
fashion than substance, the Ranters against whom Quakers wrangled
during the 1650s were often sodden and sullen bands. Ranter meetings
quickly became a rallying point for popular atheism, class resentment,
and antiauthoritarianism, which are ready to be tapped in any age. Thus,

the rarefied mysticism of the Ranter writers of 1650 was quickly transmuted into a crude materialism. The sacramental debauchery that made the first Ranter meetings such dizzying spectacles of negated Puritanism could only become sheer venality over time. As with all expressions of political resentment, the inspired gesture of contempt soon becomes an irritating tic.

It is important to correlate the real significance of Ranterism with the radical collapse of 1649-50. The "Ranter moment" was the key dialectical *aporia*, or eclipse, between the failed hopes of Seekers, Levellers, and Diggers in the 1640s and the tougher Quaker resurgence of the 1650s. For that reason, we will discover Ranters to be very important to the evolution of the Quaker movement. In a word, Quakerism was both the repudiation and the reformulation of Ranterism.

In the 1640s, religious idealism among a new generation of Puritans gave rise to the radical politics of the Levellers and Diggers. Beginning with the Ranters and continuing with the Quakers, radical religion and politics were inverted. Thus, Leveller and Digger political ideas were reborn as new forms of religious expression.[86] But these new spiritual politics were no less powerful simply because they no longer aspired to transform the political superstructure. The broader cultural politics of the Ranters and Quakers, attacking the entire social infrastructure, threatened entrenched power much more pervasively than Leveller petitions or Digger communes ever had.

Notes

1. From the "Letter of Joseph Salmon to Thomas Webbe" in *A Collection of Ranter Writings from the 17th Century*, ed. Nigel Smith (London: Junction, 1983), 201-02.
2. Jean-Paul Sartre, *Nausea*, with Introduction by Hayden Carruth, (New York: New Directions, 1964).
3. These characterizations by Rufus M. Jones and by the 1911 edition of *The Encyclopaedia Britannica* are quoted by Jerome Friedman in the Preface to his *Blasphemy, Immorality, and Anarchy: The Ranters and the English Revolution* (Athens, Oh.: Ohio University, 1987).
4. John Webster, *The Vail of Covering, Spread over All Nations* (1653).
5. Letter of Dorothy Howgill to George Fox, 1652, A. R. Barclay MSS., 32.
6. J. F. McGregor, "Ranterism and the Development of Early Quakerism," in *The Journal of Religious Studies*, 9 (1977): 349-63.

7. See Anonymous, *A Justification of the Mad Crew in Their Ways and Principles* (1650).
8. See Laurence Clarkson's anecdote in *The Lost Sheep Found* (1660), in Smith, *Ranter Writings*, 180.
9. For Coppe's biographical details, I rely primarily upon the article on him in *The Dictionary of National Biography* (Oxford: University Press, 1917), 4:1115.
10. Richard Coppin, *Divine Teachings* (1649), Part 2, Chapters 3 and 8.
11. Coppin, *Teachings*, Part 3, Chapter 3.
12. A. L. Morton, *The World of the Ranters: Religious Radicalism in the English Revolution* (London: Lawrence and Wishart, 1970), 73-74. Also see Friedman, *Blasphemy*, 17-58.
13. The Ranter closest to Coppin, particularly in terms of a more composed writing style, is Jacob Bauthumley, whom we will not treat here. His *Light and Dark Sides of God* (1650) is a serene, metaphysical treatise, utterly lacking in Coppe's provocational style. Friedman categorizes both Coppin and Bauthumley as "philosophical Ranters," but sees the latter as more mystical and the former as more intellectual. (Early Friends called the more speculative and sedate exponents "civil Ranters.") Bauthumley does indeed write with an almost transfixed tone, often prefacing his remarks with "I see...." The main text begins by addressing God, affirming that "My seeking of thee is no other but thy seeking of thy selfe: My delighting enjoying thee, is no other but thy delighting in thy selfe, and enjoying of thy selfe after a most unconceivable manner." Ironically, Bauthumley was the most savagely prosecuted of the Ranter leaders. He was not only cashiered from the army and imprisoned, but also bored through the tongue.
14. Friedman, *Blasphemy*, 77.
15. Smith, *Ranter Writings*, 56-57.
16. Smith, *Ranter Writings*, 55.
17. Smith, *Ranter Writings*, 66.
18. Smith, *Ranter Writings*, 79.
19. Smith, *Ranter Writings*, 70.
20. Smith, *Ranter Writings*, 82-83.
21. Morton, *Ranters*, 99-100.
22. Friedman, *Blasphemy*, 87 notes that this idea can be traced back at least to the Adamites of the Middle Ages.
23. Smith, *Ranter Writings*, 87-88.
24. Smith, *Ranter Writings*, 89.
25. In a similar vein, Erbury wrote that "The people of God turn wicked men, that wicked men may turn to be the people of God" — as quoted by Christopher Hill in *The World Turned Upside-Down: Radical Ideas during the English Revolution* (New York: Viking, 1972), 157. Erbury seemed to account the "wicked men" to be those outside the conventions of Puritan piety, rather than individuals indulging in moral license. Erbury's own behavior remained morally conventional. Still, we can see a bridge in thinking from the antinomian Spiritualism of Erbury to the full blown inverted morality of the Ranters.
26. Smith, *Ranter Writings*, 108-09.
27. Quoted by Morton, *Ranters*, 102.

28. Friedman, *Blasphemy*, 16.
29. Smith, *Ranter Writings*, 127-32.
30. Smith, *Ranter Writings*, 129.
31. Smith, *Ranter Writings*, 131.
32. George Fox, *Journal*, John L. Nickalls, ed. (Cambridge: University Press, 1952), 195.
33. This word-play had gone right past me, and American; but is suggested in Carol Churchill's excellent play on Ranters and other radicals of the period, *The Light Shining in Buckinghamshire.*
34. Most of what we know of Clarkson's life is derived from his autobiographical statement of 1660, *The Lost Sheep Found.* It is a work of considerable candor, though it is strongly tinged by his newly adopted Muggletonian outlook. Thus, it manifests the tone of general self-condemnation typical of a repentant convert. Also see the article on him in *The Dictionary of National Biography* (Oxford: University Press, 1921), 3:461-63.
35. Thomas Edwards, *Gangraena*, Part 2, 6.
36. Smith, *Ranter Writings*, 176.
37. Smith, *Ranter Writings*, 181.
38. Hill, *The World Turned Upside-Down*, 159.
39. Thomas Curtis to George Fox, January 5, 1659, Swarthmore MSS., 3.87.
40. Smith, *Ranter Writings*, 182.
41. Gerrard Winstanley, *A Vindication* (1650), 3.
42. Winstanley, *Vindication*, 4.
43. Winstanley, *Vindication*, 7.
44. Smith, *Ranter Writings*, 167-68.
45. Smith, *Ranter Writings*, 169-70.
46. Smith, *Ranter Writings*, 168.
47. Smith, *Ranter Writings*, 182.
48. Smith, *Ranter Writings*, 185.
49. For Salmon's biographical details, I rely primarily upon Nigel Smith's article on him in *The Dictionary of National Biography*, *Missing Persons* volume (Oxford: University Press, 1993), 580-81.
50. Joseph Salmon, *Antichrist in Man* (1648), 1.
51. Friedman (*Blasphemy*, 144.) is taken aback by Salmon's repeated use of the "whore" as the demonic figure, finding it a distasteful lapse into misogynistic language. While misogyny may be implied in such imagery, it is important to note that Babylon and Jerusalem, demonic and divine feminine images from the Book of Revelation, along with a variety of more masculine images (Beast, False Prophet, Antichrist, Dragon) were frequently employed by many religious writers during this chaotic period.
52. Salmon, *Antichrist*, 7.
53. Salmon, *Antichrist*, 13-14.
54. Salmon, *Antichrist*, 27.
55. Salmon, *Antichrist*, 38.
56. Salmon, *Antichrist*, 47.
57. Salmon, *Antichrist*, 64.
58. Salmon, *Antichrist*, 34.

59. Salmon, *Antichrist*, 72.

60. See my previous work on George Fox's apocalyptic thought in *Apocalypse of the Word: The Life and Message of George Fox* (Richmond, Ind.: Friends United Press, 1986); and *The Covenant Crucified: Quakers and the Rise of Capitalism* (Wallingford, Pa.: Pendle Hill, 1995).

61. Smith, *Ranter Writings*, 190.

62. Smith, *Ranter Writings*, 191.

63. Smith, *Ranter Writings*, 191.

64. Smith, *Ranter Writings*, 194.

65. Smith, *Ranter Writings*, 195.

66. Smith, *Ranter Writings*, 196-98.

67. Smith, *Ranter Writings*, 198.

68. Smith, *Ranter Writings*, 200.

69. Smith, *Ranter Writings*, 13.

70. Fox, *Journal*, 46-47.

71. Smith, *Ranter Writings*, 204.

72. Smith, *Ranter Writings*, 205.

73. Smith, *Ranter Writings*, 206.

74. Smith, *Ranter Writings*, 207.

75. Apophatic spirituality, sometimes referred to as "the dark night of the soul" after the writing of St. John of the Cross, often befalls those of intense spiritual devotion. Early experiences of spiritual illumination suddenly give way to desolating experiences of darkness and the absence of God. The challenge is to learn to recognize God's presence anew, amidst the experience of absence, light in the depths of apparent darkness. An excellent contemporary guide to apophatic spirituality is Sandra Cronk's *Dark Night Journey: Inward Re-Patterning toward a Life Centered in God* (Wallingford, Pa.: Pendle Hill, 1991).

76. Smith, *Ranter Writings*, 209.

77. Smith, *Ranter Writings*, 212.

78. Smith, *Ranter Writings*, 212-13.

79. The exact source of this biblical image of divine wrath is not clear. Habakkuk 2:15f may give some indication. It pronounces woe upon those who make their neighbors drink the wine of their wrath, causing them to stagger and vomit. The cup of God's right hand will come around to them. Thus, some kind of debasing social act seems to lie behind the image of God's cup of wrath. Also see Jer. 25:15; Isa. 51:17; Psa. 60:3.

80. Smith, *Ranter Writings*, 214.

81. Smith, *Ranter Writings*, 215.

82. Smith, *Ranter Writings*, 215-16.

83. Smith, *Ranter Writings*, 222-23.

84. McGregor, "Ranterism," 356-57. Also see Smith, *Ranter Writings*, 17.

85. Henry Fell to Margaret Fell, Barbados, November, 1656, Swarthmoor MSS., 1.66.

86. See Morton, *Ranters*, 16.

CHAPTER 7

ANNA TRAPNEL AND SARAH JONES
WOMEN SEEKING AND SPEAKING

So cease thy mourning, thou weeping babe, that mourns in secret for manifestations from thy beloved, as thou hast had in dayes past; for I can testifie unto thee by experience, whosoever thou art in that state, that he is bringing thee nearer him, for that was but milk which he fed thee with whilst thou was weak, but he will feed thee with the Word from whence that milk proceedeth, if thou be willing and obedient to live at home with Jacob, which is daily to retire thy mind.

—Sarah Jones[1]

Up to this point, our Seeker profiles have included only men. The bulk of materials available to us from that period were written by and about men. Very few women had access to formal education or could participate in public discourse by speaking or writing for themselves. Women who entered such realms did so at risk to their reputation, freedom, even their lives. They might be hailed as prophets or mystics; but they might just as easily be attacked as meddlers, scolds, whores, or witches, especially if their words challenged social authority and norms.

I have delayed treatment of female Seekers until now also because they bring a crucial component to the development of English Spiritualism. The experience and expression of female Seekers is a key factor in the Quaker breakthrough of the 1650s, that will be examined in succeeding chapters. For the present, we will focus on recent research into seeking women of the 1640s and look at two such women, one who subsequently joined the Fifth Monarchist movement in the 1650s, the other who probably became a Quaker. We know even less about these two women than we do about the men we have studied. But from their tiny corpus of published works we discover two vibrant, prophetic voices of that period.

The Leveller and Digger movements—the political manifestations of Seekerism in the 1640s—were devoid of female leadership. Though two pro-Leveller petitions were organized and signed by women, they were undertaken in support of the movement's male leaders. The bold Leveller proposal to expand the electoral franchise sought only to include every free male. Further, with much of the Levellers' constituency and political leverage based in the army, its masculine cast was surely predetermined. The Digger Gerrard Winstanley's theological writings upheld the dignity of women explicitly and his communal experiment was domestic in focus. But his vision for overcoming economic oppression left patriarchal assumptions unchallenged. The traditional male-dominated household was still the basis of his platform for social reconstruction. Thus, it would seem that in movements where political rights and economic justice were brought into the foreground, gender issues remained in the background. But we shall see in the convincement narratives of early Quakers (Chapter 8) that women were as ardent seekers as men were in the 1640s.

There is little evidence that 17th-century English women harbored dreams of social equality and expanded social roles in a 20th-century sense. But the upheavals of the civil war had in fact opened to them new vistas of social experience. With men away serving in the army, and with economic dislocations and food shortages forcing mobilizations all over the country, women faced many novel situations. Most crucially, with religious authority divided and questioned on all sides, new space opened in some quarters for them to speak out.

When the specter of political and religious repression returned in 1649-50, many seeking women no doubt felt the same sense of betrayal, resentment, and despair we found among the men who turned Ranters in 1650. Indeed, there were many female Ranters, but unfortunately none of them published. From the limited information available to us, mainly in sensationalist descriptions of Ranter meetings, we find women mentioned mostly as sexual co-celebrants with men. But whatever the actual scope of their Ranter activities, we can easily imagine that their motivations were as complex as those we saw among Coppe, Clarkson, and Salmon in the preceding chapter. Still, as we shall see, there were other women who found different paths through the dark eclipse of radical hope.

Phyllis Mack's landmark study, *Visionary Women*,[2] examines some 300 women (more than two-thirds of them Quaker) who wrote or prophesied during the 1640s and 1650s. She finds among them many of the same issues that preoccupied their male counterparts: obsessive guilt, desperation to the point of suicidal tendencies, movement from sect to sect, a quest for moral perfection.[3] Interestingly, Mack suggests that the deepening Seeker quest moved in a direction rather different for women, however. The withdrawal from conventional religious forms led men to retreat deeper within themselves, laying aside their masculine religious personae as speakers and leaders in order to sit in *passive silence*, often awash in deep emotion. For women, however, the suspension of traditional religious experience led to *speaking out* in unprecedented, dangerous ways.[4] This fits with what I have found in my own research. It is common wisdom today that women are more prone than men to "tell their stories." But I had difficulty finding spiritual auto-biographies among very many Seeker and early Quaker women. Much like Old Testament prophets, they seemed more concerned to decry immorality and injustice.

Mack finds the spiritual experiences of these women often centered acutely in the body, erupting at times in explosive, inflammatory words and actions that sometimes inspired fear in, and reprisal from, male authorities. Particularly among non-Quaker women prophets, there was a tendency toward sickbed visions and prophesying in catatonic states. Mack suggests that, since women were denied the social authority to speak in church or in public, there was a need to demonstrate, both to themselves and to their hearers, the overwhelming power of God working in them, beyond any intention or effort of their own as women.[5] In that way, the female prophet could transmit divine messages without seeming to overstep her subservient role.

The expressive emphasis of feminine Seeker spirituality can be heard in this 1648 statement by Mary Cary:

> Every saint in a sense, may be said to be a prophet . . . for when the Lord hath revealed himself unto the soul and discovered his secrets to it . . . the soul cannot choose but declare them to others . . . . He that speaketh to edification, exhortation and consolation, though with much weakness, doth as truly prophesy as he that hath greatest abilities.[6]

The emphasis upon the "weakness" of the prophetic agent deflected accusations of self-importance or assertiveness against female speakers as they began to testify in some Independent and Baptist meetings in the 1640s. Since Paul's letters mentioned women's prophecy and prayer in early Christian worship (1 Cor. 11:5), this new phenomenon was permitted within certain parameters. Women were allowed to speak as members of their congregation, but not as leaders. In Chapter 3, we noted the case of Mrs. Attaway, a member of Thomas Lambe's General Baptist congregation in London. Though she began to preach independently in the mid-1640s, she never gained the approval of her congregation. As we have seen, a number of Independents and Baptists (like Attaway) dropped out to join the ranks of the Seekers. And as these informal groups met in a leaderless ethos, where the weakness and lostness of all participants was emphasized, and as the work of the Spirit upon both men and women as passive vessels was experienced with increasing intensity, a *de facto* gender parity began to develop among these "mourners after Sion."

The phenomenon of women's impromptu public preaching was one of the new abominations cited in 1646 by Thomas Edwards in his heresy-hunter's field guide, *Gangraena*. Puritan orthodoxy was clearly against women's speaking in church or on political matters. Popular sources like William Gouge's *On Domesticall Duties* (1626) were cited against female preachers.[7] Such women were sometimes called "tub-preachers," stereotyped as lower-class laundresses who would stand on their tubs and preach in the streets. They sometimes brought other women with them to deal with hecklers. Mack notes that these new women prophets often sought the sponsorship of male sectarian ministers who could attest to their character and orthodoxy (at least according to the norms of that particular sect); but they usually obtained emotional support and spiritual guidance from other women in their congregations.[8]

Clearly, the spiritual journeys of these women were an important part of the Seeker phenomenon of the 1640s, even if our sources are scant. The revolutionary shock waves of the civil war spread across all dimensions of English society, including gender relations. The crisis of legitimate religious knowledge, expression, and authority brought women— mostly uninvited—into the noisy debates and fractive politics of the period. By the time it was over, women's voices would never again be stifled quite as they had been before 1640. We begin with Anna

Trapnel, whose prophetic career fused incendiary political oracles with acute asceticism and catatonic trances.

ANNA TRAPNEL

Anna Trapnel was raised in Hackney, London, in moderately comfortable circumstances. We piece together her life and witness mostly from three tracts of 1654. In particular, *A Legacy for Saints* was published that summer, while she lay ill in London's infamous Bridewell prison. As the title suggests, she feared she might not survive the disgusting septic conditions of her cell. The tract's forty-seven pages comprise three pieces, written at different times, relating various phases of her life and testifying to God's many powerful ministrations upon her spirit.

Trapnel briefly relates the "legal convictions" she suffered as a child: pangs of conscience over the slightest sins. By these guilt feelings she knew herself to be "a child of wrath like all others." By age fourteen, she became eager to pray and hear sermons. Her prayers were at first mostly rote, but over time became more spontaneous and intense. But she had not yet escaped the religious formalities of Puritan piety. During her teens, having heard the great Independent preacher Hugh Peters preach, she forsook her parish church to congregate with these "Covenanted people." She thus began a seeking journey, running from minister to minister, finding no rest. She performed Christian "duties," the devotional regimens Puritan divines prescribed for earnest young souls. But she could not discern her election and sank deep into despair. She forsook the duties, which she now considered the vain idols of a feigned faith. Yet these renunciations only intensified her sense of desolation. She still conversed piously with respected Christians, but afterwards "looked gastly." She began to fast, but without any sense of spiritual progress.[9]

She heard people speak of "free grace" (the general redemption gospel preached by General Baptists and some Independents), but she could not find it by experience. In retrospect, she realized that she "looked first for holiness, and then for Christ." That is precisely the pitfall of Puritan piety-by-the-numbers that Saltmarsh defined in 1646. She bemoans, "Oh what a knotty piece was I for the great Jehovah to work upon! untill he put forth his mighty power, I could not believe."

Trapnel was increasingly attracted to the doctrine of free grace. Those who branded free grace as "antinomian" argued that it simply provided an excuse to sin more brazenly. But for Trapnel, the sense of God's infinite love and mercy only exposed her sins more acutely.[10]

Finally, a still, small voice came to her. She resisted it for a week until its undeniable power elicited an echo in her own spirit: "Christ is thine, and thou art his." This "raised Christ from the grave" in her, advancing her through inner desolations and consolations, refining her of corruption. That sense of indwelling moves Trapnel's testimony into the realm of Spiritualism.

In 1642, Trapnel began listening to the Independent John Simpson's sermons in London. Simpson was one of the most notorious free-grace exponents in the nation and was banned by Parliament that year from preaching (though he ignored it). In January 1643, as Trapnel heard him preach on Romans 8, she had a vision of the all-consuming fire of divine love. She testified to this experience during the meeting, probably her first public ministry. She now felt utterly certain of her redemption and began to experience many "raptures of joy," "great ravishings of spirit." As she continued to express her experiences and her doctrine, some branded her antinomian for claiming to have Christ raised up within, rendering her dead to the law.[11]

Like many on the same path during the 1640s, she found that initial period of sunshine giving way to new darkness. She became troubled and confused over questions of correct forms of worship. Like many Seekers, she studied the various approaches to the sacraments and found none of them equal to the purity of New Testament practice. Just as she had found devotional "duties" an obstacle to a true encounter with the Lord, she now realized that many placed the forms of worship above Christ. In so doing, they "rejoice more in the Administration than the Administrator." This placed a veil of confusion over the mind, a mystification worse than the veil of legalistic morality. Thus, "if we have too high an esteem of things, we shall enthrall our selves."[12]

Trapnel wallowed in severe confusion and doubt over these issues for two years. She eventually drew back from the Seeker rejection of all outward sacramental practices. She decided that the Christian should utilize the ordinances in their proper place, rather than discontinue them. She concluded: "it was not externals that caused my dissertion, for they are good in themselves; I would not be thought to make them the cause,

or put fault in them, the fault was in myself." She had gone from congregation to congregation, looking for the true way,

> But I could not be satisfied in my seeking, because I found
> not, neither was I taken off the restless frame I was in, till a
> constant overpowering word came, which was this: I say to
> thee wait, it is the mind of thy God that thou shouldst wait;
> then my spirit was quiet.[13]

She understood that she was not to look for a new way of worship. She
decided that no people or pattern could be compared to Mount Sion or the
church of the New Testament. She made a clear statement against the
overweening idealism of Seekers: in their "rambling from Mountains to
Hills, sometimes they fall into a deep valley ere they are aware, and while
they are down, may again find it a long time ere they can get up."[14]

Her crisis had begun in 1644. One contributing factor was the death
of her mother in 1644 or 1645 (she had already lost her father, a ship-
wright, during childhood). Her mother's dying words, spoken three times,
were "Lord! Double thy spirit upon my child."[15] An echo of Elijah's
prayer for his successor Elisha, these words seared Trapnel with the
firebrand of prophetic vocation. At the beginning of 1646, she prayed
that God would pour the Spirit anew upon her and lead her to sinless
perfection. Over the following summer, she was stricken with serious
physical illness and suffered considerable pain and weakness. She
understood this illness to be God's work, not to punish her, but to reveal
divine glory. Indeed, the physical pain seemed to dispel the spiritual
darkness; delirious raptures mortified the power of sin in her. Friends
that gathered around her bed thought she was dying as she spoke ec-
statically all night. But by late summer, she began to convalesce. *A Legacy
for Saints* features ten pages of visions and messages received during
that period.[16]

In opting against the Seeker movement, it would seem that Trapnel
was influenced by John Simpson, who took a moderate Spiritualist
position toward the sacraments. He saw baptism as unnecessary to salvation and let his members decide for themselves whether to receive the
rite.[17] And with the freedom of expression Simpson evidently allowed
women such as Trapnel in his congregation, there was good reason for
her to settle there. She realigned herself with Simpson not long before
he became pastor to an Independent congregation at Allhallows,

London, in 1647. The congregation retained a relationship with the Allhallows parish church. The parish had a rotating lectureship that featured some of the most radical preachers in London, making it a center of millennial ferment.[18] Allhallows became the platform for increasingly political witness by both Simpson and Trapnel.

A Legacy for Saints concludes with a piece that Trapnel wrote in May 1646, just before her critical illness. Sounding very much like R. Wilkinson (but two years before the publication of *The Saints Rest*), she prophesies that God will continue to prod the saints onward; there must be no "resting on any thing below himself." Like the ancient Israelites, they will be led through a wilderness of testing and purification. The dragon will pursue the woman (the true church) in the wilderness, but will not reach her (see Rev. 12:13ff). Antichrist will come, looking like the Lamb, but goring the saints with its two horns: political repression and subtle deceits. The dragon will prevail enough to scatter the saints (the children of the woman) for a time (a reference to the Seeker phenomenon). Religious freedom will be in the hand of Antichrist (the Presbyterian majority in Parliament), but the saints that dwell steadfastly with Christ shall not be moved. By the time this prophecy was published in 1654, she felt that she had seen it further fulfilled in the control Oliver Cromwell had taken over the nation as Lord Protector. Earlier, she had viewed Cromwell as a latter-day Gideon, leading Israel in victory over its enemies (first Royalists, then Presbyterians) while refusing to accept kingly authority. But with the creation of his sovereign position as Lord Protector in December 1653, Cromwell wielded more power than Charles I had ever enjoyed.

By this time, Trapnel had followed John Simpson into the formation of the Fifth Monarchist movement. The same crushing political events that had led the Ranters into public outrage led others to organize resistance. In December 1651, Simpson and another radical Independent minister, Christopher Feake, organized a meeting at Allhallows Church to rally the radical cause. The Fifth Monarchist movement emerged from that meeting. They saw England's repressive regimes up to the present as the four demonic monarchies of Daniel's vision. King Jesus was coming soon to establish a fifth monarchy, his own government on earth. They were disgusted at the Rump Parliament (cleansed of its Presbyterian majority at the time of Charles' execution in January 1649) for not abolishing tithes or granting formal religious toleration. They wanted to replace the Rump with a Church-Parliament composed of leaders of the gathered congregations of Independents, Baptists, and others—a kind of Jewish Sanhedrin, according to historian Bernard Capp.[19] Mary Cary had prophesied in that vein in 1651:

> There must be such a time, when the saints must be so lifted up out of the dust, as they must be the top and the head of all nations: and whatsoever kingdom and nation will not serve them must perish.[20]

Cary participated in the Fifth Monarchist coalition.

Their agenda must have influenced the Independent Cromwell when he forcibly disbanded the Rump in April 1653 and created a new, Nominated Parliament comprised of hand-picked religious leaders and army radicals. We have already noted that this body was nicknamed "Barebones" for one of its colorful members, the irrepressible Separatist preacher, Praise-God Barbone. But there were only about a dozen actual Fifth Monarchists chosen for this new body. In her disappointment with its incoherent composition, Anna Trapnel later dubbed the Nominated Parliament the "Linsey-wolsey-Party."[21] It was hopelessly divided from the start and dissolved itself in December 1653. The Council of State made Cromwell its ruling executive as Lord Protector that same month. For the rest of the decade, England was ruled more or less by military *junta*. Henceforth, most radical frustrations focused on Cromwell.

Capp identifies a sense of betrayal as the key animating energy of the Fifth Monarchists.[22] Their incendiary oracles of political resentment echoed some concrete Leveller proposals, such as calls for annual elections of Parliament. But most of all, they prophesied a new age of peace and prosperity, appealing to many who were weary of unrest. The Fifth Monarchist agenda was loose and its alliance of radical congregations unstable. Its greatest support was in London, particularly among Independent and Baptist artisans. Consequently, Fifth Monarchists tended to support the Dutch War because it would reduce foreign trade competition, protecting English manufactures.[23] Their political views were more sectarian and biblicist than liberal. For example, their proposals for legal reform were based upon the Mosaic codes of the Old Testament. And while they would have abolished capital punishment for theft, some of them advocated execution for adultery, blasphemy, and Sabbath-breaking.[24]

Fifth Monarchists shared with Quakers an eschatological emphasis upon Christ's direct government in England through the agency of the saints. But they tended to predicate those hopes on gaining state power, rather than on undertaking social reordering from the grassroots as Quakers attempted. Like the Zealots in Jesus' day, whose revolutionary program could not think beyond a temple-centered society, the Fifth Monarchists were fixated upon control of the state. That mentality generated copious negative political energies, but no coherent positive agenda. An extreme Fifth Monarchist faction led by Thomas Venner attempted a violent insurrection in 1657. They were easily captured by state militias and denounced by most of the Fifth Monarchist leadership. Thus we find a coalition somewhat like the religious right in the United States during the 1980s and 1990s – borrowing some aims and tactics from liberalism, but essentially reactionary in mentality, tending in extreme cases to militia activity.

Murray Tolmie concludes that the Fifth Monarchists were fixated upon "the saints"—leaders of the gathered Separatist, Independent, and Baptist congregations—as the agency of divine intervention in England's political destiny. The predestinational convictions held by most Fifth Monarchists made it impossible for them to embrace the Leveller agenda and its republican concept of the secular state as a sphere of moral action in its own right.[25] The traditional Reformed vision of a purified church and a Christian magistracy, both comprised of God's elect, continued to guide Fifth Monarchist politics, despite their inability to articulate any coherent institutional form.[26]

The Fifth Monarchist movement offered women some recognition and freedom. As Mack notes, women could testify and vote in religious meetings, act as spies, and hold their own meetings. But, following Independent and Baptist precedents, they could not speak as leaders. And the women's meetings had their agendas set by male leaders.[27JM] Having drawn back from Seekerism in 1646 and finding encouragement from John Simpson and other male leaders of the Fifth Monarchist movement, Anna Trapnel was content to remain in their camp, often in a supportive role. Her prophecies were routinely precipitated by political events. But, as a woman, she did not share in the political aspirations of the movement's leaders. Her catatonic states were a feminine counterpart to the impotent strivings of Simpson, Feake, and the other Fifth Monarchy Men.

The rise and fall of the Barebones Parliament, together with the ascendance of Cromwell as Lord Protector, made 1653-54 the apotheosis of Fifth Monarchist ferment. Early in 1653, Fifth Monarchists cherished utopian hopes for the new body. But after it dissolved itself and Cromwell rose to unprecedented power, Simpson and Feake went on the attack, prophesying the fall of the Protectorate within six months. In January 1654, they were arrested and held at Windsor Castle. The same month, the Welsh Fifth Monarchist leader Vavasor Powell was called by the Council of State to account for his political agitation. Anna Trapnel was among a group of supporters who followed him to Whitehall. As they waited outside the chambers, she fell into a trance, praying and singing for eleven hours. She was removed to a room at Whitehall where she spent the next twelve days in fasting, prophecy, and "singing in the Spirit."

Much of her outpouring was taken down by an impromptu "Relator," who published the material anonymously in 1654. The title of the seventy-six-page book, *The Cry of a Stone*, suggests both the catatonia of Trapnel's ecstatic states and the words of Jesus as he entered Jerusalem, that if his disciples did not proclaim him king, the very stones would cry out. Accordingly, Trapnel's prophetic outburst at Whitehall proclaimed Christ as the true political King of England over against Oliver, the Gideon-gone-wrong.

Trapnel claimed that two nights before Cromwell was made Protector in December, she had had a dream or vision of a company of children with light shining around them. A voice informed her that God would abide among them while others died in the wilderness of the Protectorate regime.[28] This "Children of Light" vision evokes the emerging Quaker movement better than the Fifth Monarchist coalition. But Quakers had not yet arrived in London and Trapnel would have known of them only by rumor, if at all.

Singing her prophecies in verse much of the time, Trapnel witnessed to Christ as counter-Protector:

> Oh it will be well worth your time
> To follow the sweet Lamb
> Wherever he goes, oh after him say,
> Oh Lord we come, we come.
>
> Oh here is a General, and he
> is a King of them too,
> A Protector, Conservator,
> Oh draw neer him up to.

> He will be all things to Souldiery
> That their hearts can desire,
> Oh he will be weapons to them,
> He will be their match and fire.[29]

This sounds much like the "Lamb's War" rhetoric of the Quakers, in which Christ is both leader and armament to the faithful. But (like many Quakers during the 1650s) Trapnel did not completely separate this spiritual warfare from the military victories of the New Model Army. Indeed, the same song goes on to extol England's recent exploits in Scotland and the Dutch War. For Fifth Monarchists, the liberation struggle of the 1640s segued into England's nascent imperialism and trade protectionism in the 1650s. This was an aspect of Cromwell's leadership they evidently did not mind.

Near the end of her twelve days of ecstasy, Trapnel sang:

> Oh therefore come! Oh come thou Christ!
> Oh shew thy self now here,
> Oh come! come King Jesus, declare
> How thou art drawing near.
>
> Oh he hath said that he will reign,
> Therefore Rulers shall flye,
> Oh he hath said that he'll cast out
> The fourth great Monarchy.
>
> Oh therefore Clergy, and you State,
> Nothing at all you shall,
> When that the Lord Christ he doth speak,
> You utterly shall fall.[30]

Trapnel shared much in common with early Friends in preaching Christ's second coming. But whereas their witness emphasized a present, unfolding reality, starting among the common people,[31] the Fifth Monarchist approach tended to be more predictive, aspiring to state power to enact a top-down transformation of English society.

The Relator notes that, when she was in trance states, Trapnel seemed not to notice the noisy throng of curious observers gathered around her, but prophesied undistracted. She later explained to the Relator that she sometimes fell silent during trances because she was periodically swallowed up into God's glory, unable to speak.[32]

Trapnel's prophetic career was now in high gear. Soon after her sensational appearance at Whitehall, she felt led to travel to Cornwall, where conservative Puritan control could prove dangerous. Before going, she stayed up all night to pray with ten "sisters" in London.[33] Her activities in Cornwall soon led to arrest under various accusations of "witch," "vagabond," "imposter," "whore," and, most pointedly, "a dangerous seditious person . . . to move, stir up, and raise discord, rebellion, and insurrection."[33] She spent some fifteen weeks under detention in Cornwall, followed by eight more weeks in Bridewell prison, London.

As we noted earlier, it was during her time in Bridewell that summer that Trapnel published *A Legacy for Saints*. After her release and recovery, she published *Anna Trapnel's Report and Plea*, an account of her Cornwall journey and subsequent detentions. The tract counters various aspersions against her character, lashing back at the Cornwall jury that convicted her:

> Oh jurors, when you say you are for the Lord Protector, I am sure you do not mean the great Lord Protector of heaven and earth. . . . Oh that you did love King Jesus he would never fail you, he would teach you to make your indictments truer . . . he would teach you not to use his children as witches, and vagabonds when they come into your parts. . . . And be it known unto you, that Jehovah Protector is my King, Priest, and Prophet whose Kingly power I obey, and all government consonent with it.[35]

Like many Quaker women and men who suffered unjust punishments, Trapnel knew how to use her suffering to heap coals upon the heads of her persecutors.

The Bridewell imprisonment and its filthy conditions were an acid test of Trapnel's prophetic conviction. When she first arrived, the prison matron thought that she had seen her before, as one of a group of "ranting sluts" that had declaimed in exalted language and behaved immorally. Trapnel calmly replied that she was content to be counted among the vile, but that she led a pure life. As she settled into her vermin-infested cell, she was tempted to regret her situation, but remembered how her Lord had suffered between two thieves. Within twenty-four hours, she fell ill with fever and chills. Her female supporters came to help and even stayed in the cell with her. Though she feared she might die in that horrible place, she rebuffed offers of release, being unwilling to promise not to prophesy, "for what the Lord utters in me, I must speak."[36]

After these feverish activities, Trapnel's prophetic activity slowed. She was released from Bridewell the same month John Simpson was freed from Windsor, July 1654.[37] Both of them retreated from political agitation for the next year. Both were arrested again in late 1655 for separate provocations against the Protectorate. After this, Simpson began to preach restraint, for which he was accused of apostasy by his congregation, leading to a split in 1656.[38] Trapnel migrated to theological positions further from Spiritualism and antinomianism. She was baptized sometime in the 1650s and abandoned free-grace for the doctrine of election. Still, she had further outbreaks of catatonic trance-singing in 1657 and 1658.

During a two-week trance event in June 1658, she was visited by Quakers. When they grumbled at some of her prophecies, she began singing louder and faster.[39] Her later life is unknown to us.

As Capp summarizes,[40] relations between Fifth Monarchists and Quakers during the 1650s were complex. Neither group was an organized, membership-based movement at that time. They held many religious ideas and political views in common. Both groups preached in strongly apocalyptic categories of Christ's return to rule on earth. We have already noted some examples where Trapnel's prophecies merged with early Quaker testimony. She was reported by third-party sources to have preached to mixed gatherings of Quakers and Fifth Monarchists. Leaders of the latter movement occasionally had approving words for Quakers and their leaders. But the Quaker Spiritualist tendency to interpret Scripture typologically, in terms of personal experience, rather than literally, aggravated Fifth Monarchists, including Trapnel. Again, Fifth Monarchist biblical literalism translated to political statism. By contrast, the more "inward" interpretations of Friends, while starting out on a more personalistic and apolitical level, had far-reaching political ramifications, owing to the personal and communal transformations wrought by the Lamb.

In general, Fifth Monarchist popularity declined as the Protectorate wore on. The movement was caught in a blind alley of narrowing political options. Meanwhile, other radical spirits followed different and ultimately more productive channels of spiritual renewal and social witness. We move now to a different feminine trajectory of seeking, that of Sarah Jones.

SARAH JONES

We know almost nothing about Sarah Jones.[41] She is thought to have been a widow living in Bristol. She may have been married to a dyer.[42] She was connected with two other female writers of the 1640s, Katherine Chidley and Sarah Wight, both probably Independents like herself. She is thought to be the author of two published tracts, one in 1644, the other in 1650.[43] The first piece is only eight pages and the second a mere three. Both are nonetheless stunning.

Written in 1644, *To Sions Lovers* appeared during the early stages of the civil war, while popular hopes for a national reformation were still high. The title page bears the epigrammatic advice:

> Looke not to Scottish, nor Dutch, New England, nor Olde,
> Behold the paterne, the Apostles fellowship, and so goe up
> by the Tents of the Shepheards (Song of Sol. 1:8).

This is a warning not to replicate existing partial reformations or to escape to America, but to aspire to the New Testament model of faith and order.

Jones addresses a brief preface to "Worthy D. [Doctor] Gouge." This is the same William Gouge we mentioned earlier, the author of a classic Puritan guide to gender relations. His strict piety had earned him the epithet "arch-Puritan." His moderate opposition to the Episcopal hierarchy had gotten him in trouble twice, in the 1620s and again in the 1630s. In 1643, at age sixty-five, he was named to the Westminster Assembly of Divines, the body Parliament created to define the creed and government for a national Presbyterian church. He proved to be one of the Assembly's most zealous members.[44] It is rather surprising that Sarah Jones, given her views, would appeal to such a conservative figure. But she mentions an early personal acquaintance with Gouge, through her deceased father (indicating that she probably had grown up in at least moderately comfortable socioeconomic circumstances). Apparently, the power politics of the Presbyterians had not yet utterly alienated her. As we noted earlier, Phyllis Mack has observed that women were less prone than men to cut all ties with institutional religion. So, while Jones goes on to state strongly egalitarian views, she appeals to Gouge for his judgment, under a concern for ecclesiastical and national unity.

She asks Gouge to elucidate two key ordinances of the church: baptism and the laying on of hands (the ordination of ministers and elders). She fears that a new settlement of the national church will simply continue the unscriptural and hierarchical practices prescribed under episcopacy. She asks for a clear judgment on these ordinances, to allay accusations (by Independents, Baptists, and others) that the Presbyterian order is antichristian. But she goes on to advance her own view that sacramental authority should belong to the congregation itself: take the advice of the Assemblie of the Saints, and so of the spouse of Christ . . . let her have her due . . . right; as she is the Eldership to lay on hands by whom she shall appoint." This is an appeal for an Independent, congregationalist approach to church order: leaders are elected by the vote of the congregation and ordained under its corporate authority.

Jones notes that the continuation of unscriptural practices of baptism has led some (i.e., the Baptists) to seek a second baptism, simply compounding the problem. Further,

> some are seekers out of a Baptisme looking for Elyas as John
> the Baptist to bring it from heaven, forsaking all fellowship
> till Christ shall send forth new Apostles to lay on hands; All
> this is (as I conceive) is for want of the knowledge of those
> two middle principalls. . . . [45]

Here, in 1644, we find a clear and concise definition of the Seeker position. But Jones rejects the Baptist and Seeker positions because she still hopes for some form of national church. If the "two middle principalls" can be rightly reformed, the national church may yet be salvaged. Baptism (sealing the believer into covenant) and the laying on of hands (recognition and empowerment of leaders) are crucial. A truly reformed church must define these ordinances well. But she locates the issue not in the realm of "Priestly" questions of correct sacerdotal technique, but under Christ's "Kingly" office: it is the authority of Christ's wife, the gathered congregation, to decide who and how to consecrate.

Jones adds a postscript to her brief preface, explaining rather apologetically that she has had a few copies of this tract printed for her own use, in order to seek the counsel of others besides Gouge. By prefacing her views under the rubric of seeking men's counsel, Jones maintains her safe status as a woman subject to male authority. But she also exposes Gouge and the Westminster Assembly to overt public pressure to reform the English church more thoroughly. Describing the main text that follows, Jones uses an interesting, gendered image for her authorship: "I presume to father this naked child without Scholasticke phraises, or Schoole learning to dress it and garnish it." Yet the writing is forceful and the vision far-reaching.

In a time of military and ideological warfare, Jones testifies that God has created a new "threshing instrument." It is "the Congregations of the Saints; as shee preachers hold forth Christ, publish the Gospel, take in and cast out, exercising the power of Christ."[46] The term "shee preachers" (an obscure reference to Psa. 68:11) does not refer to women preachers as such (though at one point Jones mentions "male and female" leaders elected by congregations) but to the collective body of believers as a feminine entity. She presents the autonomous, democratic congregations of the Independent movement as the cutting edge of reform. They are fenced cities, truly able to discern, cast out, and fend off sin, because decision-making power rests in the body as a whole.

But she also exhorts readers to "be silent there [i.e., in the fenced cities], for the Lord our God hath put us to silence and given us water of gall to drinke, because wee have sinned." Independents were not known for a silent practice of worship or spiritual discernment. Jones may refer to some practice that was emerging among some radical Independent congregations or worship groups. She prophesies that "God shall put many to silence, and then they will heare what the spirit speaketh to the Saints."[47]

A central principle of this tract is that truly gathered congregations exercise the power of Christ in their midst:

> Thrones set up for Judgement in the gates of Sion, executing
> the power of Christ to judge each other; then there would be
> little or no worke for Lawyers, especially among the Saints.[48]

So this "order of the Gospel" would establish not only ecclesiastical but civil order, obviating oppressive regimes in both realms. Jones' emphasis on Christ's power rising in the group to order them anticipates George Fox's Quaker preaching in the 1650s. She observes that great energies are wasted in struggles between Presbyterians and Independents vying for power. The most important work is for every gathered congregation to move on with the work of electing, choosing out from among themselves, ordaining, investing by their owne power given her from Christ, shee being in his stead the Eldership to appoint her Officers . . . dwelling together in one Parish.[49]

Jones cites the practice of prophesying described by Paul in 1 Corinthians 14, where "males" are to speak one at a time, the others judging. She also echoes Jesus' advice in Matthew 18, in which members sort out differences among themselves.[50] Jones hopes this congregational, democratic system will become standard in England's national church. She prophesies in the oracular first-person:

behold I will make the tipicall congregation nation [i.e., ancient Israel] one congregation under the Gospel a new threshing instrument, so the power is given to her, not to her officers . . . her overseers being one with her, not Lords over her.[51]

Thus, leaders must derive power from the congregation itself, not from a hierarchy over the congregation.

She is also clear that the saints must withdraw from impure, "mixed" congregations (the present parish system). They must gather their own congregations, covenant together, and become accountable to one another. Until now, they have tried to heal Babel. Having failed, they must separate themselves from its confusion and gather into purified flocks. Here is a moral rigorism intolerant of the compromises inherent in an all-inclusive parish system. Congregations are to be fenced cities, "walled by the power of Discipline." Echoing the Song of Solomon 6:4, Jones describes this purified church as "terrible as an army with bannors, comly as Jerusalem beautifull as Tirzah." She concludes, "Oh, that wee might submitt one to another in all that is good. O that the time were come that the wolfe might lie with the lamb, and a little childe should lead them."[52]

We know nothing of Sarah Jones' thoughts or movements during the rest of the 1640s. No doubt, she must have been discouraged by the repressive tactics of the Presbyterians in Parliament and their protracted power struggles with the Independent party. She may also have bemoaned a shallowness and ineffectiveness even among the democratic congregations she had found so liberating in 1644. Many radical congregations and worship groups lost vitality as the liberation drama of the 1640s sputtered and failed. The crisis of spiritual knowledge and authority only deepened during this period. But we can also guess that for those very reasons Jones must have deepened spiritually and connected with other Spiritualists through the discipline of silence that she witnessed in 1644. As we have heard obliquely from sources in the army and elsewhere, a new sense of power and authority coalesced among those who gathered penitently to "wait upon the Lord." Consequently, our next (and last) word from Sarah Jones manifests a different tone and content from her earlier prophecy, intimating a deep spiritual immersion and a new basis of hope.

This is Lights appearance in the Truth is not really the title of a tract but the first line of a three-page epistle to an unspecified group of "dear Lambs of the Life, Dark vanished, Light shines forth." Published in 1650, the letter's first line clearly sets it apart from the ferment of the Ranters, who equated light and darkness. Various individuals and groups made use of Paul's term, "children of light," from Ephesians 5:8. We saw Anna Trapnel utilize that imagery as a Fifth Monarchist. But we know that already in the late 1640s, a network of Spiritualists in the Midlands, gathering around the still obscure figure of George Fox, were calling themselves "Children of the Light" (see the next chapter). Sarah Jones' 1650 epistle may have been written in the flow of that incipient Quaker movement. It seems possible that she was one of the new style of female leaders emerging within that network.

Jones speaks to the weary, disconsolate spiritual condition of Seekers in 1650. Their travails have brought them "to the loss of all things," a bereft state in which she repeatedly addresses them as "dear babes." In contrast to the bold, annunciatory tone of *Sions Lovers*, this epistle is tender, maternal, gently encouraging. Rather than continue struggling spiritually and politically, or bolt into the extravagant gestures of the Ranters, Jones exhorts her "babes" to

> sink down into that eternal word, and rest there, and not in any manifestations that proceeds from the word . . . for those that build upon the manifestations, and not upon that that manifests, sets up an Idol in the heart, which the Lord God will shortly throw down.[52]

To sink down is to cease struggling against the dark eclipse overspreading English radicalism. It is to discover the living Word within, the source

of all revelations. One must dwell a while in the darkness in order for
the spiritual eye to adjust and behold this hidden light. As one discovers
and abides in this light, the sense of darkness vanishes.

This state of deep resignation must be learned despite the strong temptations that inevitably come. Again, Jones counsels to

> sink down into that measure of life that ye have received, and
> go not out with your in-looking at what is contrary to you,
> for if you do you will miss of the power that should destroy
> it, for as you keep in that which is pure . . . it will work and
> operate so, that it will overcome what is contrary.[54]

To be teased out by fears, distractions, desires, curiosity—whatever
is contrary to that sublime, ineffable Presence within—is to leave that
Presence, the one power that overcomes such temptations.

> And so, you, dear babes, that are little and weak in your own
> eyes . . . look not at your own weakness, but look at him who
> is calling you in his eternal love, who will make the weak
> strong . . . Ah my soul, canst not thou say so by experience?
> yes surely.

The key is to avoid reasoning with the voice of the serpent, which only
darkens God's counsel within; "but in the power of the Lord shut him
out . . . had Eve done so, she had not been overcome."[55]

In such troubled times, however, all have been overcome in one way
or another. She counsels:

> while the trouble and conflicts are upon their spirits . . . stand
> still and see the salvation of God, which is the light of his
> Covenant, which will stretch forth the hand of his power as
> he did to Peter when he feared the proud waves would have
> prevailed over him.

Such counsel must have been powerful in the dark night of eclipse in
1650. In the quotation at the head of this chapter, we see Jones utilizing
a biblical typology that became central among Quaker writers in the
1650s: the Jacob-Esau conflict in Genesis. This typology can also
be found in Winstanley's *Fire in the Bush* the same year.[56] Although
they were twins, Esau was born first. An adept hunter, he was always
questing about here and there. By contrast, the second-born, Jacob, the

favorite of their mother Rebekkah, lived quietly at home. Those who would live in the second birth must give up Esau's restless, seeking nature and "live at home with Jacob, which is daily to retire thy mind; though the gadding, hunting Esau persecutes thee for it, thou shalt receive the blessing."[57] Esau's persecuting takes two forms: the inward agitation of the mind that will not stop questing and the outward hostility of those who would make all conform to their formal religion.

In contrast to the revolutionary dynamism of her earlier tract, Jones' tone and message here are quietistic, deeply immersed in the hard-won state of resignation of one who has "come down, come down to the Word of his patience." Yet something is gestating in this deep place:

> Oh how my bowels yernes in that living Word! yea, that ye may not fall short, but be crowned with Immortality and glory; for oh the glorious day of the Lord God hasteth to be revealed to those that are kept faithful in his Word.

The apocalyptic hope of the 1640s has died. It lies buried in the chastened hearts of those who had hoped for the kingdom of God on earth. But there is a slight glimmer here that the "glorious day of the Lord" looms even yet.

To say more would be to get ahead of our story and to anticipate the fresh socio-spiritual synthesis that emerged soon after in the Quaker movement. But Jones' epistle is a revealing transitional document. It is a strong prototype of the epistles of spiritual counsel published George Fox in 1652 and after.[58] We do not know whether Jones had by this time left the Independent churches that gave her so much hope in 1644. But there is a possible line of development from the silent worship groups in which she was already participating by 1644 and the various "Children of Light" that dotted the Midlands by 1650. The name "Sarah Jones" appears on a Yorkshire Quaker petition against tithes that was signed by "7,000 Handmaids" of the Lord and published in 1659. Mary Garman admits that this may be a different woman with the same name. But, given the wide-ranging movements of early Quaker prophets, male and female, it is quite conceivable that the writer of our 1650 epistle was itinerating as a Quaker preacher nine years later.[59]

Although Jones rejected the Seekers in 1644, they were quite numerous around Bristol, and their Spiritualist ferment had clearly exerted influence on her by 1650. Like R. Wilkinson and Anna Trapnel, she warned

the faithful that "ye may not rest short of [God] himself." We may assume
that her concern for consensual spiritual discernment, or "gospel order,"
was still lively, even if it does not lie within the purview of her 1650
epistle. It was now being grounded on a deeper foundation, a chastened
spirit of resignation that could pierce deeper but also more compassion-
ately into all spiritual conditions. A new fusion of intense spiritual experience, moral rigor, and group spiritual discernment was in the making.

Notes

1. Sarah Jones, *This is Lights appearance in the Truth* (1650), 2-3.
2. Phyllis Mack, *Visionary Women: Ecstatic Prophecy in Seventeenth-Century England* (Berkeley: University of California Press, 1992).
3. Mack, *Visionary Women*, 89.
4. Mack, *Visionary Women*, 185-86. She makes this point specifically in regard to Quaker men and women, where it may be more strongly the case. But the observation may apply to the more advanced Seekers as well.
5. Mack, *Visionary Women*, 34,112.
6. Mary Cary, *The Resurrection of the Witness* (1648), quoted in Mack, *Visionary Women*, 90.
7. Mack, *Visionary Women*, 53.
8. Mack, *Visionary Women*, 97.
9. Anna Trapnel, *A Legacy for Saints* (1654), 1-4.
10. Trapnel, *Saints*, 6-7.
11. Trapnel, *Saints*, 8-14.
12. Trapnel, *Saints*, 19.
13. Trapnel, *Saints*, 20.
14. Trapnel, *Saints*, 20.
15. Anna Trapnel, *The Cry of a Stone* (1654), 3.
16. Trapnel, *Saints*, 23-40.
17. Bernard Capp, "John Simpson (1615-62)," in *The Dictionary of National Biography*, *Missing Persons* supplementary volume (Oxford: University Press, 1993), 602-03.
18. Murray Tolmie, *The Triumph of the Saints: The Separate Churches of London 1616-1649* (Cambridge: University Press, 1977), 109.
19. Bernard Capp, "The Fifth Monarchists and Popular Millenarianism," in *Radical Religion in the English Revolution*, ed. McGregor and Reay (Oxford: University Press, 1984), p. 170.
20. Mary Cary, *A New and More Exact Mappe or Description of New Jerusalems Glory* (1651), quoted in Mack, *Visionary Women*, 101.
21. Anna Trapnel, *Stone*, 11.
22. Capp, "Fifth Monarchists," 174.

23. Christopher Hill, *The Experience of Defeat: Milton and Some Contemporaries* (New York: Viking, 1984), 61.
24. Capp, "Fifth Monarchists," 173.
25. Tolmie, *Triumph*, 185.
26. Tolmie, *Triumph*, 190.
27. Mack, *Visionary Women*, 107, 123.
28. Trapnel, *Stone*, 13.
29. Trapnel, *Stone*, 26.
30. Trapnel, *Stone*, 71-73.
31. See my previous two books on George Fox, early Friends, and their apocalyptic spirituality and politics: *Apocalypse of the Word: The Life and Message of George Fox* (Richmond, Ind.: Friends United Press, 1986); and *The Covenant Crucified: Quakers and the Rise of Capitalism* (Wallingford, Pa.: Pendle Hill, 1995).
32. Trapnel, *Stone*, 14 15.
33. Mack, *Visionary Women*, 97.
34. *English Women's Voices, 1540-1700,* ed. Charlotte F. Otten (Miami: Florida International University Press, 1992), 57.
35. Anna Trapnel, *Anna Trapnel's Report and Plea* (1654), in *Voices*, 77.
36. Trapnel, *Report*, 72.
37. Bernard S. Capp, *The Fifth Monarchy Men: A Study in Seventeenth-Century English Millenarianism* (Totowa, N. J.: Rowman and Littlefield, 1972), 102-03.
38. Capp, "John Simpson," 602-03.
39. Stevie Davies, *Unbridled Spirits: Women of the English Revolution: 1640-1660* (London: Women's Press, 1998), 247-48.
40. Capp, *Men*, 182-83.
41. I rely here on the information gathered by Mary Garman in *Hidden in Plain Sight: Quaker Women's Writings, 1650-1700*, ed. Garman, Applegate, Benefiel, and Meredith, (Wallingford, Pa.: Pendle Hill, 1996), 21.
42. She is so described in the *McAlpin Catalogue* of seventeenth-century English literature at Union Seminary, New York (New York: Union Theological Seminary, 1930), 5:357.
43. Only the initials "S. J." appear on 1644's *To Sions Lovers*; but the piece is generally attributed to Jones.
44. "William Gouge (1578-1653)," in *The Dictionary of National Biography* (Oxford: University Press, 1917), 8:272.
45. Sarah Jones, *To Sions Lovers* (1644), Preface.
46. Jones, *Lovers*, 3.
47. Jones, *Lovers*, 3.
48. Jones, *Lovers*, 5.
49. Jones, *Lovers*, 6.
50. Jones, *Lovers*, 7.
51. Jones, *Lovers*, 8.
52. Jones, *Lovers*, 8.
53. Sarah Jones, *This is Lights appearance in the Truth* (1650), reprinted in *Hidden in Plain Sight*, 35-37.
54. Jones, *Lights*, 35.

55. Jones, *Lights*, 36.
56. Gerrard Winstanley, *Fire in the Bush* (1650), 49-50.
57. Jones, *Lights*, 37.
58. See, for example, Fox's very similar counsel regarding temptation in Epistle #10 of his *Works* (Philadelphia: Gould, 1831), 7:20-21.
59. Garman, *Hidden in Plain Sight*, 20.

CHAPTER 8

THE QUAKER APOCALYPSE
FROM SEEKING TO SUFFERING

Wisdom Hath uttered forth her voice to you, but the eye and ear which is abroad, waiting upon the sound of words without you, is that which keeps you from your Teacher within you; and this is the reason that in all your seekings you have found nothing; such as your seeking is, such is your finding. . . . Therefore . . . come out of the manie things; theres but one thing needful, keep to it . . . that into my Mothers house you all may come, and into the Chamber of her that conceived me, where you may embrace, and be embraced of my dearly beloved one, Love is his name, Love is his Nature, Love is his life [see Song of Sol. 3:1-4].

—Sarah Blackborow[1]

The Quaker movement became a recognizable phenomenon in northern England during the summer of 1652. It quite unexpectedly galvanized dispirited Seekers and depleted Ranters into a fresh, refocused burst of energy. For years, the energies of thousands of England's most devout souls had been kept in an unbearable tension of utopian expectation. The Ranter rebellion released that pent-up energy in an explosion of rage, nihilistic glee, and hedonism. The Quaker catharsis expressed itself in behavior that initially struck many as Ranterism, but proved to be of an entirely different order.

The Quaker emergence of 1652 remains largely inexplicable unless we first retrace the 1640s through the personal experiences of George Fox.[2] His odyssey shared much in common with the quests of many Seekers of the period. But Fox's path of discovery ultimately redirected seeking within a new frame of reference, one that reasserted, even empowered, the utopian expectations of Seekers—albeit by way of a dread-filled, desolating inner apocalypse.

George Fox's Early Years

George Fox was a grave eighteen-year-old when the civil war broke out in 1642. Raised in the Midlands county of Leicestershire by devout Puritan parents, he was often deeply troubled by the "wantonness" he found among many, young and old. He was even more dismayed to find superficiality and hypocrisy among "professors," those considered to be pious models of Puritan faith. He withdrew from such company for the sake of his inner sense of integrity. Apprenticed to a shoemaker, young Fox was both astute and scrupulous in business. His reputation for honesty brought business to his master. His work also included shepherding, which provided this tender teenager some refuge from the human company he found so disturbing. Like some other Seekers we will note, he found solace in the natural world.

In the summer of 1643, the year of Parliament's Solemn League and Covenant, Fox went into deep personal crisis. He was invited to share a jug of beer with two Puritan friends, which he gladly did. But when the first glass led on to others and to drinking to one another's health (an oblique form of oath-taking), he was offended and left. Fox was badly shaken by the experience of seeing two supposedly model Christians (one of them his own cousin) drink excessively and make banter of religious language. Feeling tainted by the incident, he was unable to sleep that night. Soon afterward, Fox left home "at the command of the Lord," who said to him, "Thou seest how young people go together into vanity and old people into the earth; and thou must forsake all, both young and old, and keep out of all, and be as a stranger to all."[3]

Thus began years of wandering in search of a sense of peace and integrity. During the 1640s, Fox, like thousands of Seekers, visited many religious groups, heard many preachers, and read many books. But he varied from the classic Seeker trajectory that shifted allegiance from Presbyterians, to Independents, to Baptists, finally forsaking all. Fox visited groups but did not join; he desperately sought the counsel of many ministers, but did not follow any of them: "they could not speak to my condition." He undoubtedly learned from many sources; yet he found all of them confused and compromised. He lived in constant fear of being contaminated by them.

Fox wandered through the Midlands over the next months, disoriented and depressed, keeping mostly to himself. Near despair, he was beset with many temptations, including suicide. By the summer of 1644, he had arrived in London for a stay with his uncle, a man named Pickering who was prominent among General Baptists.[4] Fox came on the scene at an auspicious moment for the Baptists there. The Calvinist Particular Baptists challenged Independent leaders to debates concerning infant baptism and won many to their cause. The more Anabaptist-influenced General Baptists also expanded rapidly. Both groups welcomed the ministry of untrained preachers, common men of the trades. General Baptists permitted the speaking of women more than any other group. Fox undoubtedly learned much from his stay in London during such heady times. Still, the religious and political confusion of the day made London appear to him as "under a chain of darkness." He writes of the Baptists: "they were tender then." Still, "I could not impart my mind to him [his uncle] nor join with them, for I saw all, young and old, where they were."[5] By sometime in the autumn, he returned to the Midlands.

Over the next couple of years, Fox alternated between sojourns at home in Leicestershire and travels through other Midlands locales, including Coventry, a future center of Ranterism, where "there were many tender people." He began to have "great openings" in his understanding of the Book of Revelation. But Puritan clergy sought to steer him away from that dangerous text.[6] Still under spiritual oppression, he continued to seek counsel from many sources. Some would have had him married, others encouraged him to train for ministry, while others suggested military service to Parliament. One minister advised him to smoke tobacco and sing Psalms; another suggested bleeding. But Fox disliked tobacco, was too depressed to sing, and even failed to draw blood. By this time, he was clear that he could never go back to parish religion; but neither could he join any of the dissenting groups he encountered. Despite his struggles with despair, Fox began to impart his insights through preaching and debate. Though by no means a national figure, this severe twenty-two-year-old began to attract attention in the Midlands. Thomas Edwards' *Gangraena* contains an entry dated June 1646:

> There is a shoemaker in Coventry or thereabouts, a famous
> Preacher, who goes from Coventry and those parts up and down
> Glostershire Warwickshire, Wostershire, preaching and venting
> erroneous points of Antinomianism, Anabaptisme, preaching
> against Tythes, Baptisme of Children: A minister of the City of
> London being in Glostershire heard him preach and heard of his
> large Diocese, and perambulations from place to place.[7]

Given what we know of Fox's doctrines and movements in 1646, this
could well be a description of him and his activities.

THE CHILDREN OF THE LIGHT

By early 1647, Fox was spending significant time in Nottinghamshire,
forming a network of small groups. The work centered around Mansfield,
where a community of General Baptists had "shattered" into two groups.
One group continued to meet for worship. A woman in her mid-forties
named Elizabeth Hooton was one of its prominent figures. The other
group met more for discussion and recreation. Fox later described them
wryly as "the greatest football players and wrestlers in the country."[8] He
met with both groups and won over most of them, preaching the light of
Christ, exhorting them to turn to it and walk in it. But some members of
the more libertine group soon found Fox's moral strictures oppressive
and fell out (more about this episode in Chapter 10). Those drawn to
Fox's preaching began calling themselves "Children of the Light."[9] They
were not unique among Spiritualists in the use of this name. In the
preceding chapter, we saw the Fifth Monarchist Anna Trapnel use it.
But the name continued to be used in the movement for years to come,
alongside "Friends" and the epithet "Quakers."

Elizabeth Hooton is the first ally Fox mentions by name in his
Journal. Though he describes nothing of his association with her, the
influence of this woman twenty years his senior may have been important. For the next three to four years, Fox's travels took him repeatedly
back to the Mansfield area. During that time, his despair slowly lifted
and his ministry took shape. It was not long after encountering Hooton
that Fox had a key experience that relocated spiritual authority decisively within:

> As I had forsaken all the priests, so I left the separate preachers
> also, and those called the most experienced people; for I
> saw there was none among them all that could speak to my
> condition. And when all my hopes in them and in all men
> were gone, so that I had nothing outwardly to help me, nor
> could tell what to do, then, Oh then, I heard a voice which
> said, "There is one, even Christ Jesus, that can speak to thy
> condition," and when I heard it my heart did leap for joy.[10]

Forsaking the counsel of both clergy and dissenters, Fox found his true
help within. His "desires after the Lord grew stronger" and he gained a
deeper sense of God's endless, eternal love. Even so, his sorrows became more acute, tempting him to despair, as his inner conflict came
more fully into view. Two thirsts became evident within him: one for
outward means of comfort and strength, the other for God's inward
empowerment. Though he was torn between these two desires, "the Lord
did stay my desires upon himself from whom my help came, and my
care was cast upon him alone."[11]

His deep inner struggles evidently surfaced at times in audible sounds:
during this period he came to discern two kinds of "thoughts, groans
and sighs" in himself. The first were the groans of the flesh, which could
not endure the fire of God's refining power and "could not be patient in
all trials . . . and could not give up self to die by the Cross, the power of
God." But he also heard himself give forth other

> groans of the spirit, which did open me, and made interces-
> sion to God, in which spirit is the true waiting upon God for
> redemption of the body and of the whole creation [see Rom.
> 8:18-27]. And by this true spirit, in which the true sighing is,
> I saw over the false sighings and groanings."[12]

Thus, a peculiarly visceral sense of spiritual struggle developed in Fox's
own experience and in his spiritual counsel to others. Sighing and groaning
(and perhaps trembling) may well have been an ecstatic element in worship among the Children of the Light by this time, as it was later among
early Quakers. These physical expressions of spiritual experience became
key elements in the Quaker transformation of religious seeking.[13]

We know less about Hooton's experience during this period, except
that she became a central figure among the Children of the Light around

Mansfield and that her home in the village of Skegby became a meeting place for the group. These activities led to a period of estrangement from her husband and to many years of itinerant ministry.[14] These dramatic developments in the lives of both Hooton and Fox may suggest that the interaction between them was significant. It is possible that this woman twenty years Fox's senior helped him move into a deeper surrender to the inward authority of Christ's light. Likewise, Fox may have mobilized Hooton toward a more public ministry and leadership. Both of these movements transcended traditional masculine and feminine gender formations and social roles. In some way, Fox and Hooton may have elicited the undeveloped "shadow" gender in one another. Such an eclipse of ego-invested gender identity would surely send both through painful experiences of the "dark night of the soul." But that passage would also open new channels of divine knowledge and authority within. The power of God was neither the unexplored feminine within Fox nor the undeveloped masculine within Hooton. Rather, these were the gateways to a divine power still more deeply within each—yet also vastly beyond.

The interaction between Fox and Hooton, then, was probably intimate, but not likely sexual as such. Sexual liberation had been a route of transcendence among Ranters. It wrought temporary release but no enduring power. Fox and his followers were strongly against sexual freedom, on grounds that were not only moral. The moral stance was founded in an epistemology—a way of knowing—that eschewed the pleasure of sexual release (except within a marriage covenant) in order to drive the individual deeper into the personal resources and divine power locked within. As we shall see, the interaction of feminine and masculine was an important factor in generating the enormous energy of the Quaker movement. But while that energy boiled over into sexual freedom in a few cases (which were strongly condemned by the movement), it was typically channeled along lines that were physically cathartic (groaning, sighing, weeping, quaking) but not sexual as such. It may seem highly speculative to construct such a dynamic around Fox and Hooton, given that neither divulged anything so significant about their relationship. But the dynamic we shall see in subsequent Seeker conversions reveals a pattern that may indeed have been set at the beginning between these two.

Significantly, it was during the same period that Fox records defending women's right to speak in the church. At a public debate among several ministers in Leicestershire, a woman asked the ministers a question. One minister replied that women were not allowed to speak; "Whereupon I was rapt up, as in a rapture, in the Lord's power." Fox challenged the ministers, advancing his principle that without the leading and power of Christ, *neither* men *nor* women may speak in church, whereas *with* the leading and power of Christ, *both* men *and* women are anointed to speak. The entire assembly broke into chaos, but Fox continued debating with several people at a nearby inn. Although most opposed him, "there were several convinced that day; and the woman that asked the question aforesaid was convinced, and her family; and the Lord's power and glory shined over all."[15]

As Fox began to discern the different "thirsts" within himself, he also began to discern different "natures" at work in others as well. He gained a reputation as a discerner of spirits; many came to him for counsel.[16] Slowly, the bouts of depression became less paralyzing and passed more quickly. Around Mansfield, where he spent most of his time, Fox was noted both for his controversial views and for his assiduously moral life. Years later, local residents remembered him as an energetic tradesman (in shoemaking) who never uttered an idle word and gave all he could spare to the poor. Even those who disagreed with him acknowledged his integrity.[17]

Fox received a decisive vision in 1648:

> I saw there was a great crack to go throughout the earth, and a great smoke to go as the crack went; and that after the crack there should be a great shaking. This was the earth in people's hearts, which was to be shaken before the Seed of God was raised out of the earth. And it was so; for the Lord's power began to shake them, and great meetings we began to have.[18]

We hear a powerful fusion of apocalyptic imageries (the earthquakes in Rev. 11 and 14) with the dynamics of personal and group spirituality. It is described here in terms very similar to those witnessed the same year by Gerrard Winstanley in *The Breaking of the Day of God*.[18] That powerful fusion would become central to Fox's preaching, profoundly affecting thousands of Seekers. The apocalyptic earthquake of physical trembling continued to intensify among the Children of the Light in Nottinghamshire and Leicestershire.[20] The work also spread north into Derbyshire:

> Thus the work of the Lord went forward, and many were
> turned from darkness to light within the compass of these
> three years, 1646, 1647, and 1648. And divers meetings of
> Friends, in several places, were then gathered to the Lord's
> teaching . . . for the Lord's power brake forth more and more
> wonderfully.[21]

Note also the language of the "seed" in Fox's 1648 vision. We found this in the writings of other Seekers in the 1640s. As the light metaphor expressed the revelatory aspects of God's presence within, the seed metaphor expressed a new sense of divine power.

Fox began to speak not only at religious meetings but at fairs and before magistrates as well, inveighing against immorality and social injustices. The latter included the national church tithe system, low wages set by magistrates for seasonal agricultural workers, and the cheating of simple country folk by merchants.[22] He preached an increasingly apocalyptic message, warning people of the coming day of the Lord, calling them to repentance.[23]

Faith healings occurred around Mansfield and elsewhere. In 1649, in the home of Elizabeth Hooton, Fox performed an exorcism on a local woman. The event frightened neighbors and inspired rumors of witchcraft. Fox had become a disturbing presence around Mansfield. He was beaten up and put in the stocks for impromptu speaking at a parish service. The constable finally intervened in his behalf and he limped out of town, badly bruised "and bruised inwardly at my heart." Though he was shaken by this first of many mob attacks to come, he was also reassured by the fact that "some people were convinced of the Lord's Truth and turned to his teaching."[24] His ministry continued to become more confrontational.

Thus, by 1650, Fox's personal transformation was more or less complete and most features of his ministry were in place. Although he was still an obscure figure, he had formed a significant network in the Midlands. He was noted for a keen discernment of spiritual states, faith healings, moral rigor, socioeconomic concern, and apocalyptic warnings. He aroused cathartic, visceral responses in his hearers, polarizing groups into two camps: those who were smitten by his message, and those who smote back.

DERBY: 1650-1651

That earliest phase ended in the autumn of 1650, on a trip to Derby. On October 30, Fox spoke up during a public lecture where a number of army officers were present. He proclaimed the day of the Lord and called them to follow the light within them, warning that they were not to debate Christ but *obey* him. An officer brought him to the local magistrates, who questioned him for eight hours. What scandalized them was Fox's claim to moral perfection through the indwelling of Christ. He was sentenced to six months in prison under the Blasphemy Act (which we noted in Chapter 6 had been passed in August to quell the Ranter movement). "And so they committed me as a blasphemer and as a man that had no sin."[25] His claim apparently sounded suspiciously like Ranter preaching of freedom from sin through sin. Although Fox's *Journal* does not mention it, Elizabeth Hooton had accompanied him to Derby. She was arrested and imprisoned about the same time for interrupting a parish minister's sermon.[26]

Continuing to develop his apocalyptic outlook and message, Fox considered his prison time to be Derby's day of visitation.[27] He heaped burning coals upon the heads of his persecutors by circulating prophetic warnings to them. A steady stream of local clergy came to him, challenging his claims to perfection. He accused them of "preaching sin to the grave" and sounded the familiar Spiritualist theme of "Christ in you, the hope of glory." The pure light within purifies those who walk in it. But "they could not endure to hear of purity, or being made pure here."[28] Fox also published at least one general epistle of spiritual counsel. It contains themes similar to those we found in Sarah Jones' piece from the same year (see Chapter 7), but with a stronger emphasis on moral empowerment in the light.[29]

Thus, imprisonment amplified Fox's message in the area. It brought to him not only antagonists but local sympathizers as well. And through various seeking networks, Fox's Derby apocalypse began to attract wider attention. He corresponded with Seekers, including one Richard Farnworth in western Yorkshire.[30]

In the spring of 1651, as his six-month sentence neared completion, Fox was joined in prison by a number of men who had been pressed into service by the army. Their service was required to put down a Royalist uprising. By this time, after the defeat of the Levellers and the purging of radicals from the army, it was harder to rally men to "the Good Old Cause." As Fox noted, the "deceit and hypocrisy of the officers" had become evident to many. The imprisoned men rallied around Fox, who probably reminded them of the radical army chaplains of the 1640s. They wanted him to be their officer.

Fox reports that army commissioners offered him a captaincy if he would fight for the Commonwealth.

> But I told them I lived in the virtue of that life and power that took away the occasion of all wars, and I knew from whence all wars did rise, from the lust according to James's doctrine (James 4:1ff.).

The process of deep inward surrender over the past seven years had formed within Fox an unshakable resolve. He had faced down every dread and desire, leaving only the holy dread that meets every earnest soul with tender love, but confronts every deceitful heart with its own vanity:

> And they said they offered it [the captaincy] in love and kindness to me because of my virtue, and such like flattering words they used, and I told them if that were their love and kindness I trampled it under my feet. Then their rage got up and they . . . put me into the dungeon amongst thirty felons in a lousy, stinking low place in the ground without any bed.

He was kept under detention for another six months.[31]

So it was October 1651 before Fox was finally released from Derby. He was ready, and the times were ready for him. The churches were fighting among themselves, the Levellers had been defeated, Seekers were in disarray, and the boiling rage of the Ranters had been reduced to a simmer.

> I saw that when the Lord should bring me forth, it would be as the letting of a lion out of a den amongst the wild beasts of the forest. For all the professions [i.e., defined religious groups] stood in a beastly spirit and nature, pleading for sin . . . and imperfection as long as they lived. And they all kicked and yelled, and roared, and raged, and ran against the life and spirit which gave forth the Scriptures, which they professed in words. And so it was.[32]

Fox had picked up a thread in Derby. And from there he found a seam in the apparently hopeless situation. He now moved quickly to open that seam into a fully apocalyptic tear, a rending of the veil over the entire social order, beginning with religion.

Yorkshire and Beyond

Fox moved now with a new focus. After a brief passage through his Midlands network, he traveled north to Yorkshire. His twin objectives appear to have been to meet privately with ready allies and to attack publicly his avowed opposition, the parish "priests." The mob attack in Mansfield, followed by imprisonment at Derby, had helped to clarify the importance of a confrontational approach: "Now the Lord had showed me, while I was in Derby prison, that I should speak in steeplehouses to gather people from thence."[33] Even as Fox's Christian pacifism became explicit, his sense of apocalyptic conflict sharpened. This was an experiential, here-and-now apocalypse—that is, conflictual events in which the day of the Lord, the second advent of Christ, was revealed (the literal meaning of the Greek verb *apokalypto*) in the hearts of those present, creating a climate of crisis and decision for or against this incursion of divine power and authority on earth.[34]

Reaching Yorkshire, Fox went straight to Balby, where he met with Richard Farnworth and others. Farnworth was still in his early twenties (and Fox twenty-seven) when they finally met. From age sixteen, Farnworth had been troubled by severe pangs in his conscience, "the wrath of God revealed against sin in me." He had sought to appease the wrath and attain salvation through prayer, memorization of Scripture, listening to sermons, and finding spiritual counsel. He had led a strict life, eschewing all sports and idle pleasures. But he gained no inner assurance from his efforts and was scorned by his neighbors in Balby. In classic Puritan fashion, he went into crisis because he felt no assurance that he was truly among God's elect. He felt nothing within but condemnation:

> and curses rung in my ears, cursed, cursed, cursed art thou . . . and the pure was stirred up in me, and wounded the Serpent time after time, yet not meeting with any true shepherd that could direct . . . where the fold was, I wandered to and fro."[34]

As he continued attending the parish services in the late 1640s, Farnworth became annoyed that ministers "began to rail and bark like dogs against heretics and schismatics." He asked them to show where the new groups (such as Baptists and Seekers) were wrong, for he had begun to find fellowship among them. (He evidently had contacts in the army as well, since he specifically mentions "soldiers who feared God.") But speaking up for dissenters only made Farnworth a new target for clerical attack.

Feeling he was surely the most miserable creature on earth, Farnworth heard a voice within saying, "I will teach thee freely my self, and all the children of the Lord shall be taught of the Lord, and in righteousness shall they be established."[36] That divine promise may have come to consciousness partly through his correspondence with Fox in Derby. Still, Farnworth's friends persuaded him to return to parish worship one more time. But he now found it so oppressive that he knew he could never go back. It was in this state of resolute "waiting upon the Lord" that Farnworth was found by Fox and united with him.

Fox quickly moved on (probably at Farnworth's suggestion) to the home of a Lieutenant Roper, where he met a small group of advanced Seekers, notably James Nayler, Thomas Goodaire, and William Dewsbury. All three readily joined with Fox. Of these, Dewsbury left the most extensive testimony of his seeking and transformation. Aged thirty by the time he met Fox, he had lived in "lightness and vanity . . . untill I was about eight Years of Age," when deep sorrow for sin seized his heart.[37] The troubled boy was apprenticed at age thirteen to a cloth-maker in Leeds, where he found many people seeking. Slowly, he lost faith in the sacraments, services, and counsel of the established clergy. He gave these up, finding no assurance of his election through their practice. All he felt was God's relentless wrath. His malaise led to physical weakness and difficulty in his apprenticeship.

When the war broke out, he joined the Parliamentary army for a while, hearing that there was a true "fear of the Lord" among the soldiers. But where he was stationed in Scotland, he found only formal observance. He worshiped for a while among Independents and Baptists, but his mind was finally turned inward to wait in God's counsel and hear what the Lord would say. The word came:

> Put up thy Sword into thy Scabard, if my Kingdom were of
> this World, then would my Children Fight . . . which Word

enlightened my Heart, and discovered the mystery of iniquity, and that the Kingdom of Christ was within; and the
Enemies was within, and was spiritual, and my Weapons
against them must be spiritual, the Power of God.[38]

For Dewsbury, this was a key moment of inner "convincement" (the
17th-century meaning for Friends was closer to "conviction"). The resolution to turn inward changed everything. It redirected the focus of
struggle from outward, political, and military warfare to inward,
spiritual warfare. He immediately left the military and went back home.
As had happened with Fox, Dewsbury's discovery of inward spiritual
authority only deepened his turmoil at first. He felt the plagues of Egypt
unleashed upon his soul:

and in this condemned estate I lay crying in the depth of misery, without any hopes of deliverance by any thing I could do
to pacifie the Wrath of God, till the Administration of the
Prophets, that witnessed to my Soul there was free redemption
laid up for me, to wait for his coming; there I waited until the
Administration of John; and . . . he was a burning and shining
Light, who discovered more of the mystery of iniquity in
me . . . and the cry of my condemned Soul was great, and could
not be satisfied but breathed and thirsted after Christ, to save
me freely through his Blood . . . and in this condemned estate
I lay waiting for the coming of Christ Jesus, who in the appointed time of the Father appeared to my Soul . . . and my
dead soul heard his voice, and by his voice was made to
live...and sealed me up in the everlasting Covenant of life, with
his Blood. . . . And I witness these Scriptures fulfilled in me, in
the year according to the account, 1645.[39]

Through the turn within, this advanced Seeker experienced the history
of salvation—from the fall from grace in Genesis, to the experience of
the law's condemnation for sin, to the prophets' oracles of the Messiah's
coming, to John the Baptist's ministry of repentance, to the raising up
of Christ within—was replayed in himself, the great saga of salvation
recapitulated on the inner landscape of the human soul.[40]

Dewsbury drives home this point at the end of his testimony,
insisting that this transformation did not come through Bible reading or

listening to sermons, but "by the Inspiration of the Spirit of Jesus Christ, who alone is found worthy to open the Seals of the Book [see Rev. 5-8] . . . for he alone opened the Seals of the Book in me, and sealed it up to my Soul by the Testimony of his own Spirit."[41] We recognize here a different way of knowing. The Scriptures are "opened" to the individual not by intellectual explication, but as their testimony is played out in personal experience.

We saw something like this in R. Wilkinson's stages of spiritual rest on the way to an inward Canaan. We also found in Joseph Salmon's *Antichrist in Man* the idea that Scriptural history is confirmed by one's experience of spiritual mystery. Dewsbury had traversed this territory by 1645 and was surely moving in Seeker circles around northern England in the late 1640s. But, like other Seekers during those years, he found himself in a state of suspension, rather than true peace. He writes that he was led into a wilderness to be tempted by the devil. Slowly, he learned to wait upon God's counsel, groaning under the power of sin until the Lord finally freed him in the year 1651[42]—the year he met Fox. That state of agitation and expectation had finally driven Seekers like Joseph Salmon over the brink into despair and rage. Dewsbury was among those who found the strength to wait quietly a little longer. Fox's preaching of moral perfection inspired a new confidence of Christ's overcoming power. Fox's deep discernment of spiritual states and his emotionally cathartic style may also have helped to ground Dewsbury's advanced Spiritualism more acutely in the body.

Another element in Fox's catalytic effect was his overt attack upon the established church. Certainly, all Seekers shared a sense of disillusion with the mainstream faith and its institutional practices. They had given up on all the churches. But not even the Ranters attacked the religious establishment on its own "turf," as Fox now began to do. He was critical of Cromwell, the army, Parliament, and the wealthy for their roles in oppressing the people. But he viewed the established church as the primary agency holding people captive in alienation from the true liberating power of Christ within themselves. And it was in local parish "steeplehouses" that Fox elicited the most violent reactions to his message. He not only called people to listen to Christ as their inward teacher; he now emphasized Christ as their *free* teacher, in contrast to the tithe-supported ministry of parish "hirelings."

That message struck a chord in the North, which had been a backwater of Puritan reform in England. The northern parishes were poorly supported by the national hierarchy, which often assigned poorly equipped and spiritually bankrupt clergy to such "hinterlands." There was long-standing popular resentment toward the national church in the North, fostering a lively sectarian and Seeker scene in the 1640s. After 1650, as the Commonwealth sputtered in its reformation of church and state, Fox touched off a powder keg of revolt. The Quaker movement quickly developed as a ground swell of nonviolent, revolutionary resistance to the struggling Puritan establishment. As Fox moved from community to community, he not only sought out Baptists, Seekers, and Ranters; he also met with tithe-resisting individuals and groups. One key to the movement's spread was the sympathy of some local justices and army officers in the North, allies who provided Quakers legal shelter from enraged clergy and gentry.

On another level, it is also intriguing to speculate whether the Quaker movement represented a resurgence of the old Celtic Christian tradition in the North.[43] Celtic Christian emphases upon the indwelling of Christ, the inclusion of all creation in God's redemptive work, the spiritual authority of women, and the cross as real personal triumph through suffering[44]—all these themes found conspicuous expression in the Quaker movement. Although they were filtered through the thought-forms of Reformation, they still constituted a strong counterpoint to the dominant Puritan message. Of course, Celtic Christianity as such would not have been a conscious motif for these Seekers and early Friends. But in a backwater of the English Reformation, this very old, isolated stream of Western Christianity would have continued as an undercurrent in the faith of country folk. Fox came to the edges of the Celtic realm in West Yorkshire. As he moved westward into Westmorland, Cumberland, and northern Lancashire, where the movement exploded in 1652, he entered the largest area of vestigial Celtic tradition in England.[45]

But Fox first moved further north in late 1651, coming to a Ranter enclave in Cleveland. As we noted in Chapter Six, the term "Ranter" quickly became an epithet applied to a wide variety of rowdy, expressionistic, or libertine groups. It is not possible to ascertain whether this northern group had any serious connections to the Ranters of the South and Midlands. We at least can surmise that its members followed the general tendency of the Ranters: they had advanced far into the Spiritu-

alism of the Seekers, but had fallen into despair. As Fox states it, they
"had tasted of the power of God, but were all shattered to pieces and the
heads of them turned Ranters." He attended their large meetings without interrupting them. Afterwards, however, he told them that they had
not learned to "wait upon God to feel his power to gather their minds
together...for they had spoken themselves dry and had spent their por-
tions and not lived in that which they spake. . . . They had some kind of
meetings but took tobacco and drank ale in them and so grew light and
loose." Thus, Fox identified the speculative tendency that had always
been in the Spiritualist stream and which had become extreme in
Ranterism—that is, rarefied mystical concepts spun out in the midst of
a life unsubjected to God's Spirit. Fox exhorted them to meet again to
feel themselves gathered into Christ's direct teaching. In that state, they
could speak as the Lord revealed things to them. But then they should
enact in their daily lives what they had learned from Christ. Speaking
truth without living it had made them "dry and barren." "Thence came
all their loss, for the Lord would renew his mercies and his strength if
they would wait upon him." He records that the leaders resisted this
teaching, whereas most of the group was convinced and became a stable
Quaker meeting.[46]

Fox's anecdote offers a revealing perspective in the Seeker-to-Quaker
transformation. Here and elsewhere, Fox affirmed the spiritual insights
and experiences of the Seekers and even the Ranters. But he criticized
them for becoming enamored of spiritual *ideas* and *experiences*. Their
tendency to indulge in "words without life" was ultimately no different
from congregations gathered according to creeds or even from parish
churches. Fox offered a real alternative to the dead end of Seekerism:
namely, an emotionally charged, physically grounded, morally defined
renewal of the "waiting upon the Lord" that Seekers had already practiced for some years.

Further, Fox's sense of "waiting" shifted the emphasis from intense
expectation of future intervention by God in human affairs to one of
intense *enactment* of present divine power breaking forth within and
among worshipers. A waiting that had been largely a waiting *for*
became a true waiting *upon* the Lord, real subjection to Christ's Spirit,
not in worship only, but in the concrete acts of daily life. That deeper
surrender paradoxically released enormous new spiritual energies. The
apocalyptic earthquake experienced in the bodies of those who trembled

in the grips of that power was the catharsis emblematic of Seekers becoming Quakers.

By the end of 1651, Fox had captured the apocalyptic import of these developments in a phrase that summarized his subsequent preaching: "God [or more often Christ] is come to teach his people himself."[47] The much-speculated second coming of Christ is clearly indicated here. Christ's direct teaching and leadership is placed in direct opposition to the clerical establishment. Yet the second coming is revealed through a profoundly different way of knowing, reached by way of the cross: surrender to God's will in God's time. Only through a deep immersion in the unfathomable realm of God's time does one break the spell of the world's time and the dominion of those who rule it. And only from that baptism of Spirit and fire does one *return* to challenge that regime fundamentally. Also suggested here is a sense of *peoplehood*, a gathering of transformed men and women that will constitute some a prophetic presence in society.

Fox's *Journal* account of his itinerant preaching reads as though he were almost always confrontational and harsh. He undoubtedly was in many cases, especially where he recognized pride and deceit in his hearers. But to the earnest Seeker, he could be very tender. For example, John Taylor wrote many years later of his first encounter with Fox. He recalls that

> he took me by the hand and said: "Young man, here are three scriptures thou must witness fulfilled. This is the word of the Lord God to thee: thou must be turned from darkness to Light; and from the power of satan unto God; and so thou mayst come to the knowledge of the glory of God. And thou shalt be changed from glory to glory." And this indeed, with what else he said, did make such impression and took such deep root in my heart, that I was settled.[48]

Three key elements of Fox's counsel may be recognized in this brief account. First, there was an element of gentle intimacy with the tender Seeker, taking him by the hand. Second, Fox spoke with a sense of divine authority that others recognized. Third, rather than counsel, as Puritans did, that one must *infer* divine favor obliquely by feelings of assurance or habits of piety, Fox insisted that one must *experience* divine power immediately within and then outwardly and concretely through moral transformation.

WESTMORLAND AND LANCASHIRE

Throughout 1652, Fox's preaching continued to gather momentum. He passed again through Nottinghamshire and Derbyshire, and revisited new allies in West Yorkshire. By now, they had begun calling themselves "Friends." In radical circles, that usage was not unknown; but it quickly became the new movement's defining name. No doubt, they drew upon John 15 in their understanding of the word: the intimacy between their inward teacher, Jesus, stood in stark contrast with the hierarchy and formality they experienced in the presence of their putative teachers, the parish clergy; moreover, the intimacy of that inward communion translated into an intimacy and egalitarian ethic among these new-found Friends.

It was not until May-June that he circulated in the Northwest for the first time. In June, Fox preached to large gatherings of seeking people in Northwest Yorkshire and Westmorland, convincing many of their leaders, men and women who went on to become key figures in the Quaker movement. One of them was Francis Howgill, aged thirty-four, a long-time Seeker and Spiritualist preacher. Like most seeking individuals we have studied, Howgill had been a sober-minded child, praying three to four times a day from the age of twelve. By fifteen, he had alienated his own parents with his religious zeal. But his strivings only deepened his melancholy over the next five years. Like Fox, he went from one counselor to the next. They attempted to "apply the promises" of salvation to him, "but it was only words, for the witness of Christ showed me that the root of iniquity stood."[49] Finally, he gave up on parish ministers and spent his time alone at home or wandering in nature, disconsolate.

Then there appeared more beauty in those called Independents." He joined them, feeling that their separation from the established church afforded greater integrity:

> but at last I saw it was but in words, that they would do things, and choose officers . . . and so made themselves an Image and fell down to it; yet there was some tenderness in them at first, but the doctrine was the same with the world's.[50]

The democratic election of congregational officers practiced by the Independents, a practice that Sarah Jones had found so liberating in 1644, rang hollow to Howgill. Despite its congregational processes, Independency offered more words than power.

> Then they whom they called Anabaptists appeared to have more glory, and walked more according to the scripture . . . and I went among them; and there was something I loved among them; but after they denied all but such that came in their way . . . I saw the ground was the same...that they had separated themselves and made another likeness.[51]

Thus, Howgill was attracted to the scrupulous Baptist attention to biblical norms of worship and church order. But their sectarian hostility to all other groups was off-putting. They stood on the same "ground" of outward, biblical expertise, lacking inward, transforming power.

> Then some preached Christ within, but they themselves were without, had but words, and they said all must be within (unto which my heart did cleave), and they spoke of . . . God appearing in man, and overcoming the power of the devil. And . . . a true love I had to all that walked honestly in what profession soever, and I hated reviling one another, and that they should smite one another, and persecute one another, and with the sufferer I always took part. . . . But still I saw, though they spoke of all things within, that they enjoyed not what they spoke . . . till at last I saw none walked as the ministers of Christ.[52]

Thus, upon hearing the Spiritualist preachers, "that [light] in my conscience bore witness that it must be so." The shift toward inward knowledge turned Howgill away from sectarian strife, just as it had turned Dewsbury out of the army. A growing compassion, especially for the oppressed, was a trait typical of the Seeker turn. Yet he still found Spiritualist claims to be more theoretical than practical. Even those who preached it did not *possess* the transforming power they proclaimed.

Howgill gave up on all these groups and their teachers. As had happened to Fox, only then was it revealed to him "that the Lord would teach his people himself . . . and so I waited, and many things opened in me of a time at hand."[53] He began to preach this message; many were impressed. Yet he continued to feel something lacking. Finally, when

Fox came, Howgill felt "the day of the Lord was made manifest . . . for I was overthrown, and the foundation swept away, and all my righteousness and unrighteousness was judged and weighed and all was found too light." Hearing Fox preach of the light of Christ, he immediately believed; "and so not only I, but many hundreds more . . . were all seen to be off the foundation . . . and we saw our nakedness, and were all ashamed, though our glory was great in the world's eye; but all was vanity."[53]

The joy of this moment of discovery soon turned to terror, however:

> And the dreadful power of the Lord fell on me with fear and terror. . . . Mine eyes were dim with crying, my flesh did fail. . . . I became a proverb to all. . . . And I sought death in that day, and could not find it; it fled from me. . . . I became a perfect fool, and knew nothing, and was as a man distracted. All was overturned, and I suffered the loss of all in all that I ever did. . . . And as I did give up to all his judgments, the captive came forth out of prison and rejoiced. . . . And then I saw the cross of Christ, and stood in it, and knew the enmity slain upon it, and the new man was made, and so peace came to be made, and so eternal life was brought in through death and judgment. And then the perfect gift I received . . . the holy law of God was . . . written upon my heart, and his fear and his word, which did kill, now makes alive.[54]

Note that Howgill's Quaker convincement led him through the Ranter territory of utter distraction, making him the "perfect fool" that Salmon and others became. Yet, by *standing still* in that place, rather than running out into rage, Howgill was taken beyond, into genuine personal transformation. The excruciating crisis and travail entailed in such a fundamental shift in one's way of knowing and acting are well portrayed here. Normal human knowledge was revealed to be a way of death, "which must be slain on the cross of Christ Jesus, if ever you will come to true peace."

As an exemplary Spiritualist leader, Howgill offers us one of the best narratives of his spiritual journey and Quaker transformation. He concludes, warning others on the seeking path:

> Arise! and come away; lie not groveling in the earth; nor seek
> to know God in your fallen wisdom, for the well is deep. . . .
> You are further off in running out, and seeking in your earthly
> wisdom and comprehension, than you were before. . . . [56]

So the Quaker turn eschewed lateral moves from one group and teaching to the next, and involved instead a deeper, more disturbing search within. In another source, Howgill describes this new mode as "a narrow search."[57]

But this was not simply an individual transformation. Howgill traversed this desolation with others in his circle who had also been convinced by Fox. He testifies,

> the Lord of Heaven and Earth we found to be near at hand;
> and as we waited upon him in pure Silence, our Minds out
> of all things, his Dreadful Power . . . appeared in our Assemblies, when there was no Language, Tongue nor Speech from
> any Creature, and the Kingdom of Heaven did gather us, and
> catch us all, as in a Net . . . that we came to know a place to
> stand in, and what to wait in, and the Lord appeared daily to
> us, to our Astonishment, Amazement, and great Admiration,
> insomuch that we often said one unto another, with great joy
> of Heart, "What, is the Kingdom of God come to be with
> men?" . . . And from that Day forward our Hearts were knit
> unto the Lord, and one unto another, in truth and fervent
> Love, not by any External Covenant . . . but we entered into
> the Covenant of Life with God. . . . [58]

One can well imagine that men and women passing through such dread-filled straits were bonded powerfully together as they met in silent worship. Waves of groaning, sighing, and sobbing moved through the group. Sometimes the entire assembly was wracked with intense trembling. These visitations of the Lord's power made the apocalypse they had felt while hearing Fox a continuing reality. Slowly, through personal struggle, mutual encouragement, and shared worship, a solidarity formed, preparing them to face severe challenges in the months and years ahead.

Other Seeker leaders who were gathered by Fox over the course of just a few days in the Sedburgh area included John and Ann Audland, John Camm, Richard Hubberthorne, and Edward Burrough (aged just eighteen). None of them left as extensive a record of their seeking and convincement as Howgill did. *All of them would be dead within the next twelve years*, owing to their relentless itinerant ministry and the lethal effects of English prisons. They came out of the North like human torches: the faster they ran, the brighter they burned. By the end of the summer of 1652, the Quaker apocalypse was sending shock waves all over the North, and garbled, disturbing reports filtered southward.

The first such report in published form was an anti-Quaker tract play-fully entitled *The Querers and Quakers Cause*. Appearing in May 1653,[59] this anonymous piece noted that there had been many Seekers in York-shire for some time. Now great numbers of them were drawn into ab-surd doctrines and practices, breaking forth in trembling and trances. No doubt in reference to George Fox, the tract's Preface quips that seeking outside the established church had left these souls so weak that even a fox could break down their stone wall.[60]

The format of the tract's main text is a set of thirty queries the author circulated to Yorkshire Quakers, together with counter-queries offered in response by a Quaker-sympathizing Seeker, followed by the author's counter-responses. He notes that Zwingli had faced similar enthusiasts in Zurich and that the Swiss reformer had found their trances and fits contrived. The author suggests that the regularity of Quaker fits indi-cates that they are self-induced. He characterizes them as delusions that have boiled over into "holy rage." He cites bizarre phenomena: strange noises, bodies swelling and moving in an unseemly manner. He raises sexual innuendo, suggesting that at Quaker meetings, men and women often collapse on the ground together. The author alleges that Quakers have defended adultery and fornication as fruits of the Spirit, although the Quakers' advocate insists that this is not their way. Like many future anti-Quaker writers, the author is disturbed by the effects of Quaker meetings on women: the gatherings "draw out wives and children all over the land to spiritual madness." Meetings of 200–300 Quakers oc-cur in Malton, where they gather "to compare notes of entranced madnesse." Their meetings have no predictable pattern. They may show up suddenly in Malton, Wakefield, Kendall, and elsewhere: "they run far from home to follow these quaking Communions."[61] Besides becoming dangerous to themselves, Quakers are a threat to social authority in all forms. They leave their homes and employment to wander the countryside and preach their message. They disrespect the

Bible, clergy, and magistracy, obeying only what they receive from within. This is the shortest route to anarchy and atheism. Magistrates and Parliament must act quickly to repress this movement, or the entire nation will be swallowed up in "Divine permission in tumults, madnesse, disorders, and Anarchicall licentiousnesse."

The Quakers' advocate counters that these people do not scorn Scripture but in fact come closer to its doctrine and model than any other group. The only thing this movement may swallow up is the clerical establishment.[61] A germinal statement of Quaker pacifism comes at the end, after the author decries Quakers as a public enemy worse than the Dutch (with whom England had recently been at war). The advocate responds that Quakers are a weaponless people, against "that hire" (i.e., military service), discovering the deceit of it according to Scripture.[63]

LANCASHIRE AND CUMBERLAND

The epicenter of the Quaker explosion moved from Yorkshire to Westmorland and down into Lancashire during the summer of 1652. Perhaps the key event in Lancashire was Fox's preaching at the parish church in Ulverston and the convincement of Margaret Fell. Fell was a member of the lower gentry, the wife of the local M.P. and justice, Thomas Fell. She and her husband were ardent in their desire to know and serve God. They "inquired after the way of the Lord," going to hear the best ministers, inviting them to visit their home, Swarthmoor Hall. They had a preference for the dissenting tradition, and used their influence to install more left-wing clergy in their parish. Thus, rather than leaving the church as less privileged Seekers did, local elites could sometimes seek within their own parish. Nevertheless, like the classic Seeker type, Fell was subject to nagging misgivings: "This I hoped I did well in, but often fear'd I was short of the right way: And after this manner I was inquiring and seeking about twenty years."[64]

Judge Fell was away on business when Fox was brought by one of his associates to Swarthmoor Hall. The house being open to traveling ministers of many varieties, they stayed the night. The next day, there were parish services at Ulverston. Fox accompanied Fell and her children there, but did not enter the building until the service had begun. After some singing had finished, he asked the minister if he might speak and was given permission. As Fell recalled many years later, Fox preached

> that Christ was the Light of the World and lighteth every Man that cometh into the World, and that by this Light they might be gathered to God. . . . The Scriptures were the Prophets' words, and Christ's and the Apostles' words, and what, as they spoke, they enjoyed and possessed, and had it from the Lord: And said, Then what had any to do with the Scriptures, but as they came to the Spirit that gave them forth. You will say, Christ saith this, and the Apostles say this; but what canst thou say? Art thou a Child of Light, and hast thou walked in the Light, and what thou speakest, is it inwardly from God? etc. This opened me so, that it cut me to the Heart; and then I saw clearly, we were all wrong. So I sat down in my Pew again, and cried bitterly: and I cried in my Spirit to the Lord, We are all Thieves, we are all Thieves; we have taken the Scriptures in Words, and know nothing of them in our selves. So that served me, and I cannot well tell what he said afterwards.[65]

Fell recaptures well the kind of crisis Fox induced in the earnest Seeker. That is, he made it clear that human expertise in Scripture, even ardent moral and devotional adherence to the Bible, was still fundamentally alienated from the experience and faith of those who wrote the Bible. There was no way *back* to authentic New Testament faith, except the way *in* to the deep spiritual baptism that the apostles knew. Anything less was rote formalism: not just a pale imitation but a counterfeit faith.

Fox returned with Fell to Swarthmoor Hall after the services ended. Fell recalls,

> I was stricken into such a sadness, I knew not what to do; my Husband being from home. I saw it was the Truth, and I could not deny it . . . I received the truth in the love of it: and it was opened to me so clear, that I had never a Tittle in my Heart against it; but desired the Lord, that I might be kept in it, and then I desired no greater Portion.[65]

Fox had opportunities to talk further with Fell, her family and the servants. Fell records that there was a general convincement among them. Fox soon left, but Nayler and Farnworth showed up about two weeks later, looking for him. Then Judge Fell returned. On the way home, he had been met by neighbors and the parish minister, who gave disturbing reports of Fox's effect on his family and even suggested it to be witchcraft.

> So my Husband came home greatly offended: And any may think what a Condition I as like to be in, that either I might displease my Husband, or offend God; for he was very much troubled with us all . . . they had so prepossessed him against us.

Farnworth and Nayler succeeded in moderating the Judge somewhat. But at dinner that evening, "whilst I was sitting the Power of the Lord seized upon me, and he was stricken with Amazement, and knew not what to think; but was quiet and still. And the Children were all quiet and still, and grown Sober. . . ."

Later that evening, Fox returned and had conversation with Thomas Fell. He offered none of the courteous addresses usually offered to a man of the judge's rank. After a considerable discussion, "my Husband came to see clearly the Truth, of what he spoke, and was very quiet that Night." The next day the minister from Ulverston came and tried to set the Judge against Fox again, "But my Husband had seen so much the Night before, that the Priest got little Entrance upon him."[67] Once Thomas Fell was able to discern that Fox was not a charlatan, this young prophet probably appealed strongly to his radical religious and political sympathies.

Fell does not narrate the extremity of crisis and desolation that many Quakers of lower rank described concerning their convincement. Generally speaking, Seekers of higher social class and greater educational advantage seem to have had less "liminal" experiences. That is, they went through less intense personal disorientation and were less shaken loose from their social locations. But this does not mean that their transformation was easier. It often took longer. Phyllis Mack[68] notes, for example, that Quaker women in the more culturally complex and sophisticated South seem to have had longer struggles and greater problems with ambiguity than their counterparts had in the North. A longer process for Fell may be indicated by two letters from Richard Farnworth nearly a year later, counseling her and her household to

> take heed of getting above the cross and so you run astray from the love . . . take heed of running into extremes in any

thing, let your moderation be known to all men for the lord is at hand . . . bide in that which is pure and it will keep you pure."[69]

Fell's stability, combined with the legal shelter her husband could offer the movement in that area, soon made her a key actor among Friends. She almost immediately became the administrative anchor for the fledgling movement, coordinating communications, offering spiritual counsel, and reining in errant individuals. Henceforth, Margaret Fell became the key feminine counterpart to Fox. Like Hooton, a woman considerably Fox's senior (ten years older), Fell offered Fox a new feminine antipode. Hooton's interaction with Fox had produced a type of fearless, itinerant female prophet, of which many were to come. Fell embodied a new model: woman as center of a domestically grounded Quaker lifestyle and bearer of an increasingly rationalized female spiritual leadership among Friends. Just as Fox's early movements had brought him back to the Mansfield area many times before 1652, his frequent visits to Swarthmoor Hall after 1652 nurtured a new dynamic that became dominant in the Quaker movement in later decades. Again, there is no evidence for any sexual liaison here. Though Judge Fell did not become active in the movement, he remained a loyal ally until his death in 1658. We will treat Fox's eventual marriage to Margaret Fell in Chapter 11.

During 1653, Fox's movements north into Cumberland were fruitful. John Burnyeat narrates the effect of Fox's preaching on himself and others in his area. He was a twenty-two-year-old farmer when Fox came preaching "unto thousands that was in Error, seeking the Lord, but knew not where to find him, although he was not far from us."[70] Burnyeat was among those reached by Fox's preaching of the light of Christ within. Convincement brought "great Affliction" with it, like nothing he had ever known. This was "the Day of Jacob's Trouble," an allusion to Jacob's wrestling with God all night (Gen. 32). Burnyeat struggled desperately with a convicting presence in his conscience, hoping to receive a blessing. He now found worthless his former assurance that Christ had imputed righteousness to him. He desired a Savior to save him from further sin, not only to blot out past sins. "Then Paul's state was seen, to will was present, but to do many times power was wanting" (see Rom. 7:14-25).[71]

He and the other newly convinced Friends met together, groaning and crying to the Lord, waiting for help, resolving to obey, no matter the cost. It was a day of "horror and terror under the indignation of the Lord . . . we were given up to bear the indignation and wait till it was over." Slowly, in this weak condition, they gained a new sense of the right way. But families, friends and neighbors were offended by their strange behavior. They were scorned, criticized, and rejected. Like Israel, seeing the sea before them and the Egyptians behind them, they expected nothing but death.

Burnyeat observes that they still did not know "true striving," which is "out of self," "standing still out of our own thoughts, willings, and runnings." But other Quaker ministers came through the area and guided them "in what to wait, and how to stand still." Evidently, there was some degree of technique to early Quaker spirituality, or at least some kind of guidance that helped refocus spiritual energies from ego-centered striving to true surrender. Slowly, "a hope began to appear in us, and we met together often, and waited to see the Salvation of God." True power began to break forth: "great dread and trembling fell upon many, and the very Chains of Death was broken . . . many Souls eased . . . the Prisoners of hope began to come forth." They began to gather into the Lord's direct teaching and covenant.[72]

But Satan saw his kingdom threatened and began to rage. The Beast began to make war against the Lamb (see Rev. 13, 19). That is, the clerical establishment agitated against the new local Quaker community, leading to public whippings, imprisonments, fines, and slander. It was typical of early Quaker convincements that as the inward warfare began to resolve itself, conflict shifted to outward, social fronts. Quaker ministers demonstrated and preached a plainness of speech, dress, and lifestyle that often created friction with family, cost friendships and jobs, and could provoke violence from neighbors. The Quaker eschewal of customs of social flattery and deference offended social superiors and made neighbors suspicious.

And as if these Quaker codes of conduct did not create enough trouble, many Friends were led to their local "steeplehouse" to confront the state-sponsored worship of their parish, leading to further violence and imprisonment. "The Lamb's War," a term derived from the Book of Revelation, was used by Friends to describe the highly conflictive inner and outer turmoil Quaker preachers elicited wherever they went.[73] For the first forty years of the movement, until legal toleration finally came, the Quaker appeared to neighbors as a Seeker who had gone looking for trouble. Indeed, in these early decades, before any formal membership had been instituted, one "showed up" in Quaker records mainly by "bearing the cross" through fines, imprisonments, mob violence, whippings, dunkings, and other forms of official and unofficial violence. The suffering of these early Friends remains an inexplicable masochism unless one understands the deep inner apocalypse that began it all, and the mystical fellowship these Friends enjoyed with one another in Christ, who had endured the pain and humiliation of the cross for their sake.

THE APOCALYPSE OF GENDER: CELESTIAL FLESH

Many newly convinced Friends wrote to Fox, Fell, and others, seeking further instruction and encouragement. In 1652, Dorothy Howgill (wife of Francis) wrote to Fox following his visit. She recalls Fox telling her that "a pure light was arising in me...yet I could not believe because I felt no such thing . . . but now I know thou hast the anoynting of the Holy one and thou knowes all things . . . thou art my own heart and my soule lyes in thy bosom."[74]

Exalted language like this was commonly directed by Friends toward those who had convinced them, and most of all toward George Fox and James Nayler. Shortly after her convincement, Fell and her children wrote to Fox as

> Our dear father in the Lord. . . . We are your babes. . . . Take pity on us, whom you have nursed up with the breasts of consolation. . . . Oh, our dear nursing father, we hope you will not leave us comfortless, but will come again. . . . My own dear heart . . . you know that we have received you into our hearts. . . .[75]

Mary Howgill addressed Fox as "Dear Life" in a 1656 letter.[76] Such letters were also addressed to Fell. For example, John Audland wrote to Fell, exclaiming that she "inhabits eternity," finding her countenance "more bright than the sun." He went on to confess that his soul was refreshed by her and that by God's power he was "kept bold to declare the way of salvation."[77]

Language of this sort substantiates the points raised earlier in regard to Fox and Hooton. In the kind of deep immersion experience that Quaker convincement entailed, a guiding, nurturing persona—masculine or feminine—was extremely helpful. The sense of being reduced to almost infantile vulnerability made a loving and trustworthy father-figure or mother-figure the soul's anchor until the ego could re-form around a new way of knowing, speaking, and acting in the world. Early Quaker letters are frequently punctuated by poignant cries for help and tender expressions of affection. Fox and Fell constituted the pillar of smoke by day and the pillar of fire by night to lead these straggling children of Israel through the wilderness.

Their role continued to be crucial even after empowerment came and public ministry began. Audland's letter clearly indicates that he drew courage from Fell to risk his life daily in ministry. One is reminded of the chivalric knights-errant, who undertook quests of strength and bravery, carrying the ribbon of an inspirational feminine figure at court. The minimal organization and errant ministry of the early movement drew coherence from the constancy of Fox and Fell as masculine and feminine reference points.

The strongly gendered imageries and overtones of Quaker language, which could arrive at surprising phrases like "nursing father," sometimes stimulated the prurient Puritan imagination to suspicions of orgiastic sex at Quaker meetings. Years later, Fox muted much of this exalted language in Quaker records, crossing it out of letters that had been collected over the decades at Swarthmoor Hall. For example, he toned down Mary Howgill's "Dear Life" to read "Dear Friend." By that time, he was at work to shift the focus of Quaker awe from himself to the gathered fellowship as a whole (a move we will study in Chapter Eleven). But the near-adoration of Fox and Fell during the 1650s is crucial to understanding the Seeker-to-Quaker transformation.

Most disturbing to Puritan authorities were Fox's sporadic claims to be "the Son of God," which continued as late as 1661.[78] This issue had arisen as early as his Derby arrest in 1650. During his interrogation, his claims to perfection led straight to his assertion of Christ's indwelling. Asked if he or his associates were themselves Christ, he answered, "Nay, we are nothing, Christ is all."[79] During a trial at Lancaster late in 1652, Fox was charged with claiming to be equal with God. He denied making such a claim, but countered that "he that sanctifieth and they that are sanctified are all of one in the Father and the Son, and that ye are the sons of God. The Father and the Son are one, and we of his flesh and of his bone" (Heb. 2:11; Eph. 5:31).[80] In 1653, Fox wrote a letter "to Margaret Fell and to every other friend who is raised to discerning."[81] Apparently aiming to clarify his own words and speculation upon them, Fox did not back away from his earlier affirmations:

> Accordinge to the spirit I am the sonne of God and accordinge to the flesh I am the seed of Abraham which seed is Christ, which seed is but one in all his saints. . . . Accordinge to the spirit I am the sonne of God before Abraham was . . . the same which doth descend, the same doth ascend and all the promises of God are yea come out of time from god, into time to that which is captivated in the earth in time, and to it the seed which is Christ, they are all yea and amen fetched up out of him, where there is noe time. . . . and as many as received the word, I say unto ye: yee are gods, as it is written in your law [John 10:34]. . . . Now waite all to have these thinges fulfilled in ye, if it never be so little a measure waite in it, that ye may grow to a perfect man in Christ Jesus.

This passage is not terribly coherent. But it clearly shows that Fox claimed sonship, though in a sense that could be claimed by others who wait faithfully upon the Lord and grow into perfection in Christ. Those who had gone through the harrowing convincement process of death to the self had found a "measure" of freedom from captivity in earthly time and its realm of cause and effect. Thus, to be a child of God in the Spirit was to be "before Abraham was." To have Christ within was to be of Christ's flesh and bone, eating it and becoming the same substance with it.[82]

We confront again the "celestial flesh" theology we found in Chapter 2. We recall Schwenckfeld's point that, as the Word of God made flesh, Christ had introduced a radically different mode of existence into the world. As all creaturely descendants of the first Adam are subject to alienated consciousness and sin, so all those reborn in Christ the second Adam partake of his pure, sinless life. This is not Luther's imputed righteousness; it is a lived righteousness that comes, not through any amount of human striving, but by a deep baptism of death to self and a moment-by-moment dependence upon the Spirit's leading. Though

Schwenckfeld was unwilling to claim perfection, he did emphasize significant moral regeneration through the believer's communion with Christ's celestial flesh.

Fox was willing to push the matter further, placing himself in a provocative position toward Puritan authority and inviting his Friends to follow. But he rarely used the term, "celestial flesh." The imagery of God's seed was particularly important to Fox—it suggests a fundamentally new being and will, a transcendent subjectivity. In Christ, the seed of Abraham, who was before Abraham and even before Adam, the believer participates in an utterly new form of existence. One is no longer determined by the cause-and-effect relations of natural creaturehood, but is drawn into a trans-temporal realm by the apocalyptic in-breaking of the risen Lord, standing beyond time.

The celestial flesh tradition extends all the way back to the Alexandrian tradition of the early church and is sometimes fraught with metaphysical speculation and a Hellenistic distaste for material existence.[83] But with early Friends, as with Schwenckfeld, we find an existential emphasis upon a new way of being, a moral breakthrough in Christ. This is a new, apocalyptic mode of existence, in which natural categories still exist but are no longer determinate ("neither male nor female, Jew nor Greek, slave nor free"). It inspired the claim of some early Christians to be a "third race" of humanity, absorbing and transcending in Christ every dualism of human identity. This bold theology both reflects and inspires new formations in social status, gender relations, and economic class.

The altered states produced in Quaker worship and the distance these experiences produced between Friends and their neighbors indeed produced novel interrelations between men and women, prophetic challenges to the wealthy and powerful sectors of English society, and scandalizing plainness in speech, dress, and lifestyle. These social implications are implied in a tract by Francis Howgill, responding to a published Puritan attack. Answering the accusation that Quakers claim equality with God, Howgill first warns that "all our words are as a parable to thee, and thou knowest not what we say, although thou hast catched and snatched up some of our words brokenly to quarrell with; yet we are hidden from thee, and a gulfe is between thee and us...first a terrible day must come upon thee." This new mode of existence is opaque and objectionable to those standing outside it. Howgill proceeds to elaborate on the Quaker understanding:

He that hath the Spirit of God, is in that which is equall, as God is equall, and his wayes equall; And he that is joyned to the Lord is one spirit, there is unity, and the unity stands in equality it selfe. He that is born from above is the Sonne of God, and he said, "I and my Father are one." And when the Sonne is revealed, and speaks, the Father speaks in him, and dwells in him, and he in the Father. In that which is equall in equality it selfe; there is equality in nature, though not in stature. Goe learn what these things mean, the understanding and learned will know what I say, and this is neither damnable nor blasphemous; but on the contrary, it is saving and precious to them that believe. . . . the Son is glorified with the Father in the same glory he had with him before the world began; the glory is in purity, equality, immortality, and eternity.[83]

The Quaker egalitarian social ethic arises from this principle of unity and equality with God. One leaves the social hierarchies of the world as one crosses the abyss into new existence in Christ. In this new realm, there is unity and equality in nature, though not in stature. And as Christ is of a stature vastly beyond those who follow him into this new realm, so a difference of spiritual statures was evident in the Quaker movement. Earlier, we saw Fox's reference to different "measures" of the light in different people. The key is to be faithful in whatever measure one has been given. To those who are faithful in a little, more will be given.

Here we return to the preeminence of Fox among Friends. Not only did he manifest the keen discernment of spirits, prophetic bearing, miraculous works, impeccable morality, and theological integration of a leader among many gifted leaders. He was also the first among them to enter and map this mysterious realm. Notwithstanding the previous attainments of the other leaders, Fox had taken them a step further and awakened in them an unearthly sense of divine power. In a similar manner, leaders who were convinced by Fox through the summer of 1652 formed a certain elite around him. As the towering female figure in that group, Margaret Fell took a special place in this Quaker firmament as Fox's feminine consort. During those early years, the movement inhabited a realm of such apocalyptic intensity and social liminality (i.e., living outside the usual social boundaries), that this order according to celestial flesh was the primary organizing factor.

Fox had an uncanny quality. Critics complained that he bewitched people with his piercing eyes, taking them by the hand as he spoke to them. His deep sense of one's spiritual condition no doubt took many individuals aback. And his occasional faith healings imbued him with an aura of miraculous power. In the eyes of many Seekers, such an aura may well have conferred upon Fox the stature of the long awaited new apostle who could reproclaim the true Christian faith and gather an authentic church for a new age. Hence, the Seeker expectation of an extraordinary figure coming to perform "mighty acts of power" constitutes an additional layer of meaning around Fox's singular role in the transformation of Seekers into Quakers.[85]

LONDON

By early 1654, a plan was devised to invade the South and Wales. In particular, three urban centers known for large Seeker and Ranter populations were targeted. Francis Howgill and Edward Burrough went to London; John Audland and John Camm went to Bristol; and Richard Hubberthorne, Christopher Atkinson, and George Whitehead went to Norwich.[86] The Norwich mission struggled with mixed results. The Welsh, Bristol, and London missions were major successes that ultimately shifted the center of the Quaker movement southward.

The "official" Quaker missionaries to London were not the first to arrive. Isabel Buttery and another woman came from the North in the early months of 1654 with a large supply of Quaker tracts, particularly Fox's *To All That Would Know the Way to the Kingdom* (1653). Indeed, it was often Quaker women who first opened new territory for the movement, and often suffered the severest reprisals.[87] Buttery began holding meetings in the home of a London merchant, Simon Dring. By June, however, she had been arrested and sent to Bridewell for selling Quaker literature in the yard of St. Paul's Cathedral on a Sunday.

Howgill and Burrough were aided during their first months in London by John Audland, John Camm, Richard Hubberthorne, and Anthony Pearson. (Pearson was a Lancashire justice who had been convinced by James Nayler during the latter's trial at Appleby in 1653.) Arriving sometime early in July, these northerners were aware of the sophistication and dangers of the metropolis. Many there were eager to hear the Quaker missionaries, but were prone to argumentation. Pearson wrote to Fox during the first days of work there:

> we found very many who have a true principle of honesty in them; but they are for the most part so high flown in wisdom and notions, that it is hard to reach them: nothing can enter till their wisdom be confounded; and if they be judged, then presently they rage . . . and so the simplicity is trampled upon. Much wisdom is to be used amongst them, until the truth be clearly understood; and then to speak to that in their consciences, and to the raising up of the witness [within], to let them see themselves; and then to pass judgement upon them, and so to keep them from disputing and questioning. This we found to be the most profitable ministry; and few words must be used; for they have [held] the Truth in notions; and all cry out, "What do these men say, more than others have said": but to bring them to silence confounds their wisdom. . . . Oh! that none might come to London, but those who are raised up into the life of Truth...whose words may have authority: for there are so many mighty in wisdom to oppose and gain-say, that weak ones will suffer the Truth to be trampled on; and there are so many rude savage apprentices and young people and Ranters, that nothing but the power of the Lord can chain them. . . . Very many societies have we visited, and are now able to stand: many honest hearts are among the Waiters, and some that are joined to the Ranters are pretty people. The living power of God was made manifest to the confounding of all, and we were carried above ourselves, to the astonishment of both ourselves and others: we were made to speak tremblingly amongst them in dread and much fear.[88]

Pearson's rich description of the London scene confirms several points we observed previously. In terms of religious ideas, various Seekers had already articulated nearly every point of Quaker preaching. The London seeking scene was saturated with Spiritualist literature and intellectual discussions. The reference to a group called "Waiters" in London is interesting. They may have been a specific group of Seekers waiting for a new revelation from a new apostolate.[89] But, as Pearson emphasizes, their seeking and waiting had to be redirected, by confounding the intellect and provoking an intense experience of divine judgment within. Only then would the Quaker apocalypse of power, rather than novel ideas and experiences, be revealed. Finally, while some Ranters harassed Quaker preachers, others were "pretty people": they had already tasted the "cup of astonishment," the first part of the convincement process, and were ready to take the next steps forward.

The Quaker tactics among these groups are known from reports written to Margaret Fell that summer. In late July, Richard Hubberthorne wrote that on the preceding Sunday they had divided into three groups: Howgill and Pearson visited the Waiters, Camm attended an Independent meeting, and Burrough and Hubberthorne took on the Baptists. The Baptists ejected Hubberthorne and Burrough when they tried to speak. The Independents listened to Camm but argued with him. Pearson and Howgill were allowed to speak, and only one Waiter objected and asked some questions.[90] Clearly, the seeking Waiters provided the best opportunities for Quaker preaching. Those most receptive to the Quaker message, those who seemed to come under the power of inner conviction, were invited to Quaker silent meetings in order to feel the power break forth more fully, and to receive further teaching and counsel.

Burrough wrote to Fell about another Sunday that summer. Howgill went to the Baptists but was refused permission to speak. He left and joined Hubberthorne at a Waiters' meeting, where both spoke. Howgill went on for an hour: "and some women was struck and teares came from their eyes." One Waiter objected to the Quaker claim to have gone beyond religious forms, saying that "none was without forme, but Christ the son of God." Howgill answered that it was "Hee that spoak unto them." Such surprising claims to the personal authority of Christ in the Quaker speaker must have shocked many. In the same letter, Burrough also mentions Gerrard Winstanley's presence at the meetings they had organized (noted earlier, in Chapter 5). Winstanley confided to them his sense that "we are sent to perfect the worke which fell in their hands."[91]

Indeed, many whose radical hopes had burned bright during the 1640s found renewed life with the arrival of the Quakers. John Lilburne, the most charismatic of the Leveller leaders, was also reached by the Quaker mission. In 1655, he was languishing in the Tower of London, deep in despair of his failed political hopes—indeed, of life itself. He had lost everything, even his wife, "my old and real idol." He was visited by a number of Quaker preachers who counseled him and left him Quaker tracts to read. He slowly began to understand his "dark night" experience in the light of the inward cross. About this time, George Fox had written a statement to Cromwell, renouncing all violent options against the state. This political implication of the cross was not immediately clear to Lilburne, a former lieutenant colonel in the Parliamentary army. But through his convincement process, coming to "a further point of death," he was able to make his own public disavowal of all violence. Lilburne died the next year. But his convincement, like Winstanley's, suggests that many radicals from the 1640s found their political hopes confirmed, yet placed upon a profoundly different foundation, by the Quaker movement.[92]

Pearson reported from London, "great is the harvest like to be in that city; hundreds are convinced, and thousands wait to see the issue, who have persuasions that it is the Truth."[93] Howgill and Pearson described a meeting at Moorfields, where a Ranter opposed Howgill, persuading some of the hearers. Then Pearson spoke and they agreed with him. Finding themselves no match in debate, several Ranters fell down and "imitated a power." Howgill and Pearson admonished them for their parody of quaking. Friends generally felt they were getting the better of hecklers and opponents among dissenting groups. But they decided it was "best not to meddle with the priests and their congregations." So many in London had abandoned the parishes already; that Quakers found no shortage of dissenting groups to visit.[94] Even within the first month, large numbers were drawn to the Quaker meetings, leading Howgill to write that they would soon have to rent space in London.[95] That step was taken before the end of 1654, when Friends made the Bull and Mouth Tavern their base of operations, a center of almost continuous silent meetings, debates, teaching, and counsel.

Susanna Blandford was a seeking spirit who "travelled between hope and fear" during her teenage years, praying and fasting, but reaching no lasting peace. She knew of Friends and had even met some in the North, but was put off by rumors of their bizarre behavior. Three years elapsed before she encountered them again, this time in London. She had been attending various dissenting congregations there when she heard Howgill enter and speak at a large meeting at Allhallows (this was probably John Simpson's congregation, where Anna Trapnel belonged). She was deeply moved and began attending Quaker meetings.[96]

Rebeckah Travers, the young widow of a prosperous London merchant, was also convinced. Some years later, she wrote to Friends about

those early days of the movement in London. Many of them had been
Seekers like her:

> Do you not remember, we cried to the Lord to shew us of his
> wayes, and he heard; and to give us of his counsel, and he
> was entreated? for though the groanings of his own Seed was
> felt in many of us, yet when to the Light we were turned, we
> knew that that lived in us that was ready to betray it and
> murther it, and we saw many as wise as ourselves had been
> lost before us, who begun in the Spirit, but ended in the flesh.[97]

We hear the familiar theme of groaning for redemption and the example
of the Ranters, whose flight into nihilistic abandon was a constant danger to all who pushed antinomian Spiritualism to its limits. She reminds
Friends that

> when the Messengers of the everlasting Gospel came amongst
> us . . . we who received it did not come to the knowledge of
> the way of life without deaths many . . . we learned by the
> things that we suffered, and by subjection we came to the
> dominion."

> Well Friends, the pains of hell hath been felt . . . deep an-
> guish hath surrounded, and we have waited for the command-
> ment of life, as they who roare on their beds with pain do
> wait for ease . . . yet by obedience we came to live, and this
> is the life that shall never end.

Travers thus emphasizes that Quaker preachers offered not sublime
mystical transport but a traumatic passage through death to a realm where
God's will is known first-hand and power to obey is received.

Burrough and Howgill reported to Fell in August the great strain they
experienced in keeping pace with the work and dealing with the wiles
of a city where "the serpent's wisdom is grown fully ripe." Yet hundreds
had been convinced, with strong effects of the Spirit upon their bodies,
"which strikes terror in the hearts of many." These outbreaks of power
altered popular perception of the Quakers: "Many begin to consider of
us, and think there is something more in it than a bare notion; at first
they looked upon it to be no more: but it sinks deep inward in many."[98]
Among the convinced Seekers by the end of that summer were William

Erbury's newly widowed wife, Mary, and their daughter, Dorcas (noted briefly at the end of Chapter 4).

While Quakers made their fastest inroads among Seekers and some Ranters, they also made headway among other dissenting groups. Despite attempts to shut Quakers out of their services, Baptists proved quite vulnerable to the Quaker mission. Even within that first summer, Burrough and Howgill perceived the fear and resentment that their incursions among Baptists generated.[99] Both Particular and General Baptists lost large numbers to the Quakers in the 1650s. Writing in 1655, Burrough believed that the Baptists had grown complacent with their spectacular gains during the 1640s, and many of them had prospered financially; thus, the day of the Lord caught them by surprise.[100] Quakers seized the moral high ground from Baptists as they resisted tithes and suffered for their public witness routinely. Baptist leaders felt so vulnerable to Quaker agitation that some of them called for state protection against Quakers invading their services. Such measures were unseemly for a group that itself had made such great gains in agitating against Presbyterians and Independents.[100] As T. L. Underwood's recent study has shown, Baptist-Quaker debate centered on the question of primitivism: who made the stronger claim upon New Testament purity of faith and practice? While Baptists were strong scripturalists, making each reform according to the dictates of the New Testament, Quakers tended to emphasize being possessed by the same Spirit that had possessed the apostles who founded the early church and wrote the New Testament.[101]

By the summer of 1655, James Nayler, who had come out of the North to join Howgill and Burrough in London, elevated the Quaker sensation to new levels with his charismatic preaching and his success in debating the leaders of various churches.[102] By the end of that year, his preaching was drawing curious members of the nobility, officers of the army, and high ranking governmental officials. [103]

But real convincements occurred mostly among the middling ranks, particularly those "panting souls" who had long searched for a new and living way. Martha Simmonds, narrating her long quest, wrote that she had spent seven years in search of "an honest Minister," "wandering from one Idolls temple [i.e., parish church] to another, and from one private meeting to another," for "I saw my soul in death." Yet she could not find the true substance of faith; "and the more I sought after them the more trouble came upon me, and finding none sensible of my condition, I kept in it, and kept all close within me." She stopped "running after men" and abandoned religion altogether for another period of seven years, "living wild and wanton not knowing a cross to my will." Yet "something I found breathing in me groaning for deliverance, crying out, oh when shall I see the day of thy appearance." Finally,

> the Lord opened my eyes to see a measure of himself in me, which when I saw I waited diligently in it . . . I found this Light more and more increase, which brought me into a day of trouble, and through it, and through a warfare and to the end of it, and now hath given me a resting place with him; and this is my beloved, and this is my friend O daughters of Jerusalem.[104]

If her seven-year phases are meant literally and not merely as a figure of speech, Simmonds would have begun seeking around 1641, have given up around 1648, and have become a Friend in 1655. We find here a strikingly clear statement of a woman looking for spiritual authority among religious leaders, seeking "an honest Minister," "running after men." Her seeking was finally fulfilled in finding that authority within herself, a "beloved" and "friend" she recommends to all "daughters of Jerusalem." The language here echoes the Song of Solomon, particularly the third chapter. Simmonds, the sister of Giles Calvert and the wife of Thomas Simmonds (the two chief publishers of early Quaker literature) was convinced by James Nayler and became part of an inner circle around him.[106]

Quaker preachers claimed to live and speak by the same power and Spirit that moved the prophets and apostles. They claimed to regather the long-mourned authentic church. These bold assertions were answered by doubters' demands for unambiguous signs of apostolic authority, like those recorded in Acts. Nayler reported such demands "that I must prove my call by a miracle there, or else by some book that was infallible as the Scriptures."[107] That taunt, combined with the intimacy of the inner circle around Nayler, all in the highly charged atmosphere of London, augured for eventual trouble, which we will come to in Chapter 10.

The demand for conclusive proof or some overwhelming sign of spiritual authority was the constant refrain from more conservative Seekers, the classic type Saltmarsh described. The more Spiritualist Seekers described by Saltmarsh preferred religious ideas and esoteric knowledge.

Quaker preachers like Nayler found themselves in a position like that of Paul, who remarked,

> Jews demand signs and Greeks desire wisdom, but we pro-
> claim Christ crucified, a stumbling block to Jews and fool-
> ishness to Gentiles, but to those who are called, both Jews
> and Greeks, Christ the power of God and the wisdom of God"
> (1 Cor. 1:22-24).

The daily cross of Quaker convincement remained repellent to many Seekers of both types. But this was where the power arose.

BRISTOL

John Camm and John Audland moved on from London to Bristol, arriv-
ing on September 7, 1654. Camm (aged forty-nine) and Audland (a mere twenty-two) proved a formidable team, combining seasoned judgment and youthful fire. The large Seeker community in Bristol yearned for some kind of breakthrough and eagerly beset the two. Reporting to Burrough and Howgill in London just two days after their arrival, they described the scene: people

> groan to be delivered and they meet every day; if we go into
> the fields they follow us; from us they cannot be separated; if
> we sit silent a long time, they all waite in silence.[108]

Young Charles Marshall was one of the eager Seekers who immedi-
ately attached himself to the Quaker missionaries. He was raised in Bristol by strict religious parents who had him reading the Bible by age five or six. He went with his mother to Independent and Baptist meetings. He found some life among them, but felt they were frozen in credal formulations. With adolescence came disillusion and, like many Seekers, he often walked mournfully alone in the woods and fields. Yet even the beauty of nature accentuated his misery:

> as I walked, and beheld the creation of God Almighty, every
> thing testified against me, heaven and earth, the day and the
> night, the sun, moon, and stars, yea, the watercourses and
> springs of the great deep, keeping in their respective places;

and grass and flowers of the field, the fish of the sea and fowls of the air, keeping their order; but man falne, the chief of the work of God's hand degenerated.[108]

The natural integrity of the creation only made his own disorder more clear to him. Marshall was still only seventeen in 1654. He describes the Seeker meetings around Bristol at that time:

And in those times . . . there were many who were seeking after the Lord; and there were a few of us who kept one day a week in fasting and prayer. . . . We sat down sometimes in silence; and as any found a concern on their spirits, and inclination in their hearts, they kneeled down and sought the Lord; so that sometimes, before the day ended, there might be twenty of us pray, men and women; on some of these occasions children spake a few words in prayer; and we were sometimes greatly bowed and broken before the Lord in humility and tenderness.[110]

This is one of the best descriptions we have of (a least one form of) Seeker worship: a leaderless, nonsacramental fellowship of "broken" hearts waiting silently upon the Lord, speaking only as led by the Spirit. But there was no sense of power.

A letter from Camm to Burrough and Howgill, dated September 13, 1654, shows that the mission developed quickly, even within the first week. That day, they had met to worship with a group of Seekers. Camm describes the scene:

There wase many with the gloryousest words in prayer that I ever herd. There was the trimed harrlot gloriously deckt, and we were by and hard them and we went unto them and we boor them long till the power of the Lord took hould upon us both.

Evidently, the Seeker worship that Marshall described as broken-hearted was still too composed and too eloquent for these fire-breathing Quaker rustics from the North. Camm continues, "I was forst to cry out amongst them. My life suffered and if I did not speak I should be an exampell amongst them, and in much tenderness I spoke unto them and sillence was amongst them all." However,

> there is much wisdom which is from below in them, but it
> is truly confounded, and they see it their enemye ... the
> serpent which hath beguiled them, and robbed them of their
> simplicity, they have many of them cast off their butyfull
> garments which was without, but now the butyfull garments
> within is seen ... and shame doth cover their faces, for now
> they see themselves naked. There is a pure simplicity in them
> that would forgoe all for the Truth.[111]

Indeed, the plain, simple dress and manner of these northern Quakers was one of the first features that struck Bristol Seekers. Barbara Blaugdone recalled that their behavior and example preached even before they spoke.[112] Elizabeth Stirredge was threatened by their plainness.[112] But Camm's letter suggests that as these Seekers began to renounce their fine clothing, their inner struggles intensified. Camm and Audland labored day and night to help these tender souls through the crisis, often working from six in the morning until one the next morning.

Marshall befriended Audland and Camm within the first week after they arrived. He describes one of the initial breakthrough events. Early one morning, Marshall took them to a spring outside town where he had often gone "to seek the Lord" alone. They drank from the spring and waited quietly for some hours. Then Audland, trembling, suggested that they go back into the city, where a seeking group was meeting. They brought that group, along with people from the streets, to an open field. Camm spoke first, with his usual tenderness. Then Audland stood up trembling and said, "I proclaim spiritual War with the Inhabitants of the Earth, who are in the Fall and Separation from God." Marshall writes that "these words dropped amongst the Seed" in the hearts of those gathered. As Audland continued to preach, some fell on the ground, others cried out as they heard their condition laid open to them. From that apocalyptic point, meetings grew continually larger.[114]

Marshall recalls the "Tears, Sighs, and Groans, Tremblings, and Mournings" these Seekers experienced as they saw what separated them from true communion with God:

> Oh! the strippings of all needless Apparel, and the forsaking
> of superfluities in Meats, Drinks, and in the plain self-
> denying Path we walked ... we were a plain broken-hearted,

> contrite spirited, self-denying people . . . our Meetings were
> so large that we were forced to meet without doors . . . in
> Frost and Snow. . . . [The Lord] laid Judgment to the Line,
> and Righteousness to the Plummet, and gave to us the Cup of
> Trembling, in which was the Wine of Astonishment, which
> was in mercy to our Poor Souls, that could not be redeemed
> but by Judgment poured on the nature that had separated us
> from God.

We recall the "wine of astonishment" from the recantations of the Ranters
Coppe and Salmon. Quaker preaching took Seekers through the same
territory of utter disorientation and despair. But counsel, prayer, and encouragement brought them through the eclipse into a purer, unalloyed experience of divine presence and power. Further, simplification of lifestyle
worked symbiotically with inner "waiting upon the Lord" to ground the
convinced in a plainness and steadfastness that could face many challenges.

Still, transformation came slowly, and not without failures along
the way. Marshall recalls trying to defend the Quaker message against
critics before he was ready. He later realized that he had attempted to
speak by his own wisdom and strength. This experience complicated
his mind and captivated his spirit again for a while. He was desperate to
recover the new life that had begun in him:

> I was willing and running and striving, being in great fear
> and sorrow; and the more I toiled and laboured, kindling
> sparks of my own, the more my sorrow was increased; for as
> yet I had not learned the state of resignation.[114]

Slowly, he was helped to see his error and resumed the path of transformation, becoming a leading minister among Bristol Friends.

Barbara Blaugdone took up the cross of plain speech and habits, which
led to other challenges over the coming months and years. As she became a Quaker prophet, her witness cost her her employment. As an
itinerant Quaker minister, she was imprisoned for three months and suffered one severe flogging. The turmoil of her "Spiritual Journey" (her
own very modern-sounding term) thus led to outer travels and travails.[116]
Again, standing still sets the finder on a new course of errantry.

Elizabeth Stirredge had been a melancholy child, troubled by many
fears. Her mother warned that her chronic despondency would make

her ill, advising her to "delight thyself in something." She tried dressing finely but found little joy in it. Levity left her feeling guilty. She was twenty when she went to a Quaker gathering in Bristol. She recalls that Audland's voice pierced her heart and she went off alone to

> mourn to the Lord." Thus began, like the first day of creation in Genesis 1, "the first day's work in my heart . . . to divide the light from the darkness, and when the separation was made, then could I see my way in the light.

But this only intensified her sorrow and dread for several months. The next year, William Dewsbury came to Bristol to augment the ministry of Camm and Audland. In a private conversation, Dewsbury counseled, "Dear lamb, judge all thoughts and believe, for blessed are they that believe and see not." The fears that had hardened her heart eased, and her transformation advanced.[117]

CONCLUSION
APOCALYPSE AND ATONEMENT

The heady days of the 1640s captured the utopian imagination of a generation of Puritans just coming of age during the civil war. The bloom of youth burst forth from the confines of Stuart monarchy and state-sponsored religion and through a progression of alternatives. Traditional forms of authority and mainstream norms of piety were made to look pallid and hypocritical as the upheavals of the war swept away the "plausibility structures" that had made old ways appear self-evidently valid. The flower of a radical Puritan and Spiritualist counterculture came to political expression with the Levellers and Diggers. It found religious expression in the broad Seeker phenomenon. To many, it appeared that the utopian age of the Spirit—the age of the Lily—prophesied for centuries by figures such as Joachim of Fiore and Jacob Boehme—was dawning.

But the eager longing of that generation, like a fragile flower, could not withstand the heat of political repression, the cold, political calculation of England's new elites, or the withering power of sin abiding in personal life. The idealism of youth foundered first upon political disappointment and then upon its own moral impotence. "The grass withers, the flower fades, when the breath of the Lord blows upon it; surely the people are grass" (Isa. 40:7). Surely, there were human villains to blame—most of all Cromwell, who had seemed to promise so much. But those who saw most clearly discerned God's own hand in that day of eclipse. Thus, the Ranter Joseph Salmon wrote eloquently of the "wine of astonishment" the Lord had made him drink.

"The grass withers, the flower fades, but the word of our God will stand forever" (Isa. 40:8). The demise of the flower serves the maturing of the seed. Human expectation died, but the deep genetic coding of the biblical promise, God's reign on earth, abided deep in the hardened earth of their hearts. It would live again, but only by breaking open the heart, through a revelation of divine power shaking the earth, and freeing the seed to rise to new life.

That apocalyptic revelation was preached first by George Fox, then by a broadening circle of men and women across England, Wales, and Scotland. It was witnessed in words, but it also erupted in the body and through new, egalitarian codes of human interaction. It tore the new patch the Puritan regime had sewn onto the social fabric. It jarred people, disturbing their accustomed sensibilities. The recurring theme of Fox's preaching, and of the convincement narratives we have reviewed, is *power*. This was not the power that Parliament or the New Model Army had *wielded* against the king, or the power the Levellers had sought to seize, or the power of rage that galvanized the Ranters. Fox repeatedly described it as the power of God revealed through the cross of Christ, received by individuals *yielding* to its light within.[118]

The convincement narratives reviewed in this chapter show many of the Seekers-turning-Quakers to have started as hyper-Puritans whose idealistic moral absolutism made them unbearable to themselves and to those around them. It also alienated them from their Puritan pastors, for the standard Puritan counsel meant to reassure the average parish member only heightened their sense of personal depravity.[118] They became post-Puritan as they were drawn to the Spiritualism of the Seekers. But they were ultimately disappointed by Spiritualist promises of a new spiritual and moral power (that did not come,) an authentic church (that did not form), and a new age (that did not dawn). Saltmarsh and others described a basic divide among Seekers. On one side were the post-Protestants who still awaited new apostles who would revive the faith and church of the New Testament; on the other side were the incipient liberals who no longer dreamed of "primitive Christianity revived" but instead saw the new age of the Spirit dawning in their midst already, a new fellowship that was post-church and perhaps implicitly post-Christian. The first type of Seeker may have predominated in the North, the second type perhaps more numerous in the South, especially in London and the army.

The Quaker movement drew large numbers from both Seeker types. It sounded Protestant themes of renewing the church to primitive, apostolic purity, but made no attempt to reinstitute the sacraments, ordained ministry, or liturgy. The *Stillstand* was confirmed yet ended: the day of the Lord had dawned, Christ had come to teach and lead his people himself. Seeker innovations in silent worship were retained but transfigured by a new revelation (ironically, a revelation that Quakers claimed had been available throughout history to all peoples). Waiting in *history* for a new revelation was transformed into waiting in the *mystery* of revelation, which in turn would act back upon history through a gathered Quaker movement in English society. Waiting *for* God to act became waiting *upon* a God who acts now. The idolatries of hope were exchanged for a living faith. The future invaded the present. A movement was born of a sensed moment.

In this way, the Quaker apocalypse was also an atonement. The light's desolating power brought each vain idol, each private sin, before the judgment seat of God. Sin was not to be simply cloaked by Christ's righteousness (as taught by the leading Protestant reformers); nor was it redefined as mere neurosis (as the Ranters suggested and the liberal Enlightenment would later codify). The individual followed Christ to and through the cross, to be crucified to these things. Only there could the transforming power be revealed. Only through that painful passage could the wellsprings of love begin to flow, over spreading selfish designs with self-giving compassion for others.

Atonement began between God and the individual, as the latter stood in the unrelenting gaze of the light. It also mediated the gender-gap between men and women, as the interaction between masculine and feminine spiritual energies brought individuals to a closer encounter with God and with one another. It reconciled the culture-gap between North and South, as northern rustics *razed* the consciousness of sophisticated southerners—and as the latter more subtly brought a more cosmopolitan quality to the movement. Finally, it mediated other polarities in economic status, political power, and religious standing as convinced members of the gentry, magistracy, and even the clergy aided their poorer, less learned, and more legally vulnerable Friends.[120]

The term "Friend" evoked a new social zone. Men and women, ministers and congregants, gentry and tenants, justices and tithe-resisters became "Friends," at-one in the new fellowship of the cross. Anti-Quaker critics were not slow to discover the subversive effect of such polymorphous friendship upon the social hierarchies of their day. But friendship also kept opening toward the outsider, even the hostile critic. Quakers prefaced stinging prophetic warnings to their persecuting opponents— clergy, justices, even Cromwell—with the salutation "Friend. . . ."[121]

We close this chapter with a vision of the broadening, reconciling, transforming appeal of the Quaker movement. This was the "spreading power" of Christ that Winstanley had theorized in 1648-49, and that he now saw enacted among Friends. In Chapters 10 and 11, we will see a countervailing force also at work from the earliest phase of these Children of the Light: the narrowing, focusing tendency toward coherence and consistency. But first, we will examine two Seekers, Isaac and Mary Penington, whose long and difficult journey to Quaker convincement is marked by uncommon intellectual acumen and poignancy.

Notes

1. Sarah Blackborow, *A Visit to the Spirit in Prison* (1658), 7-10.
2. In recent years, there have been various reassessments of the centrality of Fox in Quaker beginnings. Barry Reay, in *Quakers and the English Revolution* (New York: St. Martin's, 1985), has suggested that Fox became preeminent only as he outlived other gifted Quaker leaders. Certainly, other remarkable figures helped shape the movement in important ways. Their trajectories will also receive attention here. But all alternate roads lead back to Fox. Earliest correspondence among Quaker leaders consistently shows deference to his judgment. "Great man" versions of history have rightly gone out of fashion in recent years. A "warts and all" style of biography is well exemplified by H. Larry Ingle's recent treatment of Fox, *First Among Friends: George Fox and the Creation of Quakerism* (Oxford: University Press, 1994). Ingle and others are rightly suspicious of "hagiographic" treatments of a figure like Fox, which predominate among Quaker publications. See his critique of my work on Fox, as well as that of others (and my response) in "The Folly of Seeking the Quaker Holy Grail," *Quaker Religious Thought* 75 (May 1991): 17-29. It is indeed important not to

make a larger-than-life character out of Fox. But, as we shall see, the antinomian chaos through which many Seekers and Ranters had drifted for years made it necessary to have an awe-inspiring and trustworthy figure around which to gather. Otherwise, one easily reverted (as many did) to the traditional religious authorities of clergy and church tradition, or continued drifting into a solipsistic personal religious universe (as some others did). Thus Fox became the touchstone, even a quasi-divine figure, for weary Seekers and depleted Ranters. Steven M. Tipton, in *Getting Saved from the Sixties: Moral Meaning and Cultural Change* (Berkeley: University of California, 1982), notes a similar dynamic among 60s countercultural youth becoming devoted to various gurus during the 70s. For the early years of Fox's life, we are dependent almost entirely on the account he gave many years later (1675-76) in his *Journal*. References here are taken from the John L. Nickalls edition (Cambridge: University Press, 1952).

3. George Fox, *Journal*, 3.
4. For the identity of Fox's uncle, I draw upon Ingle, *First*, 35.
5. Fox, *Journal*, 4.
6. Fox, *Journal*, 8.
7. Quoted by Henry J. Cadbury, "Then and Now," in *The Friends Intelligencer*, Sixth Month 29, 1946: 389-90. Cadbury, a Harvard University New Testament scholar who also pursued Quaker historical research in his spare time, deemed this a probable reference to Fox, given his shoemaking trade, his activity around Coventry at the time and the doctrines he had already embraced.
8. Fox, *Journal*, 337. Elizabeth Hooton's son, Oliver, described them as meeting "to play shovel board."
9. The preceding information on the Mansfield-Skegby group comes from a collection of remembrances written by Oliver Hooton and other members of that group some forty years later, in 1686. They are to be found in the "Children of Light papers," Box A Portfolio 10.42 at the Library of the Society of Friends, London (Hereafter cited as LSF).
10. Fox, *Journal*, 11.
11. Fox, *Journal*, 12.
12. Fox, *Journal*, 14-15.
13. I am grateful to Michelle Tarter for her fresh insights into the powerful physical dynamics of early Quaker spirituality. See her article, "The Milk of the Word of God," in *New Voices, New Light* (Wallingford, Pa.: Pendle Hill, 1995), 47-88.
14. Rosemary Moore, "Leaders in the Primitive Quaker Movement," *Quaker History* 85 (Spring 1996): 29.
15. Fox, *Journal*, 24-25.
16. Fox, *Journal*, 21.
17. Henry J. Cadbury, "Inquiry into Fox's Early Years," Friends Quarterly 17 (April 1971): 70-74 cites this information collected by early Quaker leaders John Camm and Francis Howgill, responding to allegations made in an anti-Quaker tract.
18. Fox, Journal, 22. George Arthur Johnson, "From Seeker to Finder: A Study in Seventeenth-Century English Spiritualism before the Quakers," Church History 17 (1948): 299-315, sees this as a decisive moment in Fox's development, one that sets him apart from the general Seeker trend.

19. Gerrard Winstanley, *The Breaking of the Day of God* (1648), 114.
20. Gervase Bennet, a judge in Derby who imprisoned Fox in 1650, was the first person Fox remembered hearing use the term "Quakers." Fox later retorted, "For long before thou in scorn called them Quakers hath the People of the Lord God been known about Mansfield, Nottingham and some parts of Leicestershire and thereabouts." See Cadbury, "Inquiry."
21. Fox, *Journal*, 27.
22. Fox, *Journal*, 26, 37-38.
23. Fox, *Journal*, 36, 38.
24. Fox, *Journal*, 45.
25. Fox, *Journal*, 52.
26. Moore, "Leaders," 29-30.
27. Fox, *Journal*, 69.
28. Fox, *Journal*, 56.
29. Fox, *Journal*, 58-60.
30. Moore, "Leaders," 30.
31. Fox, *Journal*, 65.
32. Fox, *Journal*, 70.
33. Fox, *Journal*, 85.
34. For a fuller explication of the apocalyptic coherence of Fox's ministry, see my earlier work, *Apocalypse of the Word: The Life and Message of George Fox* (Richmond, Ind.: Friends United Press, 1986).
35. Richard Farnworth, *The Heart Opened by Christ* (1654), 9.
36. Farnworth, *Heart*, 11.
37. William Dewsbury, *The Discovery of the Great Enmity of the Serpent* (1655), in his collected works, *The Faithful Testimony...* (1689), 44.
38. Dewsbury, *Discovery*, 50.
39. Dewsbury, *Discovery*, 51-51.
40. The early pages of Fox's *Journal* also manifest this scheme of personal transformation.
41. Dewsbury, *Discovery*, 54.
42. Dewsbury, *Discovery*, 52-53.
43. I am grateful to Joanna Kirkby, who was at Woodbrooke College during the autumn term, 1996 for this insight.
44. I am dependent here on the Introduction to *Threshold of Light: Prayers and Praises from the Celtic Tradition*, ed. A. M. Allchin and Esther de Waal (London: Darton Longmans and Todd, 1986); and the Introduction to *Celtic Christian Spirituality: An Anthology of Medieval and Modern Sources*, Oliver Davies and Fiona Bowie, eds. (London: SPCK, 1995).
45. On the areas of Celtic Christian strength, I draw upon *Celtic Christian Spirituality*, p. 11.
46. Fox, *Journal*, 79.
47. I find this phrase for the first time in Fox's *Journal* on page 78, just before his meeting with the Cleveland Ranters. He may have used it earlier, but I am taking his first usage of it here to indicate a development in his preaching at that time.
48. John Taylor, *An Account* ... (1710), 13.

49. Francis Howgill, *The Inheritance of Jacob Discovered* (1655), in his collected works, *Dawning of the Gospel-Day* (1676), 41.
50. Howgill, *Inheritance*, 41.
51. Howgill, *Inheritance*, 41.
52. Howgill, *Inheritance*, 42.
53. Howgill, *Inheritance*, 42.
54. Howgill, *Inheritance*, 43.
55. Howgill, *Inheritance*, 43-44.
56. Howgill, *Inheritance*, 45.
57. "Francis Howgill's Testimony Concerning Edward Burrough," in Burrough's *Works* (1672).
58. Howgill, "Testimony."
59. Also see Francis Higginson, *A Brief Relation of the Irreligion of the Northern Quakers*, published that same year. It is reviewed in my book, *The Covenant Crucified: Quakers and the Rise of Capitalism* (Wallingford, Pa.: Pendle Hill, 1995), 136-38.
60. Anonymous, *The Querers and Quakers Cause* (1653), Preface "To the Indifferent and Impartiall Reader."
61. Anonymous, *Querers*, 45.
62. Anonymous, *Querers*, 32-37.
63. Anonymous, *Querers*, 46. The author counter-responds to the use of the term "hire," apparently thinking the advocate has raised the Quaker critique of "hireling" clergy. But from the context, it seems clear the advocate has addressed the question of military service.
64. Margaret Fell, *A Relation of Margaret Fell . . .* (1690) in *Hidden in Plain Sight*, ed. Mary Garman, et. al. (Wallingford, Pa.: Pendle Hill, 1996), 245.
65. Margaret Fell, "The Testimony of Margaret Fox Concerning her Late Husband George Fox," in *Hidden*, 235.
66. Fell, "Testimony," 236.
67. Fell, "Testimony," 237.
68. Phyllis Mack, *Visionary Women: Ecstatic Prophecy in Seventeenth-Century England* (Berkeley: University of California Press, 1992), 146.
69. Richard Farnworth to Margaret Fell, et. al., Swarthmore MSS., 3:47, LSF. Also see 3:46.
70. John Burnyeat, "An Account of John Burnyeat's Convincement," in his collected works, *The Truth Exalted* (1691), 1.
71. Burnyeat, "Account," 2.
72. Burnyeat, "Account," 6-8.
73. I have treated the theological dimensions of this apocalyptic holy war theme more fully in *Apocalypse of the Word* and the social and political dimensions of it in *The Covenant Crucified*.
74. Dorothy Howgill to George Fox, 1652, A. R. Barclay MSS., 32, LSF.
75. Margaret Fell, with her children and servants, to George Fox, 1652, reprinted in *A Sincere and Constant Love: An Introduction to the Work of Margaret Fell*, ed. Terry S. Wallace (Richmond, Ind.: Friends United Press, 1992), 103-04.
76. Mary Howgill to George Fox, 1656, A. R. Barclay MSS., 41, LSF.
77. John Audland to Margaret Fell, n.d., Caton MSS. 3/137, LSF.

78. I am grateful for Richard Bailey's work on Fox's "son of God" claims and early Quaker usage of the term, "celestial flesh" in *New Light on George Fox and Early Quakerism: The Making and Unmaking of a God* (San Francisco: Mellen, 1992).

79. Fox, *Journal*, 52.

80. Fox, *Journal*, 134.

81. Swarthmore MSS., 2.55, quoted in full by H. Larry Ingle, "George Fox as Enthusiast," *Journal of the Friends Historical Society* 55.9 (1989): 265-70.

82. George Fox, *The Great Mystery of Babylon Unfolded and Antichrist's Kingdom Revealed unto Destruction* (1659), Works (Philadelphia: Goold, 1831), 3:398-99; cited by Bailey, *New Light*, 78.

83. See Paul L Maier, *Caspar Schwenckfeld on the Person and Work of Christ* (Assen, Netherlands: Van Gorcum, 1959), Chapter 6 on the derivations of Schwenckfeld's Christology. Also, R. Emmet McLaughlin, *Caspar Schwenckfeld, Reluctant Radical: His Life to 1540* (New Haven: Yale University Press, 1986), 88-89 finds the influence of Hilary of Poitiers' *De Trinitate*.

84. Francis Howgill, *Darkness and Ignorance Expelled* (1659), 22.

85. I am unable to confirm Bailey's interpretation of Fox as a self-styled "avatar" of God or Christ. The biblical and Spiritualist categories of his thinking, as I have sketched above, provide the only solid ground for interpreting Fox's bold statements. To reiterate, in order to validate the spiritual liberation he claimed for his movement, he had to pose himself as the extraordinary apostle, possessed of an extraordinary measure of God's Spirit, who could inaugurate such empowerment. He also had to be ready to face the probable consequences *vis a vis* the Puritan authorities. As we shall see later, Fox proved more adroit than Nayler at parrying the establishment's worst blows.

86. Fox, *Journal*, 174.

87. See Phyllis Mack, "Gender and Spirituality in Early English Quakerism, 1650-1663," in *Witnesses for Change: Quaker Women over Three Centuries*, ed. Elisabeth Potts Brown and S. M. Stuart (New Brunswick: Rutgers University Press, 1989).

88. Anthony Pearson to George Fox, July, 1654, in A. R. Barclay, *Letters, etc. of Early Friends* (London: Harvey and Darton, 1841), 10-14.

89. In *The Trumpet of the Lord Sounded Forth in Sion* (1655), Burrough addresses Seekers and Waiters together as representing the same position. See Burrough, *Works* (1672), 109.

90. Richard Hubberthorne to Margaret Fell, July, 1654, Caton MSS., 3/107, LSF.

91. Edward Burrough to Margaret Fell, summer 1654, Caton MSS., 3/63, LSF.

92. John Lilburne, *The Resurrection of John Lilburne* (1656). For the reformulation of revolutionary practice in early Quaker spirituality and politics, again see my recent book, *The Covenant Crucified.*

93. Anthony Pearson to George Fox, July 1654, Barclay, *Letters*, 14.

94. Francis Howgill and Anthony Pearson to Margaret Fell, July 10, 1654, Caton MSS., 3/74, LSF.

95. Francis Howgill to Margaret Fell, July 1654, Caton MSS., 3/66, LSF.

96. Susannah Blandford, *A Small Account . . .* (1698), reprinted in *Hidden*, 286-302.

97. Rebeckah Travers, *A Testimony Concerning the Light and Life of Jesus* (1663), 10.

98. Edward Burrough and Francis Howgill to Margaret Fell, August, 1654, in Barclay, *Letters*, 15-18.
99. Edward Burrough and Francis Howgill to Margaret Fell, August 29, 1654, Caton MSS., 3/62, LSF.
100. Edward Burrough, *Trumpet*, in *Works*, 105-06.
101. See J. F. McGregor, "The Baptists: Fount of All Heresy," in *Radical Religion in the English Revolution*, ed. McGregor and Reay, (Oxford: University Press, 1984), 58-61.
102. T. L. Underwood, *Primitivism, Radicalism, and the Lamb's War* (Oxford: University Press, 1997).
103. See Alexander Parker to Margaret Fell, July 28, 1655, Caton MSS., 3/96, LSF.
104. James Nayler to Margaret Fell, November 3, 1655, Swarthmoor MSS., 3.80, LSF.
105. Martha Simmonds, *A Lamentation for the Lost Sheep of the House of Israel* (1655), 5-6.
106. For a fuller treatment of the liaison between Nayler and Simmonds, and the tragic turn it took for both, see Chapter 5 of Gwyn, *The Covenant Crucified*.
107. James Nayler to George Fox, April-May 1656, Swarthmoor MSS., 3.76, LSF.
108. John Audland and John Camm to Edward Burrough and Francis Howgill, September 9, 1654, A. R. Barclay MSS., 158, LSF.
109. Charles Marshall, *Journal* (London: Barett, 1844), 3.
110. Marshall, *Journal*, 4.
111. John Camm and John Audland to Edward Burrough and Francis Howgill, September 13, 1654, A. R. Barclay MSS., 157, LSF.
112. Barbara Blaugdone, *An Account of the Travels, Sufferings and Persecutions* (1691), in *Hidden*, 275.
113. Elizabeth Stirredge, *Strength in Weakness* (London, 1795), 11.
114. Charles Marshall, "Testimony," in Camm and Audland, *The Memory of the Righteous Revived* (1689).
115. Marshall, *Journal*, 7.
116. Barbara Blougdone, *Account*, in *Hidden*, 274-84.
117. Elizabeth Stirredge, *Strength*, 1-19.
118. For just a few examples, See Fox's *Journal*, 174. Among his epistles, see his *Works*, 7:125, 193, 322.
119. For a fine study of this phenomenon, see Larry Kuenning, "'Miserable Comforters': Their Effect on Early Quaker Thought and Experience," *Quaker Religious Thought* #76 (October 1991): 45-59.
120. Again, these social dimensions of early Quaker witness are more fully explored in Gwyn, *The Covenant Crucified*, especially Chapter 3.
121. For example, in 1650, Fox addressed searing letters to the mayor, justices, and clergy of Derby as his "Friends." See the *Journal*, 53-55.

CHAPTER 9

ISAAC AND MARY PENINGTON
THE SEED RAISED

Be no more than God hath made thee. Give over thine own willing; give over thine own running; give over thine own desiring to know or to be any thing, and sink down to the seed which God sows in the heart, and let that grow in thee, and be in thee, and breathe in thee, and act in thee, and thou shalt find by sweet experience that the Lord knows that, and loves and owns that, and will lead it to the inheritance of life, which is his portion.

—Isaac Penington, 1661[1]

Isaac and Mary Penington were the most highly placed individuals to join the Quaker movement during its first and most revolutionary decade. Isaac's father was a wealthy London merchant who became a key political actor during the civil war. Between the years 1638 and 1649, the senior Isaac Penington held various positions as Sheriff, Alderman, and Lord Mayor of London, Member of Parliament, and Lieutenant of the Tower.[2] The elder Penington was a member of John Goodwin's Independent congregation and a friend of John Milton's.[3] He was one of the judges presiding over the trial of Charles I, but refused to sign the sentence of death. Nevertheless, he was condemned as a regicide at the Restoration and died in the Tower in 1661.

In his devotional biography of Isaac Penington, Joseph Gurney Bevan remarks that it "would be gratifying to trace the steps of the childhood of a man, in whom the simplicity of a child so long survived the weakness."[4] The younger Penington was born around 1616, but little is known of his early development. But it seems clear that, while the elder was embroiled in the political upheavals of that era, the younger

265

joined the struggle on a deeper, more inward level. He would later write that he had felt his heart pointed toward God from an early age. He sought the Lord earnestly, hearing sermons and reading books, especially the Bible. But he came to fear other people's interpretations of Scripture, preferring to pray and wait for understanding. Like so many of the most scrupulous young Puritans, he was "tangled up" in the doctrine of predestination, fearing that, in spite of all his seeking and yearning, the Lord "might in his decree have passed me by." He mourned and wept secretly in this condition for some years, driving himself to physical illness at times.[5]

He began studies at Cambridge in 1637.[6] We do not know the details of his academic attainments, but William Penn later described Penington as the most educated of first-generation Friends.[7] Evidently, the intellectual stimulation of university life did much to overcome his melancholy. His theological vision developed at great speed. He recalls a brief period (perhaps while still at Cambridge) in which all was sweet and pleasant. But the intensity became unbearable, and he prayed God to lessen the measure of light he was receiving. This plunged him into darkness and confusion. He later realized that he had hurt his own soul as he "limited the Holy One of Israel."[8] Still, he experienced God's sustaining mercy and by the late 1640s he was helping to lead one of the dozen or so Independent congregations in London.

Between 1648 and 1656, Penington published twelve tracts and books, charting his dramatic course from Puritanism, through advanced Spiritualism, into a serious engagement with Ranterism, to the threshold of Quaker convincement. While most of these works range from pastoral to mystical, two are political statements, revealing a keen and insightful interest in the conflicts of the day. We will review most of this pre-Quaker corpus, as it exhibits some of the most developed thought to be found among Seekers. We will also look at the acute seeking career of Isaac's wife, Mary, and the Quaker breakthrough they experienced together.

Earliest Writings

Isaac Penington was about thirty-two years old when Giles Calvert published his *Touchstone or Tryall of Faith* (1648). The tract displays a youthful confidence and a pedagogical style perhaps derived from

Penington's ministry among Independents. But it is addressed to all religious parties of the moment, warning that continued contention over religious and political issues will damage everyone's spirits and the national situation generally. Like Saltmarsh, he suggests that the only way forward is to "wait quietly upon God" rather than to enforce any settlement upon a divided people. He does not develop how such a waiting process might proceed.

He describes the religious scene as a "flitting age" in which people take up one practice today and another tomorrow. They alter their faith according to the force of an argument rather than the influence of the light within. So he warns all to "take heed of suddennesse, of sudden judgements."[9] But what follows tends toward standard Puritan pastoral counsel. He still embraces predestination, but acknowledges the problems many suffer in discerning their election. Some are too quick to decide they are saved. Their confidence will not stand up to God's trials, which must come to all. Others (like many of the Seekers profiled in the preceding chapter) are too quick to conclude they are damned. They cannot "apply the promises" to themselves and are prone to suspect the worst. In both cases, the problem is impetuosity. Souls in both conditions should "bewaile their own ignorance . . . and . . . pray and wait for light and help." At this point, Penington clearly writes with confidence in his own election and gifts in pastoral counsel.

In the next year, 1649, *The Great and Sole Troubler of Our Times* was published. Here Penington evinces a new appreciation for the ambiguities in spiritual discernment. He bases his comments on Jeremiah 17:9f.: "The heart is deceitful above all things, and desperately wicked, who can know it? I the Lord search the heart, I try the reins." Undoubtedly, not only pastoral experience but his own spiritual deepening had revealed just how difficult true self-knowledge could be. He acknowledges that deceit is everywhere in the world; but there is "nothing like the human heart for subtlety, secrecy, and depth of deceit." The heart is "a Fountaine, a Sea, an Ocean of wickedness." It is simply too deep for the intellect to plumb. Only God reaches to the bottom of it. God lets down a bucket to lift up and pour forth the utter perversity of the heart:

> what a man may seem most free from, and think himself wholly mortified unto, God chuses to draw forth and discover to him and others. Drunkenness out of temperate Noah.

> Incest out of chaste Lot, Unbelief out of faithful Abraham,
> Rigid sharpnesse out of meek Moses, Impatience and curses
> out of patient and blessing Job, Pride out of newly broken
> and humbled Hezekiah. And I have often found, that what
> evil I have dis-relished in others, and thought God might justly
> be meet with them for, it was soon after opened, and let loose
> in mine own heart.[10]

Penington had come to see the human condition as self-contradicting madness. And if God forces any remedy upon a man, "he roars and cries out, as if the healing were a loss of happiness."[10] The heart is threatened by everything it encounters, especially by God. Evil is not just a defect in the heart, it is the totality of its condition.

This crushing vision of human wickedness was precipitated in part by the political madness of 1649: the beheading of Charles, the army's manipulation of Parliament, and the defeat of the Levellers. Penington saw parties eliciting the worst from one another. First "the Kings party" seemed noble and brave until it came under pressure for reform; then its base nature revealed itself. Then came "Parliaments party" with its rhetoric of religious reformation and political liberty; but its self-serving motives soon became clear. Then came the army with "the highest and most beautiful forms of Religion . . . with a flaming zeal" to establish righteousness and liberty: "Who would think to find Self like lurking close here too?" Finally, the churches themselves, with their sacraments and devotions, have been spoiled by self-interest and human designs that

> smell so strong, that they are offensive to all, but such as are
> engaged in them. Blush oh Heavens, and be astonished oh
> Earth, how are ye both stripped? There's no vertue nor
> strength left in either of you.[12]

Evidently, he was now approaching the Seeker position opposing the sacraments and rituals of all the churches.

Still, Penington was willing to see a redemptive pattern in all this disillusion. "God is ripping up the heart of man, opening it up, stirring the sink, causing a noisome savour that offends every nostril." All should quietly endure this purging time:

> When we come to know our selves, nothing will be more
> burdensome to us then our selves, and nothing will be more
> welcome then that sword which is sharp enough, and that
> hand which comes resolutely enough . . . to let out the very
> lie of our hearts, which once done will make us happy.[13]

Thus, in 1649, Penington witnessed to the same "fiery triall"
that Saltmarsh had described in 1647 and that would become an
uncontrollable wildfire by 1652 in the North. But the times were not
yet ripe. We see him sliding quickly into the dark abyss that came
upon many advanced Spiritualists and political radicals that year.
Penington had reached the limits of his Independent faith and was
starting to slip away.

THE RANTER ECLIPSE

By early 1650, Penington was in full-blown crisis. A letter of February
18 to an intimate friend describes his state of extremity. All knowledge
and spiritual sense has been

> confounded, condemned, taken from me, made odious to
> me. Very shy have I been of new Notions. . . . I can neither
> receive any thing that is new, nor return to any thing that is
> old: but every thing is darkness, death, emptiness, vanity, a
> lye. . . . I am perfectly weary of my self and all things, but
> continually more and more beset with what I hate. [All reli-
> gion has been] violently torn from me, peece by peece. . . .
> [He briefly enjoyed a] kind of fools Paradise, yet not without
> intermixtures of anguish; but I was quickly weary of it, and
> turned out of it too. I am weary of all things, of Religion,
> Reason, Sense, and all the objects that these have to con-
> verse about: but yet there is somewhat in stead of these that I
> would fain finde within . . . which if once my spirit might be
> satisfied in, I should find some rest; till then I cannot but
> remain truly miserable, and fit for nothing, but to torment,
> and be tormented.[14]

Penington describes the Ranter eclipse poignantly. Heaven and earth, their rottenness exposed, had passed away. He was briefly immersed in the same "fools Paradise," the euphoria of pure nihilism, that had coursed through figures like Coppe and Salmon. But that quickly staled for him. The intellectual "objects" of religion and reason that had fascinated him endlessly were of no value. But hints of "somewhat in stead of these," a non-intellectual *sense*, occasionally suggested the possibility of another way not yet manifest.

Penington parted company lovingly with the Independent congregation he had served, promising to return to them if he felt free to do so.[15] It seems unlikely that he joined in the sensational theatrics of the Ranters—alias, "The Mad Crew," "My One Flesh." But from the four vivid pieces he published in 1650, it is clear that he moved in those circles and befriended at least one leading figure. We will follow his passage through extreme eclipse with a brief look at each of these four tracts.[16]

A Voyce out of the Thick Darkness appeared in late March or early April. It includes the February letter quoted above. Penington relates some observations of the recent past (probably late 1649, before his crisis arose) concerning the political and religious hopes of seeking people. Politically, he recalls having shared the fervent desires of the Leveller movement, although with less optimism about the tactics they employed. A political pessimist tending toward quietism, Penington counsels patience and submission under these new, gloomy circumstances. God is displeased not only with the self-serving tactics of those in power but with the rebelliousness of those governed. "It is the stiffnesse of the neck, and unbrokennesse of the Spirit that chiefly makes all our yokes so harsh."[17] He also counsels readers to place less expectation upon human leadership. Parliament, the army, Cromwell, and the Levellers all had disappointed radical hope by 1650.

On the religious front, Penington addresses the two forms of Seeker expectation that we have seen repeatedly in this study. He shares Saltmarsh's dissatisfaction with the first, more Protestant version of Seekerism. Why should we hope for the restoration of a New Testament Christianity that was so frail even in its primitive state that it quickly declined with the passing of the apostolic generation?[18] Penington moves on to the "new age" Seekers' expectation of a new dispensation terminating all previous ones. Some even claim to have tasted of it. Like Francis Howgill (see the preceding chapter), Penington is attracted to that notion but repelled by the fact that those who claim to have entered this new dispensation contradict its glory by the way they live. They boast that all is theirs, yet they possess nothing truly. In fact, they "wallow in filth and wickedness." Again, we see clearly the line of development into Ranterism from the advanced Spiritualism of the "new age" Seeker.

Penington admits that he was disgusted by the Ranter tendency until the crisis overtook him as well and he knew himself unworthy to judge anyone. He warns all against condemning the Ranters. This is no ordinary case of libertinism. God's deepest passages in people are those most hidden; often the deepest love comes by way of the bitterest cup. "There is a wine prepared for all to drink of, to empty them of all their glory, which the people of God must begin with. God will have no glory stand in his way: Religion is the highest glory, stands most in his way, therefore that must first down."[19] Just as Paul wrote that anguish and distress must overcome all, first the Jew then the Gentile (Rom. 2:9), Penington reasons that the messianic woes of an impending new age must initially overcome those who have arrived first at its threshold. Nature has its glory as well. In its day, religion dashed the lesser glory of nature. Now religion's glory must be quenched by something greater. Meanwhile, the nauseating "wine of astonishment" "lays the creature dead drunk" to spiritual sense. "These persons [Ranters] have been made to drink this wine. . . . Let him that standeth take heed, lest he fall. Consider what ye will do when ye come to drink of this cup."[20] (We heard a similar warning from Salmon in his recantation of 1651.)

Penington ultimately sides with those who expect a new, more glorious dispensation. It will be like the pouring of the Spirit at Pentecost, but more transformative. The Spirit will be a perfect guide, giving real victory over sin and evil. "And . . . herein lies my heart, this is all the little hope that is left me (or rather that is a little revived in me) after the bitter death and losse of all."[21] He invites all to join him in mourning for what is lost and in waiting for deliverance to come.

Light or Darkness followed in May, responding to Ranter rhetoric. The title evokes themes of Jacob Bauthumley's *Light and Dark Sides of God* and Laurence Clarkson's *The Single Eye: All Light, No Darkness; Or, Light and Darkness One*. With Jeremiah's vision of the void (Jer. 4:23-26), he launches into an amazing Ranterlike Preface. Though he has always sought wisdom, he is now stripped of it and feels more at ease with folly. Content to be a fool, he no longer tries to see to the bottom of things. As to what follows, he challenges the reader: "This Light, This Darkness (be it what it will) is of a deeper kinde then thine is . . . and thine eye cannot discern it." By his foolish words, he hopes to entangle those who think themselves wise.

He notes that some thought his last publication advocated "pure sporting with sin." He clarifies that he was not contemplating *acts* of sin but the *nature* of it. But even sin must ultimately be of service to God: the divine judge is glorified in condemning and conquering it. Hence, the human eye can see only the unloveliness of sin, but the true eye sees the unloveliness pass away. This comes very close to the Ranter preaching that sin is only perceived as such, and that through the indulgence of sin one renders sin righteous. He quotes Job's words (Job 9:22) that God destroys both the perfect and the wicked. But he adds that this desolation is not for the *destruction* of religion but for its *purification*. Only through such all-consuming fire can the primitive glory, the original beauty of all things, be again revealed.[22]

Included here is a letter, dated April 20, 1650, to a recovering Ranter Penington addresses simply as Anne. He has seen her written letter of recantation, "which doth wonderfully please me." "So where are you now, Sweet Anne? You see the rottenness of your former foundation, are you sure you now build upon firm ground, upon the inmost Rock?" She has retracted her former statement that God is all things. But Penington suggests to her that there is "everything besides the Lord, and yet nothing but the Lord." Everything is so full of the creature as to be empty of its Creator; yet the Creator so floods all things as to drown all independent being and action. Both truths must be seen within a larger framework.

His quarrel with her (and everyone else) is that she measures all things by her own measure. He concludes with breathtaking judgment:

> And this is the whole work of man, to be picking out the colour that suits with his eye, and to be exalting in it, and laying all others flat. And as often as he changes his eye, his light, his colour, still he takes the same course, and therefore still in all his changes deserves to come under the same condemnation.[23]

This searing observation has particular relevance to the shifting and contentious tides of that day—and to the lateral moves many Seekers made from one shade of doctrine to the next. It seems Anne has also reaffirmed the existence of hell. But does she know what hell is? "He that can be content to please himself in escaping Hell, where others must scorch in inutterable torment, is he righteous? Oh how my Soul loaths all that which all men call Righteousness!" He concludes that false righteousness stands more in the way of true righteousness than wickedness and misery do. His rhetoric veers back and forth between compassionate humanism and contemptuous misanthropy.

Penington leaves off tormenting Anne and vents his own noxious vision of God as a sadistic destroyer. He suggests that God projects creatures as mere shadows, infuses them with a shadowy life, and endows them with an instinct for self-preservation. Then God takes sport in hunting down and destroying them. All humans are idolatrous; they can only liken God to this thing or that. The only difference is in the degree of refinement. The human eye can see nothing except by colors. It sees the colors of good and evil, but not the *substance* of what is colored. Thus, truth lies hidden beneath paint. "O God, How art thou miscoloured! Man thinks he hugely pleaseth thee by putting the finest kind of paint upon thee, not understanding how it disfigures thee. . . . But know, O Man, O refined'st Man, God loaths to be lovely in thine eye."[24] God "is a dreadful God, and in no wise desireable . . . true substantial sight can never enter into any, until after perfect death."

Thus, Penington concludes that divine judgment only *begins* by condemning unrighteousness and justifying righteousness. Then righteousness itself must be judged and unrighteousness justified. Then *both* are condemned forever. Only then can truth break forth with its true luster and swallow up condemnation and the fear of it. Only God's Son, who was obedient through all, will stand in this day of trial.[25] He enjoins all to keep silence and tremble before the wrath of God, who comes to devour all:

> for as I live, saith the Lord, I will feed on thee, and devour thee, and thou shalt never be any thing more but what thou art in me, but what I by the power of my life, by the warmth of my stomach, convert thee into within my self.[26]

Penington thereby answers the rarified mystical principles of Ranter monism with a hideous countervision of oneness—everything consumed

and digested by a wrathful God. This stretches even apocalyptic categories. It vents the bitterness of a soul that has lost faith in God's love,
because "love" itself is a "color" we love. *Light or Darkness* marks the
nadir of Penington's quasi-Ranter phase. He has plumbed the depths of
Ranter despair and found it superficial and glib. For a brief time, the
bitterness of mortification robbed Penington of his beautiful simplicity,
just as Job was finally robbed of his patience. Some of Penington's friends
assumed that he must have committed some terrible sin to have fallen
so low.[27]

The Preface to *Severall Fresh Inward Openings* (appearing in July)
is addressed "To all Persons, of all Sorts" with the salutation,

> Mine own dear flesh without (or outwards,) Mine own Life
> and Spirit within (or inwards,) where-ever dispersed, how-
> ever clouded. I am of kin unto you, of your flesh and of your
> bone; My Life, my Spirit, my Substance is one with yours;
> why are we so strange to one another? Who knoweth how
> sweetly and harmoniously we lay tumbling together in the
> same womb of Eternity, before we were brought forth in
> these severall strange shapes, wherein we now appear. What,
> shall a few momentary varieties and contrarieties (fitted only
> for some present design) make perpetuall inroads upon ever-
> lasting Unity?

This is the classic Ranter rhetoric of oneness. It partakes of the same
unity/variety dialectic we found in Salmon's *Heights in Depths*. Salmon
and Penington both probably derived these concepts from reading recent English translations of Jacob Boehme's works.[28]

Elaborating, he declares that the present estrangement must continue
a little longer. The coexistence of differing spiritual dispensations has
not yet ended. But the "time is at hand, wherein time shall be no more;
and then whatever had a Being in time, shall cease to dust. . . . For the
mean time, Farewel: For I must retire into Desolation, which is seizing
upon all things." Only those who see beyond this cosmic collapse
can do anything other than weep. "And he who indeed beholds this,
may skip and leap in the flames, even while they are fastning upon and
burning up himself." This passage very closely approximates Salmon's
description of his Ranter phase—a holy nihilism. Penington articulates
the *via negativa* principle of spiritual immolation for the sake of a purer

love: once every thing loved and hoped is destroyed, "then I shall be sure to meet with none but God, to love none but God, to desire none but God."

The tract's main text explains that this devastation is for the sake of breaking down the "partition wall" of alienation from God. If Christ had not already undergone this desolation in the cross, there would be no hope at all. Following Paul's words in Ephesians 2:14-16, Penington argues that the mystical unity of all things is achieved through Christ's reconciling all things into one body in himself through the cross. The enmity sown throughout the entire creation is itself slain in Christ.[29] By this line of argument, Penington affirms much of the mystical monism of the Ranters but reasserts the Christocentric and apocalyptic framework for the ultimate (rather than essential) unity of all things.

He then turns to the Ranters with "A Word to the Mad Folks." He acknowledges many of these to have been "very eminent" in religious experience, ideas, and deportment. They have been on the forefront of reformation. "But now ye are dead to all this . . . He that built you, hath made you desolate." Nothing can describe their misery (or his), for "you are slain to your religion."[30] To the extent that they are dead (as he is), he joins with them. "O that ye were indeed dead! O that ye were as sober and silent as those who are in the grave!" Then they would wait until God raises them to something truly new and redemptive. Instead, they have set about to destroy the faith of others and build something new. "Come Sirs, Let us be still. . . . Let us not be too forward to throw away Christ. . . . Let us not be imagining a new Christ, while we are blaming others for imagining an old." That is, they are *living before their time* and this is sin. They are both dead and alive: dead to a shallow faith, alive to one inferior even to that. Too hasty to conceive and deliver, they have miscarried. They must wait for a more certain revelation.[31] This is the most trenchant critique of Ranterism to appear from any quarter, by one who shared their sense of despair and had truly listened to them and had learned from them. The logic here is similar to that in the epistle of Sarah Jones the same year.

Next comes an open letter to "the Captain of that Generation, whom my Soul loveth, whom, of all persons, my spirit . . . turneth most vehemently towards, and most vehemently from." The addressee here may be Laurence Clarkson, whom we recall was known as the "Captain of the Rant."[32] "Your brave resolute spirit, that dares trample upon Heaven and Earth, laying your levelling line to all things, is of much value and excellency with me." But his "creaturely way of managing this from principles of reason . . . deceiving many, this I cannot swallow." Clarkson (if that is the identity of the addressee) speaks of God being all, all things being good, all alike. Penington wonders whether he understands what he is saying. He suspects the latter will soon be as sick of these new principles as he became of the old ones.

Then Penington asserts pregnantly, "my spirit in the dark saith thus: It will be so one day." God will be all, but not as anyone now can conceive it. He is even willing to agree (theoretically) that this reality has already arrived for those so deeply in union with God as to live perfectly in God. But a change in our imaginations will not transform anything. The only posture of integrity in this dark night of distress is silent humility. "Nothing is more beseeming, though nothing more dificult to the fool, then silence. . . . O God, what a strange kind of Night this is, which affords not rest, which admits of no stilness!" Anyone can trample upon Christ and the apostles, but who can speak or act as gloriously as they did?[33] Penington seems to embrace the Seeker principle of waiting for the authoritative revelation of new apostles. Meanwhile, prophets have become fools. Only when

> their brains are weary of imagining, their tongues of expressing, and their hearts speak plainly, that all is vanity . . . and at last faint . . . then it will be time for him, who truly understands things, to speak, when every mouth else is stopped."[34]

Penington sees a new dispensation about to issue forth—but not yet.

Until then, "Seek. It is a time of scarcity, of want, of loss; Seek." The meek, the tender, the broken-spirited, those who hunger for righteousness, "these are fit to seek, these God onely desires to have seek him. The high, the lofty, the unrighteous ones; let them alone (saith God) let me deal with them."[35] An all-consuming day of wrath is descending. If any condition is safe, it is meekness. God's anger comes from love and is subservient to it. "If any thing scape, it is like to be righteousness and meekness, if any person scape, it will be he in whom these are found."[36]

Penington's final statement of 1650, *An Eccho from the Great Deep* (published by Calvert in November), was his longest publication that year (132 pages) and his cumulative response to Ranterism. He addresses another affectionate preface "To the Mad Folks," confessing that

I cannot but own you before all the world as the greatest objects both of my delight and expectation: I am most pleased in beholding you; your sickness is more lovely in my eye then that health which others enjoy . . . My expectations, of the next discovery of Light, Life and Glory, are fastened upon you . . . My heart tells me that ye are not thus shattered, broken, and made so odious for nothing.

The place of eclipse is thus the place to watch for the next appearance of light. Yet he continues in his distaste for Ranter ideas and immorality:

It is not your new Fabrick but your old desolations that kindle in me any desire towards you. . . . As ye live, I loath you; nay I loath your life more than the life of any else: So far as ye are dead I cannot but hug you. . . . But oh how I long to see your new life, with all the motions of it swallowed up by death! There is a cup prepared for you . . . which shall wash you clean within, and make you vomit lustily, even till ye are quite emptied of all that froth and scum of vanity, which now swims up and down in your stomacks, and fumes up into your brains. . . . The child is not yet born in you that knows how to chuse the good or refuse the evill. This is not the Land of promise wherein ye now set up your rest, but a strange land.

After chiding the Ranters, Penington turns yearningly to God, pleading in tones and imagery infused by the Song of Solomon:

O my Beloved, where dwellest thou! where is thy Temple . . . ? O let us at length see the conquest of love. Swallow up all in thine own perfection . . . Visit thy fainting Spouse [Song of Sol. 5:8]. . . . Her spirit is quite spent . . . yield up thy self at length to the desire, which thou thy self hast kindled in the bosom of thy Beloved. . . . Is there no cure for this love, no rasing it out of the heart, nor no attracting its object into the heart? O God why art thou so coy? why dost thou so disdain the low estate of thy Spouse? What credit will it be unto thee to have it said and seen, when all things shall be opened to all eyes and spoken in all eares, Behold a Soul burnt up into perfect misery by the flames of its own love!

Though the image of God "swallowing up" all things remains, the hideous sense of a devouring ogre is gone. The erotic ethos of desire for God has replaced it. This was not seen in Penington's writings even before his crisis. Something new is emerging from his dark night of the soul.

The main text of *Eccho* constitutes Penington's most programmatic theological statement before his Quaker convincement. It is too comprehensive to be treated here. Only a few salient points will be mentioned. He begins with a rebuttal of the Ranters' most sensational questions: whether God is a being distinct from nature, whether good is ultimately distinct from evil, whether there is any such thing as a devil. In retrospect, we see that many of the Ranters' positions are precursors of the Enlightenment's rebellion against the ideological dominance of Christendom.

Penington had used the metaphor of the seed all along. But now this figure begins to assume a special importance. He writes of "the two Principles, Seeds, or Creations, their different Natures, Motions, and Ends." Both are God's work, both excellent in their kind and to the ends for which they were intended. The first is beautiful, worthy, desirable in appearance, but weak at the root; it eventually corrupts and dies. The second appears weak and undesirable, but has a strong root and endures. The first begins with life and ends in death; the second begins with death, shame, and confusion, but grows steadily to perfection.[36] We recognize here Paul's imagery in 1 Corinthians 15:35-50 of physical and spiritual bodies, first and second Adams, differing seeds. The incommensurate qualities of these opposing dimensions of existence will become one of the great themes of Penington's Quaker writings.

But life in the second birth, the spiritual seed, is not a simple advancement upon the first. Here Penington addresses the experience of captivity, subjection to Satan's tyranny, which happens even to those who have been born again in the seed. This experience recapitulates the history of Israel, which was delivered into Canaan, the land of rest, only to be carried off into Babylon.

> How bitter, how painful it is to a spiritual man, to finde his spiritual life dying and decaying!" The secret to survival is to endure this captivity quietly. "There is no way like to lying still, and yeelding up even the spiritual life as sacrifice, following Christ as a Lamb or Sheep to the slaughter.[38]

He summarizes this most painful lesson:

> Man is ordained to walk retrograde to himself, to go quite
> contrary ways . . . to throw down all that he builds, to build
> all that he throws down, to go so many degrees of death as he
> hath gone degrees of life . . . he is but a vain fool in all, a fool
> living, a fool dying; a fool weeping, a fool laughing; a fool
> making himself a sinner, a fool making himself a Saint.[39]

In these meditations, we hear hints of Ecclesiastes, a favorite text of the
Ranters. Yet like Ecclesiastes (and Job, that other disturbing figure in
Israel's "anti-wisdom" literature), Penington is unwilling to curse God
and surrender to rage. He muses that the difference between God's seed
(here in the collective sense of a people) and everyone else is not that
the former are exempted from utter befoolings,

> but that in their running through them they still remain the
> same. They are like God . . . whatever their clothes, what ever
> their appearances may be, yet their Substance, their Life is
> still the same.[40]

Penington applies what may be the ultimate Seeker text, appropriately enough
from the Lamentations of Jeremiah: "The Lord is good to those who
wait for him, to the soul that seeks him. It is good that one should wait
quietly for the salvation of the Lord. It is good for one to bear the yoke in
youth, to sit alone in silence when the Lord has imposed it" (Lam. 3:35-28).
Penington's answer to the Ranters displays the difference we noted in Chapter
2 between Eckhart's mysticism and Tauler's Spiritualism: Spiritualism still
upholds the ultimate unity of all things; but humans come to this truth only
by way of the harrowing experience of the cross.

LATER PRE-QUAKER TRACTS

Given the tone of withdrawal and repose that comes over Penington's
last bulletins of 1650, it is not surprising that his publications slowed
considerably during the first half of the 1650s. But it is surprising that
his next two works were political. Nevertheless, Penington continued
his war on two fronts: just as he had formerly challenged Puritans and
Ranters alike, he now confronted both government and the governed
during a time of growing cynicism.

The Fundamental Right, Safety and Liberty of the People (1651) addresses the declining situation under the Rump Parliament. The preface to Parliament criticizes its narrowminded view of the public good. This remnant of a Parliament once had the people's cries for it; now the people cry against it. The most basic problem is that Parliament operates without a real constitution (only a provisional one drafted by the Army Council). The present Parliament should enact a full constitution, dissolve itself, and hold elections. A new Parliament would then exercise constitutional power. Penington also challenges "the sorrowful people of this sick nation" to bear this present miscarriage of government patiently. In the meantime, they should continue the work of personal reformation: "If every man could once espy and grow most weary of his own faults, there might be some hope of amendment." At the same time, people should not pin their hopes on political actors, as they did over the past decade.

He redirects true hope toward a third party existing between government and the governed, as the true catalyst of both political liberty and moral reformation. This mediating party is the gathered people of God. Their religious freedom is the most efficient engine for the development of all political liberties. God's word to Pharoah, "Let my people go that they may serve me," reminds all that *political* liberation begins with *religious* liberation. "This is a ticklish point, and of more consequence to the welfare of Nations then they are aware of." Penington's insight here is crucial, both theologically and historically. Theologically, political freedoms find their proper perspective in light of the human freedom/obligation to serve God (albeit according to individuals' own religious leadings). Historically, hindsight confirms that the struggles for religious freedom in the 16th through 18th centuries were indeed the catalysts for broader conceptions and implementations of human rights *per se*.

In 1653, as Cromwell's Protectorate loomed, Penington took up his pen and entered the fray a second time with *A Considerable Question about Government*. The tract's query is this: which serves the good, safety, and welfare of the people best: absolute or limited authority? Penington is willing to consider the advantages (efficiency and continuity) of even an absolutist regime (provided the ruler possesses wisdom and integrity). Yet he concludes that, while absolute authority may be theoretically best, limited authority is safest. Undoubtedly referring to the Fifth Monarchist ferment around London, he observes that it is popular to speak of "the saints" ruling the world. He agrees that the saints will indeed rule with divine justice when the Spirit is poured out upon all flesh. But without the Spirit, self-styled saints will provide the worst government.[41] He surely alludes to the total ineptitude of the Barebones Parliament that year. He concludes wearily, "Oh that this so long-captivated-Nation, could lift up their eyes towards, and wait for, the salvation of God."

Of his final pre-Quaker works, we will briefly treat with only the last and largest, *Expositions with Observations on Several Scriptures* (1656). A large compendium (778 pages) of biblical meditations written mostly in 1655, it contains a brief personal statement in which Penington looks back upon his crisis of 1650. Even five years later, he confesses,

> I am now a dark thing, still in the dark, being neither what I
> formerly was, nor yet formed into a vessel by the Potter: Not
> yet perfectly broken . . . and very little made up.

He goes on to speculate that God has bestowed three lights (or revelations) upon humanity over time: the primordial light of nature, the Jewish light of the law, and the Christian light of the gospel. Each was given by God, but was corrupted by the ways humans appropriated it to their own ends. Human control rendered each light useless to God's purposes. In spite of this brokenness, however, individuals can still be faithful whatever their station. The heathen need not make himself a Jew, nor the Jew a Christian. It is better to be a heathen or Jew of God's making than a Christian of one's own making. Who knows? he adds provocatively, God might thrust aside the Christian and choose the heathen or the Jew ahead of him. We detect here a post-Christian universalism developing in Penington's thought.

Penington's scheme of three lights is typical of his tendency to elaborate his insights (though it also is typical of the dispensationalist stream in Spiritualism). He shares much in common with early Quaker preaching of the light, and its power to redeem individuals even apart from a knowledge of Scripture. But, as we shall see in Chapter 11, Penington eventually ran into conflict with the Quaker leadership over his concept of multiple lights/dispensations.

So, even in 1656, Isaac Penington continued to sit upon the ash-heap of his desolation. He was content, like Job, to receive both good and bad from God (Job 2:8,10). But he began to find consolation in the company of a fellow Seeker with corresponding depth and desolation.

Mary Proude Springett

Mary Proude was born around 1626 into a wealthy family in Kent.[42]
Both of her parents died when she was three. She was sent to live with a
family she later described as "loose Protestants," basic church-goers.
But she sought more. The first Scripture that stayed in her mind (at age
eight) was the Beatitude, "Blessed are they that hunger for righteousness, for they shall be filled" (Matt. 5:6).

Around the age of twelve, she was sent to live with a more devout
family. She was distressed to think that she was not a true Christian. She
wanted to pray spontaneously but could only read the prayers of others.
Then she began to write her own prayers. She was drawn to Puritan
preachers and was disturbed in the 1630s to hear of Archbishop Laud's
persecution of them. Her foster family accused her of being proud and
schismatic for attending Separatist meetings, suggesting that she did so
only to look for young men. This was untrue; nevertheless, she longed
for a proposal from a good man, a partner in the search for true righteousness. Her prayers were answered in the person of Sir William
Springett, a colonel in the army for Parliament's cause. They were married in 1644, when she was aged 18. She was more advanced in seeking
than he, but they "pressed much after godliness," deciding together to
renounce the singing of Psalms and the use of sacraments. They explored the Independents and Baptists, but found no satisfaction.

William and Mary Springett had only about two years together before he died in military service. Their daughter, Gulielma (who would
one day marry the Quaker William Penn), was born a few weeks later.
Mary, a widow aged twenty, scandalized people of her rank when she
declined to have her daughter "sprinkled." Deep in grief, she found no
comfort in hearing the preachers she had once appreciated. A desperate
seeking began to overtake her:

> In this restless state, I let in every sort of notion that rose in
> that day, and for a time applied myself to get out of them
> whatever I could find; but still, sorrow and trouble was the
> end of all; and I was ready to conclude, that though the Lord
> and his Truth was; yet that it was made known to none upon
> the earth; and I determined no more to enquire, or look after

> him, for it was in vain to seek him . . . and so for sometime
> look no notice of any religion, but minded recreation (as it is
> called,) and went into many excesses and vanities, as foolish
> mirth, carding, dancing, and singing.[43]

Not only grief but class privilege contributed to Mary Springett's sense of perdition. The wealth, ease, and social life of elite circles undercut the earnestness of her seeking, just as it gave Isaac Penington the time and resources to intellectualize endlessly. Leisure helped make both of them the most miserable of Seekers. Indeed,

> in the midst of all this my heart was constantly sad and pained
> beyond expression. After such follies, I did retire from all people
> for days, and was in much trouble. [She told herself,] I do this
> because I am weary and know not what to do; it is not my
> delight, it hath not power over me; I had rather serve the Lord
> if I could indeed feel that which performeth acceptably.

She often retreated with her daughter to the country, where she found comfort in the quiet of more natural surroundings. She found no religious doctrine or fellowship helpful; she was ashamed to be counted religious at all, preferring the conversation of irreligious friends.

Like other Seekers we have seen, Mary found her prayer life reduced to sighs and groans. She tried to trust simply in God's daily guidance, waiting to see what each day would bring, responding to opportunities as her heart led her. Before she had met any Quakers, she had a dream of a lovely, affable youth dressed plainly in gray. He embraced a group of elderly poor people, seeing their hidden worth. He beckoned Mary to come to him. She also saw the Bride (i.e., the Heavenly Jerusalem of Rev. 21), a beautiful virgin, like a sister to him. She concluded, "Christ has come, but few know it."[44]

Around this time, 1654, she married Isaac Penington, seeing in him a new partner appropriate to the desolate territory she now occupied:

> My love was drawn to him because I found he saw the deceit
> of all notions, and lay as one that refused to be comforted by
> any appearance of religion, until he came to his temple . . . he
> was sick and weary of all that appeared, and in this my heart
> cleft to him, and a desire was in me to be serviceable to him

in this his desolate condition, for he was alone and miserable in this world, and I gave up much to be a companion to him in this his suffering.[45]

Probably part of what she "gave up" to be with Isaac was some degree of her ebullient social life. She had considerable social grace and wit, which delighted many, even though it often left her in a spiritual malaise.

That same year, Quakers were invading London and causing a stir. Mary recalls that she heard of them but resolved not to investigate. She did read one tract by Fox, finding the plainness of its language "very ridiculous, and so minded them not, but scoffed at them in my mind." Yet she had a recurring desire to go to their powerful meetings for worship. "I was weary of doctrines; but I did believe that if I was with them when they prayed I could feel whether they were of the Lord or not."[46]

In 1656, while Mary and Isaac were walking in the park, a young Quaker passed by, denouncing them for their pride in wearing "gay vain apparel." Mary was offended, but Isaac engaged the young man in conversation and invited him to their home. The Quaker realized he was no match for Isaac's "fleshly wisdom" and promised to return the next day with a Friend to answer all his questions and objections. This was meant to be George Fox himself, who was in the area. But some circumstance prevented Fox from coming, and two other Friends came instead.

During that conversation in the Penington home, Thomas Curtis of Reading paraphrased a verse of Scripture that struck home immediately with Mary: "He that will know my doctrines must do my commands" (see John 7:17). This addressed the doctrinal impasse she had experienced for some time. The only way to *know* the truth would be to *do* it. The plainness of these Friends communicated to her that to understand their teaching she would have to adopt some version of their way of life. That moment precipitated a great crisis. She wanted to renounce many "vain things" that she felt were decadent. But this stimulated a countereffect, a more intense desire for those very things.[47]

She struggled for months without peace of mind, until "a stroke of the Lord's judgment brought me off" vain language, costume, fashion, titles, etc. Evidently, she interpreted some painful incident as a sign that it was time to "take up the cross to my honor and reputation in the world, which cost me many tears and nights' watching, and doleful days."

She recalls that she never once disputed the doctrines of Friends; it was their moral regimen that challenged her. We can appreciate the difficulty she faced. Polite London society was an elaborate game of manners and honor. In her situation, how would she adapt to a northern, rural, countercultural ethic? No one of her rank had tried it. She faced harsh responses, especially from family; "but as I gave up out of reasoning or consulting how to provide for the flesh, I received strength and so went to the meetings of these people."[48] Friends reported seeing the Peningtons at their meetings in Reading before the end of 1656.[49]

But as we noted in the preceding chapter, those of higher social rank, particularly those in the South, had to struggle through a more complex and ambiguous cultural framework than that of most northern country folk, who became Quakers through an intense, but briefer convincement process. As Mary Penington recalls,

> I longed to be one of their number, and minded not the trouble, but judged it to be worth the cost and pains, if I came to witness such a change as I saw in them, and such power over their corruptions. . . . In taking up the cross, I received strength against many things that I once thought it not possible to deny; but many tears did I shed and great bitterness of soul did I know before this.[50]

The simplicity of these Friends, which Mary first found repulsive and threatening, slowly became a way of liberation from the highly mannered life of upper-class London society.

THE STRUGGLE OF THE INTELLECT

Isaac Penington's future son-in-law, William Penn, remarked years later that many Quaker ministers, men and women, visited the Peningtons during that period. But Isaac's advanced insights and Scriptural understanding caused him to receive the message "with great mixture"; "he had much to lose and part with, before he came to be that blessed little child . . . which inherits the kingdom of God."[51] Penington's own account of the process confirms that the obstacles which stood most in the way were intellectual ones. He felt a remarkable love flowing in his heart toward these Quakers. Yet, every time he drew them into debate, the more I argued, the more I seemed to prevail . . . they seemed a poor, weak, silly, contemptible generation . . . daily my understanding got more and more over them, and therein I daily more and more despised them."[52]

Something kept him engaged with Friends, however. By early 1658, the Peningtons were starting to succumb. A February letter of Richard Hubberthorne to Margaret Fell reported that they had been to a general meeting of Friends in Buckinghamshire and had grown "sensible unto the knowledge of Truth."[53] Their convincement culminated at the end of May, when they attended a large general meeting in Bedfordshire, at the country home of John Crook, a Quaker justice. George Fox's *Journal* reports that some three to four thousand Friends and others were present at this gathering, which lasted three days. It was apparently Fox's preaching that thrust Isaac over the precipice.[54] This seems to have been Penington's first encounter with the movement's central figure.

In his *Journal*, Fox summarizes the main points of his sermon at that meeting.[55] The seed, the promise of God sown in all souls, was a major theme. Something in Fox's evocative language and visceral emphasis spoke to Penington's condition. He reported feeling the words reach his heart, quickening the deadness within, raising the seed. He said to himself,

> This is he, this is he, there is no other: this is he whom I have waited for and sought after from my childhood; who was always near me, and had often begotten life in my heart; but I knew him not distinctly, nor how to receive him, or dwell with him.[56]

So, at age forty-two, Isaac Penington felt a melting and breaking of his heart, and surrendered to God "both in waiting for the further revealing of his seed in me, and to serve him in the life and power of his seed." This is a concise statement of the way Quaker spirituality shifted the Seeker sense of "waiting upon the Lord" from simple *expectation* of future developments to a sense of present *service* to God in a process that is already transforming the individual.

Like other convinced Seekers, Penington felt much worse before he felt better. The ensuing travails were

> not to be uttered: only in general I may say this, I met with the very strength of hell. The cruel oppressor roared for me,

and made me feel the bitterness of his captivity, while he had any power: yea the Lord was far from my help, and from the voice of my roaring. I also met with deep subtleties and devices to entangle me in that wisdom, which seemeth to make wise in the things of God, but indeed is foolishness. . . . And what I met with outwardly from my own dear father, from my kindred, from my servants, from the people and powers of the world, for no other cause but fear of my God, worshipping him as he hath required of me, and bowing to his seed, which is his Son . . . the Lord my God knoweth . . . who preserved me in love to them.[57]

The intellectual wisdom he had served so assiduously was not easily dethroned. Probably during this critical period, John Crook wrote a letter of counsel and encouragement. He confided that he too had struggled with the intellect,

until I came to see the Candle lighted in my own House, and my heart swept from these thoughts and imaginations and willings and runnings, to die unto them all, not heeding of them, but watching against them, lest I should let my mind go a whoring after them.[58]

In his own memoir, Crook testifies that in Quaker convincement he was,

as it were, beheaded for the testimony of Jesus: for I found by certain experiences, that until man be truly crucified with Christ, he cannot bear a true testimony for Christ; for it is but a bearing witness to himself, which is not true.[59]

Note the Quaker definition of "true" here. Even a witness that is propositionally "true" is false if it comes from a source that is not itself "true." Here truth is defined in the biblical sense: a steadiness, consistence, or faithfulness on the part of the speaking or acting subject. In the fullest sense, only God is true. To know and speak the truth, one must be grounded in the divine presence within. Crook counseled Penington, "be not discouraged, O thou tossed as with Tempests, nor be dismayed in thy self . . . none was beset and tried, and tempted, as the true seed was who was a man of sorrows . . . be thou still in thy mind, and let the Billows pass over, and Wave upon Wave."[60]

Some of the challenges were interpersonal and social. Those around him, including his kin, were enraged at his adoption of plain manners. The elder Isaac Penington threatened to disown him.[61] We will note later that this prominent Quaker son of a Puritan regicide was the target of many vicious attacks, particularly during the Restoration years of conservative backlash.

Penington summarizes: "But some may desire to know what I have at last met with? I answer, I have met with the Seed. Understand that word, and thou wilt be satisfied and inquire no further."[62] The encounter with the seed showed Penington that these Quaker rustics were indeed grounded in an entirely different order of spiritual knowledge:

> there is a great difference between comprehending the knowledge of things and tasting the hidden life of them . . . I fed on the sweetness of the former, until finding the true manna of the latter.[63]

Isaac Penington's Early Quaker Writings

Much of Penington's subsequent Quaker writing is devoted to spiritual guidance for Seekers and others struggling toward the same breakthrough. We will examine some of the more striking points in his early Quaker writings that elaborate upon his own transformation.

In his first piece as a Quaker writer, *The Way of Life and Death Made Manifest* (1658), Penington looks back upon nearly two decades of "grievous shakings" in English religion and politics. Over those years, many had settled into one new church or another, "save onely of a few, whose Spirits God had so reached, that their wound was incurable . . . they remained miserable, lost, scattered, and confounded."

> But the Lord hath in infinite mercy visited them, in the season of distress; and there hath a little foolish thing broke forth (at which the wise, and the religious in the Spirit of this world cannot but stumble) which hath . . . discovered a foundation on which they can settle."[63]

He beckons fellow Seekers to the path he has taken out of apostasy: "keep to the sense, keep to the feeling" of the seed's life within. There is a time of waiting, sorrow, and cleansing, of feeling the bitterness of having forsaken the Lord. Slowly, the evil power of alienation from God will wither and decay.[65] Speaking from his own experience, he testifies,

> I found my return very difficult . . . I could receive nothing, but cry out impossible, impossible, impossible. . . . But at length it pleased life to move in a low way . . . and by sinking low . . . out of the reason . . . trusting myself to it . . . at length there was some appearance of the deliverer, in such a poor, low, weak, despicable way, as could never have been welcomed, had not the soul been first brought to distress. . . . And then coming out of that into the feeling, into another part; here was a seed sprung up into a child . . . and I am daily strengthened in him, and daily weakened in that part which lived before.[66]

So Penington describes a fundamentally new sense of being, much as we saw in many convincement narratives in the preceding chapter. But here we find the struggle of the mind more acutely detailed.

Though most of Penington's Quaker writings are devoted to spiritual guidance, he closes this first Quaker work with a remarkable description of the Quaker movement as a whole:

> We are a people whom God hath converted to himself . . . the seed of his own life. . . . We, many of us, sought truly and only after God from our childhood . . . but the honesty of our hearts was still betrayed . . . we knew not how to turn to that of God in us . . . we came to great distress and misery beyond all men. . . . Now it pleased the Lord at length to pitty us, and to inform our minds toward himself, to shew us where life lay, and where death lay, and how to turn from the one, and to the other.

> Now our work in the World, is to hold forth the vertues of him that hath called us, to live like God . . . to live like persons of another country, of another kindred, of another family.

> We are also to be witnesses for God, and to propagate his life in the world . . . to fight against the powers of darkness everywhere, as the Lord calleth us forth . . . the Lord must go before [us]. . . . God is rough with transgressors, and we come

in the same spirit. . . . Now the very root of this severity is good, and of God, and hath love and sweetness at the bottom of it; yea in pittie, love, and bowels do we use the sword [of the Spirit]. . . . And though we seem enemies to all sorts of men, for the Lord's sake: yet we are not enemies, nor could do the least hurt to them any way, but are true friends to their souls, and bodies also . . . for we fight not at all with flesh and blood, but with the powers and principalities which led from God.

There is one great palpable argument that we are of God, which is this, all the World is against us, the Worldly part every where fights with us . . . the rage of man every where riseth up against us. . . . Therefore let men be sober, and take heed what they do, lest they be found fighters against God. . . . Yet I do not speak this for my own sake, to avoid my share in the cross: for the reproach of Christ is our riches. . . . It is very sweet, pleasant, and profitable for us to be found sufferers for God; but we know it will not be profitable for you to be found persecutors.[67]

Again, there is a sense of a emergent type of humanity here. To come out of alienation from God is to become an alien in an alienated society, "a stranger in a strange land" (Exod. 2:22). A retiring soul himself, Penington nevertheless defends the movement's confrontational ministry and politics. Wherever the life of the seed in people's hearts has been buried by deceit and treachery, it must be exposed. According to the Quaker understanding of truth, any belief or practice—religious or otherwise—is deceit if it disregards or represses the witness of God within.

The Axe Laid to the Root of the Old Corrupt Tree (1659) offers critiques of both types of Seekers. Here Penington characterizes the 1640s as a period of intensive reformation that spun off Presbyterian, Independent, and Baptist churches. Each new church had

a more simple and honest thing stirring there . . . according to the blessing of the Lord (which was not to the form but to the life that was stirring within). . . . But they, fixing there, lost the life and simplicity to which the blessing was, and met with the death and curse, which is proper to the form. . . .

> [Then] There was one more pure appearance, neerer to the
> Kingdom then all these, which was seeking and waiting; but
> death overcame this also, making a form of it, and stealing in
> some observations from the letter of the Scriptures concern-
> ing the Kingdom, whereby their eyes were with-held from
> beholding the inward principle and seed of life within, to
> look for some great appearance of power without (such as
> was among the Apostles) to set things to rights; and so they
> were held captive by the same spirit.[68]

So the expectation that supernatural works of power would "set
things to rights" froze the gaze even of Seekers in the wrong direction.
But some were not satisfied to stay long there, and progressed to
the advanced Spiritualism that broke out in the army and elsewhere.
They contented themselves with "high notions, yea most pleasant
notions concerning the Spirit, and concerning the life"— *but not the life
itself.* The expectation of a new dispensation released great powers
of utopian imagination, which led on to libertinism, another form of
captivity[69]

With the restoration of monarchy and the national church in 1660,
many whose hopes had swelled in the 1640s and withered during the
1650s felt acutely abandoned by God and hounded by conservative civil
and religious authorities. Penington continued his work to gather these
lost sheep. In 1661, he published a message *To All Such as Complain
that They Want Power.* The Quaker movement was about power—not
human power, but divine power coursing through surrendered human
minds and bodies. Penington notes that this power does not flow in
a way that one expects. It begins as "a weak, fooling thing." The seed
is sown mysteriously, it grows mysteriously, and its power comes
mysteriously. He confesses that in his own period of darkness, he had
believed "that my condition required the manifest appearance of a
very great power to help me." This only kept him from the power of the
seed that was already within him.[70]

He goes on to describe three ways that God's power appears to the
believer. First, it comes by *repentance*, turning from darkness to light.
Second, it comes *under the cross.* Everyone yearns for spiritual power,
but most fly from the cross wherever it appears. The cross is Christ's
yoke, which actually is rest from one's own energies. Here the power of

God can begin to flow. Third, power springs up *under the fear of God*. It appears in those who distrust their own strength and wisdom, who feel no power to do God's will, but fear not doing what the light requires. This power *must* work contrarily to human expectation and desire, for three reasons. First, in respect to God: God's power must operate by God's own nature, not by our own. Second, in reference to the human creature: we must experience the exhaustion of our own power; otherwise, we would be tempted to exalt ourselves and abuse the divine power. Third, in reference to the "enemy" within: Satan can never be conquered and cast out by human power, which must give way to God's power.

In *Some Directions to the Panting Soul* (1661), Penington continues to develop images for the mystery of the seed's life and power. The epigraph that begins our present chapter comes from this brief tract. He also elaborates on the theme of divine knowledge as manna, based on the story of the Israelites in the wilderness. He warns that one must not store up this knowledge for use according to one's own wisdom. Just as the Israelites were commanded to gather manna from the ground each morning for that day's consumption, so "use what is received fresh every day." Because light is given according to each specific situation and necessity, one must learn to depend upon the light to show the way day by day. The heart is thus kept close to God and the spiritual senses are continually exercised, making it easier over time to recognize the true shepherd's voice.[70]

Finally, *Concerning God's Seeking out His Israel* (1663) reverses the seeking equation by describing the steps by which God seeks out souls and gathers them into a flock. The scattered sheep are found in many conditions: wounded, languishing, starving. First, God leads them into a wilderness, to wear out what is left of their old nature. Then God raises a little seed in some hidden way. One must learn to love these small beginnings. One must wait "to feel the savor of life in thy breast day by day"; "breathe unto the Lord to reveal what is proper for thee at present." Penington emphasizes,

> watch against thy understanding . . . for it will still betray thee. . . . And mark this: That which God sows and brings up in thee is a sensible plant, not a knowing mind; and thy right judgment is only in the sensibleness of that plant, not in the understanding or comprehension of thy mind.[72]

As R. Melvin Keiser has pointed out, we find in Penington's Quaker writings a shift toward language of the five senses and of feeling. There is a visceral sense to his descriptions of life in the seed; it is not an abstraction of the mind but an experience mediated by the entire body. Keiser also points out that Penington's new "method of living and the basis for thinking is waiting." In place of the inquisitive and grasping intellect, the "sensible plant" grows, receiving water from the fountain daily. That this is not a state of paralysis, may be seen in the paradoxical language he uses in a letter "To Friends of Both the Chalfonts":

> Oh be faithful, be faithful! travel on, travel on! let nothing
> stop you, but wait for, and daily follow, the sensible leadings
> of that measure of life which God hath placed in you, which
> is one with the fulness, and into which the fulness runs daily
> and fills it, that it may run into you and fill you.[73]

This is the "peace of mind" that Penington quested after heroically for ten years and more, before finally succumbing to it. It had always been there in the sizable shadow of his intellect, a quiet spring of healing water.

CONCLUSION

The Peningtons became important participants on the London Quaker scene. They moved in 1658 to a home at Chalfont, near London. They opened it to Friends as a place for worship and other meetings. This use of their home gave Mary Penington great satisfaction. She recalls the elation she felt in worshipping God beyond all forms, "in that which was undoubtedly his own; and that I need put no stop to my spirit in it but swim in the life, and give up my whole strength to that which melted me and overcame me in that day."[74] This was the first time she had been able to worship wholeheartedly. Though she was strongly committed to the movement, Quaker plainness did not entirely quench Mary Penington's social sparkle. The famous diarist Samuel Pepys knew her and remarked that she was not always grave in her conversation and could still be quite witty.[75]

But the Peningtons soon experienced their share of the persecutions that besieged all Friends. Over the remaining twenty-two years of his life, Isaac was imprisoned six times, totaling five years. He lost much of

his estate to relatives who sued him. He was sentenced to *praemunire*
(forfeiture of all property to the crown) and banishment for refusing to
swear (a Quaker testimony to honesty in all language), though neither
sentence was enacted. Two of his imprisonments came at the instigation
of the Earl of Bridgewater, who was enraged that Penington would not
doff his hat or address him as "my lord." Prison time took its toll on
Penington's health; he died in 1679, at age sixty-three.

The next year, as "testimonies" of various prominent Friends were collected in memory of Isaac, Mary contributed one, which concludes thus:

> Ah me! he is gone! he that none exceeded in kindness, in
> tenderness, in love inexpressible to the relation as a wife.
> Next to the love of God in Christ Jesus to my soul, was his
> love precious and delightful to me. My bosom-one! that was
> as my guide and counsellor! my pleasant companion! my
> tender sympathizing friend! as near to the sense of my pain,
> sorrow, grief, and trouble as it was possible. Yet this great
> help and benefit is gone . . . such was the great kindness the
> Lord shewed me in that hour, that my spirit ascended with
> him in that very moment that his spirit left his body; and I
> saw him safe in his own mansion, and rejoiced with him, and
> was at that instant gladder of it, than ever I was of enjoying
> him in the body. . . . This testimony to dear Isaac Penington
> is from the greatest loser of all that had a share in his life,
> Mary Penington.[76]

Clearly, both were remarkable individuals, first as Seekers, then as
Quakers. Mary Penington died in 1682.

In *Concerning God's Seeking out His Israel* (1663), Penington concludes with a meditation "Concerning the Two Covenants."[77] He asserts
that the covenant of works and the covenant of grace are the same seed,
the same standing principle of life. They come from the same light, but
their terms and manner are different. The covenant of works (associated
with Moses) is of a working nature, and is blessed in active obedience.
The covenant of grace (associated with Christ) is blessed by God's promise alone; its will is not found in human liberty but in God's appearance
to it. The second covenant must "walk through" the first, into its many
dark paths, even into its captivity. All dispensations mingle these two
covenants. There is no pure covenant of works or of grace. That is, God's

promise lay at the heart of the laws of Moses, just as the gospel preached by Jesus came with definite demands. A pure covenant of works would not allow salvation (i.e., it would all be a matter of human endeavor, which is ultimately futile). A pure covenant of grace would not allow destruction (i.e., the desolation of the self is necessary to the appearance and work of grace). Both are necessary aspects to the one covenantal reality of the seed.

Penington continues: the covenant of grace is to all humanity; God seeks all and visits all with light. Those who turn and follow the light are blessed and ingrafted into the living vine (the church universal). But God gathered a people after the flesh of Abraham (Israel) and later a people after the spirit of Abraham (the church) to work in the world in a "peculiar" (particular) way. Here we find the incipient liberalism of a universal knowledge of God bonded with the biblical vision of God gathering and working through a specific people in history. This single-covenant/dual-mode teaching is at the heart of Quaker witness.[78] Penington articulates the far-reaching universalism of the Quaker message as it stands in tension with its stubborn, prophetic particularity. To sum it up bluntly, there is "that of God in every one," and there is a peculiar way that the people of God called Quakers must dress, speak, do business, and live in the world.

Notes

1. Isaac Penington, *Some Directions to the Panting Soul* (1661), in *Works* (Glenside, Pa.: Quaker Heritage, 1994), 2:205.
2. John Punshon, "The Early Writings of Isaac Penington," in *Practiced in the Presence: Essays in Honor of T. Canby Jones*, ed. Snarr and Christopher (Richmond: Friends United Press, 1994), 61.
3. Christopher Hill, *The Experience of Defeat: Milton and Some Contemporaries* (London: Faber and Faber, 1984), 118. Also see Murray Tolmie, *The Triumph of the Saints: The Separate Churches of London 1616-1649* (Cambridge: University Press, 1977), 111-16 on the elder Penington's role in John Goodwin's attempt to establish a gathered church on the foundation of a local parish. Penington Senior, a rare hybrid as a "parochial Independent," was eventually a key actor in removing Goodwin.
4. Joseph Gurney Bevan, *Memoirs of the Life of Isaac Penington* (London: Harvey and Darton, 1830), 1-2.

5. Isaac Penington, *A Brief Account of My Soul's Travel Towards the Holy Land,* in *Works* (London: Phillips, 1784), 3:97-98.

6. "Isaac Penington (1616-79)," in *The Dictionary of National Biography* (Oxford: University Press, 1917), 15:742.

7. Hill, *Defeat,* 128.

8. Penington, *A Brief Account,* 99.

9. Isaac Penington, *A Touchstone or Tryall of Faith* (1648), 22.

10. Isaac Penington, *The Great and Sole Troubler of Our Times* (1649), 11.

11. Penington, *Troubler,* 13.

12. Penington, *Troubler,* 24.

13. Penington, *Troubler,* 31.

14. Printed in Isaac Penington, *A Voyce out of the Thick Darkness* (1650), 18-20.

15. Bevan, *Memoirs,* 10.

16. I am aided in the sequencing of these four pieces by *The Catalogue of the Thomason Tracts, 1640-1661* (London: British Museum, 1908). Thomason was a doctor living in London during that period, who collected over 22,000 tracts, manuscripts, and newspapers over two decades. He bought most new publications as soon as they came out, and marked the date of purchase on each. These notations are an invaluable aid to research on the period. They are not infallible, but generally reliable. Thomason collected all four Penington tracts in 1650. The dates he gives are more than one month apart. They will be taken here as reliable.

17. Isaac Penington, *A Voyce out of the Thick Darkness* (1650), Preface.

18. Penington, *Voyce,* 5-6.

19. Penington, *Voyce,* 10.

20. Penington, *Voyce,* 11.

21. Penington, *Voyce,* 15.

22. Isaac Penington, *Light* or Darkness (1650), 7-11.

23. Penington, *Light,* 16.

24. Penington, *Light,* 19.

25. Penington, *Light,* 22.

26. Penington, *Light,* 23.

27. Penington, *Brief Account,* 100.

28. Giles Calvert, publisher for both Salmon and Penington, had published English translations of several works by Boehme. For a fuller treatment of Boehme's influence on Penington, see R. Melvin Keiser, "From Dark Christian to Fullness of Life: Isaac Penington's Journey from Puritanism to Quakerism," *Guilford Review* 23 (Spring 1986): 47-53.

29. Isaac Penington, *Severall Fresh Inward Openings* (1650), 2-9.

30. Penington, *Openings,* 25.

31. Penington, *Openings,* 26.

32. Penington apparently also was acquainted with Abiezer Coppe. There is a very brief, undated letter from Penington to Coppe, excoriating him for speaking out of his imaginations, calling him a fool. Penington MSS., 2:254, at the Library of the Society of Friends, London (henceforth cited as LSF). Since all the correspondence in that collection comes from after his Quaker convincement, this brief censure may have arisen from some contact between the two after 1658. But their original acquaintance would probably go back to 1649 in London.

33. Penington, *Openings*, 30.
34. Penington, *Openings*, 31.
35. Penington, *Openings*, 44.
36. Penington, *Openings*, 46.
37. Penington, *Eccho*, 35-37.
38. Penington, *Eccho*, 99.
39. Penington, *Eccho*, 107.
40. Penington, *Eccho*, 110.
41. Isaac Penington, *A Considerable Question about Government* (1653), 7.
42. I summarize the details of Mary Penington's life from her spiritual autobiography, *A Brief Account of My Exercises from My Childhood; Left with My Dear Daughter Gulielma Maria Penn* (Philadelphia: n.p., 1848).
43. Mary Penington, *Account* , 6-7.
44. Mary Penington, *Account*, 9.
45. Mary Penington, *Account*, 10.
46. Mary Penington, *Account*, 10-11.
47. Mary Penington, *Account*, 12.
48. Mary Penington, *Account*, 12.
49. Bevan, *Memoirs, 9.*
50. Mary Penington, *Account*, 13.
51. "The Testimony of William Penn Concerning Isaac Penington," in Penington's *Works* (London: Phillips, 1784), 1:vii.
52. Isaac Penington, "A True and Faithful Relation," an unpublished testament written in 1667 while in prison at Aylesbury gaol, quoted in full in "The Testimony of Thomas Ellwood Concerning Isaac Penington," in Penington's *Works,* 1:xlii-xlvii.
53. Richard Hubberthorne to Margaret Fell, February 2, 1658, Caton MSS. 3/111, LSF.
54. "Alexander Parker's Testimony Concerning Isaac Penington," in Penington's *Works,* 1:lii.
55. George Fox, *Journal,* ed. John L. Nickalls (Cambridge: University Press, 1952), 339.
56. Penington, "Relation."
57. Penington, "Relation."
58. John Crook to Isaac Penington, in Penington's *Works* (Glenside, Pa.: Quaker Heritage, 1994), 2:298-300.
59. John Crook, *The Design of Christianity* (London: Phillips, 1791), xx.
60. John Crook to Isaac Penington.
61. Richard T. Vann, *The Social Development of English Quakerism, 1655-1755* (Cambridge: Harvard, 1969), 22.
62. Penington, "Relation."
63. Penington, *Brief Account*, 103.
64. Isaac Penington, *The Way of Life and Death Made Manifest* (1658), Preface.
65. Penington, *Way*, 69-73.
66., Penington, *Way*, 76.
67. Penington, *Way*, 89-92.
68. Isaac Penington, *The Axe Laid to the Root of the Old Corrupt Tree* (1659), Preface.

69. Penington, *Axe*, 31.
70. Isaac Penington, *To All Such as Complain that They Want Power*, in *Works* (London: Phillips, 1784), 2:344-45.
71. Isaac Penington, *Some Directions to the Panting Soul* (1661), in *Works* (London: Phillips, 1784), 2:241,245.
72. Isaac Penington, *Concerning God's Seeking out His Israel* (1663), in *Works* (Glenside, Pa.: Quaker Heritage Press, 1994), 2:396-97.
73. Quoted by Keiser, "Fullness of Life," 55.
74. Mary Penington, *Account*, 13.
75. "Isaac Penington," *Dictionary of National 6Biography*, 15:743.
76. "Mary Penington's Testimony Concerning Isaac Penington," in his *Works* (London: Phillips, 1784), 1:lviif.
77. Penington, *Works*, (Glenside, Pa., Quaker Heritage Press, 1994), 2:399-404.
78. This theme runs through my earlier study, *The Covenant Crucified*.

CHAPTER 10

APOCALYPSE AND ATONEMENT
THE QUAKER MOVEMENT AS NEW CREATION,
1646-1660

Them whom thou calls Quakers doth utterly deny thee, and all of thy Principles, and all the Ranters is by us denied; and your Practices we abhor. And in the eternal light which never changes do we see you and know you. And with that which was before the world was; do we try your spirits, and comprehend your bottom and foundation, and Race you out from the presence of the Lord, and all who are of him. . . . And this is from the Quakers which you say is not yet come to you, but is from you separated eternally.

—Margaret Fell, 1656[1]

Throughout the early chapters of this study, we encountered a number of inspired leaders and movements generating from the Seeker milieu of the 1640s. In terms of religious ideas and political initiatives, it is hard to see what early Friends added to that rich outpouring. As Anthony Pearson reported (see Chapter 8), Seekers could listen to Quaker preaching and ask, "What do these men say, more than others have said?" Yet, as Pearson added, Quaker preaching brought men and women to a different level of seeking, what Francis Howgill called a "narrow search."

Those who responded to the first Quaker prophets felt the apocalypse breaking forth in their very bodies. The quakes, groans, and swoons that moved through whole groups of people at Quaker meetings transfigured the ethereal speculations and projected hopes of Seekers into a visceral experience of the day of the Lord. Such cathartic events then initiated a process of personal transformation, a shift in the very ground of being. This unfolded not only through interior experience but through an austere moral practice that transmitted the shock waves of inner apocalypse through the fabric of familial, social, economic, and political relations. This *practical apocalypse* confirmed and integrated many of the religious ideas and political initiatives of Seekers, Levellers, Diggers, and Ranters of the 1640s. Yet these Seekers-turned-Quakers felt they had discovered the reality of their ideals in a profoundly new and living way. The sense of empowerment these women and men felt, as they discovered their own bodies to be the site of Christ's return in glory, was earth-shaking in its implications.

These first Quakers held a scandalously incarnational understanding of that reality. Through the inward apocalypse, they had been "born from above": that is, their existence had been transubstantiated. They understood themselves to partake of the nature of God, to possess in some measure the same flesh and bone (see our discussion of "celestial flesh" in Chapter 8). However, this reality was known not by mere affirmation, exalted sensation, or metaphysical speculation but rather through moral transformation. Just as Christ knew equality with God not as something to be grasped but to be poured out in the form of a servant (Phil. 2:6-8), these Friends found exaltation through suffering servanthood. Self-giving ethical action was thus understood to be the foundation of this new form of human existence in Christ, this new creation.

It was the foundation of true knowledge as well. We recall the Quaker counsel to Mary Penington, that she would know the doctrine of Christ only when she obeyed his commandments. That affirmation is found in a whole array of Quaker writings, like William Smith's *The New Creation Brought Forth in the Holy Order of Life* (1661):

> here man finds a new and living Way, which makes him a new
> and living Man, and leads him unto the living God; and this is
> the Way of Holiness in which clean feet walk, and Man that is
> in it ordered, he is in the way of Peace . . . in the holy Life of
> the Immortal Seed is his Life bound up, and he is ordered in
> the motion of it, and he doth not stir but in the holy order of
> it . . . unto good works he is Created in Christ, and his delight
> in the new Creation is in doing the thing that is good. [2]

The apocalyptic realm of new creation is defined in consistently ethical terms. Early Friends believed that through the spread of their experiential apocalypse, not only would their interior and moral lives be transformed, but the entire creation would be reordered. This is the bodily redemption for which not only the individual creature but the whole cosmos groans (see Rom. 8:18-25).

This stance implied a Copernican revolution regarding the usual understanding of atonement in Christ. No human reading of Scripture or reflection upon Jesus' death on the cross could communicate its saving power to the soul. It must be known within, through the individual's own death to self and the raising of Christ the seed within. But, again, this would be only an interior phantasm if the individual's concrete life did not evince fundamental transformation. Early Friends thus argued that there could be no *justification* by Christ's death on the cross in history without *sanctification*, the mystery of the individual's own death to self-interest and new life for others. This understanding built on the Spiritualist tradition that we first encountered in Schwenckfeld's teaching.[3] But the apocalyptic horizon of the early Quaker understanding of atonement made it a drama of reconciliation not only between the individual and God but throughout the entire social and natural order of creation.

The Quaker insistence upon saving knowledge as inwardly received and morally expressed led to statements seemingly dismissive of the historic importance of Jesus' death. But, much like Winstanley, early Friends recognized the dangers of an alienated, abstract theology that made Scripture's witness more real and authoritative than the witness of the light of Christ within. It created Christian hypocrites who mouthed the words of faith without sharing in the life of faith. Nevertheless, on various occasions, Puritan critics accused Friends of both an *antinomian* disregard for Scripture and a *legalistic* righteousness that defined salvation in terms of an austere and rather idiosyncratic set of moral codes. Not many movements in Christian history have succeeded in being accused of both!

These charges, although mutually contradictory, point toward the real paradox in early Quaker consciousness. Taken as a "style of ethical evaluation,"[4] early Quaker faith was a volatile synthesis. Coming at the end of the Reformation, the movement was infused with the Puritan concern for an authentically biblical faith, church order, and ethics. This quest had reached its acute form in the first type of Seeker, who gave up on all churches in order to search for and await an authentic "primitive

Christianity revived." So the *posterity* of New Testament faith and practice was the primary reference point, though it was recognized that some
new Pentecost and some new apostle would be needed to catalyze such
a renewal. Human reconstructions, no matter how scholarly or well-
intended, had failed. Again, we see the motif of Schwenckfeld's *Stillstand*
as the prototype of this first form of English Seekerism.

But early Friends also believed that they were part of an unfolding
futurity, the second coming of Christ by the Spirit, the kingdom of God
on earth. This counter-tendency had been nurtured among the second
type of Seekers seen in this study, those who believed that God would
not revive an ancient New Testament church, but would move forward
with some new dispensation, a new age of the Spirit. This proto-liberal
outlook exhibited a progressive view of history in which each new
dispensation brought humanity to a new level of clarity and divine
vocation. This side of the early Quaker paradox is evidenced by the fact
that, while early Friends often cited New Testament precedents for
their faith and practice, they made no effort to reintroduce the ritual
sacraments of baptism and communion. Early Friends emphasized the
indwelling of Christ and a typological interpretation of Scripture that
found all its history fulfilled inwardly in the mystery of faith.

These emphases were at odds with the expectations of the first Seeker
type. However, early Friends did not disregard the New Testament in
this matter. They interpreted Paul and other New Testament writers to
have *always* understood that true baptism is in the Spirit (Matt. 3:11; 1
Cor. 12:13), and that true communion is a mystical encounter with Christ
(Rev. 3:20). But above of all, sacramental reality, whether ritual or inward, must be authenticated in personal moral transformation. That is,
true baptism is a lived initiation into Christ's death (Rom. 6:3) that
crucifies the person to self and raises her or him to new life in Christ for
others. Likewise, true communion with Christ in the heavenly realm of
existence is for those who come out of alienation and rebellion from
God in real-life terms (Rev. 3:21).

Another example of the Quaker ethical synthesis is found in the
spiritual authority of women. That quantum leap in female leadership
was part of the movement from its earliest days in the latter 1640s and
had affinities to the Spiritualist idea of a new age of the Spirit unfolding.
Again, the Quaker breakthrough in gender was posited from an apocalyptic perspective *beyond* the social categories of the old order. That

perspective was ethically defined: Friends believed that their lives preached most definitively. Quaker women and men living in the peaceful and egalitarian new order of Christ on earth preached volumes by the way they dressed, conversed, and lived in the world. Still, when they were attacked by Puritans for breaking Paul's injunctions against women speaking in church, Friends did not simply insist (like many today) that Paul was wrong, or that things had changed (owing to changing times or a new dispensation). They reinterpreted the same Pauline texts in light of their new experience, arguing that, of course, women should not speak in church. For that matter, men should not speak either. Even the clergy should not speak. Only Christ should speak—through whatever obedient instrument Christ chooses.[4]

This apocalyptic style of ethical evaluation gave primary authority to Christ returned in the Spirit, recreating men and women here and now. This was the pull of *ultimate futurity* upon the present moment, opening a dramatic new realm of human being on earth. The Spirit had indeed arrived with power, not only with words. Yet early Friends continued to defend their innovations according to Scripture. Just as the first advent of Christ had fulfilled messianic prophecy in surprising ways, so the second advent could be expected to renew the church in unexpected directions. These "new" phenomena would be expected to *confirm* the older ones, while not necessarily *conforming* to them. Thus, the *posterity* of Scripture still played a role.[6] But it was the *presence* of Christ in the here-and-now that played the central, synthesizing role. Experienced as both a light of revelation and a seed of new being, the living Christ within fulfilled many of the expectations that had once flourished among both Seeker types, but only by way of a desolating cross to the willful imposition of such hopes. All idolatrous projections upon both past and future were to be offered up to the consuming fire of this apocalypse within. In sum: early Quaker preaching confirmed many beliefs of both Seeker types; but it also razed the false consciousness with which both Seeker types held their beliefs and projected their hopes.

This process was an ongoing *atonement drama* during the second half of the 17th century. Fox and the earliest leaders charted a course between the two Seeker expectations, canceling their former agendas, while simultaneously integrating their salient themes and reconciling their self-defeating differences. All this was accomplished through a servant ministry that dealt gently with every tender heart, but confronted every deceitful word and stood ready to absorb the wrath of the proud. In the egalitarian ethos of the early Quaker movement, leadership was measured in terms of miles traveled to minister to isolated Seekers in remote villages, of stripes worn on the backs of men and women who directly confronted Puritan and Restorationist establishments, and of weeks, months, or years spent in stinking, vermin-infested prisons. Most of all, it came to be measured by the stature of George Fox, that canny/ uncanny personality who had inexplicably galvanized disheartened Seekers and spent Ranters into an unprecedented surge of prophetic witness. Not only did Fox's beatings, imprisonments, and privations compare with anyone's; he could also discern and respond to many spiritual conditions, even one as sophisticated as that of Isaac Penington's.

In Chapters 8 and 9 we illustrated the *spread* of the Quaker movement from the rural North to the urban centers of London and Bristol, from rustic stalwarts like John Camm and John Audland to high-society types such as the Peningtons. We saw *suffering* as the new mode of seeking among these new Friends, a path of inward transformation and outward resistance. *Atonement* was enacted as one took on the daily cross in codes of dress, speech, and social carriage, immediately *stigmatizing* the individual in his or her family, neighborhood, and workplace. We saw how George Fox and Margaret Fell became the guiding masculine and feminine figures of the movement, a pillar of smoke by day and a pillar of fire by night to guide the children of Israel through a wilderness of privation and conflict. Fox and Fell (along with other male and female Quaker leaders) evoked the inner masculine and feminine qualities in Friends, channels for the flow of divine power and guidance, a source of courage for women to speak authoritatively in public, and for men to be the meek transmitters of Christ's nurturing love.

This and the following chapter explore the dialectical counter-motion to the spreading power of the movement: the focusing, defining and narrowing of the Quaker apocalypse into a coherent movement, a visible standing church. Through a series of defining episodes stretching from the 1640s to the 1690s, we shall see how former Seekers struggled with one another over the movement's nature and future. Some felt betrayed when the movement took on a rationalized message and organized structure; their commitment to continuing errantry carried them out of the Quaker fold, often toward more liberal and universalist vistas. Others found the movement too idiosyncratic and heterodox over the long term and dropped out, returning in some cases to more conventional Protestant churches.

Throughout this process, we will find Fox and other central leaders continuing to work out a synthesis of the Protestant and liberal tendencies of Seekerism, defending the center against tendencies on both sides. We will see that the movement bridged several key social fault-lines—North and South, Protestant and liberal, masculine and feminine—with successes and shortcomings in each case. But in the latter decades, as persecution eased, the atonement drama of the early movement lost intensity. Likewise, as the Interregnum's crisis ended and the Restoration reimposed more stable religious and political authority, the sense of apocalyptic moment also faded. Under these circumstances, the movement suffered its first large-scale defections and exhibited a more sectarian use of vindictive rhetoric and scapegoat tactics in its internal struggles.

We can therefore recognize a lively interplay between apocalypse and atonement in the early Quaker saga. As a drama of unfolding cosmic transformation beginning from within, apocalypse constitutes the context or *frame of reference* of early Quaker faith. Meanwhile, as the drama of men and women coming out of alienation from themselves, from God, and from one another, atonement remains the abiding center or *point of reference*. The daily cross of spiritual devotion and servanthood is the "privileged" vantage point where the apocalyptic "turn of the ages" is viewed. Meanwhile, the *community* of faith constitutes the key mediating term between individual experience and the larger society. These chapters follow the step-by-step definition of the Quaker community as the hermeneutic (the interpretative principle) mediating between mystery and history, and between living faith and future hope in the Quaker experience.

Rice Jones and the "Proud Quakers"

We recall from Chapter 8 that a "shattered" General Baptist community in Skegby, near Mansfield, was one of the first groups reached by George Fox's message in late 1646 or early 1647. The group had broken into two factions. He had initial success among both factions. Fox's future ally Elizabeth Hooton was a key figure in the first group. Some of its members left, but most were convinced by Fox's preaching of Christ's light within and began calling themselves "Children of the Light." The second Baptist faction had lapsed into more of a discussion group that also indulged in "vain pastimes" such as "shovel-board." Fox also convinced a number of these more recreational Seekers, including one Rice (or Rhys) Jones. According to Elizabeth Hooton's son, Oliver, Jones initially hailed Fox as God's instrument of a great new dispensation of the Spirit. But as Thomas Hyfrold, another member of that early group recalls, Jones and his friends were soon overtaken by an "exalted spirit," denied Fox's message, and broke off fellowship.[7]

Later, in 1651, Jones and some of his followers visited Fox in prison at Derby, as they passed on their way to the battle of Worcester, to fight for the Commonwealth. Continuing in his Ranter tendency, Jones debated Fox, as the latter records in his *Journal*:

> Says he to me, "Thy faith stands in a man that died at Jerusa-lem and there was never any such thing." I said unto him, "How! Did not Christ suffer without the gates at Jerusalem through the professing Jews, and the chief priests, and Pilate?" and he denied it that ever Christ suffered there outwardly. . . . And from this man and his company was the slander raised upon us that the Quakers should deny Christ that died and suffered at Jerusalem, which was all utterly false, and never the least thought of it in our hearts.[8]

Jones went on to argue that all the sufferings of the prophets and apostles were inward. Fox responded with several instances of outward, historical sufferings of God's people in Scripture. "So I brought the power of the Lord over his imaginations and whimsies; and he went his ways."

This extreme Spiritualist tendency to lose the dynamic tension between outward and inward, to swallow up history into mystery, was a pitfall of the second type of Seekers, some of whom became Ranters. We can see that Fox refused to let the power of the present experience of atonement negate its historic reference point in the death of Jesus. More than theological abstraction was at stake in the matter. The absence of tension between history and mystery caused Jones to lose not only the historical death of Jesus but his inner sense of the cross as well. Breaking free from these moorings both within and without, Jones and company went on to fight for the Commonwealth and live a vain, sporting life. William Smith later summarized succinctly: "these people have taken up a belief that they may keep their inward unto God, and yield their bodies to comply with outward things."[9] Skirmishes between Quakers and Jones' followers (sometimes called the "proud Quakers") continued throughout the 1650s. Friends were slowly able to win over a number of these opponents, but not Jones himself.[10]

EARLIEST QUAKER CORPORATE DISCIPLINE

Writing near the end of his life, Fox recalled that even the earliest Children of the Light in the Midlands of Nottinghamshire, Derbyshire, and Leicestershire had regular meetings for business: "we did meet concerning the poor, and to see that all walked according to the Truth, before we were called Quakers."[11] These twin concerns, poor relief and moral accountability, were consistent themes of Quaker organization from the start. A shared sense of the movement's moral parameters was crucial if the Quaker community was to communicate a coherent message to the world. Group solidarity was essential to facing the hostility of neighbors and official persecution. For years to come, Quaker poor relief had to focus primarily on the needs of Quaker families under duress from fines and imprisonment, although they also managed to aid some poor people beyond their own ranks as well. Most of all, the community understood itself to be the incarnation of Christ the *corpus delicti*, the tangible evidence, of Christ's reconciling work in the world. A body of diverse individualists would not succeed in this ministry even among themselves, let alone to the world.

An early document of Quaker organization is William Dewsbury's 1653 general epistle to Friends. It counseled each local meeting of Friends to chose one or two from their group "most grown in the Power and Life, in pure discerning in the Truth, to take the care and charge over the Flock of God in that place." These informal elders or overseers were to live as examples to others and see that moral standards were maintained by all. They were also to see that meetings for worship were held regularly on the first day and at least one other day per week. General meetings were to be held every two to three weeks, combining Friends from several meetings in an area. These were times for worship, reading of epistles from Quaker leaders, general fellowship, and disciplinary matters.

Dewsbury instructed elders to deal with those who "walk disorderly" along lines prescribed by Jesus in Matthew 18. That is, they should speak privately with the offender, reproving his or her behavior in plain terms. If the offender did not reform, they would take two or three mature Friends along for a second visit, admonishing the individual in love. If the individual still resisted, he or she would be reproved openly at a general meeting of Friends. Upon continued breach of faith, the meeting would break off fellowship with the offending individual until he or she repented.

The local meeting was to see to the material needs of poor or persecuted Friends. Conflicts between Friends should be dealt with speedily and fully. But Dewsbury counseled against hasty judgments. If the truth were not abundantly clear, they should send for more seasoned minds to sort it out. But in every case, "cut down all deceit." The allergic reaction of Friends to dishonesty or hypocrisy in any form was severe. But where anyone was truly open, Dewsbury advised the utmost tenderness and patience:

> wash the Disciples Feet in bowing to the pure in the least appearance, and ministering to it, to strengthen the desire raised up towards the Name of the Lord, until Judgment be brought forth into Victory, then you will have union together.[12]

Maintaining unity in a movement so minimally organized and coursing with intense energies required a great deal of work. While local leaders were able to handle most cases, itinerant Quaker apostles like Dewsbury were crucial to helping settle the more difficult or novel situations. They were also needed to communicate the evolving definition of Quaker faith and practice from group to group.

Some of these developments came from consultations among the movement's leadership. But others developed out of local situations, where an original approach was recognized to be "consistent with truth" and helpful for all Friends. We will see that the organizational structure that was applied to the overall movement in later decades derived from a number of regional innovations among Friends, melded together into a coherent framework.

The same year, 1653, a second general epistle was issued by a meeting of Quaker leaders at Skipton in the North, signed by George Fox. It added further instructions for local groups, including the detailed recording of births, deaths, marriages, and various sufferings from persecution. The Quaker apocalypse questioned many of the world's mores. But it bolstered integrity in all relationships. Thus, contracts between indentured servants and their masters were to be honored, and children were to be trained in some useful calling, "that none may live idle and destroyers of creation, and thereby become burdensome to others." Burial grounds were to be maintained by each meeting (since Friends would not be buried at their local parish grounds). Friends who had run into business debts should be counseled by their local meeting and helped to reestablish credit. Poor Friends were to be relieved out of a meeting treasury. Anyone writing Quaker tracts and books should submit them to seasoned Friends, "lest they should slip any word." Quaker marriage procedures (weddings under the corporate authority of the local meeting, rather than the authority of an ordained clergyman) were outlined.[13] Again, this was a practical apocalypse, balancing ecstatic worship and charismatic itinerant preaching with stable domestic relations, meticulous record-keeping, and scrupulous business acumen.[14]

These are not so much definitive statements as surviving documents of a makeshift but serious system of accountability by which early leaders sought to give their movement coherence. The general meeting, made up of clusters of local groups gathering every three weeks or month, was the first form by which Friends aimed to become consistent in the truth. It functioned mainly by mutualistic mechanisms of assistance, encouragement, and criticism. Local stalwarts modeled Quaker behavior and nurtured it in others, relying from time to time upon the greater authority of itinerant leaders.[15]

RECKONING WITH RANTERS

Rice Jones and his group offered only the first skirmish in an on-going struggle to forge the molten dynamics of ecstatic, apocalyptic spirituality into a coherent, sustainable life-force. It might be compared to today's scientific quest to find a "container" for the tremendous power of atomic fusion. The next challenge Quaker leadership faced was the abiding presence of Ranters in England. As J. F. McGregor notes, early Quaker documents are among the most extensive anecdotal records we have of the Ranters. But early Friends seem to have used the term "Ranter" in a loose, epithetical manner to describe anyone exhibiting immoral and incorrigible behavior or dabbling in speculative religious ideas. As McGregor observes, Ranterism was more a religious *mood* than a defined movement. To grasp the Quaker response to Ranterism is an important key to understanding their unique success in founding a viable religious society upon a radical dependence upon the Spirit.[16] In other words, the Ranter challenge was a defining moment in the trans-figuration of Seeker errantry into Quaker community.

Quaker preachers encountered Ranter groups in various locales of the North, Midlands, and London. But, McGregor suggests, even where there were no Ranter groups, Quaker preaching often generated more local upheaval than could readily be absorbed into the Quaker move-ment and its rudimentary forms of discipline. Thus, many individuals, set on fire by the Quaker message, blazed wildly around the country-side, becoming nuisances to many, including more sober Quaker con-verts. In response, a 1655 general epistle by Fox urges Friends to

> wait low in the fear of the Lord, and be not hasty nor rash, but see the way made clear . . . the unbridled will gets at lib-erty, and an exalted spirit gets up. . . . And friends, in all places, where any go abroad, as they pass by examine them, whither they are going, and what about? And if they cannot give a good account, exhort them to return back and abide faithful in their places until they see their way made clear.[17]

The fiery Quaker message and movement were scandalous enough with-out half-baked souls raging around indiscriminately.

Anti-Quaker literature seized upon examples of individuals who fell prey to erratic actions that were often associated with Ranters. The anonymously published *The Quakers Dream* (1655) cited Quakers burning their Bibles, as Ranters had done (suggesting that Rice Jones' disregard for Scriptural truth was not as isolated a problem as Fox in-sisted). Quaker meetings were not bawdy, but in other ways they were deeply disturbing. After a long silence, people would begin falling down, shaking, shrieking, howling, their bellies swelling up. These incidents frightened spectators, pets, and farm animals—even stampeded cattle. The tract describes the case of a John Gilpin, who heard John Audland preach and fell into various strange behaviors, before deciding that it was the devil, not Christ, that had entered him. He eventually condemned his brief Quaker episode.[18] Clearly, the intense, chaotic energies of

Quaker convincement did not always find the same channel of personal transformation that we saw witnessed in Chapter 8.

The fifth edition (1654) of Ephraim Pagett's *Heresiography* added both Ranters and Quakers to its catalog of religious complaints. Like most conservative literature, *Heresiography* portrayed Quakers and Ranters as variations upon the same blasphemy:

> They are a desperate, furious kennel . . . of Hereticall, Atheisticall professions . . . [that has] infected many inno- cent harmless soules, and will, if in policy they bee not suppressed, perhaps ere long root out all pietie, order, and humanity. . . . The Ranter is an uncleane beast, much in the make of our Quaker, of the same puddle, and may keep pace with him; their infidelity, villanies, and debochements, are the same, only the Ranter is more open, and less sowre, professes what he is, and as he has neither Religion, nor honesty, so he pretends to none.[19]

The Quaker claims to victory over sin were repeatedly equated with Ranter equations of sin and righteousness. The Baptist John Bunyan's first pub- lished work in 1656 was an attack upon Quakers. He believed that Friends preached the same ideas that Ranters had already vented, "only the Ranters made them threadbare in the alehouse, and the Quakers have set a new gloss upon them again, by an outward legal righteousness."[20] Again, Quakers were accused of both antinomianism and legalism. Richard Baxter, much given to theories of "popish" conspiracy, supposed that both Ranters and Quakers were actually "fronts" for Jesuit agitation. He speculated that when the Ranters' outrageous behavior turned public opinion against them, the Jesuits shifted tactics "from horrid Prophaness and Blasphemy, to a Life of extreme Austerity."[21] In a July 1654 conver- sation about Quakers and their preaching of Christ's light, Oliver Cromwell commented to Anthony Pearson that "the light within had led the Ranters . . . into all manner of wickedness."[22] Such popular associations were dangerous to the new movement. Worse, fringe elements of the movement added credibility to the comparisons with Ranters.

Friends systematically answered the published attacks of hostile crit- ics, attempting to show the difference between themselves and Ranters. They also made overtures to the government, protesting that their moral rigor was conducive to citizenship of the highest caliber, at least in relation to just and equitable government (they also warned that they would not obey unjust laws).[23] But the influence of Ranterism on seeking souls—potential converts to the movement—was perhaps the most disturbing issue for Quaker leadership.

This concern is illustrated in a letter from Thomas Lawson to Margaret Fell during the summer of 1655. Traveling in Sussex, Lawson encountered a number of Ranters who opposed him, seeking

> to justify that which they walk in, even filthyness and ungodliness . . . several of them have tasted of the good word and of the power of that word . . . their hearts were truly touched with the love of God and they led by a principle of righteousness leading to life, but being falne from it, the abomination of desolation is set . . . and by them is the way of truth ill spoken of, and they are given up to follow the motions of the wicked one and in unrighteousness they take pleasure.

We find this assessment repeatedly in Quaker literature regarding Ranters: they were among the most advanced seeking spirits of their day; they had started to come under the power of the cross; but they lapsed into despair and nihilistic behavior. None had come closer to the Quaker revelation than figures like Salmon and Penington, before their eclipse in 1650. The similarity between Ranters and Quakers thus posed serious problems:

> they have severall scriptures which they vent and spew out for to justify their shameless ways, and many simple people were afraid to receive us in whom was first groanings after righteousness, for the Ranters had cast out among them that there was nothing stood up between them and the Quakers only they [i.e., Quakers] did not see all things theirs, so were in bondage, but they would grow up to them [i.e., Ranters], and many stumbling blocks they lay in the way to stop people from owning friends.[23]

We find here a classic example of the mentality of the second Seeker type. Ranters saw their position as a more advanced stage in progressive revelation. They took a condescending attitude toward Friends, assuring themselves that the Quaker revelation would eventually catch up with their purer, more mystical vision. This rhetoric of progressive revelation (whether employed by Ranters outside the movement or Friends within the movement) could thus be used to resist any serious gathering into a stable faith community. Anyone who did not wish to submit to the cross of obedience and corporate witness could simply claim "further light."

The showdown between Quakers and Ranters came to a head during 1654, around the Leicestershire town of Swannington, where a number of Ranter-Quaker skirmishes took place. As in several episodes where the Quaker movement received new definition, Richard Farnworth was in the thick of the action. During 1654, he spent considerable time in and around Swannington dealing with Ranters. That summer, he wrote one of the definitive Quaker statements against Ranters, *The Ranters Principles and Deceits Discovered* (dated 1654 but published in 1655). Farnworth's passion for moral purity was acute; he was strongly repulsed by libertinism in all forms. He acknowledged that many Ranters had once received a pure revelation from God, but they had not remained in the burning light of divine judgment. They fled the cross, betraying Christ with a kiss, delivering him into the hands of sinners. They ranted and swaggered in wickedness, claiming to be free.[25] He stated the Quaker difference succinctly: "the liberty which Christ purchased to and for his, is a liberty and freedom from sin, and he that saith he is in Christ, ought to walk as he also walked."[26] He followed this with a great deal of language about God's purity, adding that all sins will be forgiven *except* the sin against the Holy Ghost (Matt. 12:31f), which is to sin willfully once grace is received and to speak evil of the power of truth.[27]

Farnworth described a confrontation he had on September 1 with one Robert Wilkinson of Coaton, Leicestershire. This quite possibly was "R. Wilkinson," the member of the army who published *The Saints Rest* in 1648 (see Chapter 4). That book exemplified the advanced Spiritualism that often went awry by 1650 into Ranterism. If Farnworth met the same individual in 1654, he had certainly degenerated over the intervening six years. According to Farnworth, Wilkinson claimed that he was born of God and unable to commit sin, that he was both God and the devil, that there was no God or devil but him, that the apostles were liars and deceivers, that the Bible was a pack of lies, and that there was no heaven or hell except on earth. Farnworth vigorously defended the integrity of the apostles and pronounced judgment upon Ranters: "Wo to the Ranters, this book is as a testimony against you, from us whom the world calls Quakers, and you and your wicked principles we deny, and hold them and you accursed."[28]

Farnworth's defense of the apostles, his frequent citation of biblical references (Fox and most early Friends quoted and paraphrased the Bible extensively, but did not usually cite chapter and verse), and his general moral rigorism would seem to classify him among the first type of Seeker, the radical Protestant type, whose conservative passion for a renewal of New Testament Christianity led to the Quaker movement. This type of Seeker seems to have predominated in the North. Since all the central leadership of the Quaker movement had been gathered from the North by 1652, their concern for a visible, coherent, and purified church came to bear with increasing weight upon the Quaker movement as a whole. We will find that Fox proved a mediating figure between this conservative group from the North and Quakers in the South, who were more often of the second, proto-liberal Seeker type.

Fox was not disposed to mediate between Ranters and Quakers, however. His critique of Ranterism was identical with Farnworth's. He carried on struggles with Ranters all over the country. But while Farnworth tended to anathematize Ranters with white heat, Fox sometimes made headway among them. For example, he convinced some of the Sussex Ranters who had frustrated Lawson. As Fox summarized, they had become weary of their profligacy,

> and so the Lord's truth catched them all and their understandings were opened by his light . . . through which they came to be settled upon the Lord; and so became very good Friends in the Truth and became very sober men.[28]

Late in 1654, Fox made his way toward Leicestershire for a general meeting of Friends there. This meeting was apparently planned to be a showdown with the considerable Ranter forces in the area. One of the Ranter luminaries of 1650, Jacob Bauthumley, author of *The Light and Dark Sides of God*, had a following around Leicester. Farnworth had tangled with Bauthumley and followed that meeting with a virulently hostile letter summarizing their argument.[30] Friends described figures such as Bauthumley as "civil Ranters," implying that they indulged in speculative theology and libertarian ethics, but not rude behavior. But Farnworth's antipathy suggests that such civility made Ranter ideas all the more dangerously seductive.

The general meeting at Swannington was a week long, January 8-15, 1655. Friends took on all comers—Ranters, Baptists, local clergy—daring them to "come forth and try their God." The less "civil" Ranters sang, danced, and whistled in contempt during the Quaker meetings. The scene became so chaotic that local magistrates finally summoned army troops to break up the meetings.[31]

In 1655, many incidents continued to occur in which Ranters were either rebuffed or convinced by Quaker preachers. Fox recalls learning of John Chandler, a former cleric turned notable Ranter in London. As Fox reports it, Chandler "had run into so much wickedness that he lay as a spectacle to all people; and he cried out that he was in Hell fire, and no one could minister any comfort to him." Having known that sense of dereliction in his early years, Fox asked Edward Burrough to go to Chandler. The latter was convinced and became a preacher and writer in the Quaker cause.[32l]

In 1659, John Chandler published *A Seasonable Word and Call to All Those Called Ranters or Libertines*. His knowledge of Ranterism from the inside made his tract one of the best Quaker attacks. He charged Ranters "to bethink your selves (ye that are not past feeling) of your former estates when ye were conscientious and tender . . . and commune with your own hearts, by turning in to the witness of God, that calls for purity and holiness . . . submit to the judgment of the witness" instead of fleeing from it.[32] The Quaker entered the same painful place of eclipse that the Ranter had entered and fled in 1650. The Quaker lesson was to stay there and wait for the power to come. Chandler refuted the progressive dispensationalism of the second-type Seeker and Ranter. They pleased themselves in thinking that they were in the last and highest dispensation, that they saw more clearly than the ancient Jews could under the law and the apostles could under the gospel. But having fled both law and gospel, they in fact saw the least. Thinking to be at the top of the ladder, they had deserted even the foot of it. Chandler asserted (contrary to the bulk of Reformation thought) that the apostles preached and strived for perfection, not a Ranter perfection that denied the reality of sin and evil, but one that conquered all in Christ's power.

> And know ye (Oh ye haughty and conceited ones) that there
> is never any other new dispensation, different from this, to
> be brought forth in the World; but that the Glory of the Church

in these last times is to be wrought out by the pure and powerful appearance of the Lord God, in his very way of purifying and refining his People; for through Judgment is Zion to be redeemed, and her Converts with Righteousness.[34]

This is a key statement. Despite the apparent novelties of their movement, Friends rejected the dispensational scheme of progressive revelation. That speculative outlook was replaced by a more purely apocalyptic sense of Christ's return in glory, of judgment day revealed within, exposing and burning up sin, refining and purifying the heart and mind to serve God in righteousness. Chandler concluded:

I in the love and fear of the Lord God, exhort you to listen continually to the voice of the good Shepherd, whose rod and staff hath reproved and comforted, and is reproving and comforting you; that so neither ye, nor I my self, may ever any more turn aside to folly.[35]

Another Friend, Richard Hickock, attacked Ranters in 1659. *His Testimony against the People Called Ranters* opened with the exhortation, "Return, and come down to judgement, for down to judgement you again must come, that judgement may have its perfect work, to the bringing down of your imaginations." He reported a Ranter criticism of Friends, that if everyone possessed the divine teacher within, why did they need to gather to worship together, or preach to others? Hickock answered that the same light that taught individuals also led them to meet together. Moreover, when that light moved a person to speak, whether in Quaker meetings or out in public places, "it is the spirit that speaks in them (and so Gods teachings)."[36] So the Quaker understanding of spiritual authority residing in each person did not serve an individualistic or relativistic outlook; rather, it undergirded a strong commitment to collective spiritual practice, in which Christ's authority was exercised at large in the community of faith, and Friends learn from one another in Christ's wisdom.

Starting in 1655, then, Friends began drawing a line between themselves and their Ranter cousins. Ranters could wait for Quakers to attain their more enlightened dispensation, but they would have to wait somewhere else. Quaker leadership acted first through published denunciations of Ranterism. Then, by degrees over succeeding years, the elaboration of Quaker doctrine and the tightening of the movement's internal discipline removed Ranter tendencies from among Friends. The term "Ranter" was applied to a wide variety of individuals whose ideas or behavior resisted the emerging orthodoxy and orthopraxis of Quakerism.

Friends did not mount a similar public attack on Seekers. They viewed any earnest "mourner after Sion" as a tender soul open to the Quaker revelation. But Edward Burrough's work in London among gathered Seeker groups led him to criticize them briefly in early 1656. *The Trumpet of the Lord Sounded out of Sion* attacked all existing religious groups of the day in a form reminiscent of the letters to the seven churches in Revelation. Burrough saved the "Seekers and Waiters" until last, implying that they had come closest to the truth. Nevertheless, in less than one page he unleashed a desolating exposure of the Seeker condition.

Burrough granted that among Seekers "there is a simplicity, and a calm spirit, for you have been poured from vessel to vessel, and your scent is not so strong as the former [religious gatherings]." However,

> you seek not at the true Door, nor wait not at the Gates of Life, and your seeking will end before life eternal you find; for you with the rest [of the gatherings] stumbles at the Foundation; and in him who is the Light of the World . . . you cannot believe; you are airy in your words and knowledge, and spake of that which through death you never obtained; your knowledge is high, but it ariseth out of the cursed ground, which is not removed in you; Forms outward you deny, but your Form is inward, and your chiefest Idol is in your heart; and while you say you eat and drink the Flesh and Blood of Christ [without the outward elements], in the Substance you slay him in his least measure . . . and when you speak, the mans head is covered, and the womans head is uncovered, and this is a shame, that the woman hath not power on her head: your Seeking and Waiting is in your selves, and in your own time, and the Lord is not all, and in all among you . . . and your Profession will wither as time passeth away . . . this is to you as a warning, for a Preparation to meet the Lord, and to put away your other Lovers.[37]

Burrough's critique is much along the same lines that Isaac Penington confessed in his Quaker convincement. His seeking, like that of many in London, was highly advanced, but in the wrong direction. He had attained a rarefied intellectuality but not the true wisdom of the cross. After discarding every outward form of Christian worship, Seekers had fallen prey to an inner form, the discursive mind. Some years later, Penington reflected on Seekers of the 1650s, after the Ranter crisis, commenting that they

> grew dry, barren, and contentious; losing the savor, sweet-
> ness, meekness, love . . . and remained fixing their minds on
> that which the Lord had departed from. Oh, the darkness and
> misery of this state![38]

Thus, the freshness, urgency, and tenderness that had characterized religious seeking in the 1640s had itself become a form, a reflexive human contrivance, by the 1650s.

We also note Burrough's rather cryptic remark that in Seeker worship, men spoke with their hats on and women spoke bare-headed, which was "a shame." This concern reflects Paul's advice to the church at Corinth (1 Cor. 11:2-16) and early Quaker practice in which men took their hats off when someone prayed, while women kept their heads covered. It was a standard practice among churches, including Friends, to follow this point of Scripture. Apparently, this observance had been abandoned by London Seekers and Ranters. In Burrough's criticism we again identify a Protestant-like concern for New Testament precedent more typical of Seekers and Quakers from the North. Yet, as we shall see in the next chapter, this issue of headgear ran much deeper in Quaker consciousness than a chapter-and-verse replication of New Testament practices.

Escalating Growth, Persecution, and Organization

These separations from Ranters and Seekers took place amidst burgeoning growth in the Quaker movement. Through 1656, Quaker numerical and geographical expansion were exponential. An increasing sense of panic gripped the religious and political establishments, arousing greater persecution. Fox later recalled that in 1656 thousands were being convinced all over England, Wales, and beyond, while there were "seldom under a thousand in prison in the nation for tithes and going to the steeplehouses, and for contempts and not swearing and not putting off their hats [to magistrates and other powerful figures]."[39]

The coherence of the movement was crucial not simply for its legitimacy as a standing church. Friends were not attempting to start a new denomination. They were proclaiming the day of the Lord, the reign of Christ, the outbreak of a peaceful and just society on earth. The Quaker apocalypse was a revolutionary ground swell aimed at transforming the entire society. Therefore, good order was a matter of *revolutionary praxis*, proclaiming and demonstrating God's government through consistent words and life. Friends had begun to pay an awful price for their witness. The message of reconciliation was written not only in the surging hundreds of Quaker publications, but in the blood of martyrs dying in English prisons. The atonement drama was reaching full intensity.

By 1656, the movement in the North was four years old, with large standing enclaves in Yorkshire, Lancashire, Cumberland, and elsewhere. Northern leaders sensed that it was time to regularize the pattern of local monthly meetings into a general system. Fox directed Farnworth to organize a large regional meeting of northern elders in November at Balby, Yorkshire.[40] While Fox worked to organize the newer meetings in the South, Farnworth and Dewsbury led the way at Balby, drafting the most far-reaching document to date, outlining the business of local elders and monthly meetings. The Balby epistle to "the Brethren in the North" addressed resolution of conflicts and disorderly behavior according to Matthew 18, relations between family members, masters and servants (following the pattern found in New Testament texts such as Ephesians 6:1-9), poor relief, marriage procedures, business ethics, and record-keeping. Elders were increasingly important as catalysts for this ordering work, but the document emphasized that they were to act as examples and not as lords over God's rightful heritage. The document concludes:

> Dearly beloved friends, these things we do not lay upon you as a rule or form to walk by, but that all with the measure of light which is pure and holy may be guided, and so in the light walking and abiding these may be fulfilled in the Spirit—not from the letter, for the letter killeth, but the Spirit giveth life.[41]

Here we find an attempt to balance the need for an ordered, visible church, beginning to take on a nearly Baptist profile, with a sustained Spiritualist emphasis upon the direct government of Christ's Spirit.

Clearly, a consolidation process was under way in the North. Besides the work done at Balby, a second layer of organization had already come in place, with *quarterly meetings* comprised of groupings of monthly meetings, more or less by county. Fox wanted to make this northern innovation a national norm as well, though it would take a while for organization in the more recently missionized areas to catch up. Finally, the first national gathering of Friends was held at Skipton, Yorkshire late that year. But again, it would take time to make this third layer of consultation a fully representative and functional *yearly meeting*.[42]

Meanwhile, in the South, organization in London took a significantly different path.[43] Sometime in 1655 or 1656, a fortnightly business meeting was established to "manage Truth's affairs." As Burrough later described it in 1662, the meeting was to consist principally, but not exclusively, of men most established in the new faith. It was to mediate conflicts within the community, aid in the resolution of any Friend's financial or business difficulties, keep records of births, marriages, sufferings, and burials, care for the poor, and help find employment for those who lost their livelihood on account of their faith. It seems significant that Burrough's language couched disciplinary action in a more neutral language of "disagreements," rather than the "disorderly walking" that northern documents normally mentioned. It would be a gross misrepresentation to suggest that London Friends were moral relativists. But the more complex cultural environment of that large urban center made moral questions more ambiguous at times. And (as we shall see) there was a greater tendency to contest spiritual authority in London than in the North. Consequently, London elders were charged to deal with any who acted slightingly or contemptuously toward Quaker ministers, while simultaneously confronting any self-seeking or lordly manner found among the ministers themselves.

Burrough emphasized the need to make decisions carefully and to suspend judgment when the group lacked certainty. Such suspension was not indefinite; yet it was necessary until more seasoned leaders could be assembled to help discern the matter. In describing these methods, he formulated the best early statement of the Quaker principle of decisions made in unity. The service of truth must proceed

> not in the way of the world, as a worldly assembly of men,
> by hot contests, by seeking to outspeak and over-reach one

another in discourse, as if it were a controversy between party and party of men, or two sides violently striving for dominion, in the way of carrying on some worldly interests for self-advantage; not deciding affairs by the greater vote, or the number of men, as the world who have not the wisdom and power of God; — that none of this kind of order be permitted in your meeting. But in wisdom, love and fellowship of God, in gravity, patience, meekness, in unity and concord, submitting one to another in lowliness of heart, and in the holy Spirit of truth and righteousness, all things [are] to be carried on; by hearing and determining every matter coming before you, in love, coolness, gentleness, and dear unity.[44]

Today, we are likely to consider this egalitarian business method in terms of advanced democracy. However, Burrough's language makes it clear that early Friends understood it most of all as faithful to the example of Christ and the apostles. Laying down self-interest and willfulness in mutual service to God's will constituted a corporate bearing of the cross in the particular circumstances of lived faith. In each concrete circumstance and dilemma, therefore, Friends understood themselves enacting the atonement, the reconciling love of God in Christ, weaving together the threads of their lives into the fabric of God's new creation.

For Seekers most deeply convinced by early Quaker preaching and example, such corporate methods of discernment represented the *transfiguration* of seeking, not its end. Seeking God's will together in each new circumstance was both a continuing commitment to the personal search for truth and a cumulative enterprise in which the local meeting and the overall movement struggled to build a consistent, abiding body of witness, an edifice of collective experiment and discovery. Nothing less would validate the Quaker proclamation of Christ's return to teach, lead, and govern a new people, the vanguard of a new human society.

Sometime after this fortnightly business meeting was established, two other business meetings were settled in London expressly for Quaker women. Perhaps as early as 1656, but no later than 1659, the male leaders of the fortnightly meeting felt the need for a parallel body of female leaders and asked the ministers present in London at that time (including Fox, Burrough, Howgill, and Hubberthorne) to advise in establishing it. A second women's meeting, called the "Box" Meeting owing to the collection box they kept, was organized to serve the needs of poor Friends. This weekly meeting apparently developed out of a conversation between Fox and Sarah Blackborow about the growing needs of poor and persecuted Friends in the city.[45] Blackborow, Ann Downer, Rebeckah Travers, and Mary Elson became prominent among London Friends, partly through their leadership in these meetings.

Although the North produced several significant women ministers, and although Margaret Fell was the movement's early coordinator, northern business meetings had been organized for male leaders. Women could attend and speak in such meetings, but the formal authority of the meetings was vested in those local male leaders identified by the group. It remains a question whether the northern Friends, more typically concerned with New Testament precedents, would ever have initiated women's meetings on their own. The more complex urban environment of London made this less charismatic, more fully rationalized form of female leadership thinkable—and in fact, necessary.

By the time the women's meetings were organized, the London Quaker scene had been severely rent by a division concerning James Nayler. A bitter conflict broke out in 1656 between some of Nayler's female followers and Burrough, Howgill, and Hubberthorne. None of the male leadership among London Friends succeeded in mediating the conflict. It may well be that London Friends recognized the need to define a distinctly feminine sphere of spiritual authority to help heal the continuing rifts of the Nayler controversy. But, as we shall see in the next chapter, this London innovation eventually became an integral part of the larger movement.

THE NAYLER CONTROVERSY

The first major conflict in the Quaker movement erupted around one of its most gifted leaders, James Nayler. His charisma as a preacher and his ability to debate theological critics made him especially effective in the high-powered atmosphere of London. The details of his Quaker career and debacle have been narrated by a number of scholars.[46] We will treat here only those aspects that relate to our present concern.

In Chapter 8, we noted the dynamics of masculine and feminine in the breakthrough of Seekers into the Quaker movement. A rigorously conservative sexual morality was held in tension with a highly affectionate style of expression among early Friends. The charged energies of masculine and feminine fueled the Quaker struggle to live an austere life and to challenge repressive authorities. Quaker leaders often exemplified attractive masculine and feminine virtues. That modeling helped their followers discover the same qualities within themselves. Sometimes the powerful energies that were unlocked within followers were projected upon their leaders and expressed in exalted erotic language in letters to them. We saw one of the most clear-cut examples of this in the convincement narrative of Martha Simmonds, who, using language from the Song of Solomon, described the discovery of her "beloved" within. She was the sister of Giles Calvert and wife of Thomas Simmonds, the two main publishers of Quaker materials, and quickly became a prominent leader in London. During late 1655 and early 1656, while Burrough and Howgill were on a mission to Ireland, Simmonds became Nayler's closest ally and confidant. For his part, Nayler had left a wife and family to the care of local Friends in Yorkshire. He was acutely overtaxed by the mass popularity of his ministry in London.

It is easy to overemphasize the role of Nayler's female followers. In fact, a number of key male followers (including Thomas Simmonds) also formed tightly around him, separating him from the rest of the Quaker leadership. Nayler later confessed that he had been drawn by sexual desires for at least one of the women around him, but he always insisted that no sexual liaison took place. The issue was more one of *enmeshment* between Nayler and his followers. This was most overt between Nayler and Simmonds, but it was shared and fostered by the group as a whole. When Burrough and Howgill returned to London, Simmonds resented their incursion and was soon locked in bitter conflict with them. Nayler, failing to mediate the situation, withdrew to the Simmonds' home and lapsed into severe depression. Those closest to Nayler exalted him in escalating terms and isolated him from the other Quaker leaders. The gendered tensions that energized early Quaker spirituality at its best now imploded and a vortex of chaotic energies swirled around Nayler.

One of the issues that had flared up between Simmonds and the northern leaders in London was their growing tendency to deliver long, didactic vocal ministry in meetings, marginalizing group participation. One gains the impression that the leaders were attempting to squelch the ecstatic dynamics that had burgeoned under Nayler's leadership. At one meeting, Simmonds countered with a "filibuster" of her own, singing the words "innocency, innocency" repeatedly for an hour or more. The ecstatic and didactic tendencies now stood in severe tension, in a manner similar to the problems Paul addressed in the church at Corinth (see especially 1 Cor. 11-14).

Fox did not intervene in the situation until late summer 1656. He concurred with the other northern leaders and ordered Nayler to judge his followers' adulation and reclaim his role as a servant-leader. Fox and Nayler nearly reconciled in September, but the antagonism of Nayler's coterie elicited an imperious response in Fox, sundering relations. Nayler, increasingly alienated from Fox and the northern leaders, resented their impositions. As the charismatic leader of the movement in London, viewed by many as the emerging true leader of the movement, Nayler felt that he possessed the same divine authority claimed by Fox. Fox certainly had used exalted language to describe himself many times. Yet Fox's incisive insight into others and his compassionate response to tender souls had always operated across a sense of distance, a separateness from others. This trait had preserved him through all kinds of challenges. By contrast, Nayler's followers had begun to cast him in messianic terms. Nayler had surrendered himself to a small group of devotees whose adoration for him was mixed with personal ambitions and grudges. The Nayler group drifted dangerously into something akin to the Ranter sense of "my one flesh." Other Quaker leaders could not penetrate the miasma. Margaret Fell's letters to Nayler, underscoring Fox's advice, failed as well.

In October 1656, Nayler and his followers enacted a prophetic sign of Christ's return in the flesh of common people. They led Nayler on a horse through the streets of Bristol, laying garments in his path and singing "holy, holy, holy." Dramatic enactments were not unusual among early Friends, who were known to perform various "signs," like walking naked through the streets. Moreover, Nayler knew that he was not himself the Messiah. By this time, however, some of Nayler's followers believed him to be Christ. Parliament, desiring to take a decisive action against Quakers, seized upon this confusion to punish Nayler savagely as a blasphemer. Fox wrote to Parliament in Nayler's defense, but ambivalently: he was no longer sure of Nayler's self-understanding and intentions.[47]

In the aftermath, Martha Simmonds published her interpretation of their symbolic action in Bristol and expressed her view of Nayler:

> Why should it seem a strange thing to you to see Christ reign in his Saints . . . and make our bodies fit for himself to dwell in, seeing our bodies are ready to bow to his will? And is it not more for his glory, though it be a greater cross to your wills, to purifie these bodies, and pour out the dregs thereof, than to bring down that body that was crucified at Jerusalem . . . ? [Through] much tribulation, anguish of spirit, and sufferings of the flesh, he hath now fitted a bodie for himself, who hath conquered death and helle, so perfect is he that he can lay down his life for his enemies . . . this vessel is as precious to me as that which was tortured at Jerusalem, seeing the same Father hath prepared them both.[48]

Other men and women in the Nayler group were less sophisticated in their messianic understandings. Together, they had tapped a dangerous potential in the exalted consciousness of Quaker spirituality. Nayler's only serious error was his rejection of the collective discernment of Quaker leadership. That was the absolutely essential counterbalance to heady Quaker claims to moral perfection and Christ's indwelling. Simmonds' placement of Nayler on a par with Jesus of Nazareth was not only bad theology; it also bore the bitter fruits of alienation, accusation, and general hell-raising within the Quaker movement— hardly an atonement.

This breach in the Quaker ranks provided religious and civil authorities just the provocation they needed to turn official policy and public opinion against the movement. From that point onward, official persecutions and mob violence against Quakers became steadily worse.

The Nayler incident also provided an opportunity for critics to attack the unorthodox theology of Friends. The Baptist Thomas Collier published *A Looking-Glasse for the Quakers* in 1657, finding the messianism of the Nayler group to result from a low regard for Scripture and the historic atonement of Christ. He lost no time in identifying Quaker doctrine as a rehash of Ranterism:

> And what the Quakers is more or less, let their own consciences be judge; only they smooth it over with an outward

austere carriage before men, but within are full of filthyness, pride and abomination, which by degrees breaketh forth; Witness Naylors exaltation. . . . [Quakers are] the most dangerous and pernicious Principle that hath yet appeared in the likeness or pretence of truth in this latter age.[49]

Collier had previously sparred in print with Burrough and Nayler. Nayler had accused Collier of limiting God to the Bible. Collier had countered that God limits us to the Bible.[50] As a personal and social enactment of the historic cross of Jesus, the Quaker atonement drama was a profoundly creative process. But it was vulnerable to misunderstanding from outside the movement and to misguided energies within.

If Nayler's act had been part of the concerted wisdom and will of the movement, Friends would probably have closed ranks with their typical readiness for conflict and suffering. As it was, however, the conflictual tactics they often employed toward state-sponsored parish churches now turned inward on the movement itself. Nayler sympathizers interrupted Quaker meetings for worship and harangued Quaker ministers, just as many Friends had done in parish "steeplehouses" all over England. The Quaker movement had been by no means innocent of the Ranter politics of rage and resentment. Its unprecedented attacks upon the religious establishment had drawn many to the cause. Now the same energies, never amenable to spiritual authority in any form, ripped through the movement itself, particularly in London.

Women were not the only ones besetting Quaker meetings in 1656 and 1657, but they were the majority. Given the rage that focused upon Fox, Burrough, Howgill, and other male Quaker leadership, it seems impossible to imagine that the London Quaker women's meetings were not organized partly to mediate these conflicts. After terrorizing London meetings for nearly a year after the Bristol incident, Martha Simmonds and most of the key figures in the Nayler episode gradually reconciled with the movement.[51] One can imagine that leaders of the London women's meeting, such as Rebeckah Travers, who had herself been close to Nayler, helped to build bridges between alienated parties.

But all leadership was tested severely for the rest of the decade by the aftermath of Nayler's fall. Richard Farnworth withdrew to the North in 1658. Rosemary Moore suggests that he was probably exhausted with the conflicts in the South and perhaps divided in his loyalties, since Nayler had been a fellow Yorkshire Seeker and Quaker traveling companion.[52] Farnworth did not return to London until late in 1661.[53]

Nayler survived Parliament's barbaric treatment, confessed his error to Friends by 1658, and was released from prison in 1659. Fox initially refused to meet with him; but, through the mediation of several leaders, particularly Hubberthorne and Dewsbury, there was a tacit rapprochement in early 1660. Before that time, Nayler had already returned to effective ministry in London. But at Fox's insistence, he agreed to return home to Yorkshire that summer. It may be that Fox aimed to "retire" Nayler permanently. However, with Farnworth continuing to minister locally in Yorkshire, it is possible that Nayler left London to recuperate more fully under the care of his old friend. Tragically, we can only speculate: robbed and beaten on his way north, Nayler died later in the home of a Friend.

Robert Rich

But not all Friends made peace. Robert Rich was among those closest to Nayler in 1656. Letters between them during Nayler's imprisonment show that Rich harbored deep resentments against Fox and opposed Nayler's reconciliation. Rich wrote to Nayler in 1657 of a conversation with Fox, in which the latter had dealt gently with him. But Rich concluded that Fox was "wise as an Angel of Light . . . King of the Locusts . . . whose name and nature is to destroy."[54] Sometime around the beginning of 1658, Nayler wrote back to Rich, urging him to join with him in making peace with Friends, whatever their failings:

> better it is to suffer with them for a little time than to be tormentors of them . . . he who now rejoyces to see those scattered with wind...shall receive his reward according to his work . . . truly my peace flows as a River...Dear Heart, do not hearken to that which would perswade thee that I would lay any evil upon thee, or burthen the innocent in thee.[55]

In what may have been his last communication, Rich urged Nayler not to reconcile: "O my deare heart, enter not thou into their secrets . . . for as the Lord lives their nakedness shall be no longer hid."[56] Rich departed England for Barbados, where he lived the next twenty years.

Robert Rich was a classic London Seeker-turned-Quaker. He came from a wealthy family and was a well-established London merchant when he became a Friend in 1654. He sacrificed much in terms of wealth and social standing as a Quaker activist. At the end of 1656, Rich stayed with Nayler on the platform when the latter was pilloried, even licking Nayler's forehead after it was branded. After leaving Friends and England, Rich decided

> that the whole Body of Truth was not circumscribed within the Bounds of any one particular Persuasion, but lay scattered and dispersed amongst the Outcasts of Israel, (i.e.) The several Parties and Opinions which did all . . . lay claim to Religion . . . and hereby attaining to a more universal Spirit, he found freedom in his mind to dive into the several Forms of Professors now appearing...with a design to cull out the Gold (i.e.) that which was good in all, and to reject the Dross . . . this work necessarily is critical, and exposes one to the dislike of most parties not willing to have their mistakes and misapprehensions exposed to them.[57]

In other words, he returned to seeking. Rich was no longer disposed to cast his lot with any one group, but instead opted to sample and taste the best of each. This "more universal Spirit," finding pieces of a larger, ineffable truth in many religions, manifests the classic liberal mode of seeking down to this day. We found an early example of it in William Walwyn (Chapter 5), whose Socratic style of questioning various groups made him unpopular among most of them. The liberal seeking sensibility finds its Protestant Seeker counterpart brittle and narrow-minded, too intent upon embodying the visible church, too apt to bog down in legalisms of form and belief. Rich clearly felt the Quaker movement had veered in that direction.

Rich died in 1679. *The Epistles of Mr. Robert Rich to the Seven Churches* was published the following year by unnamed associates in London. In it, Rich addressed seven Christian bodies in London: Roman Catholic, Episcopal, Presbyterian, Independent, Baptist, Quaker, and a group he calls "the Church of the First-Born." In 1666, he had sent donations of thirty pounds to each of these churches for the relief of their London members after the Great Fire. He commended the good traits he found in each, while criticizing their shortcomings, in a manner similar to the letters to the seven churches of Asia Minor in Revelation 2-3.

His epistle to Quakers, who had refused his donation and sent it back, contained much criticism. He deplored the organization and disciplinary actions that evolved in the 1660s and 1670s:

> Now dear Friends, can you . . . believe that this violent and rigid sort of Practice, will render your Feet beautiful upon the Mountains? or will attract the Hearts of any wise or ingenuous People towards you? . . . the Dispensations in which God administers Himself to the World at this day, do most naturally call for a more sober moderate, tender, and loving Spirit amongst Christians, than this wherein you are exercised.[58]

Rich saw history moving on, new dispensations calling for more practical cooperation and doctrinal latitude among churches. Along those lines, the Latitudinarian movement, an early liberal initiative in England at that time, sought to define a basic body of universally acceptable doctrine among Christians.

He concluded his counsel to Friends:

> Cast off your Judging, Censuring, and Imposing Spirit, and give the Witness of God in every one its just Right, its due Scope and Latitude, and usurp not Authority over it. . . . Give Christ his Prerogative in Spirituals, He must and will have it; Give Caesar his due in Temporals, who may of undoubted right challenge it.[59]

He concluded that this separation of inward and outward realms would offer the shortest route to both internal peace among Friends and toleration by the government. In effect, Rich advocated a mysticism that detached itself from the lost political battles of the Commonwealth period.

This attitude is made more clear in his epistle to "the Church of the First-Born." It is not clear what this body was, if indeed it was a distinct fellowship. The name—used among early Friends, including some of the movement's central leadership, in earlier days[60]—evoked the sense earliest Friends shared of being the vanguard of a new humanity, the first-born of the new creation. One of the named recipients of Rich's gift to this church was a William Blackborow, probably the husband or some other surviving relation of Sarah Blackborow, who had died in

1665. It may be that a London group of separated Friends, or a dissident faction still within the fold, continued to use this name. But from Rich's language to them, it appears that they were seeking again. He wrote to them that over the years he had encountered

> several Celestial Pilgrims journeying towards Sion, with their Faces thitherward, by whose sprinklings, in many of their Books and Papers, I have bin often refreshed and comforted.

He recommended the Greek philosopher Cebes, Thomas â Kempis, Nicholas of Cusa, Henry Nicholas, Jacob Boehme, William Erbury, John Saltmarsh, and James Nayler, among others. He commended the Church of the First-Born as standing most inwardly near to God, released from all formalities into the deep mysteries of God. He hailed it as the true Mount Sion and urged it to reveal itself to the world.[61] But one suspects that by 1680, this vanguard of new humanity had become a self-styled elite, the stranded first-born of a stillborn new age of the Spirit.

With Robert Rich we find one Seeker trajectory leading back out of the nascent Religious Society of Friends, to seek again. Notwithstanding his ongoing animus against Friends, a generous-hearted, liberal-minded Christian ecumenism flows through Rich's last testament. Like Sebastian Franck in the previous century (see Chapter 2), Rich celebrated the church invisible, the mystical fellowship of saints across and beyond all Christian boundaries. He saw the continuing Quaker insistence upon a defined, visible church as an apostasy. Friends continued to fight a losing battle against powers that had long since reclaimed control of England; worse, they had become brittle and reactionary, entrenching themselves as a mirror-image of the repressive powers that persecuted them. Thus, Rich accused Friends of "hardening" into a certain set of practices—the very accusation Friends had made against Baptists and others.

But we are getting ahead of ourselves. In our final chapter on early Seekers and Quakers, we will resume following the Quaker atonement drama as it continued after 1660. We will chart the ongoing Quaker struggle to exercise a prophetic faith and establish a visible church in the face of withering persecution.

Notes

1. Margaret Fell, *A Testimonie of the Touchstone* (1656), 36.
2. William Smith, *The New Creation Brought Forth, in the Holy Order of Life* (1661), 48-49.
3. Schwenckfeld does not affirm moral perfection in this life, but comes close to that position at times, countering the emphasis upon continuing sin taught by most Protestant reformers. See Joachim Wach, "Caspar Schwenckfeld: A Pupil and a Teacher in the School of Christ," in his *Types of Religious Experience Christian and Non-Christian* (Chicago: University Press, 1951), 166-69.
4. I am here borrowing terminology from Steven M. Tipton's sociological study, *Getting Saved from the Sixties: Moral Meaning in Conversion and Cultural Change* (Berkeley: University of California, 1982), which received extensive attention in Chapter One of this study.
5. Key Quaker defenses of women's ministry are: Richard Farnworth, *A Woman Forbidden to Speak in Church* (1655); George Fox, *The Woman Learning in Silence* (1656); and Margaret Fell, *Women's Speaking Justified* (1666). For a summary of Fox's teaching on the subject, see Gwyn, *Apocalypse of the Word: the Life and Message of George Fox* (Richmond, Ind., Friends United Press, 1986), 149-50.
6. T. L. Underwood, *Primitivism, Radicalism, and the Lqmb's War: The Baptist-Quaker Conflict in Seventeenth-Century England* (Oxford: University Press, 1997) points to the strong claims early Friends made to New Testament precedent for their doctrines and actions. This primitivist theme was especially strong in early Quaker literature defending the movement against Puritan and Baptist attacks.
7. See the collection of statements concerning this earliest identifiable group of Quakers, the "Children of Light papers," Portfolio 10.42 at the Library of the Society of Friends, London (hereafter cited as LSF). The occasion for this handful of statements, mostly dated forty years later, 1686, is mysterious. Each seems to stress the point that they used the name Children of the Light only after Fox came to them. And each devotes attention to the defection of "Rice Jones' company." The fullest statement is by Oliver Hooton, which unfortunately has been partially lost.
8. George Fox, *Journal*, ed. John L. Nickalls (Cambridge: University Press, 1952), 63.
9. William Smith, *A Few Words unto a Peculiar People* (1669), 1; quoted by William C. Braithwaite, *The Beginnings of Quakerism* (London: Macmillan, 1912), 46.
10. See Fox, *Journal*, 178, 338; and Thomas Hyfrold's statement in the "Children of Light Papers."
11. George Fox, unpublished paper "Concerning our Monthly and Quarterly and Yearly Meetings..." (1689), in *Letters, etc. of Early Friends*, ed. A. R. Barclay (London: Harvey and Darton, 1841), 331.

12. William Dewsbury, "Epistle" (1653), in *The Faithful Testimony of that Faithful Servant of the Lord...* (1689), 1-4.
13. Unpublished epistle, Portfolio 36.19 at LSF; see Arnold Lloyd, *Quaker Social History, 1669-1738* (London: Longmans, Green, 1950), 2.
14. For a fuller exposition of the early Quaker concern for marriage and domesticity, see Barry Levy, *Quakers and the American Family* (Oxford: University Press, 1988).
15. Fuller treatments of the origins of Quaker organization *per se* can be found in two excellent studies: Hugh Doncaster, *Quaker Organization and Business Meetings* (London: Friends Home Service, 1958); and Michael J. Sheeran, *Beyond Majority Rule: Voteless Decisions in the Religious Society of Friends* (Philadelphia: Philadelphia Yearly Meeting, 1983).
16. J. F. McGregor, "Ranterism and the Development of Early Quakerism," *The Journal of Religious History* 9 (1977): 350.
17. George Fox, Epistle #83 (1655), in *Works* (Philadelphia: Gould, 1831), 7:94-95.
18. Anonymous, *The Quakers Dream: or, The Devil's Pilgrimage in England* (1655), 3-7. The report on Gilpin was taken from Gilpin's own publication, *The Quakers Shaken* (1653). The cover to *The Quakers Dream* features a series of four cartoon woodcuts of Quakers in various activities, all suggesting sexual libertinism and general antinomianism. For another published case of a convincement that led to strange and self-destructive behaviors, see John Toldervy, *The Foot out of the Snare* (1656).
19. Ephraim Pagitt, *Heresiography: or, a Description of the Hereticks and Sectaries Sprung up in these latter times*, fifth edition (1654), 145.
20. John Bunyan, "A Vindication of Some Gospel Truths Opened..." in *Works* (London: Virtue and Yorston, 1859), 1:93.
21. Richard Baxter, quoted by A. L. Morton, *The World of the Ranters: Religious Radicalism in the English Revolution* (London: Lawrence and Wishart, 1970), 91.
22. Anthony Pearson to Margaret Fell, July 18, 1654, Swarthmoor MSS., 3.34, LSF.
23. I have dealt much more fully with the posture of early Friends toward civil order and the state in *The Covenant Crucified: Quakers and the Rise of Capitalism* (Wallingford, Pa.: Pendle Hill, 1995).
24. Thomas Lawson to Margaret Fell, July-August 1655, Swarthmoor MSS., 1:242, LSF.
25. Richard Farnworth, *The Ranters Principles and Deceits Discovered* (1655), 1-2.
26. Farnworth, *Ranters*, 5.
27. Farnworth, *Ranters*, 7.
28. Farnworth, *Ranters*, 19-20.
29. George Fox, *Journal*, 212.
30. Richard Farnworth to Jacob Bauthumley, January 4, 1655. Samuel Watson MSS., p. 162. The language of the letter is perhaps the most severe and antagonistic I have seen among early Quaker writings. William Dewsbury also tangled with Bauthumley sometime in the winter of 1654-5. The latter was more philosophical than confrontational and did not attempt to answer Dewsbury's attack. See William Dewsbury to George Fox, Swarthmoor MSS., 3:22, LSF.
31. George Fox, *Journal*, 181-82. Also see McGregor, "Ranterism," 352-53.
32. Fox, *Journal*, 196-97.

33. John Chandler, *A Seasonable Word and Call to All Those Called Ranters or Libertines* (1659), 6-7.
34. Chandler, *Word*, 10-11.
35. Chandler, *Word*, 19.
36. Richard Hickock, *A Testimony against the People Called Ranters* (1659), 5-6.
37. Edward Burrough, *The Trumpet of the Lord Sounded out of Sion* (1656), in *Works* (1672), 109.
38. Isaac Penington, *Many Deep Considerations* (no date, probably 1663), in *Works* (Glenside, Pa.: Quaker Heritage, 1995), 2:375.
39. George Fox, *Journal*, 280.
40. Braithwaite, *Beginnings*, 310-11. Also see Rosemary Anne Moore, "The Faith of the First Quakers: The Development of their Beliefs and Practices up to the Restoration" (Ph.D. Thesis, University of Birmingham, 1993), 138.
41. Barclay, *Letters*, 277-82.
42. Fox, *Journal*, 284-85. For further background on organizational developments of that year, see Braithwaite, *Beginnings*, Chapter 13.
43. I am aided here by Braithwaite, *Beginnings*, 320, 339-40; and Barclay, *Letters*, 294-310.
44. Barclay, *Letters*, 305.
45. On the women's meetings in London, see Braithwaite, *Beginnings*, 340-42; Irene L. Edwards, "The Women Meetings of London," *Journal of the Friends Historical Society* 47 (1955): 3-21; Bonnelyn Young Kunze, *Margaret Fell and the Rise of Quakerism* (London: Macmillan, 1994), 143-50; and William Beck and T. Frederick Ball, *London Friends' Meetings* (London: Kitto, 1869), 343ff.
46. See Braithwaite, *Beginnings*, Chapter 11; Emilia Fogelklou, *James Nayler, the Rebel Saint* (London: Benn, 1931); William G. Bittle, *James Nayler, 1618-1660: The Quaker Indicted by Parliament* (Richmond, Ind.: Friends United Press, 1986); Leo Damrosch, *The Sorrows of the Quaker Jesus: James Nayler and the Puritan Crackdown on the Free Spirit* (Cambridge: Harvard University Press, 1996); and my own treatment of Nayler in *The Covenant Crucified*, Chapter 5.
47. Fox's initial letter to Parliament, before Nayler's trial, is highly garbled and ambiguous. Later, before Nayler's punishment, he published a second letter to Parliament more clearly defending Nayler. See *Covenant Crucified*, 168-69,
48. Martha Simmonds, Hannah Stranger, and James Nayler, *O England thy time is come* (1656), quoted by Moore, "First Quakers," 170.
49. Thomas Collier, *A Looking-Glasse for Quakers* (1657), 7,12.
50. Collier, *Looking-Glasse*, 13.
51. Phyllis Mack, *Visionary Women: Ecstatic Prophecy in Seventeenth-Century England* (Berkeley: University of California, 1992), 210. The treatment of the gender dynamics of the Nayler episode, pages 197-211, is one of the high points of her excellent study. On Martha Simmonds in particular, see Kenneth L. Carroll, "Martha Simmonds, a Quaker Enigma," *Journal of the Friends Historical Society* 53 (1972): 31-52. According to Carroll, there are reports of Simmonds and others starting to quiet down in late 1657, after Nayler had written statements from prison condemning the disturbance of meetings. But after that, Simmonds disappears from Quaker records, until her death in 1665, apparently a Friend in good standing.

52. Moore, "First Quakers," 177.
53. For more on Farnworth, see Tam Llewellyn-Edwards, "Richard Farnworth of Tickhill," *Journal of the Friends Historical Society* 56 (1992): 201-209. Apparently, Farnworth married another Yorkshire Friends minister, Mary Stacey, in July 1658, which would account partly for his more retired life over the next three years.
54. Robert Rich, *Hidden Things Brought to Light* (1678), 42.
55. Rich, *Hidden*, 43.
56. Rich, *Hidden*, 44.
57. Rich, *Hidden*, Preface by "J. W." Geoffrey Nuttall, "The Last of James Nayler: Robert Rich and the Church of the First-Born," *Friends Quarterly* 60 (1985): 527-34 speculates that this may in fact be John Webster, the former associate of William Erbury (see Chapter Four).
58. Rich, *Hidden*, 101-02.
59. Rich, *Hidden*, 103.
60. See Nuttall, "The Last of James Nayler."
61. Rich, *Hidden*, 105-16.

CHAPTER 11

CORRESPONDENCE AND COHERENCE
QUAKER SELF-DEFINITION, 1660-1700

I speak as one that seeth the end of all distinctions, and separations by Names . . . there are of the People called Seekers, Baptists, Independents, and others . . . [those] whom I as truly own, and with whom I have more Unity, than with divers which are called by the Name of Quakers.

—John Perrot, 1662[1]

So in Faith and Patience in the Power of the Lord, all in your own measure received of God stand, stand still all in the pure unity with the Lord, and with one another in his living Dominion rest in peace, God will give you an answer to all your Prayers and Tears.

—William Dewsbury, 1662[2]

The Quaker movement featured an unprecedented counterattack upon the national church system and its enfranchised clerical elite. Parish "priests" were denounced as false prophets even as they stood in their own pulpits. The academic training that formed the basis for their rule by expertise was challenged as false knowledge. But even Independent and Baptist ministers and their congregations were challenged for limiting God to the Bible and for fixing their knowledge of divine truth idolatrously in set creeds. All churches were denounced for their tendency to encourage "profession without possession"; that is, to establish doctrinaire belief systems without a foundation in personal experience of God and without practical grounding in a faithful, morally rigorous life.

The *inductive* approach to faith—namely, belief according to the data of actual experience and moral method—was a religious correlate to the emerging modern sciences of the 17th century. In terms of a philosophical stance toward truth, we could say that early Friends held to the *correspondence theory*. One embraces only those beliefs that can be verified by the corresponding facts of experience. Thus, as we saw in the preceding chapter, the historical atonement of Christ witnessed in the gospels was verified to Friends in two primary ways: in their personal experience of reconciliation with God through the harrowing "daily cross" of Quaker convincement; and in their social practices (the Lamb's War), which generated intense conflict, but also offered egalitarian reconciliation to all parties. Likewise, they believed in the return of Christ and the end of the world because their personal encounter with Christ had brought them through a deep experience of death and resurrection, discredited the world's institutions in their eyes, and empowered them to realize the kingdom of God in their daily lives.[3]

But of course there is no such thing as pure experience. We frame all experience within certain assumptions and expectations. The Quaker movement emerged within a Seeker milieu that had developed a set of shared radical Protestant and Spiritualist understandings over the previous decade and more. Quaker preaching did not embrace all Seeker assumptions, however, as we have seen. On the one side, it did not fulfill the more Protestant Seeker expectation that the new apostles would reinstitute the sacraments of the New Testament church. On the other side, it did not embrace the Spiritualist doctrine of progressive dispensations of truth, each new one making the previous one obsolete. Quaker preachers defined all historic revelations as developments from one light. The covenantal integrities of successive peoples of God are the historic expressions of that one dispensation.

As the movement grew, matured, and responded to attacks from without and controversies within, a body of shared understanding inevitably developed. That process increasingly set the movement off from other movements and tendencies around it. We have seen how Friends vehemently drew a line between themselves and Ranters. We also noted their more sympathetic but resolute critique of Seekers. The Nayler episode precipitated the first serious internal rift in the movement. For a movement under increasing persecution, this internal conflict was acutely painful and threatening to all parties, inspiring severe invectives between them for a while. But the hostile pressures of the outside world and the ongoing atonement drama of the movement augured for reconciliation among nearly all combatants—at least for a while.

In these developments we see a counterforce operative in early Quaker fidelity to truth. In philosophical terms, this counterforce has affinity to the *coherence theory* of truth. That is, all truths attain their validity within a holistic framework. A belief is verified by being consistent or harmonious with a larger system of beliefs. The emerging coherence of Quaker witness embraced many beliefs in common with traditional Christian orthodoxy. But this coherence was established less by means of rational deduction or biblical proof-texts than according to appropriate practices of moral living, Spirit-led worship and ministry, and decision-making based upon corporate procedures for discerning God's will. This strong feature of early Quakerism has much in common with the modern *operationalist* theory of truth, established by science and mathematics. Here the *methods* of verification are emphasized: there is an appropriate set of procedures to verify any given truth-claim. (Again, recall the Quaker counsel to Mary Penington, that true knowledge of Christ's *doctrine* comes through obedience to Christ's *commands*.)

Thus, as time went on, Quaker rhetoric increasingly sounded themes of consistency of faith and practice, the unity of Friends in faith and practice, and the need to verify individual truth-claims according to methods of corporate discernment. For instance, during the 1660s, when the Restoration regime feared Quakers as plotters of armed insurgency, Friends began to articulate their pacifist position more clearly, emphasizing that they had submitted peacefully to previous persecutors in the 1650s and would continue to live *consistently* in this manner of obedience to Christ's teaching and example.[4] Concomitantly, struggles within the movement were increasingly decided by principles of consistency with the earliest practices of the movement, and appeals for the continued unity.[5]

Coherence had an added dimension of meaning in the Quaker case. All Quaker language and action was aimed to communicate truth to an alienated social world. Every aspect of Quaker life was thus understood to be a *testimony* to the world of Christ's Lordship. A coherent code of Quaker faith and practice was thus vital to the distinctively holistic understanding of Quaker witness and evangelism. Suffering under persecution epitomized a whole system of signs held up by

Quakers to the world, signifying Christ's sacrificial death, resurrection, and return in the bodies of the faithful.

All along, Friends confronted concrete dilemmas that had to be solved in practical ways. Friends showed shrewd tactical thinking in a variety of ways. For example, the strategy to invade the South in 1654 targeted areas where rapid success seemed most likely. Also, Margaret Fell's coordination of the movement and its finances from Swarthmoor Hall in the years displayed a great deal of practical ability. These examples highlight one more aspect of the emerging truth among early Friends. According to the philosophy of *pragmatism*, true statements are those which lead to desirable results. In coordination with the other dimensions of early Quaker truth we have just noted, Friends displayed a clear-eyed pragmatism that should not be ignored.

True atonement, or reconciliation, invites all parties into its divinely bestowed peace. But the truth of that atonement and the faithful consistency of that peace are forged out of the interaction of different elements. We have identified those elements here according to representative philosophical theories: correspondence, coherence, operationalism, and pragmatism. We will see how the interaction of the elements fared as the Quaker movement defined itself into a stable, viable entity. (We will return to a further consideration of these same elements for today in our Conclusion.)

THE RESTORATION AND PERSECUTION

The late 1650s saw the gradual collapse of the English Commonwealth. As all attempts at a viable republican government proved half-hearted and contradictory, popular longing grew for the more stable era of the Stuart throne. Quakers, the major embodiment of English radical religion and politics in the 1650s, became the prime target for the venting of both governmental and popular frustration. Particularly in London and Bristol, Friends meetings came increasingly under mob attack. These hostile pressures forced greater solidarity and consolidation within the movement. Organization slowly developed in the South to meet the needs of those suffering persecution, and to sustain a healthy religious and social life among Friends.[6] The breaches caused by the Nayler controversy slowly healed.

When the Commonwealth finally succumbed at the end of 1659, Friends grieved bitterly for the "Good Old Cause." Many of them had been soldiers in Parliament's forces against Charles I and had supported the political agendas of Levellers. They had abandoned political hope in Parliament and the army, finding that the kingdom of God unfolded more effectually through their grassroots movement. But they had still looked to the army as the most friendly ally among the powers, the political force most likely to offer official toleration. When these forces finally acceded to public clamor for a resumption of monarchy, the future appeared dim. Still, the apocalyptic world view of Friends was able to entertain the most ironic rereadings of history. Quaker literature in 1660 interpreted the Commonwealth's failure to be God's judgment upon the hypocritical and self-seeking politics of both Parliament and army. Friends were willing to view even the restoration of the Stuart throne as a potential victory for God's larger purposes. For his part, Charles II seemed interested in granting Friends official toleration.[7]

But the restored monarchy was much reduced in political power; moreover, the Cavalier Parliament of the 1660s was determined to punish all radicals who had frustrated the power and policies of England's "natural rulers" for two decades. From the foundation of the world, polities of all kinds, from primitive tribes to great nations, have consolidated order and renewed allegiances by stigmatizing "the other," by "scapegoating" those who cannot or will not fall in line. The negativities of an entire society—its fear, hate, and guilt—are piled upon hapless individuals or groups who are abused, imprisoned, killed, or otherwise "disappeared" (the term recently coined from Latin American liberation struggles) from public consciousness.[8] *This is the pathological version of atonement, the formation of social solidarity at someone's expense.* This is the poisonous "way of the world" that Christ came into the world to end. Wherever Christ is truly received and his followers live by his example, preaching universal reconciliation and bearing one another's burdens, Christians come to "the end of the world," the end of this principal perpetuating mechanism of alienated human culture. But, as history has repeatedly proved, Christians have found ways to reincorporate scapegoat mechanisms into the life of the church itself.

Quakers (and, to a lesser extent, Baptists) became the most visible scapegoats of the Restoration regime. They were viewed as the most obvious threat to the reconstituted national church and the Stuart throne.

ere even more hated; but like most nonconforming groups,
ntly stayed underground. By keeping their meetings at regu-
... .ld visible to the public eye, Quakers bore the brunt of popular vilification and the first systematic official repression. In the light
of Christ's cross, they understood their sufferings as a redemptive act
of free self-offering that exposes the shame of human arrogance and
dominion, while simultaneously offering forgiveness and fellowship to
all. The cross is the place where the self-perpetuating cycles of violence
and recrimination end. It is the place of true atonement, healing, social
renewal, and peacemaking. But Parliament and the restored hierarchy
of England's church would have none of it.

So the Quaker atonement drama entered its most acute phase. It is
amazing that, from 1660 to 1689, as fines against Friends accumulated
into the tens of thousands of pounds, as imprisonments escalated into
the tens of thousands, and deaths from miserable prison conditions
mounted to hundreds, Friends steadily increased in numbers and continued building a stable and enduring religious society, perfecting their
unique worship and ministry, marriage procedures, decision-making
methods, and social customs. Still, the sustained pressures of persecution produced damaging internal stresses.

THE PERROT CONTROVERSY

John Perrot was an Irish Friend convinced by Burrough in 1655.
He quickly developed into a charismatic minister among Friends in
Ireland and England. In 1657, he joined a quixotic group of Friends on
a mission to Europe and the Middle East. Their aim was nothing less
than to convert the Pope in Rome, the Great Sultan at Adrianople, and
the populace of Jerusalem. On that journey, Perrot had written epistles
to Friends back in England. One letter "To all which wander from the
true Order" (1657) addressed those Friends who had taken up James
Nayler's cause and withdrawn from or attacked the main body of Friends.
He warned that

> God almighty will certainly withdraw himselfe from such
> as withdraw themselves from the congregations of his Saints,
> Saying in their hearts God is everywhere, thereby tempting him

in their high hearts and proud wills, denying and forsaking
the holy assemblings and congregations of the Saints.[9]

Clearly, he shared the leadership's concern for the continued unity and
coherence of the movement.

But Perrot was arrested by the Italian Inquisition and sent to the mad-
house in Rome, where he was tortured and severely mistreated for three
years. As Kenneth Carroll summarizes, the long periods of isolation
and physical abuse evidently drove Perrot more deeply within himself.[10]
He continued to write epistles and tracts during his imprisonment,
a number of which were published in England before and after his
release. His language became increasingly mystical, exalted, and incoherent. In 1660, Perrot urged Friends to desist from taking off their hats
during vocal prayer in meeting. He now viewed this practice as a formality incompatible with worship in the living Spirit of God. He shared
this new light with Friends as further progress in God's revelation,
further liberating them from Christendom's dead conventions.

That letter reached England in advance of Perrot's release and return
in the summer of 1661. It disturbed George Fox and other leaders who
were just putting the Nayler episode behind them and scrambling to
respond to Restoration repression. It also reactivated the animosities of
those who had resented Fox's stern response to Nayler. Many of Nayler's
admirers flocked to Perrot's support. Though they did not indulge him
with the same messianic epithets they had lavished upon Nayler, one
can hear in both cases a language of child-like innocence. Letters to
both Nayler and Perrot addressed them as "poor babe" and "innocent
lamb." A cult of spiritual childhood was fostered among these Friends,
who claimed innocence of intention, felt wounded by any form of criticism coming from within the Quaker "family," and were prone to view
leaders such as Fox and Fell as repressive "father" and "mother" figures.
Once again, a form of emotional enmeshment threatened to quench the
fire of judgment and dull the edge of spiritual discernment.

For his part, Fox was ready to play the strict father again, if necessary. He immediately took a strong stand against Perrot's statement
regarding the hat. Upon his return, Perrot first defended Fox against his
critics in Bristol and London. But during the autumn of 1661, when Fox
and other key leaders bore down heavily on him in a series of evening
discussions in London aiming to bring him back into unity on the hat

issue, Perrot began to feel abused. He insisted that his conscience did not lead him to remove his hat in prayer. He respected those who felt genuinely led to do so, but could not follow their example out of mere conformity. He believed that this position should have satisfied Fox, unless Fox really did intend to impose his will upon the entire movement, as critics murmured.

We detect in Perrot's position an insistence upon *correspondence* (that is, that each individual must come to his or her own inner conviction on any question) in tension with the leadership's growing concern for the movement's *coherence*. His variance is attributable in part to his absence from England for more than four years of crucial developments in the movement. He was thereby out of touch with the organic processes that had led to the increasing emphasis upon unity. In November, Perrot asked for an open hearing among Friends to reconsider Quaker hat policy. But the leadership was not willing to open any wider the floodgates of controversy. In December, Perrot left London to return home to Ireland for a while. After a friendly parting, he believed the other ministers had accepted his nonconforming position. But epistles from Fox shortly thereafter made it clear that reconciliation had not been achieved.[11]

Perrot's case for individual conscience seemed impeccable on its own terms. Friends had preached the primacy of personal experience and the individual conscience since the beginning. But Fox had always viewed the issue of individual conscience within a larger, corporate framework. Again, the status and future of the Quaker movement as a visible church was at stake. Fox accused Perrot of introducing new views. He argued that removal of the hat in prayer was not a "form," but a "custom" among Friends from the beginning. It was Perrot's "sophistical" reasoning that had made a form of it. Fox associated Perrot's refusal to remove his hat with Ranter practices and with a 1656 incident in which Nayler had slighted Fox's prayer by refusing to remove his hat. Finally, and most tellingly, Fox judged Perrot's position according to its effects upon those who sided with him. Some withdrew from worship and fellowship with Friends. Fox believed these dissidents to be filled with a "dark, earthy spirit" that would not take off the hat in prayer, but would then go to the parish clergy to be married: "then this dark earthy spirit could bow, and put off its Hat to its own."[12]

This last point deserves elaboration, as it may express the heart of the issue from Fox's perspective. Quaker men were not unique among

Christians in removing their hats during vocal prayer. But they were notorious for refusing to remove their hats before the clergy, magistrates, and other human authority-figures. The point of early Quaker egalitarian social codes was to bring all low before God. So while Friends were not supposed to feel or express awe toward any human, they were to "fear the Lord" in every aspect of life. Taking off the hat in prayer, in addressing God, was thus an essential part of the Quaker symbolic system. *Solidarity in reverence toward God was integral to solidarity in defiance of human authorities.* The former was the *raison d'être* of the latter. Fox viewed the resistance to the hat gesture as a resistance to authority in its true form. Once one snubbed divine authority, one could cynically acknowledge authority in any form.

The Perrot controversy rattled the movement, particularly in the South. For a time, it alienated some eminent Friends, including the Peningtons, from the northern leadership. The Welsh Quaker leader Richard Davies spent time in London during this period and was with the Perrot faction for a while. As he later recalled, they met mostly to inveigh against the Quaker leadership as dead and formal, even as the latter were bearing the brunt of persecution. The Perrot faction believed themselves to be the vanguard of "a more Glorious Dispensation, then had been yet known among Friends." Similarly, Thomas Ellwood, friend of the Peningtons and another well-born recruit to the movement, was "taken with the Notion . . . of a Spiritual Dispensation."[13] Clearly, the "progressive revelation" logic predominant among southern Seekers and Quakers was a driving force among Perrot's supporters.

Isaac Penington, a friend of Perrot's, ventured into print amid the controversy. *Many Deep Considerations* did not take an overt position for or against Perrot, but it speculated that even the most eminent instruments of the Lord could stumble and fall if they did not maintain a spirit of brokenness and humility. Certainly, many Perrot sympathizers felt that Fox had become imperious by this time. Penington emphasized that unity could not be achieved simply by virtue of uniform thought and action; surely diverse practices could come from the same Spirit. Speaking in the oracular first-person, Penington prophesied, "I will beget a deeper life in you, and bring it forth after a deeper way of dispensation than ye have yet been acquainted with."[14]

Francis Howgill took Penington to task for this publication in a June 1663 letter. With tender affection, Howgill acknowledged that Penington's actions were well intended, but admonished him firmly not to publish such views again. He argued that to speculate on the fallibility of the movement's leaders only exposed a flank to hostile critics assaulting Friends from every side. Finally, he warned,

> it is a dangerous word to speak of a further dispensation than that whereby eternal life comes to be witnessed unto the creature and while many have talked of this they have neglected and undervalued that which they have attained unto and so gaze and wonder at they know not what, and so lose what they did already enjoy; but a growth and increase in life and power and glory we have always spoken of, but still it's the same and not another, and them that have spoken of another dispensation, have grown weary as Israel did of the manna, and . . . undervalued heavenly food, and last of all fed upon an husk. And them that have spoken of these things unto us would have had their necks out of the yoke and so run out. . . . Thou saist theres no certain knowledge of the life by any administration [i.e., dispensation]. We say, yes, as the tree is known by its fruits and as a cause may be known by its effects . . . was not Christ manifestly the son of God by his works? and is not the spirit manifest by the life?[15]

This is a key Quaker answer to the progressive dispensationalism of the southern Seekers and Quakers. The notion of successive revelations led to idle speculation and a neglect of the Spirit's present work in personal transformation. This was the manner in which so many Seekers had lost the Spirit, some of them lapsing into Ranterism, others into endless doctrinal "jangling." In place of new waves of revelation obviating old ones, Friends preached the return of Christ, a revelation that would grow in continuity with itself. While Penington speculated that no one knows absolute truth, Howgill countered with a functional, moral argument that the truth of revelation is known by its fruits in one's life. Finally, by this time, the Perrot faction had come to the further conclusion that meeting at set times was also a dead formality. They instead chose to meet only as determined by the Spirit. Quaker leaders identified this novelty as a handy rationale for starting to meet secretly, thus ducking persecution. That issue underlies Howgill's allusion to those who wished to slip "their necks out of the yoke." The dispensationalist outlook was thus prone to fractionalizing politics, in which the unity and visibility of the church would be slowly diminished, ultimately leading to an individualized, private faith.

In June 1662, Perrot was among a group of Friends arrested at a meeting in London. He was held in Newgate prison with Edward Burrough and John Crook, and for a while seemed ready to be reconciled with the Quaker leadership. But he unexpectedly volunteered to exile himself to Jamaica in return for release from prison. In Jamaica, he followed his own course until his death in 1665. He professed undying love for Friends, even for Fox. There was no contentious nerve in the man. But one can easily imagine that the deep inner communion and guidance that had helped him survive unbearable abuse in Rome had become so absolute that he dared not submit to authority working through any external means.

Richard Farnworth had resumed ministry in London in the latter half of 1661, around the time of Perrot's return from Rome. Once again, he played an important role in sorting through the issues and working to reconcile Friends scandalized by Fox's intransigence toward Perrot. In a 1663 paper, Farnworth defended the practice of taking off the hat "in humility of soul before the Lord" and identified a dualism in Perrot's position. He affirmed Perrot's insistence that all inward observances must be subject to the inward leading of the Spirit. But to imply that outward observance was insignificant would be to render worship and ethics ultimately meaningless. The shared practices of Friends mediated between spiritual and material, inward and outward, individual and world. Without that mediation, the inner aspect of the person would be subject to spiritual laws while the outer aspect would

> be subject to outward laws, worships and governments of men, as outward, useless and unserviceable things, and needs not be liable to any persecutions of suffering for righteousness' sake.[16]

As years of persecution wore on, the thought of a less arduous life surely tempted Friends to pull back from their public witness. But within the Quaker paradigm of atonement/apocalypse, self-preservation meant capitulation and the loss of hope for the world.

Fox, Farnworth, Howgill and others could be tender enough with Perrot in private to make him believe he had won them over. But in their statements to the body of Friends, they resolutely held the line against him. They were by no means ready to cede leadership of the movement to this beautiful but broken spirit drifting rapidly into a private, Gnostic mysticism. The visible faith community, the key mediating agency between the inner spirituality of the individual and the outer social world, necessarily demands some level of sacrificial witness, as long as alienated and unjust powers dominate in the world.[17] Once these convinced Seekers had found a place to stand against those powers, it was vital that the Quaker social space be maintained at all costs. As we observed in Chapter 8, the equality these Friends found in Christ with God was something not to be grasped or exploited personally but rather poured out in the form of servanthood, even to the point of death (Phil. 2:5-8).

That prophetic witness was exemplified by Edward Burrough, who in early 1663, at age twenty-eight, succumbed to illness in the same Newgate prison cell from which Perrot had escaped to Jamaica. This loss rocked the movement. Fox wrote to encourage Friends, especially the many who had been convinced by Burrough:

> Friends, Be still and wait in your own conditions, and settled in the Seed of God that doth not change, that ye may feel dear Edward Burrough among you in the Seed, in which and by which he begat you to God, with whom he is, and that in the Seed ye may all see and feel him . . . so enjoy him in the life that doth not change, but which is invisible.[18]

Note the transcendent, overcoming unity of the seed. The here-and-now emphasis of Quaker apocalyptic witness did not deny the eternal dimension of the new life Friends had found together. Rather, the nearness of eternity in the seed inspired both a breathless urgency for personal and social transformation *and* a larger sense of victory that could swallow up death and defeat. The power of the resurrection, the overcoming love of God, is the ocean of light that overflows even the vast ocean of darkness.[19]

Still, an undeniable formalism grew within the movement. The more Protestant-inflected Seekerism that had formed northern Friends, who were generally unmoved by Perrot's arguments, asserted itself resolutely. And behind that strengthened tendency lurked an incipient legalism. Fox had attempted to fend off accusations of formalism by arguing that Perrot had made a form of the hat by stepping outside the existing Quaker consensus. But even granting Fox's point, the poisoned consciousness of mechanistic conformity, once suggested, spread inexorably. Standard-ization of organization and behavior eventually repelled some, driving them out of the movement. Among those who remained, standardiza-tion slowly forced some minds into the same mechanistic observance that had repelled them in the 1640s, leading them to forsake all churches and become Seekers.

ORGANIZATION AND ITS DISCONTENTS

One important key to the changes that ensued is the gradual loss of apocalyptic horizon. Throughout the early 1660s, Friends prophesied God's judgment upon the Restoration regime for its antichristian treat-ment of nonconformists. With the eruption of plague of 1665 and the Great Fire of London in 1666, it seemed that God's displeasure was clearly expressed. Indeed, the Restoration's first administration under Clarendon fell in 1667. But it was clear that the general tenor of the Restoration would not change. Parliament would continue its cynical and unjust policies. The reign of Christ through the common people of the Quaker movement had been turned back. The end of the world—that is, the end of an alienated, violent, exploitative, and scapegoating culture—had been deferred.

The cross still ended the world within certain spheres of true Chris-tian obedience and influence, however. And within the logic of that situ-ation, Quaker leaders understood the need to consolidate and nurture the utopian life of the movement. A *microcosmic eschatology* (that is, a limited version of the end of the world, in which a tightly delimited religious community models the kingdom of God on earth) quickly re-placed the fully apocalyptic eschatology of the first period.[20] One readily shares early Friends' grief for the loss of the first period's exuberance and wide-open sense of possibility. Yet the succeeding phases, as the movement acquired a more sectarian profile, were profoundly creative in their own right.

Fox spent a long term of imprisonment first at Lancaster and then at Scarborough, 1664-66. During the latter phase, his jailers kept him from receiving or sending correspondence.[21] Howgill was sentenced to life imprisonment at Appleby (where he died in 1669). In the absence of Burrough, Fox, and Howgill, it was left to Farnworth, Dewsbury, and others to heal the Perrot rift and keep the movement alive. Farnworth, arguably the Quaker leader most passionately concerned for discipline and order, organized a meeting of eleven Quaker leaders available in London in May 1666. They produced a document aimed to resolve the Perrot controversy and establish unambiguously the stabilizing authority of corporate discernment over individual conscience. No other single document so clearly marks the moment of transition in Quaker faith and practice.

This epistle reaffirmed the Seeker hope that in the Quaker movement the true church was returning from the wilderness of apostasy. But this renewed church has found "not only many open but some covered enemies to contest against; who are not afraid to speak evil of dignities [i.e., recognized leadership], and despise government [i.e., an ordered church]." Pretending to oppose "men and forms" these enemies actually oppose "ministry and meetings." The recognized ministers and elders of the movement must be allowed to articulate the boundaries and direction of the church. When differences arise, the body of Friends will decide between parties. Those refusing to submit to the corporate authority of the church and its leadership therefore *by definition* do not possess the spiritual *rights* or gospel *authority* of membership in the body. In particular, those traveling in ministry among Friends and out in the world must be accountable to the body for their words and actions. Those continuing to act as free agents will be disowned in public and rebuffed in meetings.[22]

The high-handed, Sinai-like tone of this document startled Friends. As Farnworth lay dying of a fever just a month later, some speculated that God had struck him down for his action.[23] On his deathbed, however, he insisted that, to his own inward eye, "God hath appeared for the owning of our Testimony . . . No Lincy-woolcy Garment must be worn."[24] The imperative for *coherence* thus *corresponded* with the deepest spiritual experience of Farnworth and most Friends. But it jarred many others. The May 1666 epistle scandalized the left wing of the movement as deeply as Perrot and his sympathizers had scandalized the right wing. The most serious divisions were still to come.

George Bishop, one of Bristol's leading liberal-wing Seekers-turned-Quakers, a leader who had helped keep the movement together during the Nayler crisis, responded with a trenchant, undated criticism sometime before his death in 1668:

In the Apostles days were Pastors, Teachers, Elders, etc. but in this day the Spirit it self is the Pastor, Elder, etc. So that if the Spirit move any to Declare or Speak, that is the Apostle, Teacher, Elder, etc. So that we have not now things in the disposition of Persons, nor according to Persons, but in, or according to that power which moves in every one, which being kept to, preserves out of the Apostacy: So I know no Pastor, Teacher, Elder, etc. but as I find moving in any, to any of these things, for that is the Elder, the Apostle, Teacher, etc. and that which would be otherwise than this, leads into the Apostacy, and will seek to bring [the] dark night in again, and so will place the Thing to the Person, and not the Person to the Thing. And for my part if that day should prevail, or those things which Your PAPER seems to hold forth and enforce, I have no other Expectation, but that the same exercise we shall receive at your hands, as we received at the hands of those [persecutors] who would have held us in Captivity in the day that the Lord first visited us.

The Seed is come, and the Heir in many, who is not to be under Tutors and Governours, which must not be limited; to turn to which, or for the good of which the Ministry was sent, and in which it is to end, it being the end of the Ministry unto which its Crown is to be laid down, as to that which is worthy; and this is no derogation of the Ministry. Now for You, because You have ministered, and the Presence of the Lord hath been with You for the good of those that are to be Heirs of Salvation, to think to settle Your selves in the place of the Heir, and to enforce Your Orders, as instead, or over that; this is not to allow that the Seed is Come, or that it is of age to abide in the House for ever. You must not think, that because the Lord hath wrought by You, that therefore He will not work otherwise. This is the Error into which all have fallen that are turned from the Truth. Therefore seek not to undervalue that to which you were sent to minister; nor endeavour to keep under the Seed, for that will Break You to Pieces. The Revelation of God is to His Seed, and His Secrets he reveals to it, for which He made the World, and for whose sake it is continued; and now the Seed is raised to reign over all, which will Cast You out, and the Parable of the Husbandman will be fulfilled upon You. It is my Love that gives me this plainness of Speech, for I am Jealous of every thing that may bring dark Night over again, or that may hinder Your Work, or lose your Reward with the Lord; for the Son must abide in the House for ever, but not the Servant; therefore take heed how You set up your Laws and Constitutions over His Dominion, or how you take upon You to make Laws to His Dominion, who lives for ever. Many have attempted it, and have been Broken to pieces: and if You do the same, the same will be Your Portion from the Hand of the Lord.[25]

Bishop's prophetic denunciation and warning is stunning in its clarity. A careful reading reveals that he upheld the principle of corporate authority over individual conscience. But he extended that principle to subvert the self-asserting authority of the movement's surviving leaders. The authority of Christ ministering by the Spirit was to be recognized and honored wherever found, and not necessarily reckoned according to its conformity to the movement's leadership, no matter how trustworthy they were in their own right. Bishop identified a process of reification at work, in which Quaker was becoming "Quaker," and elders were becoming "elders." As he stated it, over time this process would "place the Thing to the Person, and not the Person to the Thing."

Note also the theme of undervaluation. In his letter to Penington, Howgill had warned that progressive dispensationalism leads the individual to speculate on "new lights" and undervalue the present work of the one light. Bishop by no means disagreed with that position. But he articulated the opposite danger: to press forward in defining authoritative leadership and bodies, "to set up your Laws and Constitutions over his [i.e., Christ's] Dominion," is to "undervalue that to which you were sent to minister"—namely, the seed of Christ abiding in the people.

In the North, the home of the movement's most "ancient" leaders, where the Perrot viewpoint had received little sympathy, the London epistle found support in most places. But in southern centers like Bristol and London, outright revolt was brewing. If Fox had remained off the scene much longer, the movement might well have collapsed, or perhaps broken into diverging northern and southern bodies. In that case, Bristol, jealous of London's cultural dominance, would probably have become a body unto itself. But Fox was released from Scarborough Castle in September 1666, just as the Great Fire broke out in London. Although he was weak and ill, he quickly made his way southward. In the closing months of that year, he moved decisively to add organizational definition to the Farnworth epistle and to begin the enormous work of personal ministry necessary to its implementation. A key early action was a reconciliation meeting in London for those who had been drawn away by Perrot. Thomas Ellwood later wrote of the great relief it offered him and others to acknowledge their error and be accepted back. During the meeting, letters were read from others unable to attend, adding to the sense of reconciliation.[26]

Isaac Penington and George Fox exchanged affectionate letters while the former was imprisoned at Aylesbury in 1667. A letter from Penington dated July 15 includes these lines:

> I feel the tender mercy of the Lord and some proportion of that brokenness, fear, and humility, which I have long waited for, and breathed after. I feel unity with, and strength from, the body [of Friends]: O! blessed be the Lord, who hath fitted and restored me . . . . I feel an high esteem and dear love to thee, whom the Lord hath chosen, anointed, and honoured, and of thy brethren and fellow-labourers in the work of the Lord. And dear GF I beg thy love; I entreat thy prayer . . . that I may be yet more broken . . . poorer, and humbler before the Lord . . . . Dear GF thou mayest feel my desires and wants more fully than my own heart. Be helpful to me in tender love, that I may feel settlement and stability in the Truth.[27]

Through his incisive but intimate personal ministry, Fox was able to win friends and allies in places where Farnworth's decree was not. Clearly, Penington sensed the Spirit's gifts in Fox. This was the charismatic leadership that Bishop had emphasized must always take priority. Penington's awe of Fox never wavered after this; as we shall see, in the years ahead, he became an advocate of both Fox and organization.

Fox needed all the help he could get in implementing his plan for a national organization of Friends. By the end of 1666, he records,

> the Lord opened to me and let me see what I must do, and
> how I must order and establish Men's and Women's Monthly
> and Quarterly Meetings in all the nation, and write to [Friends
> in] other nations, where I came not, to do the same.[28]

He began immediately in London, where the separate women's meetings had first been established in the latter 1650s. He organized five sets
of parallel men's and women's monthly meetings around London "to
admonish, and exhort such as walked disorderly or carelessly, and not
according to Truth; and to take care of God's glory,"[29] the latter being a
phrase Fox used to describe the traits of good order among Friends.

Fox devoted the years 1667 and 1668 to the intensive, grueling project
of establishing monthly meetings around England and Wales. In most
places, he had to confine himself to organizing men's monthly meetings.
Only in Bristol was he able to replicate the London pattern of parallel
women's meetings—and there in the face of growing opposition.[30]
Elsewhere, resistance to independent women's eldership and monthly
meetings was too great. He worked systematically through the counties,
coming to agreement with local male and female leadership, working
through points of resistance, then organizing general meetings of Friends
to consolidate support.[31] Fox emphasized that through the regularized
organizational structure,

> the Lord's power came over all, and all the heirs of it came to
> inherit it, for the authority of our meetings is the power of
> God, the Gospel which brings life and immortality to light,
> that they may see over the Devil that has darkened them,
> and that all the heirs of the Gospel might walk according to
> the Gospel, and glorify God with their bodies, souls, and spir-
> its, which are the Lord's. And so the order of the glorious
> heavenly Gospel is not of man nor by man.[32]

So Fox argued that true government is the power of God working through
visible, ordered bodies of those who wait upon the Lord for guidance.
The *structures* that nurtured the discipline of group spiritual discernment were not the "gospel order" itself, but simply a *regimen* by which
the group allowed Christ to exercise divine authority in its midst. To
realize that order among Friends was thus to "inherit," to take possession of and to fulfill, twenty years of development in Quaker practice.

In other words, far from an apostasy; *this was the crowning moment of the Seeker quest.*

But not all Friends saw it that way. There were four evident points of opposition. *First*, many simply did not want to become accountable as individuals to the corporate authority of their local meeting. There were still places, particularly in the South, where regular business meetings were only beginning. Over the years to come, those who continued to resist the moral scrutiny and group processes of Friends were often labeled "Ranters" and disowned.[33]

Second, continued persecution wore down even the most committed Friends. The proliferation of meetings for worship and business presented new targets for mass arrests, imprisonments, fines, and mob abuse. When laws against nonconforming religious groups were renewed in 1670, Friends reeled. Fox became gravely ill from a condition that was only partly attributable to physical disease. The Restoration's continued vehemence "oppressed" his spirit.[34] The Perrot faction's practice of meeting secretly and unpredictably had seemed cowardly to most Friends in the early 1660s. But by the 1670s, more Friends, even some in the North, wondered why they should go out of their way to be arrested. The government had begun paying informers to identify the time and place of Quaker meetings. Dissenters from Quaker organization renewed the surreptitious practice of meeting "as moved by the Spirit."[35]

The *third* point of resistance is less clearly stated in the literature of the controversy, but it seems that many desired to retain local and regional autonomy.[36] Even though the quarterly and yearly meetings were intended to exercise mainly an advisory and coordinating function, they clearly would function to standardize the faith and practice of Friends all over England and Wales. H. Larry Ingle adds that many especially resented the centralizing administrative authority of the Ministers Meeting and later the Meeting for Sufferings, both in London. Aside from and beyond the organizational structures established by Farnworth and Fox, these central bodies exerted a powerful and sometimes intimidating authority over Friends across the nation.[37] Many former Seekers had never contemplated becoming part of something so regimented. Like Bishop, they viewed Quaker organization as a return to the apostasy captivating all churches. Indeed, those who dropped out over the issue of organization often did not join another religious group.[38]

Fox's rhetoric countered these concerns by presenting the "gospel ordering" project as the appropriate countercultural response to the Restoration of the monarchy and national church. He wrote of gospel order as the *restoration* of the relations between man and woman in Eden before the Fall.[39] The mutualistic community of hearing and obeying that Adam and Eve had enjoyed with God in the beginning had been recovered in early Quaker spirituality. Now the corporate practices of spiritual discernment in the men's and women's meetings would perfect that recovery. Thus,

> faithful women, who were called to the belief of the truth, being made partakers of the same precious faith, and heirs of the same everlasting gospel of life and salvation that men are, might in like manner come into the possession and practice of the gospel order, and therein be meet-helps unto the men in the restoration, in the service of truth, in the affairs of the church, as they are now outwardly in civil, or temporal things. That so all the family of God, women as well as men, might know, possess, perform, and discharge their offices and services in the house of God.[40]

In the face of a long-term retrenchment of alienated social relations (including patriarchy) by the English Restoration settlement of church and state, the Quaker movement carried on the utopian values of English radicalism, albeit in a more contained form.

An epistle from Fox issued in late 1666 or early 1667 exhorted Friends everywhere to set up the women's meetings:

> Keep your meetings in the power of the Lord God, that hath gathered you; and none quench the spirit, nor despise prophesying, but keep your testimony in public and private.

Hence, the charismatic preaching that women had carried into the marketplaces and steeplehouses in the 1650s was to be institutionalized through regular women's meetings. These meetings, held visibly and not in secret, would constitute the next, post-apocalyptic phase of women's countercultural spiritual empowerment. Women were not to be bypassed in the consolidation of the movement: all must "come to know their duty in it, and their service in the power and wisdom of God. For now the practical part is called for." We hear the rationalization of charisma clearly stated. Fox not only invited women into this creative new phase, he acknowledged the dangers of leaving them out. The women's meetings were essential,

> so that none may stand idle out of the vineyard, and out of the service, and out of their duty; for such will talk and tattle, and judge with evil thoughts, of what they in the vineyard say and do.

There was work to be done and spiritual authority to be exercised by all. The power of God must course throughout the body of faith, "and all keeping in it, then there is none to let or stop its flowing; but through it you are all watered, as a garden of plants; by which you are nourished."[41] But except for London and Bristol, women's meetings were still years away from formation.

This leads us to the *fourth* point of resistance to gospel order. Many Friends, northern and southern, were scandalized by the idea of separate women's meetings. Northern Friends, who had been organized longest, readily took to the standardization of a structure they had helped the leaders create. But while the North had produced some of the most fiery female ministers, there was no tradition of separate women's meetings for business. Likewise, Bristol Friends were alienated by Fox's initiative. They had had a women's meeting for poor relief for some years, but not a separate women's meeting for spiritual nurture and discipline. Only London had developed this pattern. And Bristol Friends were already jealous of London's growing dominance in the movement.[42]

So the genesis of the national organization of women's meetings seems to lie in the alliance between Fox and London women Friends in the latter 1650s. There has long been speculation that Margaret Fell was involved in the plan to establish women's meetings nationally. Though there is no conclusive evidence to substantiate that theory, Fell does appear to be implicated in these developments.[43] It is possible that Fox and Fell began developing a plan while they were both imprisoned at Lancaster Castle in 1664-65. Fell was still there until 1668, well after Fox had started his organizational initiative. But she was an important catalyst for women's meetings in the North thereafter.

In view of the national movement, the women's meetings appear to be another example of Fox's mediating work between North and South, this time incorporating into the national system an experiment among

London Friends. But this aspect of organization was the hardest to impress upon Friends. For one thing, there was no clear New Testament precedent for female eldership and separate women's meetings. This question of innovation bothered Protestant-leaning Friends most. In Wiltshire, for example, Nathaniel Coleman and other elders argued that female eldership was an affront to the established authority of male Quaker eldership, that a man must rule over his wife. "But," Fox recalls,

> I told them that he and they were but elders in the Fall, ruling over their wives in the Fall, but neither he nor they must rule over widows and young women, and over other men's wives.[44]

In other words, by reenacting the gender relations of Eden, Friends transcended the curse of patriarchy in Genesis 3:16. Again, we find Fox's countercultural restorationist theology challenging Friends to organize formally the spiritual and social revolution implied earlier in their charismatic manifestations of women's leadership.

There were various issues of debate and centers of resistance in the South, especially in Bristol. But serious resistance to women's meetings also emerged in the North, in Westmorland. Two ministers from the early days of the movement, John Wilkinson and John Story, became emblematic figures of the controversy and eventual separation among Friends. A statement by Wilkinson and Story sometime early in the controversy summarized their viewpoint:

> we do approve of Monthly and Quarterly-Meetings, for the necessary Service of the Truth . . . we believe, that as it now is, it also will become our Duty, to be at Unity with our Brethren in the Service thereof . . . Yet according to that inward sense we now have, there appears to us no absolute necessity to continue Womens Meeting in the Country, distinct and separate from the Men; and therefore do conscientiously forbear to assent or encourage, to lay the Intentions of Marriage before them.

Wilkinson and Story went on to state that they fully accepted the decision of other Friends to settle women's meetings. They further promised to remain open to further light on the issue, asking for the patience of the Quaker mainstream. Finally, they invoked Paul's words, "if in any thing ye be otherwise minded, wait for God to reveal" (Phil. 3:15).[45] So, while Wilkinson and Story accepted the need for an overall organizational structure, they balked at women's meetings. The requirement (initiated Fox in 1671[46]) that couples submit marriage intentions first to the women's meeting for clearness was a key stumbling block.

THE FOX-FELL MARRIAGE AND
THE WILKINSON-STORY SEPARATION

Many different conflicts of principle and personality came under the general banner of the Wilkinson-Story controversy and eventual separation. It would be a mistake to attribute to the separatists a great deal of shared vision. What united them most was a growing resentment toward Fox and Fell. With Burrough and Farnworth dead, and Howgill and Dewsbury confined, a variety of dissatisfactions focused more specifically against Fox and Fell. This trend was accentuated by their marriage on October 27, 1669. Fell was fifty-five and Fox forty-five years old. Fell's first husband, Thomas, had been dead for eleven years. Fox notes in his *Journal* that "I had seen from the Lord a considerable time before that I should take Margaret Fell to be my wife. And when I first mentioned it to her she felt the answer of life from God thereunto. But though the Lord had opened this thing unto me, yet I had not received a command from the Lord for the accomplishment of it"—until that time.[47]

Some Friends chided Fox that it was a little late for them to start a family. Fox made it clear that he was not thinking about procreation. He also avoided speculation that he had designs on her money by explicitly excluding himself from Fell's considerable estate. Certainly, their marriage was the crowning moment of a long spiritual friendship and ministerial alliance. But they saw their wedding as an important symbolic act among Friends as well. First, it allowed them to demonstrate good order by submitting their intentions to the men's monthly meeting and then a joint meeting of male and female elders in Bristol, a place where there was much opposition. (Recall that it was later, in 1671, that Fox advised that marriage intentions be submitted first to the women's meeting.) Second, by modeling this gospel order among Friends, they intended their marriage to be "as a testimony, that all might come up into the marriage as was in the beginning . . . that all might come up out of the wilderness to the marriage of the Lamb."[48] So they enfolded their marriage symbolically into the primeval relations between man and woman in Eden, the eschatological marriage of the Lamb and Heavenly Jerusalem in Revelation 21, *and* in their current organizational program.

Nevertheless, Fox adds, "there was some jumble in some minds about it." The overtones of the marriage were far-ranging in the early Quaker psyche. The wedding disturbed some Friends on conscious and unconscious levels. It symbolized a general shift in the movement from informal alliances to more defined, contractual agreements. In so doing, it also marked a change in the manner of masculine and feminine inter- action in Quaker spirituality. The submission of marriage intentions before the women's meeting as well as the men's meetings especially threatened many. It replaced the ambiguous and evocative dynamics that had earlier energized relations between Quaker women and men with a more cut-and-dried accountability procedure. Fox and Fell had long been the preeminent focus of "transference" energies among early Friends, as we have noted earlier. Their tacit alliance had long been rec- ognized and respected by Friends. But their formal marriage produced deep, unconscious dissonances within the same Friends. Marriage *institutionalized* their alliance in leadership in new and threatening ways. That dynamic may well underlie the tactics of character assassination aimed at Fox and Fell during the 1670s and 1680s. Negative oedipal energies concentrated around them, both in some Friends' attacks upon them and in other Friends' defense of them. Consequently, the literature and extant correspondence of the Wilkinson-Story controversy display an unprecedentedly mean-spirited tone. Statements of principle are lost in a welter of caricatures and accusations of misconduct, misrepresen- tation, and outright fabrication.

The first major published attack on Fox came in 1673, with T*he Spirit of the Hat,* published anonymously by William Mucklow. Rallying the forces of those who had never been truly reconciled after the Nayler crisis or the Perrot controversy, Mucklow summarizes the dissident tradition within the movement: no one who has been reborn from above can simply conform to practices handed down by church leaders; each must discover the validity of such practices through personal revela- tion. He attacks "Foxonian unity" as a new dogma, an outward regimen that can only alienate Friends from the inner guide. "In the true Church unity stands in diversities; but in the false unity [the Church] will not stand without uniformity." Moreover, the Foxonians *impose* their false unity from the Ministers Meeting in London by assigning in advance their own representatives to speak in local meetings. These ministers then proceed to speak almost the entire length of the meeting (recall Martha Simmonds' frustration on this point seventeen years earlier). Such tactics turn everyone else into mere "hearers," passive recipients of the party line.[49]

These developments furthered the tendency that some had recognized among the "orthodox" core of Quaker leadership for some time. A coherence was being forced upon the movement. Whatever the validity of that coherence, many former Seekers felt it was being promulgated through the very conformism that they had rejected in the 1640s. They continued to insist upon unity in diversity. Individual conscience and personal revelation were thus valued over corporate understanding and obedience.

Clearly, these were important objections. The problem in the long term for these dissenters, however, was that the only unity they possessed was their resentment of "Foxonian unity." They quickly lost both coherence and cohesion once they quit protesting at the edges and separated from the movement.

Meanwhile, Fox was unswerving in his resolve. But another long imprisonment (1673-75) suspended the itinerant ministry that made him so effective in imparting his vision. The forces of entropy advanced during his absence. Increasingly ill, he responded to hostile attacks like Mucklow's with an epistle from Worcester prison:

> you have known the manner of my life, the best part of thirty years, since I went forth, and forsook all things; I sought not myself, I sought you and his glory that sent me; and when I turned you to him, that is able to save you, I left you to him: and my travels have been great, in hungers and colds, when there were few, for the first six or seven years, that I often lay in woods and commons in the night; that many times it was as a by-word, that I would not come into houses, and lie in their beds. And the prisons have been made my home a great part of my time, and in danger of my life, and in jeopardy daily. And amongst you I have made myself of no reputation, to keep the truth up in reputation . . . . With the low, I made myself low; and with the weak and feeble, I was as one with them, and condescended to all conditions, for the Lord had

> fitted me so before he sent me forth; and so I passed through
> great sufferings in my body, as you have been sensible. And
> few at the first took care for the establishing men and women's
> meetings, though they were generally owned when they un-
> derstood them: but the everlasting God, that sent me forth by
> his everlasting power, first to declare his everlasting gospel,
> and then after people had received the gospel, I was moved
> to go through the nation, to advise them to set up the men's
> meetings, and the women's, many of which were set up . . . .
> And this was the end, that all that had received the gospel,
> might be possessors of it, and of the gospel order . . . . And so
> men and women being heirs of Christ, they are heirs of him,
> and of his government.[50]

The pathos of Fox's self-description, written at a time he was not confident of living much longer, recalls Paul's lists of abuses and privations
in 2 Corinthians 11:22-29. Both of these apostolic figures had an unshakable conviction of their calling. Both relied upon their personal
stature and suffering to help convince others of their vision. Both understood the ongoing power of Christ's atonement as working through their
very bodies. This was the only authority they claimed—one that they
were not shy to exert in cases of conflict.

Yet it is also undeniable that, just as Paul's co-workers and later interpreters tried to wield his authority in struggles that went beyond his
time and place, so Fox's allies, both before and after his death, availed
themselves of his apostolic authority, sometimes in ways Fox himself
did not attempt. The "Foxonian party" became an intimidating and sometimes abusive force, extending the founder's authority through space
and time. Their efforts to defend "dear George" against attack and to
advance his cause in the face of opposition often did more to divide than
unify the movement. This was the likely danger to a movement in which
such a remarkable individual became both touchstone and totem. The
problem was intensified by the early deaths of other key leaders through
martyrdom and the rigors of their feverish itinerant ministry.

We encounter here the problems created by mimetic desire. We are
all familiar with the mimetic element in material or sexual desire:
we learn to desire according to what others desire or possess. In other
words, the objects of desire are selected because of envy. Religious de-

sire is not immune to these processes. One of the great strengths of the Seekers who became Quakers was that they had been weaned of mimetic desire in the process of passing through every new religious truth and gathering. By the twilight of 1650, every bright, shiny talisman of spiritual status had been tarnished or utterly destroyed. Those who did not give up were radically free to discover something profoundly new. More than any other individual, Fox had been able to define and direct Seekers to that *novum*, and, over time, to forge a coherent movement whose corporate structures and processes were appropriate to the truth they had found.

To the extent that Friends saw for themselves the truth of this organizational structure, they rightly moved into solidarity with Fox and the rest of the leadership. But to the extent that some embraced the organization because it was Fox's design, or because it had become the measure of what it is to be a "Quaker," then mimetic desire became the operative element. Opponents of organization rightly smelled this taint at work among some who closed ranks around Fox. They rightly decried a spirit of "formality" or "conformity" creeping into the movement. And as mimetic desire is the key energy underlying "scapegoat" tactics in communities and societies,[51] they also rightly feared that some Friends would be sacrificed in the name of "Friends." To repeat Bishop's warning,

> I have no other Expectation, but that the same exercise we shall receive at your hands, as we received at the hands of those [persecutors] who would have held us in Captivity in the day that the Lord first visited us.

There is, however, a negative-image version of the same taint that just as easily steals upon those who oppose what they consider an unjust power structure. Resentment[52] sickens dissenters when they define themselves primarily in opposition to a powerful foil, rather than adhering to their own vision and authority. That is, "what they are, we are not." That unclean spirit leads on to collaborations among individuals and groups who share the same resentment against a common foil, even if their positive agendas are opposite to one another. That is, "my enemy's enemy must be my friend."

Those were the energies that Nayler eventually confessed had overwhelmed him in 1656. In 1658, he admitted that he had been tempted to "Envy against the People of God already gathered, pretending a greater thing to come another Way." Thus, his love was disaffected

> from the Flock of God already gathered . . . to spy out their
> Failings, and delight to hear of them. [Envy is] the Old Spirit
> of the Ranters . . . . Once this spirit enters in, it is hardly
> gotten out again and if it be, it is not without much Sorrow."[53]

At the end of the preceding chapter, we saw that Nayler tried in vain to rescue his friend Robert Rich from this poisonous spirit. It was this same spirit that we heard confessed by Richard Davies after he pulled back from the Perrot faction.

John Wilkinson and John Story appear to have been ready to pull back from their alienation at a reconciliation meeting in the North in April 1676.[54] Fox was not at the meeting. Partly owing to his imprisonment 1673-75 and long recovery at Swarthmoor, he had kept some distance from the controversy, letting others work it out. In some respects, this was healthy. Having set up an organization that would survive him, Fox was allowing others to take the lead. But in practice, others took it upon themselves to be Fox's defenders and enforcers. At the meeting, Wilkinson and Story were moved to confess their envy of the movement's leadership, and they even repented in writing. They went on to visit Swarthmoor, where they had a loving meeting with Fox. But the official minutes of the April meeting failed to convey its spirit of mutual forgiveness, emphasizing instead the paper of self-condemnation by Wilkinson and Story. Those who had not attended were not convinced. As for the two dissident leaders, they soon felt betrayed. From that point onward, the controversy hardened into lasting separation.

THE PENINGTONS AS MEDIATORS AND APOLOGISTS

One of those who continued to work for reconciliation was Isaac Penington. Writing to Story in September 1676, he worked to recover his friend much as Howgill had worked to recover Penington in 1663: "I am loath to part with thee eternally. . . . Yet I would not spare being thy enemy, if at length thereby I might prove to be thy friend. They are not thy friends that stand by thee." He urged Story, "O do not bow to me nor to any man, but O that thou mightest have the discerning and sense of God's truth and Spirit in any, though never so mean and low, and bow to it." Penington witnessed that he sensed "a wrong spirit had entered thee . . . and thou art sorely inwardly hurt and languishing, and also . . . many with this wrong spirit."[55] Evidently, there was some ensuing correspondence between the two, though we do not have Story's side of the dialogue. But a letter by Penington early in 1677 presented Story with five queries, suggesting that the latter had hardened himself against further efforts at reconciliation. "Thou mayst safely outword me, but thou canst not outsense me. I fear thou has let in somewhat against the dear and precious servant and chosen minister of the Lord GF."[56]

Penington's efforts at reconciliation also extended to his dear friends Thomas and Ann Curtis of Reading, who had been instrumental in the early stages of his convincement. They had strongly sided with John Story against Fox. Writing to them in December 1677, he professed undying love for them, but challenged them vigorously. He had long observed in them a tendency to slight the movement's leadership generally, especially those of lower social rank. He warned them to "take heed of letting in anything against dear GF or oppose anything that the Lord employs him in: for if thou do so indeed thou opposest not him, but the Lord." He goes on to make a remarkable endorsement of Fox's leadership:

> I would thou hadst felt the pure glory of life in dear GF, as I have often lately felt: and how gloriously he is at work in the service of the Lord, and how the Lord is with him therein, and how brightly he sees with the anointed eye over all dark spirits . . . and how it is not his delight to rule over any, but to bring every one into the holy dominion and blessed government under the everlasting seed, that it alone may reign in and over all. O how doth my love flow to him, and what a sense hath my life of him . . . how honorable he is there, even in those very things for which he is by some despised![57]

Penington, whose seeking had been quite advanced in Spiritualism before his convincement, and who had been drawn to Perrot's cause for a while, became Fox's most eloquent apologist.

On the other side, however, Penington moved to protect tender souls against the occasional prophetic bombast of the northern leadership. In a September 1678 letter, he urged William Dewsbury to be more active in mediating the conflict. But he also warned,

O Dear WD, Be tender hearted towards God's tender ones in these parts; and take heed thou not hurt any now, in this present case, as thou formerly didst in the case of JP [John Perrot] . . . thou hast had a hand in hurting many very sorely, some of whom the Lord hath shown tender mercy but other some utterly lost, and not likely ever to be recovered. Be tender, be tender, be tender, for I [see?] the tender life wounded in these parts, and I find the tender hearted laying it much at thy door, I deeply mourning before the Lord because of it.[58]

We do not know the specific earlier incidents to which Penington refers. But for his part, Dewsbury proved himself a moderating influence within the "Foxonian party" in the 1670s. He especially opposed the publication of letters and other materials that only hurt people and magnified the schism.[59]

Both Isaac and Mary Penington wrote to encourage Friends to adopt the women's meetings, although neither had found the plan tasteful when it was first broached. Isaac recalled that upon hearing of the plan, the "reasoning part" in him spoke against it as having no benefit to Friends or service to God. Yet, as he continued to consider it in stillness from his own thoughts, "the Lord brightly opened the thing to me . . . that it was the proper way and course of life in the whole body, for every member to have its use and service in the body, every one in their place and order, as the power shall please to make use of them."[60] The leadership and spiritual authority of women was thus recognized as healthy for the body of Friends overall.

Two undated statements by Mary Penington also survive. She had viewed the women's meetings in London as being useful in an urban context, but "did not discern a womens meeting to be requisite in these parts" of Buckinghamshire. Yet she was willing to try a women's meeting, at least on the basis of worship and mutual encouragement. They embarked upon meetings with great apprehension, lest they generate conflict with the men's meeting. She intended "not to meddle with any outward business till I found the Lord's clear guidance in unity with the men." Slowly, a sense of rightness emerged from the meetings.

By the time of her second statement, Mary was more confident that the women's meeting were a proper body for "outward business." Still highly deferential toward the men, she saw the women as "inferior parts of the body, being members, though like fingers or toes." But they were at least fit for more "mean" services, such as visiting the sick, which were not "convenient" for male leadership. She did defend the place of the women's meeting in clearing couples for marriage, however. She argued that a woman would be less "bashful" to speak of her situation before other women; the women's meeting would thus discern some aspects of a proposed marriage better than the men would alone.[61]

Not all Quaker women were as deferential and self-effacing as Mary Penington. But generally speaking, over succeeding decades, the actual realization of the women's meetings settled into a status rather subsidiary to the men's meetings. This outcome was not so much Fox's and Fell's intention as the product of many protracted resistances.[62] Male leaders often proved intractable and manipulative against the establishment of a separate sphere of feminine spiritual authority. It is ironic that Quaker women, who had been so fearless as street preachers during the 1650s, were less assertive in claiming their more rationalized roles alongside Quaker men in later decades (compare the dynamics of women's charisma in the 1640s and 1650s in Chapter 7). Phyllis Mack notes that while the earlier female prophets came from lower social circumstances, the new generation of Quaker women leaders tended to come from more prosperous and educated ranks within the movement, blending spiritual leadership with economic advantage and experience in record-keeping.[63]

FROM RECONCILIATION TO RECRIMINATION

Unfortunately, many writers and actors in the Wilkinson-Story separation lacked the plain but loving spirit of the Peningtons. On the "Foxonian" side, for example, Solomon Eccles penned the following invective to John Story in March 1677:

> O John Story, What hast thou done against the Lord and thy Soul! Thou hast divided the Heritage of God; and the good Ordinances which Christ Jesus hath set up in his Church hast thou contemned, especially Womens-Preachings, and Womens-Meetings; therefore will the Lord throw contempt upon thee; and if thou dost not repent speedily, miserable

will be thy End. . . . be reconciled to GF who is God's Friend,
and the Servant of the Living God, and Great Apostle of Jesus
Christ. . . . for this is the Word of the Lord to thee, Viz. That
this year shalt thou (John Story) die, because thou hast Taught
Rebellion against the Living God.[64]

If Fox had become something like a touchstone for Penington, he had
become for Eccles a blunt instrument with which to thrash opponents.
Story was in failing health at the time, and Eccles lost no time in interpreting it as divine judgment. Nevertheless, Story lived on until late 1681.
The letter is a sad example of the decline of Christian love in the movement. The fact that it was printed by the Wilkinson-Story faction (in 1682)
in order to increase hard feelings suggests decline on both sides.

William Rogers, a leading dissident in Bristol, continued to stir up
resentment through his publication of *The Christian-Quaker* in eight
installments, 1680-82, heaping invectives upon Fox in particular. Rogers
claimed to desire a meeting with Fox, but declined opportunities when
they were offered.[65] Another dissenter, Thomas Crisp of London, published his own serial, *Babel's-Builders Unmasking Themselves*, in six
parts, starting in 1681. Crisp reprinted past statements by respected
Quaker leaders—Burrough, Nayler, Penington, and William Penn—to
bolster the argument against organization. To Crisp's mind, statements
Friends had made for freedom of conscience against the state's imposition of a national church could be applied equally against the internal
imposition of corporate discipline. Crisp also quoted and sided with
Nayler, Rich, Perrot, and later George Keith (whom we will treat in a
moment) against the central leadership. Evidently, he was willing to
ally himself with several different positions, as long as they were contrary to Fox and company. Of course, it must be observed (contrary to
Crisp and Rogers) that the assertion of behavioral and organizational
norms among Friends was in no way comparable to the state's persecution of nonconformists. But one can also appreciate the dilemma faced
by opponents of organization: where else would they go?

The Wilkinson-Story separation spun off no viable alternative to the
nascent Religious Society of Friends. The three Westmorland meetings
that sided with their local heroes, Wilkinson and Story, did not survive
to the turn of the century. The other hotbed of dissent, Bristol, produced
no recorded counter-organization to Friends. Seekers-turned-Quakers

who did not finally ally with Quaker organization drifted off in two basic directions. Like Robert Rich, some more liberal-minded individuals remained apart from all organized religion, picking and choosing among religious teachings, or drifting on toward Deism or general skepticism. Others felt the gradual pull of more theologically orthodox and socially accepted Protestant faith, often the Church of England itself. It remains to give a brief example of that latter trajectory during the last decade of the century.

THE KEITHIAN CONTROVERSY

George Keith, Robert Barclay, and William Penn were upper-class, university-educated, second-generation converts to the Quaker movement. All three bonded strongly with Fox and Fell and helped to implement Quaker organization. Barclay and Penn in particular wrote apologetical works to present Quaker faith and practice as an acceptable variant of Protestantism. All three applied their advanced theological training to reframe first-generation Quaker witness in the most orthodox terms possible.

Because this study has focused on Seekers and Quakers of the 1640s and 1650s, we have not included these three major second-generation figures. But Keith's defection from Friends in the 1690s is especially illustrative of the Protestant path some former Seekers followed out of Quaker faith and practice. The Quaker response to Keith is also indicative of the stance Friends had adopted by the end of the century. For these reasons, we will treat him briefly here.

George Keith, a Scottish convert, was convinced in 1664. After years of service to Friends in Britain and Europe, he migrated to New Jersey, where he assumed the office of Surveyor-General in 1685. In 1689, he moved to Philadelphia and taught Latin.[66] According to J. William Frost,[67] Keith was the most educated and intellectual Quaker operating in America at that time. He became a leading minister, traveling throughout the colonies. On a trip to Rhode Island, Keith engaged with a former Quaker who argued that most Quakers were heretical because they equated the light with the whole person of Christ and denied "that ever Christ as Man shall come down from Heaven to Raise and Judge the dead."[68] Truly, early Friends had emphasized strongly the *present* apocalypse of Christ's coming in terms of the light within. Any future coming was usually left unconfirmed. It was contrary to early Quaker witness to speculate upon future or past events. What mattered was to know the truth of Scripture's prophecy here and now.

But in the post-apocalyptic situation of the 1690s, when Friends were at last tolerated in England and had become a dominant force in Pennsylvania and other colonies, such allegations disturbed Keith. He responded in print with a list of fundamental Christian doctrines he claimed all Quakers could affirm. Rhode Island Friends indeed subscribed to Keith's assertions. In 1690, Keith went further by proposing to Philadelphia Yearly Meeting that membership should be limited to those who would give written testimony to key articles of Christian faith. Evidently, Keith sensed heresy among the ranks of Philadelphia Friends, who were sometimes disciplined for unquakerly conduct but never for unchristian belief. The demurral of the Yearly Meeting to act on his proposal only confirmed his unease. Keith felt that the Yearly Meeting leadership was being corrupted by its own power, which extended far into the civil sphere, while it neglected questions of basic Christian faith. True enough, the Pennsylvania situation was a bizarre inversion of the political circumstances that had formed Quaker faith and practice in England.

At the same time, however, Yearly Meeting leaders were disturbed by Keith's arrogance. They were also concerned because he dabbled in religious speculations that went well beyond belief in the resurrection. Earlier, in England, he had theorized upon the transmigration of souls. Now in Pennsylvania, he began to insist upon the bodily resurrection and return of Christ, suggesting that Friends had overly spiritualized a fundamental doctrine. These two developments in Keith's thought not only moved in opposite directions, they also diverged markedly from the experiential and practical emphases that Friends had given to Christian doctrine. First-generation Quaker witness had played out atonement and apocalypse in a single drama of personal and social transformation. Now that the drama had ended, these doctrines had become categories of speculative theology (in Keith's case) or neglect (in the case of the Quaker mainstream).

The slippage of some leading Philadelphia Friends into early liberal rationalism was already evident to Keith. He quoted Governor Thomas Lloyd as saying "We might be Christians good enough without the Faith of Christ as he died for our sins, and rose again without us."[69] By early 1692, there was overt separation under way in the Yearly Meeting, with Keith and his adherents calling themselves the "Christian-Quakers."[70] The majority of Yearly Meeting ministers, along with Lloyd's Quaker aristocracy, opposed Keith. William Penn, some ministers, and many artisans and lesser merchants sided with him.[71] Keith publicized the conflict in print, decrying the unorthodoxy of Friends. This act scandalized Friends on both sides of the Atlantic. The recent Toleration Act in England predicated the state's indulgence of dissenters on their Christian orthodoxy. So Keith's action jeopardized British Friends, even Penn's colonial charter, and exposed a flank to renewed attacks from Anglicans and Presbyterians.

Keith was censured by the September 1692 Philadelphia Yearly Meeting, despite support for him by one out of four Friends in attendance. He was condemned on the basis of the disorderliness of his actions, rather than his beliefs. Keith and his followers responded with an expanded critique of the Yearly Meeting and Quaker political leadership. They cited anomalies such as oath-refusing Quakers administering oaths to non-Quakers and the Quaker government selling gunpowder to Indians and supplying the Crown with money and troops, despite Friends' well-established pacifist position. Finally, they denounced the rapid increase in slaveholding in the colony and called for its abolition. In sum, Keithians concluded, Friends had moved into an untenable position as colonial rulers and should withdraw from government. Thus, Keith's theological concern led him to startling social and political testimonies. He stands within that Protestant-leaning Seeker-Quaker tradition in which religious conservatism could lead to radical conclusions.

The Keithian Christian-Quakers formed a separate organization in Pennsylvania. Within the year, however, Keith felt compelled to return to England to seek vindication by the mother church. British Friends were displeased with both Keith's actions and the power-politics of Philadelphia's response to him. The 1693 London Yearly Meeting criticized both sides and urged reconciliation. For his part, Keith saw Friends again side-stepping theological issues by focusing on procedural miscues. As Frost summarizes, "What began as a dispute over theology became a battle of technique."[72] Keith minded little what technique he used to expose creeping heresy among Friends and began to attack the British Quaker leadership. He was disowned by London Yearly Meeting in 1694.

Keith then organized a separatist Quaker body in England, where he was able to attract some free-floating dissidents from the Wilkinson-Story separation. We find Thomas Crisp writing on his behalf as a self-proclaimed Christian-Quaker in the 1690s.[73] But the volatile Keith could not find peace even with his own sympathizers, and rejoined the Church of England in 1700. In 1702, he returned to America on a mission to draw Presbyterians, Quakers, and Christian-Quakers back to Anglicanism. Some Christian-Quakers followed him. Others rejoined Friends. Still others helped found the first Baptist congregations in Pennsylvania and New Jersey.

While Keith's orthodox crusade followed an erratic, vituperative course back to mainstream Protestantism, the Quakers' use of proceduralism against him did not serve the future Religious Society of Friends well. As Frost summarizes, the important criticisms and reforms offered by Keith and his group were stigmatized by Quaker leadership, causing these reforms to be deferred for decades. Friends derived the following lesson from the Keithian controversy: theological renewal produces schism; therefore avoid it and continue reading early Quaker classics. Pennsylvania Friends also resisted confronting the conflict between their faith and their political power. It was not until the 1750s and the French and Indian War that Friends finally admitted their position to be untenable and began to withdraw from colonial leadership. And after fending off decades of prophetic criticism from the time of George Keith to that of John Woolman, Philadelphia Yearly Meeting finally renounced slavery in 1755. "Not until Friends had forgotten George Keith were they willing to endorse his reforms."[74]

Returning to the philosophical formulations of truth we cited at the beginning of this chapter, we could conclude that the Keithian controversy drove a wedge between the principal modes of defining truth. Keith and his followers opted for the doctrinal and deductive mode of coherence, the one that reckons the truth of any belief according to its harmony with a larger body of beliefs. That led them back toward Protestant orthodoxy. The Quaker establishment polarized toward the operationalist and inductive approach, in which one discerns the truth of any assertion through the application of appropriate procedures of inquiry. So Keith was "wrong" because he did not proceed with his theological argument in the proper manner as established by Quaker organization. Finally, the heat of controversy no doubt caused Friends on both sides to lose touch with the first mode of Seeker-Quaker truth—that is, the correspondence of this or that competing truth with one's personal experience of the light within.[75]

Clearly, there are major dangers on both sides of this schizoid split between orthodoxy (right belief) and orthopraxis (right action), between gospel and gospel order. For American Friends, the theological questions fended off in the 1690s would come back after 1800 to wreak havoc on them in the Hicksite controversy, leading eventually to separation in 1827.[76] In that case, doctrinal renewal asserted itself in a much larger sector of Quaker leadership, but was opposed by another sizable segment over a series of issues too complex to recount here. Suffice it to say that the split in Quaker consciousness between orthodoxy and orthopraxis continues to divide and disturb Friends profoundly on both sides of the Atlantic today.[77]

In light of the developments we have narrated over these last two chapters, we can see that as the atonement drama and apocalyptic horizon of the early Quaker Lamb's War faded in the last decades of the 17th century, the first truly damaging conflicts emerged within the movement. First, the long-term grind of persecution began to wear Friends down during the 1670s. Then its gradual abatement and end over the 1680s removed the centripetal forces that had held the movement together despite growing animosities. The apocalyptic hope for the world, together with meaningful witness to it through suffering, no longer fused Friends. Doctrines of eschatology (the end of the world, the resurrection, the last judgment, new creation) and atonement (universal reconciliation through Christ), both of which had been played out through intense personal and social drama, now tended to become abstractions, confusing Friends.

Over the course of the next century, a slow, subliminal drift took place among Friends. Some became more orthodox, reclaiming more biblically based doctrinal standards and beginning to see potential allies in the evangelical renewal movement of the wider church. Others found both apocalypse and atonement to be increasingly meaningless doctrines, even considering them to be ancient superstitions. These Friends came to view Christ more humanistically as a moral teacher and example. They found new allies among Deists, liberal humanists, Transcendentalists, Unitarians and others. Thus, we see the reconciliation between two types of Seekers—radical Protestant and incipient liberal—begin to break down by 1700, as the atonement drama of the early Quaker movement ended. Two streams of modern consciousness, so powerful in their personal and social dynamics when held together, thus become enervatingly conflicted, even mutually destructive, as they move apart from one another. Therein lies the fall, the alienation, apostasy, and captivity of our modern consciousness.[78] As we saw in the Introduction to this study, seeking today often plays out around this same fault-line.

Notes

1. John Perrot, *An Epistle for the Most Pure Amity and Unity* (1662), 12.
2. William Dewsbury, General Epistle from York Castle (1662), in *The Faithful Testimony of...* (1689), 211.
3. For a general statement of this Quaker "correspondence theory" of truth, see George Fox, *Journal*, ed. John L. Nickalls (Cambridge: University Press, 1952), 31-33.
4. The watershed event in this development occurred in January 1661, when a failed Fifth Monarchist uprising led to the arrest and imprisonment of over 4,200 Quakers. The Quaker protest of innocence to the king that month stands as the defining historical document of Quaker pacifism. See *A Declaration from the Harmless and Innocent People of God Called Quakers* (1661).
5. See Hugh Barbour and J. William Frost, *The Quakers* (New York: Greenwood, 1988), 46 on the rise of concern for unity and consistency.
6. An epistle from a meeting of Friends from four southern counties, dated May 1659, indicates that the South was catching up with the northern churches in organization and structures of accountability. See *Letters, etc. of Early Friends*, ed. A. R. Barclay (London: Harvey and Darton, 1841), 283-86.
7. George Fox the Younger published *A Noble Salutation to Thee, Charles Stuart* (1660), affirming God's hand in the latter's ascent to power. Richard Hubberthorne and James Nayler published *A Short Relation of the twelve changes of Government* (1660), detailing the Commonwealth's repeated acts of bad faith and affirming God's hand in its fall. Margaret Fell published *A Declaration and Information* (1660) promising Quaker support for any good government. George Fox published *A Word on Behalf of the King*, exhorting all to honor the new king, albeit on paradoxically egalitarian grounds. See Douglas Gwyn, *The Covenant Crucified: Quakers and the Rise of Capitalism* (Wallingford, Pa.: 1995), 229-33.
8. Rene Girard views the scapegoating mechanism in its various forms as the foundation of all human culture. For a summary of his daring work on this subject, see his *Things Hidden from the Foundation of the World* (Stanford: University Press, 1987).

9. John Perrot, Swarthmoor MSS. 5.40, Library of the Society of Friends, London (hereafter cited as LSF). Quoted by Kenneth L. Carroll, *John Perrot: Early Quaker Schismatic* (London: Friends Historical Society, 1971), 42. I am greatly aided by Carroll's fine study in this section.

10. Carroll, *Perrot*, 44.

11. See Perrot's letter to George Fox from Jamaica, 1664, printed in Robert Rich, *Hidden Things Brought to Light* (1678), 2-17, especially 2-7.

12. George Fox, Epistle 214 (December, 1661 or later), in *Works* (Philadelphia: Gould, 1831), 7:213-215; also quoted in full by Carroll, *Perrot*, 57-59.

13. Carroll, *Perrot*, 90-91.

14. Isaac Penington, *Many Deep Considerations Concerning the State of Israel Past, Present, and to Come* (n.d., probably 1663) in *Works* (Glenside, Pa.: Quaker Heritage, 1995), 2:384.

15. Francis Howgill to Isaac Penington, June 20, 1663, Penington MSS. 4:3-4, LSF.

16. Richard Farnworth, "Concerning Putting off the Hat in Prayer," unpublished paper, dated August 1663, a copy of which is found in the Penington MSS. 4:40, LSF.

17. This is the perspective from which I would understand the traditional Christian doctrine (classically formulated by Anselm) that God "demanded" Christ's sacrifice to atone for the sins of the world. It is a distasteful affirmation on the face of it. And I agree with those who protest that a patriarchal church has given it the ring of an abusive, authoritarian "father-figure." But if we look at it from the perspective of lived faith, we have to confront the fact (no less painful) that to embody the love of God in an alienated world sooner or later entails personal sacrifice. Injustice, violence, and moral degradation must be renounced and denounced, sometimes at great personal cost. Is the resultant suffering the will of God? No, it is the terrible side of freedom: God has made humans free not only to turn their backs upon their Creator, but even to slay God's messengers. The wounds of Christ and those who follow him are the mark of an abusive world, not an abusive God.

18. Fox, *Journal*, 437.

19. For Fox's vision of the two oceans, see his *Journal*, 19.

20. I have covered other socio-political aspects of this shift in Chapters 8-10 of *The Covenant Crucified*.

21. Rosemary Moore, *The Light in Their Consciences: Early Quakers in Britain, 1646-1666* (State College, Pa.: Penn State University Press, 2000), 185, 226.

22. Barclay, *Letters*, 318-24.

23. Josiah Coale, *The Last Testimony of that Faithful Servant of the Lord, and Minister of Jesus Christ, Richard Farnworth* (1667).

24. Coale, *The Last Testimony*, 11-12. We recall the Presbyterian Thomas Edwards' use of the "linsey-woolsey" image in his disgusted description of sectarians and Seekers in 1646 (see Chapter Three).

25. The original of Bishop's letter is not extant. It was published first (in excerpt) in William Mucklow's *Tyranny and Hypocrisy* (1673), 34-36, and later (again excerpted) in Thomas Crisp's *The Testimony of Isaac Pennington* (1681), 10-11. I have used the entire excerpt from Crisp.

26. Carroll, *Perrot*, 93.

27. Isaac Penington to George Fox, July 15, 1667, Penington MSS. 4:139, LSF. Also see two brief letters by Fox to Penington in 1667, Penington MSS. 4:2.
28. Fox, *Journal*, 511.
29. Fox, *Journal*, 511.
30. William Rogers was the spearhead of opposition to organization (especially women's meetings) and antipathy toward Fox. He published his views against the "Foxonian party" in eight installments of *The Christian Quaker*, 1680-84.
31. Fox, *Journal*, 511-28.
32. Fox, *Journal*, 514.
33. We find an anecdote of this ongoing struggle within the movement in Fox's *Journal*, 525-26. The way he narrates the incident, one can barely tell that these were individuals still within the Quaker movement up to that point. He remarks, "As they being Ranters, the world called them Quakers." But Fox would not have been meddling with them had they not been ostensibly considered Friends.
34. Fox's *Journal*, 569-78 records his physical sense of "oppression" under the weight of persecution, along with delirious visions of "man-eating priests" and the Heavenly Jerusalem.
35. See William C. Braithwaite, *The Second Period of Quakerism* (London: Macmillan, 1919), 298.
36. This aspect of organization and resistance is emphasized in Michael J. Sheeran's description of early Quaker organization, *Beyond Majority Rule: Voteless Decisions in the Religious Society of Friends* (Philadelphia: Philadelphia Yearly Meeting, 1983), 30-32.
37. H. Larry Ingle, *First among Friends: George Fox and the Creation of Quakerism* (Oxford: University Press, 1994), 257.
38. This is Robert Barclay's report in his pro-organizational book, *The Anarchy of the Ranters* (1674). See my review of it in *The Covenant Crucified*, 320-24.
39. See, for example, Fox, *Journal*, 667.
40. Fox, *Journal*, 668.
41. George Fox, Epistle 248, in *Works*, 7:283-84.
42. Braithwaite, *Second Period*, 303.
43. See Bonnelyn Young Kunze, *Margaret Fell and the Rise of Quakerism* (London: Macmillan, 1994), Chapter 7.
44. Fox, *Journal*, 667. That incident took place in 1673. Nine years later, a letter to Fox from Adam Gouldney reports that Coleman and others had established a small separatist meeting around Sutton. But "I doe not Question but that in time this spirit will be quite worn out." A. R. Barclay MSS., 147, LSF.
45. John Wilkinson and John Story, quoted by Thomas Crisp in *The Testimony of Isaac Pennington*, 30.
46. On this development, see Ingle, *First among Friends*, 254.
47. Fox, *Journal*, 554.
48. Fox, *Journal*, 557.
49. William Mucklow, *The Spirit of the Hat* (1673). See William C. Braithwaite's summary of issues, *Second Period*, 292-93.
50. Fox, Epistle 308, in *Works*, 8:61. Braithwaite also notes the Pauline cast of Fox's self-presentation here. See *Second Period*, 308.

51. Again, see Girard's explication of these linkages in *Things Hidden from the Foundation of the World*.

52. I draw here on Friedrich Nietzsche's classic treatment of "ressentiment" in *The Genealogy of Morals*, ed. Walter Kaufmann (New York: Vintage, 1967), 3-198.

53. James Nayler, *To all the People of the Lord* (1658), quoted in Gwyn, *The Covenant Crucified*, 185.

54. I am indebted to Braithwaite, *Second Period*, 303-307 for the following narrative of these crucial events.

55. Isaac Penington to John Story, September 21, 1676, in Penington MSS. 4:140-41, LSF. Page 140 is missing in this folio volume, so we have only the latter part of the letter.

56. Isaac Penington to John Story, April 26, 1677, Penington MS., 4:142, LSF.

57. Isaac Penington to Thomas and Ann Curtis, December 1, 1677; and Isaac Penington to Thomas Curtis, December 13, 1677, Penington MSS., 4:141-43, LSF.

58. Isaac Penington to William Dewsbury, September 1678, Penington MSS., 4:157, LSF.

59. See Braithwaite, *Second Period*, 318.

60. Isaac Penington paper "Concerning Women's Meetings," September 10, 1678, in Penington MSS., 4:157, LSF.

61. Mary Penington, "A Testimony to the Lord's Power at the Womens Meeting at JM's to the Service in generall," and "For those Women friends that are dissatisfied at present with the Womens meeting distinct from the Men, sharing Collectings and severall businesses apart" (both undated), Penington MSS., 4:158-160, LSF.

62. This is L. Hugh Doncaster's conclusion in *Quaker Organization and Business Meetings* (London: Friends Home Service, 1958), 17-18.

63. Phyllis Mack, *Visionary Women: Ecstatic Prophecy in Seventeenth-Century England* (Berkeley: University of California Press, 1992), 219.

64. Quoted by Thomas Crisp in *The First Part of Babel's-Builders Unmasking Themselves* (1682), 15.

65. Braithwaite, *Second Period*, 319.

66. Barbour and Frost, *The Quakers*, 79-80.

67. I am generally dependent here on J. William Frost's excellent study of Keith in *The Keithian Controversy in Early Pennsylvania* (Norwood, Pa.: Norwood Editions, 1980).

68. Frost, *Keithian Controversy*, iv.

69. Frost, *Keithian Controversy*, xii.

70. I do not know what, if any, connection Keith made with the use of the term "Christian-Quaker" ten years earlier by William Rogers of Bristol. Rogers' concerns did not seem to be as overtly doctrinal as Keith's.

71. It is interesting to note that 135 years later, the time of the Hicksite separation in Philadelphia Yearly Meeting, the class lines of conflict were rather opposite. Then, upper-class Philadelphia Quakers took the more theologically orthodox position, and many lesser artisans and merchants followed the more traditional (but incipiently liberal) Elias Hicks. See Robert W. Doherty, *The Hicksite*

Separation: A Sociological Analysis of Religious Schism in Early Nineteenth Century America (New Brunswick, N.J: Rutgers University, 1967).

72. Barbour and Frost, *The Quakers*, 80.
73. See, for example, Thomas Crisp, *Animadversions* (1694), in which he defends Keith against published attack by George Whitehead. After the death of Fox in January 1691, Whitehead became the chief foil for dissident resentment. Crisp makes several statements here that "all Christian-Quakers" should do this or not do that. Even in the grave, however, Fox continued to serve as Crisp's target. *An Essay towards the Allaying of George Fox His Spirit* (1695) distinguishes "Foxonian Quakers" from "Christian-Quakers." He follows Keith in pointing out various Quaker statements slighting the importance of the historical Jesus.
74. Frost, *Keithian Controversy*, xx.
75. A clear example of this problem of spiritual discernment in the midst of conflict is found in the life nineteenth-century American Quaker minister Joseph Hoag. His journal indicates that during the decades of controversy leading to the Hicksite conflict (see below), his ability to discern and speak to spiritual conditions in the meeting for worship declined markedly. See William F. Taber, "The Theology of the Inward Imperative: Traveling Quaker Ministry in the Middle Period," *Quaker Religious Thought* 50 (1980): 15.
76. For a full treatment of the development of the theological and organizational conflict, see H. Larry Ingle, *Quakers in Conflict* (Knoxville: University of Tennessee, 1987).
77. I have written extensively on this "great divide" among Friends. See *Unmasking the Idols: A Journey among Friends* (Richmond, Ind.: Friends United Press, 1988); the conclusion to *The Covenant Crucified*; and *Words in Time: Essays and Addresses* (Bellefont, Pa.: Kimo, 1997), Part I.
78. For another statement of this thesis, from a different angle, see the last two chapters of my previous work, *The Covenant Crucified*.

CONCLUSION

EARLY FRIENDS, THE GOSPEL OF JOHN, AND ATONEMENT IN TRUTH TODAY

In our final two chapters, we saw the Quaker movement establish definite form and direction out of the fertile matrix of English Seekerism. Over the course of that process, a specific stance toward "truth" emerged within the several visionary horizons that had been explored by individuals and groups during the previous decade. The prophetic power and resilience that made the Quaker movement the one great survivor of all these experiments consisted in its powerful integration of religious ideas, practices, and organization, mediated by George Fox and others. Over time, the "stand-still" enabling that integration struck some Seekers-turned-Quakers as stagnation and rigidity. Some left the movement in order to resume seeking toward new horizons. But most of those gathered into the Quaker pentecost of the 1650s recognized a deepening and "seasoning" in their seeking as they took part in a regularized, corporate discipline of spiritual formation. That discipline allowed many of the radical ideas and practices explored in the 1640s and 1650s to survive as a small but significant utopian sub-current in Anglo-American culture.

At the start of Chapter 11, we noted that the emerging Quaker truth-stance was constituted by four distinct aspects, or "moments," and that these can be related to four standard philosophical accounts of truth. We will review and extend that analysis here. The first and founding moment was the powerful catharsis in which seeking individuals were "convinced of the truth" (in early Quaker parlance). At that moment, the light of Christ gave them a searing, unmistakable knowledge of themselves. They were confronted as never before with their alienated conditions (including overt sins) *and* by the power of God to redeem them. These basic Christian tenets, which they had heard preached and which they had repeated endlessly before, became a staggering reality in that moment of convincement (which in 17th-century Quaker usage connoted "conviction," more than a mere rational assent).

This first moment of truth, therefore, was one of *correspondence* between propositional belief and lived experience. In philosophy, correspondence theory typically relates hypotheses to empirical "facts," or "data."[1] But inward, spiritual realities are no less "hard evidence" to those who experience them. This insistence upon a lived experience of Christian beliefs (what Fox called "possession" and not mere "profession" of truth) was an important breakthrough at the culminating—and self-defeating—moment of the English Reformation, when competing creeds and church orders had left Christendom in utter confusion. The Quaker experiential breakthrough has affinities to the inductive methods of the emerging new sciences and the rationalism of the coming liberal Enlightenment. Nevertheless, its Christian, post-Reformation logic is primary in this founding instance.

The second "moment" of truth in early Quakerism was constituted immediately in relation to the first. Quaker "convincements" took place often in direct confrontation with the clerical ruling class of the established church. These attacks against Puritan orthodoxy were not simply a rebellion against authority. They posed a counter-orthodoxy, grounded in a different basis of knowledge (epistemology)—namely, the light within each person, the direct teaching of Christ returned in the bodies of ordinary people. The authority of the light within did not reject Scripture but confirmed it, albeit on a radically different basis, and often with bold new meanings. Early Quaker preaching thus began establishing its *coherence* from the start. The bulk of early Quaker publication was devoted to asserting this new Christian coherence, especially in defense against Puritan attacks and calls for the government suppression of Quakers.

In philosophy, coherence theory suggests that the truth of any proposition is established by its consistency or harmony with a larger body of previously accepted truths. Coherence, then, implies a framework within which one interprets either ideas or the data of experience (spiritual or empirical). But simultaneously, new experiences, while corresponding to elements within that existing framework, may also alter the framework ("shift the paradigm"), sometimes drastically. Thus, early Friends interpreted their experience within the framework of the traditional

Puritan and newer Spiritualist beliefs that had formed their consciousness. But the new experience of the emerging Quaker milieu also reinterpreted and reorganized that framework.[2] (Here we can speak in terms we used in our Introduction, regarding the interaction between point of reference and frame of reference.) This made early Quaker doctrine "orthodox" in surprising ways. For example, early Friends never rejected New Testament statements regarding women's spiritual status and role in the church. But their *experience* of women's spiritual authority and leadership in the movement led them to reread and reinterpret the same texts in surprising, liberating ways (noted early in Chapter 8).[3]

The third "moment" of truth was constituted by the novel methods of the movement. Some of these had already been in formation among Seekers and Baptists. Silent worship, the non-ritual, internalized sense of the sacraments, a spontaneous, Spirit-led vocal ministry, the absence of clergy—these practices carried over from experiments among Seekers of various types. To these elements early Friends added mechanisms of moral accountability (based partly on Matthew 18, but also carrying over from General Baptist practices), communal forms of spiritual discernment and decision-making (also with General Baptist affinities), assiduous record-keeping, and the leadership of women (first as charismatic prophets, but eventually as regularized elders and ministers).

Further, early Friends established explicit behavioral codes—plainness of speech and dress, simplicity of lifestyle, relatively egalitarian relationships, nonviolent approaches to conflict, etc. These were understood to be not only expected outcomes of the convincement process but also the necessary *means* of conformity with Christ. This strong "process" aspect of Quaker truth has affinity with *operationalist* philosophical theories, which posit that a hypothesis must be verified by appropriate procedures of investigation. Here, the emphasis is upon the active means of testing a proposed idea or action, in contrast with the static framework of established truths suggested by coherence theory. (Recall the early advice to the Penington, that they would find clarity about Quaker doctrines as they engaged in Quaker practices.) However, in any given case, the appropriate means of testing are actually deduced from that static framework. (So we increasingly see how these moments, or aspects, of truth are intimately entwined and mutually implicating.)

The operational aspect of early Quakerism also has strong affinity to the experiential, correspondence aspect, which constituted the movement's first, breakthrough moment. Quaker processes of spiritual formation and group discernment functioned to nurture and reproduce a distinct Quaker experience and to bring the Quaker truth-stance to maturity. Thus, Fox wrote of Quaker organization as an *order* appropriate to the *gospel* that had first gathered Friends, and as a step to "inheriting" the spiritual space they had entered. It is also worth noting that Quaker operationalism formed ready alliances with the new sciences, in which experimental methods were recognized as foundational, and where extreme care in record-keeping was emphasized. But again, in this founding instance, Quaker operationalism must be recognized as generating within an idiomatically Christian economy of truth.

Finally, the fourth moment of truth seems the most prosaic, yet proves to be strongly interactive with the first three. While the first three moments appear to comprise the "spiritual" aspects of early Quaker truth, the fourth is the most material, practical, and grounding to the other three. From the beginning, Friends had to deal with concrete problems to be solved, questions to be answered, and strategies to be devised. Certainly, these dealings were carried out in the context of their spiritual experience, doctrinal coherence, and communal processes—that is, they were not sheerly pragmatic. But truth's fourth moment is still rightly called *pragmatic*. The pragmatist school of philosophy defines truth thus: those statements are true that lead to actions producing desirable results. Of course, a great deal of ethical qualification is required to define "desirable results," if pragmatism is to avoid becoming mere utilitarianism. But pragmatic theory defines a crucial moment of truth. It must be included within our scope of inquiry. Otherwise, it will wreak havoc outside our realm of attention.

Like operationalism, pragmatism is concerned with action, but judges truth according to *end results*, rather than means. Thus, when northern Quaker prophets looked southward in 1654, they targeted those areas where Seeker ferment was strongest, where their opportunities for success were optimal, where "the ground was prepared" for them. Likewise, when George Fox, Margaret Fell, and other key leaders vigorously confronted straying ministers like James Nayler and John Perrot, they did so in desperation to avert dangerous outcomes for those individuals and for the movement in general. But their tactics were not really at variance with the strongly confrontational ministry that had convinced most Friends in the first place. The need to "confound deceit," to attack partial and self-serving truths remained the early Quaker *modus operandi* at every moment.

Nevertheless, we found in the later stages of early Quaker organization a temptation to use rhetorical force and to scapegoat rebellious individuals. At the end of the 17th century, in Keithian controversy, we saw Friends use the procedural *means* of Quaker truth-seeking to achieve the efficient *end* of dealing with a troublesome individual. From another angle, Keith's questions about Quaker orthodoxy were answered by ruling him out of order in terms Quaker orthopraxis. This breakdown in the Quaker conversation (dialectic) of truth, a breakdown between doctrine and process, also caused Friends to ignore important ethical questions raised by Keith and his followers (including Pennsylvania's complicity in British militarism and the increasing use of African slaves). Pragmatism thus lost its accountability structure due to the stalemate between doctrine and process. Largely because these ethical questions had been stigmatized along with Keith, it took American Friends another half-century to address them and begin atoning for their pragmatic drift.[4]

To summarize, these four "moments of truth" in early Quakerism do not themselves comprise the truth that early Seekers found and attempted to keep holy as "Friends of the Truth." Rather, these comprise the framework within which early Friends found, served, and remained *faithful to the truth*. The truth itself remains a divine reality, defined by God's loving faithfulness toward humanity and all creation. What we have defined here is the *hermeneutic* of truth, the mode in which Quaker witness to the truth was defined and interpreted. Because that hermeneutic was an unfolding historic process, building on a prior Seeker process and informing later Quaker processes, it is preferable to call these aspects of truth "moments of truth." If we deny their historic character and their temporal dynamism, they become static, misleading, and even dangerous. By recognizing truth as a living, moving being, we may better remember that truth is a someone we must serve, not a static entity we can master. Hence, the four-part framework we have defined is not a "cage" designed to capture truth. Rather, it offers a guide to the dynamics of a faithful conversation of truth. It also characterizes the various roles we may find ourselves playing in that conversation. By being accountable to one another in that conversation, we form communities accountable to truth. Rooted in such communities, we are better able to speak and act truth in the world.

Early Friends came closest to identifying truth as the light of Christ within each person. Since the cathartic experience and decisive authority of the light in personal experience was the foundational, first moment of truth in early Quakerism, that affinity between truth and light is not surprising. But a privileging of the truth in personal experience, apart from its other three moments, would have produced only an exalted individualism. We saw the struggle with individualism enacted in successive stages of Quaker self-definition. The fruit of that struggle was the creation of an abiding *Religious Society of Friends*. Though that designation did not come into usage until the beginning of the 19th century, it is apt. While early Friends called themselves simply "Friends of Truth," their association was "religious" in the root sense of *rebinding* reality, renewing relationship between God and humanity, between humans, and with God's creation. It formed a "society" somewhat analogous to England's Royal Society of new scientists (which several early Friends helped found in the latter 17th century), a body anchored by a core of trustworthy "Friends" and rigorously defined by an established body of assumptions and methods aimed to advance truth.[5]

As a religious rebinding of reality, early Friends of Truth were also renewing *covenantal* reality. A biblical theme rooted ancient in Israel's relationship with its Lord, the Hebrew *berith* (usually translated as "covenant") paradoxically means both "to cut" and "to bind." I have previously explored the covenantal meaning (especially the sociopolitical dimensions) of early Quakerism in *The Covenant Crucified: Quakers and the Rise of Capitalism*.[6] As we have also found in this study, the covenantal definition of early Quakerism took place both by cutting itself off from certain dynamics of Seekerism (especially Ranterism) and by binding together a faithful service to truth derived partly from Seeker and Baptist experimentation. Again, the four "moments of truth" that we have defined among early Friends are not truth itself but characterize their *faithfulness* to the truth. Put in another way, this four-part hermeneutic describes an ongoing conversation of truth. Each moment is one phase of a larger *testimony* to the truth. In the course of that conversation, each participant *witnesses* to one moment of truth in faithful corroboration and/or counterpoint to the witness of other participants. Along the way, we become speakers in a divine conversation far greater than ourselves. This is one level of meaning in Fox's recurrent exhortation to "answer the witness of God in every one." The covenantal dynamics of early Quaker witness in general, and its definition of truth in particular, are largely hidden to our modern consciousness. But if we are to understand truth in terms of sustained, faithful words and deeds, covenant is a category we do well to recover.

Finally, the development of this dynamic faithfulness constitutes the early Quaker *atonement* drama. Atonement is a complex term with multiple connotations, some derived from ancient ritual sacrifices.[7] In the present context, we emphasize the meaning of atonement as reconciliation between humans and God, among humans, and with the creation. Routinely, societies and communities attain false reconciliation through the sacrificial elimination of scapegoats, those who cannot or will not conform. By stigmatizing difference, communal solidarities are renewed. By contrast, true reconciliation exemplified by Jesus Christ (and a number of Hebrew forerunners, such as the "suffering servant" of Isaiah 53) begins inwardly with radical surrender to God. As one comes out of alienation from the divine other within, all human forms of otherness become relative and less threatening. Recall, for example, Isaac Penington's struggle to come into communion with the seed of God within himself. It seemed so "weak and contemptible." But his surrender to the seed within opened him to the witness of rustic Quaker preachers from the North and empowered him to a new ministry of spiritual counsel to others. As one experiences God's compassion, one becomes compassionate to others. As one becomes hospitable to God's presence, one becomes hospitable to the presence of others. Atonement becomes interpersonal and social as one becomes present to others, extending divine love to those who would otherwise be excluded. Still, the rebinding of alienated parties in a manner that respects their freedom often requires initiatives of personal risk and voluntary sacrifice. Hence, the cross is taken up within, then followed out into the world.

"Friendship" is the polymorphous category of relationship that can reconcile even the most unrelated or hostile parties. The deepest friendships often begin with personal risk, even sacrifice, on the part of one party. But to reach fulfillment, friendship must become mutual, accountable, and practical.[8] The four moments of truth we have described in the early Quaker formation also describe the dynamics of any mature friendship among two or more parties. Typically, friendships include founding experiences, mutual understandings, typical modes of maintenance, and some shared goal-oriented activities. Recalling Michael Oakeshott's observations concerning modes of association (see our Introduction), friendship in truth combines both civil and enterprising features.

Early Friends attained a deeply integrative reading of Scripture. But their emphatic use of terms such as "Friends," "truth," and "light" suggest that the Gospel and Letters of John were an especially formative influence. If we are to understand the inner logic of early Quaker testimony to the truth, and the manner of atonement they enacted therein, we should review the way in which "truth" is dramatized in the Gospel of John and witnessed in the Letters of John. By themselves, philosophical theories of truth and historical analyses of Quaker beginnings cannot reach that inner logic, and ultimately prove misleading.

TRUTH IN THE GOSPEL AND LETTERS OF JOHN

In Old Testament usage, the Hebrew noun typically translated into English as "truth" is *amath*, derived from the verb root *amn*, meaning to "sustain" or "support." Its adjectival forms connote "faithful," "firm," "solid," "reliable." O. A. Piper[9] summarizes the Hebraic sense of truth: a reality that is unchanging; not simply by inertia but owing to an intrinsic energy. In Hebrew Scripture, the Lord alone is true, not only in contrast to false gods, but especially as one that people can rely on (Dtr 32:4; Psa 146:6). Divine truth is often coupled with *hesed*, "steadfast love" (Gen 32:10; Psa 25:10—note that *amath* is translated "faithfulness" in these cases). Truth is not an incidental property but the very nature of God's will. God's commandments are not arbitrary demands but have truth in them (Hos 4:1). Therefore, Israel's covenant with God demands ethical constancy (1 Sam 12:24).

The Hebrew sense of truth carries over into the New Testament's usage of the Greek noun *aletheia*, though Greek cultural influences sometimes shift "truth" to mean simply the validity of religious statements, rather than the quality of divine being (Mark 5:33; John 4:18). Still, the Platonic idea of truth as eternal reality or form, beyond or without words, is foreign to the New Testament. In Plato's system, truth gains ethical significance only as knowledge (*gnosis*) of it leads to good action. In Hebraic thought, truth is morally defined from the outset by God's faithful character. What one does determines what one is. To act morally is to do the truth.[10]

The Gospel of John is astonishing in its usage of terms that can be understood from Hebrew and Greek perspectives simultaneously.[11] John's use of *aletheia* and its cognates is the most extensive and developed of any New Testament text. While John's employment of these words evokes Platonic, Gnostic, and Hermetic thought-worlds, the overall economy of usage is thoroughly Hebraic. In John, Jesus affirms that God is true (3:33; 7:28; 8:26; 1 John 5:20). But to the traditional Jewish meaning of truth, John adds two new elements: the identification of truth with Christ, and a description of how truth is appropriated.[12] John portrays God as true to his love for the world and his plan to redeem the world by sending Christ and the Spirit of Truth into the world (3:16; 16:12-15). Thus, God alone is true, as God alone is self-determining ("I am that I am") and not deflected from divine intention by the forces or corruptions of the world. The various "I am" statements of Jesus in John witness the identity of Father and Son in this redemptive veracity.

Rather than continue with these general observations, we will now view the way truth unfolds in the gospel narrative of John. We will also examine some passages from John's epistles, where the post-resurrection situation of the Johannine Christian community is more explicit. We will find the four "moments" of truth clearly manifested.

John's Prologue (1:1-18) provides an overture to the ensuing drama. Several key themes are briefly rehearsed and interrelated in John's appropriation of a Christ-hymn of the early church. Echoing the opening verse of Genesis, John affirms that the Word (*logos*) was "in the beginning" with God and was one with God. God (subsequently identified as the Father) created all things through the Word. Thus, creation, God's formation of a *coherent* universe, constitutes the first moment of truth. In that coherence abides life, and that life is light to humans (1:4). The statement that this light enlightens every one (1:9)[13] perhaps suggests the traditional Hebrew-Jewish wisdom tradition that God may be known by contemplating the wonders and order of the creation (Psa 119). As the foundational moment of truth, the coherence of creation can enlighten human consciousness to awareness, instilling the wisdom to live in harmony with the divine patterns of life.

However, this alone proves insufficient. "The light shines in the darkness, and the darkness did not overcome (King James: 'comprehend') it" (1:5). The light "was in the world, and the world came into being through him; yet the world did not know him" (1:10). In other words, the coherence of the world (*kosmos*) was immanent and knowable to those dwelling in it, but they did not recognize it. This alienation from the light of divine wisdom and purpose, a "darkness" in both consciousness and morality, makes the world a realm of incoherence. In John, "world" (referring to alienated human society, not the natural order) is almost always used with negative connotations. Still, John witnesses that "God so loved the world that he gave his only Son, that everyone who believes in him may not perish but may have eternal life" (3:16).

This expression of persistent coherence of divine purpose leads to the second moment of truth, the incarnation of the Word/light in the person of Jesus. The Prologue attests that "the Word became flesh and lived among us, and we have seen his glory, the glory of a father's only son, full of grace and truth" (1:14). ("Grace and truth" here is probably a Greek rendition of the traditional Hebrew association of *hesed* and *amath*.) However, this second moment of truth was not conclusive for most people either. In Jesus of Nazareth, the Word "came to what was his own, and his own people did not accept him" (1:10). The Word's "own people" were the people of Israel, to whom the Word had been revealed through the exodus from Egypt, the revelation of divine Torah, the oracles of the Hebrew prophets, and the wisdom of the Hebrew sages. The prophets had also alerted Israel to look for a coming Messiah, or prophet like Moses. The incarnation, however, was fraught with human ambiguities and was resisted by the same alienated consciousness that cannot comprehend the universal light. This second moment of truth is *operational*: that is, the incarnation of the Word is aimed to communicate God's love to the world through the words, actions, and miraculous signs of Jesus, the Christ. Jesus *demonstrates* the love of God, even to the point of death on the cross. In philosophical terms, he *verifies* the redemptive purposes of God with humanity through an appropriate set of communicative actions.

We now shift from the summary affirmations of the Prologue to the narrative of John's gospel. The drama begins with John the Baptist, perhaps the most credible prophetic figure on the scene in Judea at the time Jesus emerged to public attention. John therefore embodies the vitality of the Hebrew prophetic tradition, an important thread of coherence extending from the classical Hebrew prophets, through the troubled era of Jewish exile in Babylon, down to the difficult times of the Roman occupation of Palestine. John's charismatic gift of prophetic insight makes him first to recognize Jesus as "the Lamb of God who takes away the sin of the world" (1:29). John's prophetic witness to Christ is unambiguous.

But other authorities see less clearly. Nicodemus, a high-ranking Pharisee who apparently sat with the governing body of Judea, the Sanhedrin (3:1), had been impressed by the early teachings and actions of Jesus. Coming secretly by night, Nicodemus said to Jesus,

> we know that you are a teacher who has come from God; for no one can do these signs that you do apart from the presence of God" (3:2). But Jesus counters that no one truly sees by these criteria. One must be "born from above (3:3).

As Jesus continues, Nicodemus only becomes more confused. This passage introduces an ambivalence regarding the various healings and other "signs" performed by Jesus, demonstrating the truth. They cannot be understood from a human point of view. The truth abides in a realm (or "kingdom"—3:3) radically different from the world of normal human consciousness. This way of being (ontology) is "from above," "of God" (1:13), and is like a new birth. We have already encountered this emphasis among the Spiritualist reformers from Schwenckfeld onward, manifested by their doctrines of "celestial flesh" and their inward understanding of the Lord's Supper as heavenly communion with Christ. Francis Howgill's comments regarding equality with God (Chapter 8) also echo John's themes of human incomprehension at spiritual realities. We will simply note here that truth, according to the Gospel of John, radically alters the structure of being in those who receive it. This outlook also underlies the strange manner in which the Jewish writers of John refer to their own ethnic group as "the Jews" (e.g., 2:18; 3:1).[14]

In the dark night of Nicodemus' surreptitious visit, Jesus testifies to the moment of truth that is unfolding in his ministry:

> And this is the judgment [*krisis*], that the light has come into the world, and people loved darkness rather than light because their deeds were evil. For all who do evil hate the light and do not come to the light, so that their deeds may not be exposed. But those who do what is true come to the light, so that it may be clearly seen that their deeds have been done in God [3:19-21].

The second moment of truth, the action-oriented, operational moment of Jesus' ministry, induces a crisis, a day of judgment that comes like light amid darkness. The light does not judge, but simply comes into the world. People judge themselves, either coming to the light or moving away from it, depending whether they "do what is true." The life and death of Jesus serve as the demonstration-model of truth and love in the Christian community:

> This is my commandment, that you love one another as I have loved you. No one has greater love than this, to lay down one's life for one's friends (15:12f).

Jesus' conversation with the Samaritan woman (John 4) anticipates the next moment of truth, for the Gentile mission after Jesus' death will begin in Samaria. Still, Jesus' interactions with marginal Jews and non-Jews are significant in the present moment itself, since they demonstrate the pattern of gracious inclusion for the movement that survived him. In that moment, however, Jesus the Jew and the unnamed woman of Samaria confront the incommensurability of their respective worships of the same God (4:20). Jesus prophesies the coming moment, first negatively then positively:

> the hour is coming when you will worship the Father neither on this mountain nor in Jerusalem . . . the hour is coming, and is now here, when the true worshipers will worship the Father in spirit and truth, for the Father seeks such as these to worship him. God is spirit, and those who worship him must worship him in spirit and truth [4:21,23f].

The coming moment of the Spirit of truth is already breaking into the present moment during this encounter. Yet its full realization will come only with the negation of the present moment (more on this later, regarding John 14). It is worth noting that early Friends made emphatic use of this text to undergird their claims for silent worship, beyond all liturgical forms, as the universal worship in spirit and truth.[15]

The Christian hermeneutic of truth is dramatized explicitly in John 5, in a controversy arising from healing on the Sabbath. Jesus defends his action, asserting that as the Father is "still working" on the Sabbath, the Son works with him (5:17,19). Here he clearly testifies to himself as the Son of God. He acknowledges that without the corroboration of other witnesses, "my testimony is not true" (5:31). This statement refers to the Jewish legal code requiring the evidence of two or three witnesses to sustain a charge (see Dtr 17:5f; 19:15). In support of his claim, Jesus first evokes the testimony of John the Baptist, "who testified to the truth." This recent prophet "was a burning and shining lamp, and you were willing to rejoice for a while in his light" (5:35). Again, John represents the current, charismatic authority of Jewish prophecy, combining the coherence of tradition with the corresponding authority of a living, timely Word.

But Jesus quickly moves on to "testimony greater than John's, the works that the Father has given me to complete, the very works that I am doing, testify on my behalf that the Father has sent me" (5:36). Here is the operational truth of Jesus' actions.

> And the Father who sent me has himself testified on my behalf. You have never heard his voice or seen his form, and you do not have his word abiding in you, because you do not believe him whom he has sent (5:37f).

Here the witness of inner certainty, which should correspond to the witnesses already cited, is evoked. Nevertheless, Jesus confronts the disbelief of his accusers, asserting that this inner witness of the living Word finds no place in them.[16]

Finally, Jesus cites the witness of Hebrew Scripture:

> You search the scriptures because you think that in them you have eternal life; and it is they that testify on my behalf. Yet you refuse to come to me to have life . . . I know that you do not have the love of God in you (5:39f,42).

Now the historic coherence of the Hebrew-Jewish revelation is brought to bear upon the case. The disbelief of Jesus' accusers is not mere incomprehension—it is the absence of divine love. Finally, Jesus turns scrutiny back upon his audience:

> Do not think that I will accuse you before the Father; your accuser is Moses, on whom you have set your hope. If you believed Moses, you would believe me, for he wrote about me [Dtr 18:18]. But if you will not believe what he wrote, how will you believe what I say? (5:45-47).

Moses, the legendary author of the Torah, will be the witness against those who have staked their salvation and spiritual authority upon Scripture.

So we see Jesus assemble the hermeneutic, the framework of interpretation, for the Christian revelation. It will alter significantly after his death. The significance of the Baptist's witness will fade over time. The pentecostal arrival of the Spirit of truth will merge with and redefine the inner Word of the Father, as well as the universal light of life. We find the elements of coherence, correspondence, and operationalism already at work among these witnesses cited in John 5. The missing element here is the pragmatic—the functional response to the revelation of Jesus. Jesus confronts that lack repeatedly in his attack upon unfaith. But even his closest and most lucid disciples are not yet ready to manifest the response of true Christian faith.

The issue of witnesses is raised again later, in John 8, as the controversy around Jesus becomes more hostile. Jesus notes that his accusers "judge by human standards" (8:15), while the Son judges only by divine revelation from the Father. As they continue in their confusion, Jesus shrugs, "Why do I speak to you at all?" (8:25). The ambiguities of Jesus' humanity only compound the confusion of human reckoning. But "When you have lifted up the Son of Man, then you will realize that I am he, and that I do nothing on my own, but speak these things as the Father instructed me" (8:28). Indeed, the death of Jesus becomes the defining event of his life. But these accusers of Jesus are those who will hand him over to the Romans for execution. The confusion of human reckoning is not morally neutral. It is rooted in slavery to sin. In an aside to his Jewish disciples, Jesus assures, "If you continue in my word, you are truly my disciples; and you will know the truth and the truth will make you free" (8:31f). But those who continue to prefer the twilight of human discretion to the light of divine freedom not only continue as slaves to sin—they are revealed as children of the devil, for

> you choose to do your father's desires. He was a murderer
> from the beginning and does not stand in the truth, because
> there is no truth in him. When he lies, he speaks according to
> his own nature, for he is a liar and the father of lies (8:44).

These are harsh words. They speak to the escalating direction of events, as they move from the well intentioned queries of Nicodemus, to accusations of Sabbath-breaking activity, to hostile mobs, to the eventual scapegoat strategy of a nervous priestly regime (11:45-53).

These absolute claims to truth—and the invectives against those who do not believe—are scandalous. Elsewhere, Jesus says, "I am the light of the world. Whoever follows me will never walk in darkness but will have the light of life" (8:12); and "I am the way, and the truth, and the life. No one comes to the Father except through me" (14:6). We tend to hear these as imperatives to accept a credal belief in Jesus. But we must recall that the biblical sense of truth is more holistic, rooted in consistent, faithful action. We also must recall that Jesus speaks in the operational moment of truth: it is his demonstration of divine love to which we are called. That active faith is the means of truth, the way to the Father. "Doing the truth" does demand the discipline of mind and spirit as well. But the operational emphasis of the historical Jesus should challenge the doctrinaire Christian as seriously as it disturbs everyone else.

The revelation of Jesus and the controversy around him in his Palestinian context culminate with his entry into Jerusalem (12:12-19). Viewing the throng that greets him, the Pharisees worry that the situation is out of control: "You see, you can do nothing. Look, the world has gone after him!" Just at that moment, John adds,

> Now among those who went up to worship at the festival were some Greeks. They came to Philip . . . and said to him, "Sir, we wish to see Jesus" (12:20f).

The saturation of his Palestinian ministry and the first indication of his significance in a wider Greek-speaking world signals that "The hour has come for the Son of Man to be glorified" (12:24). With his arrest imminent, Jesus withdraws with his disciples to celebrate the Passover meal and instruct them of things to come (John 13-17). As one moment of truth comes to critical definition, Jesus prepares his followers for the next.

Jesus assures his disciples,

> If you love me, you will keep my commandments. And I will ask the Father, and he will give you another Advocate, to be with you forever. This is the Spirit of truth, whom the world cannot receive, because it neither sees him nor knows him. You know him, because he abides with you and he will be in you [14:15-17].

In following the practices demonstrated and commanded by Jesus, the disciples will receive and know a new "Advocate." This "Spirit of truth who comes from the Father, he will testify on my behalf" (15:26). The Spirit will corroborate the witness of Jesus, will give evidence corresponding to the words and actions of Jesus. This new moment of truth, in which spiritual experience *corresponds* to Jesus' actions, necessarily implies the end of the previous moment, painful as that ending is:

> I tell you the truth: it is to your advantage that I go away, for if I do not go away, the Advocate will not come to you; but if I go, I will send him to you. And when he comes, he will prove the world wrong about sin and righteousness and judgment: about sin, because they do not believe in me; about righteousness, because I am going to the Father and you will see me no longer; about judgment, because the ruler of this world has been condemned [16:7-11].

With the death of Jesus, the incoherence of the world will no longer be held in abeyance. First, sin is exposed as the world spurns the love ethic of Jesus. This no mere confusion but deceit. Second, the return of the Son to the Father confirms the demonstration of God's love to the eyes of faith. Finally, the demonic force that united the earthly powers in condemning and executing Jesus is finally exposed. The post-resurrection Spirit of Truth will reveal all these things to those who abide in faith.

The coming Spirit of truth confirms and extends the teaching of Jesus:

> I still have many things to say to you, but you cannot bear them now. When the Spirit of truth comes, he will guide you into all the truth; for he will not speak on his own, but will speak whatever he hears, and he will declare to you the things that are to come. He will glorify me, because he will take what is mine and declare it to you. All that the Father has is mine. For this reason I said that he will take what is mine and declare it to you [16:12-15].

The Spirit of truth is thus a force of continuing revelation, speaking to circumstances beyond the life and times of Jesus. It also speaks more specifically to concrete circumstances than the transcendent coherence of the Father. So, as the Father gave all things to the Son, so the Son gives all things to the Spirit, which will declare all things to the community.

This leads to the fourth and final moment of truth, the *practice* of the community of faith gathered in the name and Spirit of Jesus. Keeping the faith of Jesus in changing and challenging circumstances, the community faces many pragmatic moments of truth: how shall we act out the love of God in light of Jesus' example, the teaching of the Spirit, and the coherence of the Father? Jesus presses the issue of effective discipleship with his image of the vine. To abide in Christ the vine is to be a fruitful branch (15:1-11). To bear fruit is to keep Christ's commandments, to abide in love (15:10). The Father tolerates incoherence in the world but not in the vine, and prunes away unfruitful branches (15:2,6). But through this discipline of accountability, fruitfulness is enhanced and the community rises to a scandalous level of communion with Christ. No longer servants, they become his "friends," for he has made known to them everything he has received from the Father (15:14f). *This is full partnership with the Father, Son, and Spirit of truth.*

To speak of Christian truth as it is laid out in John is to speak of *quadrinity*, a dynamic interaction between four equal partners. To speak of only a "trinity" of divine truth is to settle for an incomplete and static truth that never quite touches the ground. The fourth element, the practicing community of faith, is the pragmatic moment of truth that struggles to carry out on earth all that it has received from its three partners in heaven. But in doing so faithfully, it also speaks to and acts back upon its three covenant partners, altering and advancing the conversation of faith. Jesus promises great things to come in the practice of this community:

> the one who believes in me will also do the works that I do
> and, in fact, will do greater works than these, because I am
> going to the Father. I will do whatever you ask in my name,
> so that the Father may be glorified in the Son. If in my name
> you ask me for anything, I will do it (14:12-14).

The Father, Son, and Spirit of truth not only guide but empower the practice of the community, as it serves to advance the truth, to glorify the Father. *Prayer* functions as the means by which the faithful community invokes the active partnership of heaven in its Christian practice on earth.

Jesus also warns, however, that the community will face the same incomprehension, rejection, and even persecution that he has faced. As they are delivered from the world's incoherence, they will be stigmatized in the world, much as Jesus was. The ancient sanctifications of the scapegoat mechanism, though radically exposed by the death of Jesus, will not be discredited easily: "Indeed, an hour is coming when those who kill you will think that by doing so they are offering worship to God" (16:2). This ongoing struggle to expose and condemn "the god of this world"—the power of envy, resentment, stigmatizing rage, and pious rationalization—is the continuing practice of the true friends of Jesus.

The letters of John further elucidate the community of faith as the fourth moment of truth, since they more overtly address the situation of the church during the first decades after Jesus. In the first and longest epistle, John states the pragmatic orientation of faith succinctly:

> Now by this we may be sure that we know him, if we obey his commandments. Whoever says, "I have come to know him," but does not obey his commandments, is a liar, and in such a person the truth does not exist; but whoever obeys his word, truly in this person the love of God has reached perfection [1 John 2:3-5].

Note the equation here between truth, love, and obedience to Christ's commandments. John further presses his community:

> Little children, let us love, not in word or speech, but in truth and action. And by this we will know that we are from the truth and will reassure our hearts before him whenever our hearts condemn us; for God is greater than our hearts, and he knows everything (3:18-20).

Concrete acts of compassion will stabilize the heart against subjective doubts, testifying eloquently before God.

John's letters refer pointedly to a doctrinal conflict in the community. The apostle inveighs against "those who do not confess that Jesus Christ has come in the flesh; any such person is the deceiver and the antichrist!" (2 John 7). He urges the community, "do not believe every spirit, but test the spirits to see whether they are from God; for many false prophets have gone out into the world" (1 John 4:1). The "spirits" in question here are statements made by those claiming prophetic inspiration. There can be no certainty of the exact questions under debate here. But John poses the question of Christ come in the flesh as the acid test for discerning spirits (1 John 4:2f). It would appear that the incarnation of the Word—including the suffering and death of Jesus—had been denied by some within the community. Such denials are known more explicitly from other early Christian sources. Such denials had the effect of weakening the love ethic of Jesus. His demonstration of God's love would not constitute a moment of truth. Moreover, the mediation of Jesus as Son between the coherent purposes of the Father and the corresponding leadings of the Spirit would be sundered, and the community's practice could drift in any direction. *The atonement of truth*, the reconciliation of truth into a unified field of interactive moments, was negated by this false spirit of "antichrist." This interpretation would explain why an apparently abstract theological question is raised in the middle of so many imperatives to live out the commandments of Christ, to enact the love of God in everyday life.

Piper contrasts the truth witnessed in John's gospel and letters with the static Platonic ideal. For Plato, truth always lies beyond words; its concrete expression will always be flawed. For John, truth is an active, creative, temporal reality; it moves from provisional to final expression. Therefore, Christ is not the essence of all truths. Rather, he reveals the goal for which the world is destined. The provisional expressions of truth given final expression in the incarnate Word include not only the revelation of Moses (e.g., John 6:32f[17]) but also the Greek philosophical traditions more implicitly evoked along the way. For John, truth has an *eschatological* character, since it unfolds in history, moving toward final expression. Through the life of Jesus, the Gospel of John portrays the struggle of truth against falsehood. That historical struggle continues in the ongoing revelation of the Spirit of Truth and the evolving practices of the faithful community. The struggle is not simply to familiarize people with the truth, but that they may be transformed according to their divine destiny: to become like Christ (1 John 3:1f).18

The Gospel of John was the most popular gospel in the early centuries of the church. It was less concretely engaged than the first three gospels with the original Palestinian context and apocalyptic preaching of Jesus. But it engaged mightily with the pluralistic cultural context and competing truth-claims of the Greco-Roman world. John presented a Jesus who spoke penetratingly to the thought-world of cosmopolitan culture, but also called men and women out of the stagnating morass of paganism, into a world-historical drama of unitive truth.

Again in contrast to the other New Testament gospels, which record the sayings of Jesus, John portrays Jesus in conversation with a variety of individuals who take different positions in relation to him. A Christian dialectic emerges from these conversations, engaging various truth-stances in an evolving synthesis. John's dialectical universalism contrasts with the syncretistic universalism of Hellenistic culture, where various deities mixed and matched for the masses, while philosophy served as the more refined pastime of the privileged. The Greco-Roman world, which mixed peoples, cultures, and religions as never before in history, was one of the great seeking cultures of all time. There were so many gods to worship, teachers to follow, and philosophies to explore. The Gospel of John called various peoples into service to the one true God (John 3:33; 7:28; 17:3; 1 John 5:20). Again, this God who sent Jesus is "true" less in the sense of opposition to false gods, than in the Hebrew sense of faithfulness. In a world where human purposes are conditional, illusory, and thwarted, this God acts with undying love and sustained will to redeem those who seek to do the truth, and to reconcile them with one another. One did not choose Jesus from a long list of seeking options. Rather, "I chose you" (John 15:16). That call of truth was enormously energizing in the early centuries of the Common Era, when Roman imperialism slowly sagged under its own weight, casting a pall over political, religious, social, and economic life.[19]

The Conversation of Truth
Returning to the Seeking Dilemma Today

The Greco-Roman world of the early Christians has similarities to our world of global capitalism. There are also differences. In the Greco-Roman world, economies were determined (and slowly stultified) by an imperial political structure. In our "new world order," national politics are determined (and increasingly stultified) by the global structure of capitalism. Given that key systemic difference, religion follows a different course. In the Greco-Roman world, religions functioned partly as expressions of political allegiances. Christianity was first viewed as subversive by most political authorities, from the Jerusalem priesthood to the Roman *imperium*. Then, under Constantine, it was converted into the official religion of the Roman Empire. Today, religions (or spiritualities) are traded on a world market. For example, a very westernized, capitalist Christianity expands into Asia, while eastern spiritualities are marketed effectively in the West. Finally, global economic integration today is leading to social and spiritual stagnation, much as the progressive political consolidation of the Roman Empire slowly stifled spiritual energies in the ancient world. As the superstructure of the Roman Empire became increasingly otiose, cynical, and corrupt, men of rank increasingly withdrew from public leadership to pursue private life and philosophical speculation. Similarly, as multinational corporate conglomerates engulf the globe, we find people of means withdraw into private life, esoteric beliefs, and financial speculation. In both periods, the masses are left to seek truth in a din-filled marketplace.

We need not worry about the future of religion and spiritual life in the new world order. The crude materialism all around us will insure that we ache for a more refined spirituality. The penetration of market relations into every realm of our existence will insure that we have plenty of options as religious consumers. In terms of what the world can offer, our seeking will not be in vain. But if the Gospel of John is right, that the world can offer only incoherence, then both our seeking and our finding will be in vain. "Such as your seeking is, such is your finding," early Friend Sarah Blackborow concluded in the epigraph to Chapter 8.

In Chapter 1, we sketched the dilemma of seeking in North American culture since the 1960s. Following an intense period of "culture wars" in the 1980s and 1990s, the century ended in a quieter mood, owing perhaps to unprecedented prosperity. "Orthodox" and "progressive" forces that earlier joined battle on many fronts of religion, culture, and politics have generally withdrawn into respective comfort zones, cultural enclaves where we can continue seeking along our preferred options, where we can converse comfortably with those who threaten us less and understand us better. But this trend is dangerous in its implications. Not only does our seeking become self-referential and esoteric, but our continued indulgence of stereotypical versions of the "others" fuels alienated, paranoid politics of mutual aversion that will only breed more trouble in the future. As we noted in Chapter 1, we live in one another's unexamined "shadow" of projected fears and secret desires. Too often, we "seek" mainly to avoid those we fear and loathe.

The twin trajectories of seeking that we noted on the American scene are basically the same two formations we found among 17th-century

English Seekers. They are strongly polarized today. Orthodox traditionalists continue in a reflexive mode we might call *fundamentalist universalism*, an insistence that the traditional truths they have reclaimed (or never abandoned) have absolute, non-negotiable validity for all people everywhere. Those who do not respond to these truths are written off as "lost." They have no share in eternal salvation and pose a political opposition to the reassertion of traditional faith and values. Meanwhile, liberal progressivists continue in an inversely reflexive mode we will term *universalist fundamentalism*, a Platonic insistence that truth remains beyond the language and spiritual devotion of any group. Though truth may be encountered fleetingly and partially in rarefied mystical experiences, it is idolatrous to attempt any categorical formulation of truth. Groups (usually discounted wholesale as "fundamentalists") claiming to know and impart truth in any definitive sense are *by definition* wrong.[20] These two general orientations to truth inform a wide variety of position-takings today. Their mirror-image character suggests a fundamental problem in our orientation to one another and toward truth. Along these mutually and inversely defined trajectories, our seeking will be in vain. Moreover, as we continue to discredit and neutralize one another, the ruling interests of this age will further consolidate their power over all of us. We saw this point made succinctly by William Walwyn in the epigraph to Chapter 5.

Both orientations are essentially Platonic and Gnostic. Both assume that the truth is some static entity. They disagree on the question whether the truth may be known—or rather, on the way and extent to which it may be known. But they polarize—and captivate one another—over the question of *gnosis,* knowing. If we return, however, to the Hebraic and Johannine Christian sense of truth as something *enacted* through faithfulness and love, these polarities become academic. We act faithfully toward one another as we enter honest conversation with one another. We "seek the truth" in a manner proper to that end as we love one another enough to listen deeply to their own accounts of the truth. Like the Peningtons, some of us are tangled up in "doctrines," in propositions about truth, while others are awash in meditational techniques aimed at experience of truth. But, as Thomas Curtis advised them, "he that will know my doctrines must do my commands" (see John 7:17). Jesus summarizes that command: "love one another as I have loved you. No one has greater love than this, to lay down one's life for one's friends" (John 15:12f).

In our seeking, we have sought mainly ourselves. We have gathered truths unto ourselves, then gone off to be alone with our God, or with the few that have collected similar bouquets of truth. The call today is to lay down our lives, to befriend those unlike ourselves, to lay out to them truth as we have found it, and to allow them opportunity to do the same. In the process of this renewed conversation, we may begin to integrate the far-flung horizons that our divergent seeking have opened in recent decades. Our seeking has been rich and creative. But until we are gathered into operational and practical coherence, our seeking is as vain as the seeking of the 1640s.

The four "moments of truth" we have found in the Gospel of John and the formation of the early Quaker movement offer an appropriate structure for this renewed dialogue. Some may complain that this structure is Christian. It is. But we have seen that these mutually informing moments of truth have their correlates in philosophical schools of thought, from ancient to modern. By itself, none of these theories is credible today as an adequate account of truth. "Truth" is a disreputable word in the postmodern era for various reasons, not least being the Platonic assumptions behind our use of it. But in conversation with one another, these theories may regain credibility. Or rather, in conversation with one another, *we* may regain credibility, as we enact these four moments in the dialectic of truth as a living, active being in the world.

As a Christian, I find the truth to the extent that I faithfully follow the example of Jesus in Scripture, as I listen to the Spirit of Truth in my heart, and as I harmonize with the order of God's beautiful creation. I struggle to do this in the changing circumstances and confusing dilemmas of my life and times. I know that the "content" of truth as I know it is different from what other people know. But I believe that our different ways of being *faithful* to the truth will show structural similarities. We will find that we have certain "moments" in common. For example, my wife, Caroline, practices truth along Buddhist lines. There are great differences in what we believe. Buddhism is not even necessarily predicated upon God. But I can recognize a similar structure of faithfulness to truth in her Buddhist practice. Buddhist teaching is minimal in its cosmology. Perhaps it is even acosmic in its totally monistic outlook. Yet Buddhism affirms a basic *coherence* to reality. That coherence may be found through the discipline of meditational practice. Buddhist teachings (Dharma) themselves contain a harmony and consistency that witness coherence. Again, one knows their truth through the *corresponding* experience of meditation. The strong discipline of Buddhist practice, with its few but definite Precepts, forms an *operational* verification for the view of life the Buddha taught. Like Jesus, the Buddha's life offers a demonstration-model for his followers. And like a Christian minister, the Buddhist *roshi* models the path of truth to students. Finally, the Buddhist practitioner often encounters novel circumstances that do not readily fit within the categories she or he has already learned and practiced. One must improvise in a *pragmatic* fashion, in light of everything else that one has learned and practiced of truth along the way. Indeed, the expansion of Buddhism in the West in recent decades is a vast project of innovation and adaptation with many pragmatic moments of truth.

Caroline and I continue a faithful life conversation across the imponderable gap between Christianity and Buddhism. At moments, we listen to one another with incomprehension. But our love for one another and our devotion to the truth as we have followed it thus far continues to grow. Some of my Christian friends may reckon that I am skirting apostasy, having knowingly been "yoked with an unbeliever." I suspect that some of Caroline's Buddhist friends secretly hope that I will someday rise to the higher dispensation of that eastern wisdom. But what we know is what we faithfully enact of truth.

Meanwhile, we both continue as members of a present-day Religious Society of Friends, a denomination that manages to invite and include individuals such as ourselves, practicing diverse and apparently contradictory "hyphenated" Quakerisms, such as "evangelical Friend" and "Buddhist Quaker." This situation is not entirely satisfactory for most Friends today. Many Christian Friends are uneasy with the inclusion of non-Christian and even anti-Christian proponents who call themselves Quakers. Other, more universalist Friends are ready to include all earnest seekers—except perhaps those who make exclusive claims for salvation in Christ. Beginning with schisms in the 19th century (which were renewed during the recent wave of "culture wars"), Friends have often preferred to segregate themselves from one another. Nevertheless, the uneasy experiment continues within this tiny religious tradition which was from the start fiercely Christian in its identity, strongly universal in its implications (the light shining in every one), and socially progressive in its methods.

Whether among Friends or in wider conversation, the hermeneutic of truth presented here can be applied to any developed religious or philosophical position. It is not a means of verifying or disproving anyone's truth-claims. But it offers a way to discern the *faithfulness* of a tradition and its followers to whatever it is they claim as truth. Wherever we encounter integrity in someone's account of truth, we encounter that person as actively faithful to truth as they know it. Where we find apparent inconsistencies in someone's practice of truth, we can (with humility) query them about it. In many cases, we will learn something from them. In some cases, they may be challenged to dig deeper within the resources of their own tradition. Where clarification is achieved, where integrity is recognized, and where mutual respect is established, we may find ourselves becoming friends. In friendship, a new sense of civility grows. Upon that foundation, we may also become covenant partners in the pursuit of practical works of love and service. Again, the purpose of this model is not for philosophical discussion in comparative religion, but to advance the cause of truth as an active reality among us. While our statements of truth continue at variance with one another, we may still unite in the works of love that demonstrate truth. Such as our seeking is, such is our finding.

In the conclusion to *The Covenant Crucified*, I proposed a model for covenantal social reconstruction in the postmodern situation of global capitalism. I suggested that across our different religious traditions, we can still unite provisionally in work for social justice and peace. I also proposed that these various "found" covenants might slowly weave faithfulness and transcendent values back into society. The conversation of truth advocated in this conclusion offers a model that engages us toward that kind of covenant renewal.

This amounts to a "testing of the spirits" similar to what John urged (1 John 4:1-12). Among Christians, John's crucial criterion remains the same: "Jesus Christ has come in the flesh." But in wider, interfaith dialogue, that criterion may be generalized in the same direction that John pointed: "Beloved, let us love one another, because love is from God; everyone who loves is born of God and knows God. Whoever does not love does not know God, for God is love" (1 John 4:7f). This love is not a mere sentiment but an active way of being in the world. The Buddhist may not predicate love upon God, but the Buddha demonstrated a universal compassion that stands well alongside that of Jesus. Recall that when his disciples reported that strangers were casting out demons in his name, Jesus was not threatened, but replied, "Whoever is not against us is for us" (Mark 9:40). Loving, healing acts are all in divine conspiracy. It was only when he was attacked for an act of healing that Jesus retorted, "Whoever is not with me is against me" (Matt. 12:30).

The "query" has a place of honor in Quaker faith and practice. A well considered question can be a powerful engine of discovery. The traditional queries that Friends have posed to themselves invite individuals and groups to press forward in their growth in truth. "Are you open to the healing power of God's love?" "Do you encourage in yourself and in others a habit of dependence upon God's guidance for each day?" "Are you following Jesus' example of love in action?" "Are your meetings for Church affairs held in a spirit of worship and in dependence on the guidance of God?" "Do you work gladly with other religious groups in the pursuit of common goals?"[21] The same queries are just as challenging to the mature, "seasoned" Friend as to the newcomer.

Similar queries could serve the conversation of truth among individuals and groups of different truth-stances. In a structured discussion for the sake of inter-faith exploration and community building, queries like the following invoke truth's four moments:

1. Do you participate in a specific religion/spirituality? Do you participate in more than one? Do you hold to a specific philosophy? Does this tradition provide you a coherent outlook on the world and life? Why is this particular teaching more meaningful for you than another? Does it speak to the whole of your life? What are some of the most important truths you have received from that teaching? How have they affected your life?

2. Do these teachings correspond with your life experience? How do you know that they are true? Can you cite some examples? Do you try to live in such a way that corresponds to these teachings? How? Does living according to these teachings lead to more experiences that confirm their truth? What in your religion or philosophy does not correspond with your actual experience so far? Is that a problem? Why? Why not?

3. Who are the models of faithful or truthful living to whom you look? Are there sacred figures? Founding figures? Do you look to local

leaders in your religion for guidance and example? How do they demonstrate the truth to you? Do they offer specific methods of worship, meditation, and living? Do you find these useful and confirming to your faith? If you participate in a religious organization, how does it make decisions and settle disputes? How do those methods demonstrate truth to you?

4. How do you deal with practical problems in your life? How does your religious faith or philosophical teaching affect your response to these dilemmas? How does your life experience affect your response? Do you look to leaders for advice or direction? How do you assess the success or appropriateness of the outcome? What does failure mean? Do you see these experiences affecting your faith over time? If you participate in a religious organization, how are religious teachings, organizational structure, and styles of leadership engaged in problem-solving? Do these practical problems and solutions affect your religious tradition over time? How?

These queries are be aimed toward a general conversation to acquaint participants with one another's orientations toward truth. They involve considerable listening, storytelling, and struggle to articulate deep convictions and assumptions, perhaps for the first time. In this process, patience and generosity of spirit are essential. We must remember that we are on holy ground as we listen to others describe their best understanding of truth, of the sacred. Our task is not to believe or disbelieve the truth as they know it, but to hear it as fully as possible. Through a participant's response to these queries, we hope to discern their *faithfulness* to truth as they know it. Our listening is part of our faithful response to the truth they witness.

In the process, we may hear apparent *inconsistencies* in what one believes, or between one thing that one believes and something else one does. It may be necessary to raise questions about what we have heard. But such queries must be stated humbly, with emphasis upon what the querying individual does not understand. Many apparent inconsistencies can be clarified upon further exploration. Inconsistencies that remain may not be important. If an abiding inconsistency seems important to a listener, he or she must consider: is this inconsistency serious enough that I cannot remain in active association with this individual? Is it serious enough that I cannot work constructively with this individual? Recalling Oakeshott's two modes of association, we may encounter some individuals and groups toward whom we can be civil, but with whom we cannot work. We may encounter some with whom we can be civil best through joint efforts for the sake of a common sense of good or social betterment

Some conversations might be oriented specifically toward engagement with a common dilemma to be solved. In such cases, queries begin with the pragmatic and operational, rather than coherence and correspondence. Different starting points make for different conversations. Queries like the following would explore a common dilemma experienced from different truth-stances:

1. What is the nature of the dilemma? What are its causes? What solutions have been tried? To what extent have they succeeded/failed? Why? What other practical solutions come to mind? What would constitute success/failure? How are you related to the dilemma? How is it your dilemma? Who else shares the dilemma? How? Who needs to be part of the solution?

2. What kinds of prayer or meditation would be appropriate to contemplating this dilemma? What are the typical procedures within your religious tradition for confronting such situations? Could any of them be applied in this case? How? What might the heroes and heroines of your tradition do in this case? Are there stories within your tradition that apply to this situation? What is the counsel of your local leaders?

3. How does the present dilemma pose a dissonance for your sense of truth? How does it represent an incoherence in the larger pattern of divine will or reality? Considering the desired ends and appropriate means already discerned in the first two steps, how would such means and ends restore or create harmony in this situation? Are the ends desired and the means proposed harmonious with each other?

4. Where do you fit into this plan of action? What personal interest does it serve? What personal sacrifice does it demand? Are you willing, if necessary, to lay aside personal interest for the sake of resolution? How will this plan of action, if successful, confirm your sense of truth in personal experience? What will this plan of action, if a failure, mean to truth as you know it?

These rudimentary queries may not all fit with every possible truth-stance. In particular, those Roof calls "highly active seekers" (Chapter 1), who are not particularly settled into any one religious or philosophical tradition, may struggle to apply these questions. But it is a struggle worth entering. Even open-ended seeking carries with it many more convictions than one usually realizes. And even those with strongly held religious identities operate with unexamined (often extraneous) assumptions. Meanwhile, the most productive aspect of these queries is the opportunity to hear how participants of different truth-stances answer the same questions. The differences can be mind-reeling, even disturbing at times. But they can also reveal new realms of possibility around a shared dilemma. Again, this process tends to situate an otherwise frustrating and "godless" situation on holy ground. Situating a shared problem within overlapping realms of the sacred serves to consecrate whatever agreement on shared action can be reached.

Such processes of action-oriented conversation would substantiate the "dialectical universalism" proposed in Chapter 1. They would renew the American conversation along the lines we saw suggested by Martin Marty in *The Many and the One*. They can only be sketched briefly here. But this model would serve as one basis for the reconstruction of truth through faithful and loving interaction. Wherever people unite in constructive dialogue around questions that really matter, wherever they patiently listen and humbly query one another in love, and wherever they establish new foundations for civil concord and concerted enterprise for a more peaceful and just world—there God's realm is enacted, truth is served, love is perfected, and covenant faithfulness is renewed. In some cases, such truth may generate fear, ridicule, and violence on the part of those who refuse to enter the conversation (as seen in the Gospel of John and the early Quaker movement). But among those who participate faithfully, there is no cause for fear, for "perfect love casts out fear" (1 John 4:18).

Nevertheless, it is important to admit that at this juncture, we are still in the wilderness of uncivil disassociation and enterprises at cross-purposes with one another. Like the Seekers of the 1640s, we witness that smoke still fills the temple. Like William Erbury, we must confess that all religions dwell in the same Babylon—and that we are among them. Well, that in itself is the beginning of a new universalism. This is where our conversation must begin—with a shared sense of captivity, waiting for deliverance. Coming to this stand-still, we come into communion with one another as if for the first time. In this place of eclipse, we may find the strength to wait and listen faithfully, as Sarah Jones urged Seekers in 1650. In this thick night of darkness, we may come to feel the Spirit of truth speaking through our words, our sighs, our silences, as it did in those earliest Friends gatherings. In this place of weakness and surrender, we may find the power of God moving among us, enabling us to do things that seem utterly impossible to us now. As Isaac Penington recalled, it was their sense of utter human weakness, combined with an overwhelming sense of God's power, that made northern Quaker preachers so effective as they invaded London. To be sure, we are not yet at that pentecostal moment. But we can prepare ourselves for it as we stand still for one another in a dialogue of depth, where words are comprehended in silence and the Word is made flesh. God only knows where the stand-still will take us.

Notes

1. For summary definitions and interrelations of the various philosophical accounts of truth reviewed here, see *The Cambridge Dictionary of Philosophy* (Cambridge: University Press, 1995), 812-13; *The Encyclopedia of Philosophy* (New York: Macmillan, 1967), 2:223-32; 2:130-33; 8:240-47; *Supplementary Volume* (New York: 1996), 92-95, 572-73. Approaches that review more contemporary philosophical and critical approaches, see Barry Allen, *Truth in Philosophy* (Cambridge: Harvard University Press, 1993; Michele Barrett, *The Politics of Truth: From Marx to Foucault* (Stanford: University Press, 1991); and Theresa Man Ling Lee, *Politics and Truth: Political Theory and the Postmodernist Challenge* (Albany: State University of New York Press, 1997). An attractive philosophical approach to recouping a postmodern sense of truth is presented by Wendy Farley in *Eros for the Other: Retaining Truth in a Pluralistic Age* (University Park: Pennsylvania State University, 1996).
2. The defense of Quaker coherence reached its culminating moment with Robert Barclay's *Apology for the True Christian Divinity* (1678). Organizing his defense in terms of propositions mirroring the Westminster Confession, Barclay devotes his first two propositions to the foundational epistemology of the light of Christ in all people. He argues that Quaker witness is not a new gospel or doctrine but a new insight into the established gospel and doctrines. See *Barclay's Apology in Modern English*, ed. Dean Freiday (Newberg, Ore.: 1991), 63.
3. Also see Douglas Gwyn, *Apocalypse of the Word: The Life and Message of George Fox* (Richmond, Ind.: Friends United Press, 1986), 149-50. One of the classic early Quaker texts offering biblical defenses of women's leadership is Margaret Fell, *Women's Speaking Justified* (1666).
4. For excellent studies of these important shifts beginning in the 1750s, see Jack Marietta, *The Reformation of American Quakerism* (Philadelphia: University of Pennsylvania Press, 1984); and Richard Bauman, *For the Reputation of Truth: Politics, Religion, and Conflict among Pennsylvania Quakers, 1750-1800* (Baltimore: Johns Hopkins, 1971).
5. For the beginnings of the Royal Society and its struggle to establish reliable criteria of scientific truth, see Steven Shapin's fascinating study, *A Social History of Truth: Civility and Science in Seventeenth-Century England* (Chicago: University Press, 1994). George Fox's organizational campaign can be seen as a countercultural religious version of the Royal Society's struggle to establish reliable truth-telling in science. In contrast to the Royal Society's emphasis upon respected gentlemen (like Robert Boyle), whose wealth helped assure that they would not skew their findings for the sake of self-advancement, early Friends produced more egalitarian forms of accountability, undergirded by mutual aid, to establish their veracity in business, science, and general society. Sociologist Max Weber defines "society" in terms of interactions based upon intentions that are in turn founded upon a common body of knowledge, norms, customs, and expectations. See "Society" in *The Encyclopedia of Philosophy* (New York: Macmillan, 1967), 7:470-73. In *The Beginnings of Quakerism*

(London: Macmillan, 1912), 570, William C. Braithwaite attests that the usage "Society of Friends," can be traced back no further than 1793. The appropriateness of the term, however, is indicated by a statement by William Erbury in 1652: "Admission [in the formal churches] intimates the Church of Christ to be a corporation, as if there were a common council among them, whereas the [true] Church is a free company or society of friends, who come together, not as called by an outward but freely choosing by the inward spirit" (*The Welsh Curate*, 8). In *The Second Period of Quakerism* (London: Macmillan, 1919), 248, Braithwaite comments pregnantly upon the organizational initiatives that began in 1666: "The fellowship is still grounded in a common experience of spiritual life; but agreement with the approved practices and principles which have sprung from that experience is also essential. In other words, Quakerism has narrowed itself into a religious Society. The change was bound to come.... Quakerism had never been merely subjective."

6. Douglas Gwyn, *The Covenant Crucified: Quakers and the Rise of Capitalism* (Wallingford, Pa.: Pendle Hill, 1995).

7. For a survey of the various meanings of atonement, see John Driver, *Understanding the Atonement for the Mission of the Church* (Scottdale, Pa.: Herald, 1986). Again, in our present study, the work of René Girard has been central. See Girard's *Things Hidden Since the Foundation of the World* (Stanford: University Press, 1987). Building on Girard's work, see James G. Williams, *The Bible, Violence, and the Sacred: Liberation from the Myth of Sanctioned Violence* (Valley Forge: Trinity Press International, 1991).

8. Edward Collins Vacek reviews the three Greek words for "love" in the New Testament: *agape* (love for the sake of the other), *eros* (love for one's own sake), and *philia* (friendship, mutuality). He disagrees with Anders Nygren's classic account of *agape* as the distinctly Christian love and concludes (to his own surprise) that *philia* represents the most complete love, in Christian understanding. All three aspects of love are necessary, but come to maturity in friendship. While *agape* and *eros* tend to focus on the personal and interpersonal dimensions of love, *philia* is most suggestive of the communal dimension, in which most of our moral action takes place. See his *Love, Human and Divine: The Heart of Christian Ethics* (Georgetown, D.C.: University Press, 1994), xvi, 312. Truth as a pattern of sustained, mutual, and covenantal faithfulness, therefore, has special affinities to friendship.

9. O. A. Piper, "Truth," in *The Interpreter's Dictionary of the Bible* (Nashville: Abingdon, 1962) 4:713-17 is a succinct and compelling treatment of that important word, and informs this treatment at several points.

10. See John Breck, *The Spirit of Truth: The Origins of Johannine Pneumatology* (Crestwood, N.Y.: St. Vladimir's Seminary, 1991), 99.

11. A classic treatment of John's thematics in their bivalences is C. H. Dodd, *The Interpretation of the Fourth Gospel* (Cambridge: University Press, 1954). He follows Rudolf Bultmann in finding a strong influence of Greek thinking in John's use of the word "truth" (see 170-78). More recent scholarship has tended to affirm the primacy of Hebraic thought in John. See Breck, *Spirit of Truth*, and Rudolf Schnackenburg, *The Gospel according to St. John*, 3 vols. (New York: Crossroad, 1980). Both scholars see the Dead Sea Scrolls of the Qumran

community as the most important contemporary influence on the Johannine sense of truth. As Schnackenburg summarizes (2:236), in emphasizing the word "truth," John took on the language of his syncretistic world, opting for a word with a familiar and attractive ring; nevertheless, he remains rooted in his Hebraic-Jewish sensibility.

12. Piper, "Truth," 716.

13. The King James Version reads "the true Light, which enlighteneth every man that cometh into the world," whereas the New Revised Standard Version reads "the true light, which enlightens everyone, was coming into the world." The Greek is equally suggestive. The NRSV reading emphasizes the historic Incarnation of Christ, while the KJV reading emphasizes the light in each person, but the two readings are not contradictory. Early Friends quoted John 1:9 tirelessly to emphasize the universal presence and saving power of God. For an overview of George Fox's understanding on this foundational concept, see Douglas Gwyn, *Apocalypse of the Word: the Life and Message of George Fox* (Richmond, Ind.: Friends United Press, 1986), Chapters 3-4.

14. This sense of altered being was widespread among early Christians. Even among pagan adversaries, Christians came to be known as "the third race," neither Greco-Roman nor eastern "barbarian." See R. A. Markus, Christianity in the Roman World (New York: Scribners, 1974), 24. The name "Christian" became an anti-identity in the ancient pagan world. For example, an early Christian under interrogation was reported to have refused to give any information regarding his name, city, or race. To each question he replied, "I am a Christian." See Peter Brown, The Making of Late Antiquity (Cambridge: Harvard, 1978), 56, citing The Martyrs of Lyons. Tragically, as this consciousness was lost among Christians, it became all too easy for Gentiles to read John's references to "the Jews" without their Jewish context. That reading inspired virulently anti-Semitic interpretations of John – and Christian violence against Jews – for centuries to come.

15. See, for example, Margaret Fell, *A Call to the Universal Seed of God throughout the Whole World* (1664), reviewed in Gwyn, *Covenant Crucified*, 256-57.

16. Repeatedly in John, we find a nearly dualistic sense of separation between light and darkness, truth and deceit, faith and disbelief. Recent scholarship emphasizes that these controversial passages in John reflect the synagogue debates regarding Jesus that went on for decades after his death, finally leading to the expulsion of Christian Jews. The unhopeful attitude toward "the Jews" portrayed in these debates expresses the disappointment and rejection experienced by Jewish Christians in the 80s and afterwards who, having lost the debate, found themselves cast loose from Judaism, and increasingly exposed to persecution. See J. Louis Martyn, *The Gospel of John in Christian History* (New York: Paulist, 1978); *History and Theology in the Fourth Gospel* (Nashville, Abingdon, 1979); and Raymond E. Brown, *The Community of the Beloved Disciple: The Life, Loves, and Hates of an Individual Church in New Testament Times* (New York: Paulist, 1979).

17. See Paul N. Anderson, *The Christology of the Fourth Gospel: Its Unity and Disunity in the Light of John 6* (Valley Forge, Pa.: Trinity International, 1997). Though Anderson does not deal directly with the thematics of truth in John, his

treatment complements a number of issues raised here. Note especially Chapter 7 on the dialectical character of John 6.
18. Piper, "Truth," 4:716.
19. For various and conflicting accounts of the vitality of Christianity in its early centuries, see Wayne A. Meeks, *The Moral World of the First Christians* (Philadelphia: Westminster, 1986); Helmut Koester, *History, Culture, and Religion of the Hellenistic Age* (Philadelphia: Fortress, 1982); E. R. Dodds, *Pagan and Christian in an Age of Anxiety: Some Aspects of Religions Experience from Marcus Aurelius to Constantine* (Cambridge: University Press, 1965); Peter Brown, *The Making of Late Antiquity* (Cambridge: University Press, 1978); and *Authority and the Sacred: Aspects of the Christianization of the Roman World* (Cambridge: University Press, 1995).
20. Although the terminology is my own, I am aided in this analysis by an article by Hugh Pyper, "A Place in the Dialogue," *The Friend*, May 30, 1997: 2.
21. Queries selected from *Quaker Faith and Practice* (London: Britain Yearly Meeting of the Religious Society of Friends, 1995), 1.02.

INDEX